Sl very

The Embarrassment of Slavery

*Controversies over Bondage
and Nationalism in the American
Colonial Philippines*

Michael Salman

UNIVERSITY OF CALIFORNIA PRESS
Berkeley · Los Angeles · London

University of California Press
Berkeley and Los Angeles, California

University of California Press, Ltd.
London, England

First paperback printing 2003

Library of Congress Cataloging-in-Publication Data

Salman, Michael, 1960–

    The embarrassment of slavery : controversies
    over bondage and nationalism in the American
    colonial Philippines / Michael Salman.
       p. cm.
    Includes bibliographical references and index.
    ISBN 0-520-24071-5
    1. Slavery—Philippines—History.
    2. Philippines—History—1898–1916.
    3. Nationalism—Philippines—History.
    I. Title.

HT1271.S25   2001
306.3'62'09599—dc21   2001027449

Manufactured in the United States of America

12   11   10   09   08   07   06   05   04   03
10 9 8 7 6 5 4 3 2 1

Contents

Maps

Acknowledgments

Acknowledgments, which usually appear at the opening of books, are always written last. I feel that I am only now beginning the most difficult part of this endeavor, for I have accumulated debts that I can never repay and I feel embarrassed to reciprocate with only these inadequate words of thanks. If I always had hope that I would finish a creditable book, it was only because of the support and advice I received from so many friends, colleagues, and teachers.

This study was initially inspired by Richard Roberts's seminar at Stanford University on the comparative history of emancipation. George M. Fredrickson and my graduate advisor, Barton J. Bernstein, joined Richard Roberts to form a dissertation committee of insightful and supportive readers. They guided me toward the highest scholarly standards and allowed me the freedom to question everything. Perhaps more than anything else, I learned from them the value of intellectual diversity and disagreement as vital prerequisites for critical thought and scholarly creativity.

At critical junctures I received essential assistance from Vicente L. Rafael, the late William Henry Scott, and David Brion Davis. I met Vince when he was a postdoctoral fellow at Stanford. Since then he has been a treasured friend and colleague who has encouraged and aided me in innumerable ways, professionally and intellectually. Vince read the entire manuscript and his thoughtful and constructive comments have made it a better book.

In the Philippines, William Henry Scott welcomed me to his home in Sagada, in Mountain Province. He read aloud to me an unfinished draft of his *Slavery in the Spanish Philippines* and then discussed my own research at length. Later, he sent me documents discovered in his decades of primary research and even some family histories from his neighbors in Sagada. Everyone who writes Philippine history has benefited from Scotty's erudition and goodwill. He enriched our field and our lives.

David Brion Davis also took an interest in this project at an early date, responding to a letter and inviting me to his home for a lunch that turned into a five-hour conversation about slavery, history, politics, and religion. When I later sent him some early chapters of my dissertation, he replied with some of the most inspiring comments I have ever received. His scholarship has had a tremendous influence on my own thought; indeed, this book would not have been possible without the intellectual foundation laid out by his work on slavery and antislavery movements. He, too, read the entire manuscript of this book before publication. I cannot say how grateful I am for his incomparably learned and generous comments, criticisms, and suggestions.

In the United States and the Philippines, I was fortunate to be assisted by librarians and archivists who were always knowledgeable, efficient, and welcoming. The department of history at the University of the Philippines in Diliman kindly provided an official affiliation during my research in the Philippines, which was funded by Stanford University and a grant from the MacArthur Foundation. I also benefited from a generous grant from the Charlotte W. Newcombe Foundation. At the University of California, Los Angeles I have been profoundly influenced by many friends, colleagues, and students and have received important support from the Asian American Studies Center, the department of history, and our new Center for Southeast Asian Studies.

Many individuals read proposals, abstracts, and chapters over the years, or simply provided the kind of sustenance without which I could not have continued. For this help I would like to express my gratitude to Randolf Arguelles, Pearlie Baluyut, Neil Barker, Lew Bateman, Fred Bradford, Bill Bravman, Ernie Chavez, Miroslava Chavez, Connie Chen, King Kok Cheung, Catherine Ceniza Choy, Carol Dahl, Pete Daniel, Arleen de Vera, Laura Edwards, Augusto Espiritu, Cindy Fan, the Flavier family, Stephen Frank, Fu Poshek, Barbara Gaerlan, Susan Grayzel, Robert L. Hill, Doug Klusmeyer, Mike Latham, Wendy Lynch, Howard Malchow, Donald Moore, Hans-Reudi Morgenthaler, Don Nakanishi, Marajorie Nazareth, Kumar Patel, Shela Patel, Dean Perton, Tony Reid,

Jan Reiff, Peter Reill, Julie Reuben, Amy Roberts, Geoffrey Robinson, Jun Rodriguez, Mike Saler, Jesse Sarol, Boone Schirmer, Mark Schuster, Daryl Scott, Suzanne Shanahan, Allison Sneider, Robby Sunico, Bill Tobin, Sharon Traweek, Steven Van Evera, Joe Ward, Jeff Webb, Susan Woll, Emily Woodward, Kariann Yokota, and Henry Yu.

I thank the University of California Press for moving this project to completion and into print. Monica McCormick and Suzanne Knott, my acquisition and production editors, cajoled me at just the right moments. They offered sage advice on both style and the process of producing a book. Frances Bowles, my copyeditor, undertook a Herculean task and saved me from many errors. Those that remain are entirely my own.

If all of these expressions of thanks are insufficient, as I feel they must be, then fulfillment of this last obligation is certainly beyond human bounds. Muriel C. McClendon has taught me about realms of life that cannot be studied, and she helped me in ways that no one could request. Perhaps I have only learned to appreciate how the elusive ideal of freedom can be so powerful because I have experienced Muriel's love, an indomitable force that defies explanation and life's most brutal challenges.

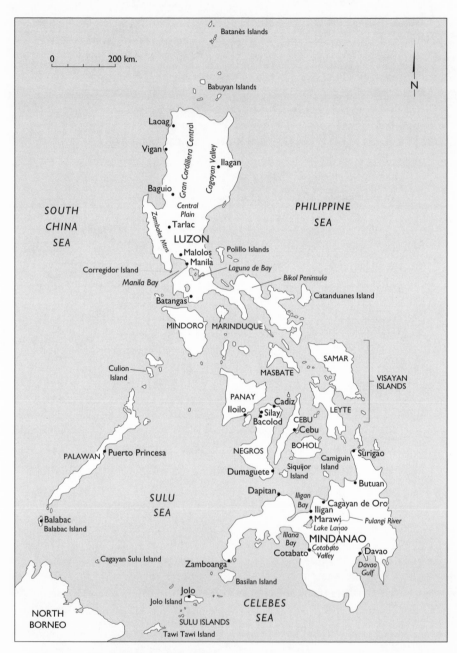

Map 1. The Philippines, c. 1900.

Introduction

The Genealogy of an Insult

In 1921, the Filipino residents of Dapitan on the southern Philippine island of Mindanao gathered in their town plaza to greet William Cameron Forbes, who had been the governor general of the Philippines from 1909 through 1913. Forbes was now touring the colony with General Leonard Wood, the newly appointed governor general of the Philippines, on an official mission to evaluate the Filipinos' readiness for independence, which the United States' Jones Act of 1916 had promised upon the establishment of a stable government. As elsewhere on their travels around the Philippines, Forbes and Wood were received in Dapitan with passionate appeals for Philippine independence. But the event in Dapitan was special in three ways.

First, Dapitan was the Filipino town on the northwest coast of Mindanao where Jose Rizal, the Filipino national hero, had lived in exile for the four years preceding the 1896 revolution against Spain and his execution for allegedly being its mastermind. Second, although Dapitan was a Catholic town, it lay within the territory of the special Moro Province that the American colonial state created in 1903 for the separate government of the Moro (Muslim) population of the southern Philippines. The first governor of the province, General Leonard Wood, broke with the previously lax practice of indirect rule in 1903 by declaring the legal abolition of slavery in the Moro societies, an act that sparked ten years of brutal warfare. Third, the ritual enunciation of nationalist aspirations at receptions for the Wood-Forbes mission in 1921 took a peculiar turn in Dapitan.

The rhetoric used by a nationalist orator in Dapitan excited Forbes's wrath. In his diary, Forbes recorded that "[o]ne little boy representing the 'rising generation' incurred my displeasure by telling me the Filipinos didn't want to continue in slavery." In addition to being a former governor of the colony, Forbes was a grandson of the great Boston merchant John Murray Forbes, who secretly aided the militant abolitionist John Brown in the 1850s. The remark clearly struck Forbes deeply as an indictment of American colonial rule in the Philippines, as he revealed in his characteristically bombastic reply:

> I made him repeat his words, and then thundered at him that I resented any such description of what America had done for the Philippines. I told him that for three consecutive years the [Philippine] Assembly had declined to approve a law penalizing slavery on the ground that it didn't exist in the Islands. I explained what slavery meant, told of our efforts to cure the Filipinos of the practice of making virtual slaves of some of their servants. I told him that his characterization of the present condition of the Filipinos as slaves was an insult to the American Government and to the Filipino people. I demanded that he withdraw his words and apologize for using them. This he did, wiping the sweat from his face, and then proceeded lamely with what remained of his speech.[1]

Why did slavery remain such a heated issue in a remote corner of the Philippines such as Dapitan in 1921? The painful disputes about antislavery laws that Forbes recollected had transpired years ago when he was governor general and were now long settled. The legal abolition of slavery in the Moro societies occurred even earlier and had never been a major subject of concern for Filipino nationalists, who defined their national community as Christian and considered the Moros a separate, and inferior, people.

Neither Forbes nor his Filipino opponent claimed that actual slavery currently existed as a social practice in the Philippines. Quite the contrary, they clearly regarded the slightest intimation that slavery might currently exist as a terrible indignity. Forbes even equivocated over whether slavery had actually existed at the time of his clash with the Philippine Assembly over antislavery laws (1909–1913), although he and his administration had argued forcefully then that slavery was practiced by many of the animist minority groups the Americans called the non-Christian tribes and also by some of their Catholic Filipino neighbors. American officials had equivocated similarly over the nature of slavery in the Moro societies from 1899 until 1903, describing it as so mild that it was not really slavery at all. Their interpretation of bondage in the Moro societies then changed quickly and completely when the colonial state moved to institute a more intrusive local rule that included abolition.

The confrontation between Forbes and the anonymous Filipino nationalist in 1921, like the series of controversies over slavery and anti-slavery laws that had preceded it, turned on the problem of what slavery meant precisely because the retrograde nature of slavery was beyond dispute. Both Forbes and the Filipino nationalist understood slavery as being inconsistent with progress and national independence. Slavery was wrong, they seem to have agreed, but what counted as slavery? As the record of their encounter shows, they could make the word *slavery* mean the oppression of servants and the condition of being colonized, as well as—by default—an unspecified kind of literal slavery.

Much of our scholarly literature on slavery outside of the Americas is concerned with precisely this question of defining the term. And yet, although there has been much debate about what should count as slavery and many scholars have commented on the sensitivities involved in labeling certain practices as slavery, I do not think we have sufficiently analyzed the continuing volatility of this issue.[2] Quite apart from situations in which individuals have had vested economic interests in labor relationships that might be delegitimized by defining them as slavery, why is it that assertions about even ancient and remote practices of slavery so often provoke defensive responses, denials, and counterassertions of cultural insensitivity?

The problem, I suggest, does not lie in the historical denotation of slavery. That is, rather than just determining what should be called slavery, a question answerable by studies that classify social practices according to translatable definitions and available data, we also need to examine the historical connotations of slavery. The primary issue I address in this book is not whether slavery, in fact, existed, but why Americans and Filipino nationalists who had no direct economic interests at stake cared so much about what should be denoted as slavery.

Indeed, however differently Forbes and the anonymous Filipino nationalist defined slavery, they both understood that allegations of the existence of slavery in the Philippines would be an embarrassment to Americans or to Filipinos and, ultimately, to both. The allegation that slavery existed in the Philippines was, according to Forbes, "an insult to the American Government and to the Filipino people." Filipino nation-

alists and American anti-imperialists had said much the same thing in
1913 and 1914, when the dispute over antislavery laws and the alleged
existence of slavery among the non-Christian tribes reached its apogee.
The participants in that controversy wielded definitions of slavery as
weapons, just as Americans divided over the colonial question had done
a decade earlier when they argued about whether the forms of bondage
practiced by Moros constituted slavery. A truer social history of indigenous institutions might tell us if slavery actually existed, but it could not
answer the question of why the connotations of slavery evoked such pas-
sions. That question requires a different kind of history, a genealogy of
how slavery came to be so embarrassing that allegations of its existence
would be taken as an insult.

It will help, then, to work backward from what we know—or, perhaps
it would be better to say, to work backward from how historians and social scientists think—about the Philippines, the United States, and the
comparative histories of slavery and its abolition. For example, students
of United States history might suppose that the Civil War and the Thirteenth Amendment to the Constitution should have settled all questions
about slavery in American territories, but that was obviously not the
case. Historians of the United States do not recognize that the country
played a role in the world history of abolition beyond its own borders.[3]
Only a few historians of the United States have been inclined to analyze the significance of American slavery and abolition in relation to a
broader field of history beyond the New World slave systems.[4]
    Rather than standing as a monumentally important case in a com-
parative field of historical knowledge, slavery and abolition in the Americas have been taken as the defining examples of the phenomena for
most of the modern world ever since the Anglo-American abolitionist
movement.[5] The privileged position of the United States in this global
historiography is taken for granted, but that assumption is obviously inadequate for an understanding of slavery and abolition in the Philippines. It also screens from view important features of U.S. history.[6] For
example, until very recently most scholars have taken Americanness as
a natural category that follows creole birth and certain cultural changes,
such as language use.[7] The slaves and freed slaves are thus typically presumed to be American when, in fact, the process of becoming American
and, more importantly, the general creation of American identity itself
need to be opened to a broader historical scrutiny. Like the global circulation of stereotyped images of American slavery in the nineteenth and

twentieth centuries, the transnational dimensions of American identity require analysis that goes beyond national historiography.[8]

Similarly, historians of the United States have been slow to take colonialism seriously as a relationship of interaction between Americans and other peoples. Despite their early critical contributions, neither William Appleman Williams nor Walter LaFeber nor their most influential students developed cross-cultural studies of colonialism.[9] With but a few exceptions, the study of U.S. foreign relations has remained state-centered and, whether critical or uncritical, fixed on the point of view of American policy makers.[10]

Concurrent with U.S. historians' tendency to isolate themselves and their subjects from the rest of the world, most of the vibrant comparative scholarship on colonialism and colonial discourse during the past two decades has bypassed subjects related to U.S. history. This is all the more remarkable given the fact that much of this intellectual work has been conducted at American universities by scholars who emphasize the importance of positionality and the political nature of scholarship. Despite their commitment to a politics of situated knowledge, virtually all of the major collections of innovative essays on colonialism ignore the United States.[11]

Important forays into the subject of U.S. colonialism and American cultural participation in a wider imperial world have been made by practitioners of cultural studies, but many historians continue to resist this literature as an intrusion into their discipline.[12] Among historians of the United States, it is still difficult to talk about the United States as a colonial power or a society that is enmeshed in a global world of social and cultural change.[13] Consequently, the historiography of the United States offers little guidance for explaining how the issue of slavery became entangled with colonial rule in the Philippines and why it continued to be a sensitive issue for American colonial officials as late as the 1920s.

One possible explanation of the embarrassment felt by the Filipino nationalist in Dapitan can be derived from the behavioral models of patron-client relations and reciprocity that have dominated much of Philippine historical and social study since the 1960s. Presented with Forbes's account of the confrontation in Dapitan, the classic literature of the patron-client school suggests that we should explain the anonymous nationalist's retreat from a face-to-face confrontation with a loud, angry American official in terms of the Filipino culture of interpersonal relations. The patron-client school's behavioralist theory virtually predicts the nationalist's flabbergasted reaction as a response to broken reciprocity between unequals.[14]

By this reading, the Filipino nationalist's desire to obtain honorable recognition in a smooth exchange with a powerful superior was answered with intemperate rejection, a charge of ingratitude, and a humiliating exposure of fault. In Tagalog (although the nationalist's ethnicity is unknown, Tagalog norms of reciprocity are the most deeply studied), one would say that he had been overcome by *hiya* (shame). This is the very quality that must be controlled in order to enact the most important reciprocal relationships founded on *utang na loob,* commonly rendered as "debt of gratitude" and, more literally, "debt of the inside." People who do not honor their *utang na loob* are derided as being *walang hiya* (without shame), and thus hardly worthy of recognition.

In the cultural system described by the patron-client school of Philippine studies, hierarchical relations are formed smoothly and consensually by gifts and grants that create debts and obligations. The point is not to pay off the debt, which need not be monetary or material, but to maintain the relationship with habitual payments so that another round of patronage (or, conversely, clientage) can be enacted in the future. People desire to be included and empowered—one might say bonded— through kinship, reciprocal exchanges, and other forms of mutual obligation. Their fear is to be shut out of such networks, unable to muster and then control the sense of *hiya* needed to establish respectful human relations and a position in the social hierarchy.[15]

There is much to be learned from the foregoing analysis. I do not think the encounter between Forbes and the anonymous nationalist can be understood fully without it. But this cannot be a sufficient and satisfactory explanation of the Filipino nationalist's extreme sensitivity to the issue of slavery. Nor can it explain Forbes's reaction.

Rather than assume an abstract and total cultural proscription against conflict with a superior, it is necessary to consider the historicity of the exchange at Dapitan and the patron-client model itself.[16] Why, for example, did the anonymous nationalist openly challenge Forbes in the first place? As a request for liberation from the slavery of colonialism, this supplication to a superior took the seemingly peculiar form of a protest. In addition, although the Filipino nationalist's reaction to Forbes's tirade may have been highly interpersonal, his terms of address were corporate and abstract; his words asserted a national desire to escape from the condition of being colonized. Filipino nationalists had used the concept of slavery in just this way since the late nineteenth century. The rhetoric of dependent reciprocity existed as an expression of ruling class desire for national hierarchy almost half a century before it became a social science theory of how Philippine social relations actually function.

We must remember that Forbes, too, considered the nationalist's charge that the United States kept the Filipinos in a state of slavery "an insult to the American Government and the Filipino people." Most historians would be quick to see ideology and a rationalistic historical frame of reference structuring his point of view, but not a more clearly circumscribed cultural pattern of interaction that might account for his anger and anxiety.[17] As this divergence suggests, most historical writing on American-Filipino colonial encounters tends to emphasize an initial cultural difference, sometimes followed by resident Americans or Filipinos being drawn ineluctably into the other's cultural orbit.[18] Such radical differences existed and assimilating adaptations no doubt occurred, but so too did more complex relationships of cultural exchange, improvisation, and understanding.

Last, why not ask whether there was something specifically and powerfully meaningful about these accusations of slavery? After all, the word *slavery* can describe relationships of great symbolic significance. The comparative historiography has shown that slavery has long provided a central metaphor for relations of power, subordination, and otherness in many different societies. To slave can mean to toil. To be enslaved can mean that one is bound or subject in countless ways. And to be the opposite of a slave can mean that one is a master, or free, or simply that one belongs as kith or kin. Enslavement can even have a positive meaning when, in the context of certain dyadic systems of relation, one is enslaved to a more luminous superior or, theologically speaking, to a god.[19]

If slavery as a social practice and slavery's symbolic meanings have always been related, the exact relationship must be a highly mediated one.[20] Wherever slavery has existed as a social relationship, its practice and its meaning have been shaped by the specific sociocultural setting, the cognitive bases for the enslavement of some and not others, and locally determined struggles between the will of masters and the willfulness of slaves. But from the postslavery perspective we share with the antagonists who faced each other in 1921, it would seem that the word *slavery* can only have references at the symbolic level and to a past that no longer exists.[21]

Like the anonymous Filipino in Dapitan, Filipino nationalists have long been very sensitive to discussions about the alleged practice of slavery in the Philippines. Indeed, the history of slavery in the Philippines remains controversial, even among the specialist community of Philippine and Southeast Asian historians.[22] In the Philippines the historical practice of indigenous forms of bondage is generally denied today by most educated Filipinos and nationalist historians, or relegated to a distant and often romanticized precolonial past.[23]

Until the eighteenth century, indigenous forms of bondage, which the Spanish officials and missionaries called slavery, were commonly practiced in almost all Philippine societies. These societies were highly localized and dyadically organized networks of kin, dependents, and allies. The people the Spaniards called *esclavos,* known as *alipin* in Tagalog and *oripun* in some languages of the central Visayan Islands, entered into their subordinate relationship through various routes, including fines, debts, purchase, capture, and inherited obligation.[24]

Far from forming singular status groups, *alipin* and *oripun* were complexly subdivided according to the origin of their subordination, whether they lived in their master's house or had their own household, and the degree to which they were in bondage (one could be half *alipin,* for example). Moreover, a great deal appears to have depended upon to whom one was bonded. The *alipin* to a powerful *datu* (chief or princeling) might enjoy prestige and being bonded to a relative might give one protection, but being a captive or human commodity in the active trans-archipelagic Southeast Asian slave trade would rip one away from all of the identity-giving dyadic relations of established social life. All of these elements that determined the condition of *alipin* and *oripun* could also change throughout the life of a given bondsperson, giving a shifting and fluid character to the practice of bondage.[25]

The consolidation of Spanish colonial rule in the Visayas and lowland Luzon during the seventeenth century gradually ended most local slave raiding as it suppressed the more outward manifestations of endemic petty warfare. Spanish colonialism also introduced new modalities of social subordination based on appointment to office, lineage, race, property in land, and the monetarization of economic relations. In an entirely unanticipated way, the colonialism of church and crown caused slavery to vanish from most of the Philippines.[26]

Spanish officials in the Philippines attempted to reconfigure the practice of slavery according to Spanish Catholic norms of just and unjust enslavement. This allowed for the purchase of slaves from international markets and the occasional enslavement of rebellious infidels, but not, in theory, the enslavement of *indios* who had submitted or still could submit to the authority of church and crown through religious conversion. Converts to Christianity became identified as subjects of the Crown's patronage, exchanging tribute in goods, cash, or labor for the royal "gifts" of Christian religion and protection. Spanish colonialism redefined the *indios* of the Philippines as "slaves of God" who also served the Spanish king, reserving worldly slavery, in theory, for infidels and outsiders who were assumed to be justly enslaved, like those sold internationally by Portuguese and Dutch merchants.[27]

Natives in the Philippines did not, of course, perceive themselves to be *indios* before colonization by Spain, nor did they consider themselves as having common identity with people outside their own locality. Anyone not from one's own village, kin group, or extended cohort of allies could be fair game for enslavement through capture in raids. But, in addition to this dramatic kind of immediately forced kinlessness, one could also become an *alipin* or *oripun* through indebtedness to kindred, and then, potentially, transferred beyond the realm of kin in commercial transactions. Consequently, the Spanish quest to sort out just from unjust slavery produced more than one hundred years of legal wrangling and contradictory opinions. In the meantime, Spanish authorities curtailed long-range slave raiding by their colonial subjects and suppressed the endemic local warfare that had also supplied captives for enslavement. As new modes of dependence took hold among the colonized Catholic *indios*, indigenous slavery disappeared from most of the northern and central Philippine lowlands. The words *alipin* and *oripun* seem to have fallen out of everyday use sometime in the eighteenth century.[28]

Spanish forms of slavery followed suit in the eighteenth century because the locally oriented colonial economy could not and did not need to compete for the purchase of slaves in the world market. The famed Manila galleon trade with Acapulco did not carry Philippine-made commodities until 1785, and then it ended weakly in 1811. Plantation agriculture for export did not begin until the mid–nineteenth century. While Spanish settlers and creoles in Cuba bought African slaves to labor on their plantations until the 1880s, the mostly mestizo planters and landlords in the Philippines' newly emerging export sectors (located principally in the hemp- and sugar-producing regions of central and southern Luzon and the sugar plantations of Negros in the central Visayan Islands) relied on local labor supplies and a range of labor relationships that did not include slavery.[29] Spanish colonialism in the Philippines was never abolitionist, but it presided over territories in which slavery ceased to be a social institution.

By the time of the revolution of 1896, slavery had not been a common practice in the Catholic Philippines for almost two centuries. But the Philippines remained ethnically, politically, and culturally heterogeneous. Although the disappearance of indigenous slavery was one constituent part of what the historian William Henry Scott called the creation of a "cultural majority" of lowland Catholics, the practice of indigenous forms of slavery persisted into the twentieth century among peoples who are today called "cultural minorities," namely the Moro societies and some of the upland animist groups who held Spanish conquest at bay.[30]

The emerging cultural geography of a Catholic majority population did not in itself produce the origins of Filipino national identity that informed the 1896 revolution against Spain, but it has structured the often-fraught relationship between Philippine nationalism and the heterogeneity of the Philippine past. In the second half of the nineteenth century, a Philippine-born intelligentsia began to imagine a new national community by taking the name Filipino, formerly applied only to the small population of Spanish creoles, and redefining it to include potentially all people born in the islands, which had been named *Las Filipinas* for a sixteenth-century Spanish king. Keen students of history, these mostly mestizo (Chinese, Spanish, and *indio*) intellectuals known as the *ilustrados* (the enlightened) projected their new sense of identity into the past, creating a mythos of an ancient historical unity.[31]

In Spanish-language writings, the *ilustrados* marked off the boundaries of national belonging in a way that defined a Filipino civilization. From their positions in Manila, Madrid, and other European cities, the *ilustrados* confidently assumed their right to lead their less cosmopolitan Christian countryfolk. But the countryfolk the *ilustrados* knew best and spoke for tended to be concentrated in Manila and the *ilustrados'* own home provinces, predominantly in the Tagalog region. Dissemination of the new Filipino communal identity thus faced barriers of communication. Spanish was the only lingua franca in the Philippines, but less than five percent of the population was fluent and literate in that colonial tongue. The order of a new national identity thus took shape through multiple translations, first and foremost into Tagalog, and then later into other native vernaculars. The resulting cultural localizations ensured that the *ilustrados'* variety of nationalism would not be the only one in play. *Ilustrado* nationalism appears to have been the only early nationalism that consistently embraced the entire Philippines rather than being regional or ethnolinguistic, but it was nevertheless exclusive and hierarchical in many ways.[32]

Under the shadow of colonialism, *ilustrado* nationalism posed a series of cultural problems revolving around perceptions of the uncivilized within its midst and at its borders. Few *ilustrados* recognized any quality of national belonging among their putatively less civilized upland animist and southern Muslim neighbors, whom they did not regard as Filipinos. Internal, intra-Filipino ethnic distinctions were less troubling at first. But they quickly became a source of concern when the 1898 revolution established the Philippine Republic and tried to insist, against the American imperialist onslaught, that it represented an indivisible Filipino nation and not a band of diverse "tribes." Thus, if *ilustrado* nationalists strove for a paradoxical timelessness in their appropriation of the Spanish colonial designations for a set of previously unconnected islands and the creole children of Spanish parents, their nation's internal divisions of race, ethnicity, religion, and culture remained uncomfortably manifold into the early twentieth century.

It was in the context of this emergent nationalism, its internal tensions, and its struggles against colonialism that Filipinos began to discuss slavery in new ways. When the anonymous Filipino nationalist in Dapitan told the former American governor general that "the Filipinos didn't want to continue in slavery," he deployed a familiar element of Filipino nationalist discourse. The early *ilustrado* nationalists in the 1880s and the popular nationalist movements that sprouted and multiplied during the 1896 revolution concurred in calling colonialism a form of slavery, but with different inflections and in different styles. No other kind of true slavery existed in the Philippines, they would say, not in 1921 or even in the ancient past.

Looking back again at the confrontation in Dapitan, we can now see that the mention of slavery carried a powerful excess of meaning for both parties. The classicist M. I. Finley once elaborated on a similar phenomenon in the historiography of ancient Greek and Roman slavery. He argued that the racial and political conflicts rooted in American slavery usually thought to explain the "volume and the polemical ferocity of work on the history of slavery . . . obviously cannot explain why ancient slavery is being subjected to a similarly massive and not much less heated inquiry. No one today need feel ashamed of his Greek or Roman slave ancestors, nor are there any current social or political ills that can be blamed on ancient slavery, no matter how distantly." I agree with his conclusion that "[s]ome other explanations must be sought" and, as he did, I "shall argue that they are deeply rooted in major ideological conflicts." [33]

In the two decades before 1921, the "major ideological conflicts" in the American colonial Philippines revolved around the colonial question itself. Were Filipinos a nation and were they modern? When would the Philippines be an independent nation-state? Could it be? Did the United States have a right or duty or even the simple power to make these determinations? Could it enforce an instructive colonial discipline to develop Filipino fitness for independence? What, ultimately, did the United States stand for on the stage of world history? Could it be expressed as a force for slavery or the champion of freedom? And what were the dimensions and internal structures of the Filipino nation that desired independence? These were questions about the identities of peoples and authority, the boundaries of belonging and civility, the meanings of freedom and subjection.

By the early twentieth century, virtually all Americans and Filipino nationalists shared the basic assumptions of antislavery ideology. To them, slavery was uncivilized and unchristian. It was either antithetical to progress, or it marked a distinctly premodern phase of social evolution. Perhaps it is easy to see that Americans would be sensitive to complaints about enslavement in their new colony, given the recent history of abolition in the United States. But why did allegations about slavery in remote places and time periods prove so much more intensely embarrassing for Filipino nationalists than did colonial publicity about other reputedly uncivilized practices such as head-hunting and animist spirituality, or even the live display of non-Christians as G-stringed savages at international expositions? Indeed, why were Filipino nationalists so affected by antislavery ideology? There had never been an abolitionist movement in the Catholic Philippines or the kind of industrial capitalist development that historians have correlated with institutional support for antislavery ideology in the leading abolitionist countries in the nineteenth century.[34] The answer, I believe, lies in the way modern nationalism and antislavery ideology pose similar problems of corporate belonging, progress, and freedom.

Almost everywhere, according to a vast range of historical accounts, when slaves passed out of slavery into another social condition there were questions about their new membership in families, societies, and polities. The questions could be answered in many ways, even to the point of accepting former slaves without lasting stigma, but they had to be asked.[35] The problem of belonging not only lingered but also intensified on a massive scale with the coming of the abolitionist movement that originated in the eighteenth century.

In contrast to the ancient practice, by individuals, of manumitting certain favored or deserving slaves, the modern antislavery movements originating in the eighteenth century began to construe their tasks in systematic and corporate terms. Their goals rapidly evolved from eradicating slavery within their own saintly religious communities, as did the Quakers, to abolishing it as a system in local, national, and international jurisdictions. Now the old problem of what to do with a few selectively freed slaves was replaced in the Americas and western Europe by the vastly different question of how an entire population of slaves would, or would not, be incorporated into the community of belonging. Nobody had ever before asked that kind of question because nobody had ever before contemplated abolishing slavery. But there was one more step beyond that. Well before the end of the nineteenth century, the abolition of slavery became a global and globalizing campaign tied to the rise of modern imperialism, especially in the colonial partition of Africa.[36]

Antislavery ideology, it has often been noted, emerged and developed with the Enlightenment, the "age of revolution," and the rise of industrial capitalism. Modern nationalism crystallized during this epoch, too. Under these circumstances the first worldwide campaign for human rights did not call upon self-determining nation-states to end slavery as much as it took part in the determination of which people were fit to govern themselves as nations and which needed to be colonized in order to fulfill the higher good of eliminating slavery.[37] Decolonization in the twentieth century left in its wake a world composed of nation-states, the kind of entities that could join the United Nations and have representatives sign its 1948 Universal Declaration of Human Rights and later conventions against slavery.

Our present postslavery and postcolonial world is also a nationalist world—a world structured by compulsory nationality—committed to a discourse of freedom.[38] We are all, equivalently, expected to belong to one self-determining nation or another. Nationalism projects this belonging back into the immemorial past as if it were a natural condition, just as the discourse of liberal freedom tends to represent itself as if it were also founded in nature. Not only are we encouraged to believe we are everywhere born free, as Rousseau said, but we are also taught that we are all born equally into nations.[39]

The history of indigenous slavery in places such as the Philippines can thus appear to be doubly anomalous. It controverts the modern presumption of freedom and it contradicts the projection of nationality into the past by recollecting old boundaries between persons and groups who are supposed to constitute a single people. For these reasons I think Orlando Patterson recognized something fundamental about the making of the modern world when he advised readers of *Slavery and Social Death* that "[s]lavery, for all who look to Enlightenment Europe and revolutionary America as the source of their most cherished political values, is not the peculiar institution but the embarrassing institution."[40] Many of the Filipino and American participants in the controversies over slavery felt the deep sting of this embarrassment, but so far no historian has explained how and why the embarrassment of slavery spread beyond its European and American origins.

While antislavery ideology clearly originated and first took hold in some European and American societies during the eighteenth century, the history of its development extends far beyond those geographic and temporal limits. Nevertheless, the historiography of abolition continues to treat antislavery ideology and discourse as distinctly Western phenomena. Far from being peculiar to peoples in Europe and the Americas, the history of the American colonial Philippines shows that the postabolition sense of slavery as an embarrassment spread through struggles over the cultural elaboration of colonialism and the oppositional desires of anticolonial nationalism. Slavery became a lasting source of anxiety, and a potential insult, for modern Filipinos and Americans precisely because we have lived within the hegemony of both antislavery ideology and nationalism.

In recent decades, scholars have tended to explain the worldwide abolition of slavery as, ultimately, the result of the globalizing drives of capitalism and imperialism acting upon the Americas, Africa, and Asia.[41] The historiography of abolition in Africa and Asia has paid ample attention to antislavery as a colonial ideology and discourse, but it has said little about how and why the colonized found it desirable.[42] Even when this literature has argued that slaves were primarily responsible for freeing themselves in the face of official hesitation and prevarication, it still treats antislavery ideology as an externality originating from the metropolitan centers of capitalism and colonialism.[43] It is, of course, crucial that we recognize the difference between slaves who did not want to be slaves and the reconceptualization of the world embodied by anti-slavery ideology. Many freed slaves may not have come to see the world through antislavery glasses, but, assuredly, antislavery ideology eventually took hold among at least the leading segments of virtually all polities in the twentieth century.

There is, in fact, a pronounced methodological duality in the currently dominant historiography of emancipation, not only in Africa and Asia, but also in the Americas.[44] Conventionally, this literature begins by introducing the rise of European and American antislavery ideology and recounting how it became historically effective to the point of abolition. Once here, the literature almost universally turns away, however, from questions of ideology and culture to examine the lives of freed people sociologically. That is, freed people and their former masters become the subjects of a material history of social and economic struggle. Meanwhile, the sense that slavery and its antitheses become meaningful through the workings of ideology fades away. This is nowhere more visible than in studies that treat the "meaning" or "problem" of freedom as a set of material questions about land, access to resources, and labor.[45]

The dominant historiography of emancipation exposes a history of economic contradictions and the failure of liberal ideology to live up to its promises, but it does not exhaust the problem of understanding the meanings of emancipation and freedom. As David Brion Davis advised, "metaphorical usage tells us nothing about the sociological character of particular forms of servitude," but it is equally the case that "sociological analysis and typology tell us nothing about the meanings people have attached to various kinds of dependency, constraint, and exploitation."[46] The liberal discourse of freedom must have something more to it that evades criticism of its economic contradictions and social mystifications.[47] Hegemonic ideologies must appeal to some desire among the subordinated in order to be hegemonic. There must be something in the discourse of liberal freedom that continues to be positively desired across so many different sociocultural contexts, despite one hundred and fifty years of astute criticism.[48]

So far, however, the principal critique of these materialist histories of emancipation in Africa and Asia has come from an archly ahistorical vantage point. The anthropologist Igor Kopytoff has argued that abolition in African societies only "allowed the social organization of dependency to purge itself, so to speak, of the accumulated dissatisfactions within it." Abolition, he suggests, rather than initiating dramatic changes, only "gave greater stability to the continuing social structure of dependency." Consequently, political structures remained unchanged unless they were "altered by forces other than abolition," because "the lowering of one kin group simply makes room for the rise of another."[49]

Scholars familiar with Philippine studies will immediately recognize the similarity between Kopytoff's homeostatic model of abolition in Africa and prominent models of patron-client relations in the Philippines. Like Kopytoff, the patron-client school discounts the significance of historical change. It tends to dismiss egalitarian ideologies and rhetoric as alien encrustations on a persistent, deep cultural desire to attach oneself to a chain of hierarchy. Names of leaders and followers may change, but, the patron-client school asserts, the principal organization of society will not change unless there is a massive intervention from outside the system.[50]

A much more nuanced and, indeed, novel reading of the persistence of seemingly traditional modes of servitude has been offered by Gyan Prakash in a history of labor bondage in Bihar, India. In a fascinating argument, Prakash shows how the British colonial discourse of freedom successively redefined a group of servile laborers called *kamias* as suffering first from slavery, then debt-bondage, and then a psychological inability to actuate freedom. Not just a gloss of alien ideas on a native social reality, colonial discourse and juridical action reshaped both the representations and practices of exchange between these *kamia* laborers and their *malik* superiors. This made the *kamias* "unfree" in a way that was formerly impossible in a society that did not hold freedom to be a natural state, but it also presented them with new points of struggle in their relation to *malik* dominance. The aim of the project, writes Prakash, "is to make visible the process by which freedom and commodity fetishism came to don the garb of naturalness in Indian history."[51]

Although Prakash's historical subject is quite different from my own, we are perhaps converging on adjacent themes. In his conclusion, Prakash alludes to the postindependence Indian state's perception of debt-bondage as a sign of backwardness and unfreedom in a national society that it would like to depict as modern and free.[52] Although he does not explain why this element of the colonial discourse of freedom developed a particularly strong hold on the representatives of the nation, Prakash's reference to the naturalization of freedom in "Indian history" does provide an important clue. In assimilating precolonial and colonial societies into the narrative of the nation, nationalist historiography posits independence as the recovery of a self lost to colonialism. This historiography develops its own ideological power by predicating national freedom as a natural state violated by the repressive power of colonialism. While the *maliks* and *kamias* were apparently forced to remake their social relationship in congruence with the discourse of freedom, nationalists in the Philippines (and perhaps India?) actively desired antislavery ideology as a sign of modernity that enabled national self-recognition and representation in a world of nations.

No historian has satisfactorily explained how and why dominant political movements in Africa and Asia gave the disciplinary regime of antislavery ideology the willing consent (as well as enforced accommodation) necessary to make it internationally, if not universally, hegemonic in the twentieth century.[53] This stands in rather interesting contrast to Benedict Anderson's influential text, *Imagined Communities,* in which he argues that the form of nationality that crystallized in the eighteenth-century revolutions became "modular" and thereby well-nigh global through its adaptation to the particular desires of distinct nationalist movements.

From my perspective, Anderson repositions our understanding of nationalism in two ways that help explain why modern anticolonial nationalists would also be deeply affected by antislavery ideology. First, Anderson considers nationality a special and distinctly modern form of community, a "cultural artefact" historically distinguishable from other kinds of polities and associations. Whereas other forms of large-scale community, such as dynastic states and religions, funneled together vertical ties of secular and sacred hierarchies that cut through space and providential models of time, modern nationality depends upon our recognition of simultaneous horizontal relationships that spread across homogeneous time and fill finite territories with delimited populations. The conceptual revolutions needed to imagine for the first time the vast, anonymous relatedness of modern national belonging coincided and in many ways overlapped with the redefinitions of identity, society, and otherness in the rise of antislavery ideology.[54]

Second, Anderson brings us inside the powerful communication of belonging that is both a structure and an effect of nationalism. He insists, quite originally, that we should not classify nationalism as "*an* ideology," but rather treat it "as if it belonged with 'kinship' and 'religion.'" As such, Anderson takes quite seriously the frequent self-conceptualization of nationalism as "a deep, horizontal comradeship," albeit one that is necessarily limited to the members of the nation and compatible with gross inequalities in social life. This leads him to an appreciation of the often-tragic calls to love, memory, and sacrifice made in the name of the nation—that is, to an understanding of nationalist discourse as a rhetoric of particular desire. As an international phenomenon, nationalism thus produces a paradox of sameness and difference: Everyone has a nationality, but each nationality is understood to be internally unique. Nationalists thus seek conformity to an international disciplinary regime because, ironically, they desire its mode of particularity and difference.

Anderson's historical theorization of nationalism has, of course, been criticized by specialists in various national histories as well as challenged more broadly by so-called primordialists, such as Anthony Smith, who root the history of nationalism in older ethnocultural groupings.[55] Among scholars concerned with anticolonial nationalism, Partha Chatterjee has been the most persistent critic.[56] He is therefore, perhaps, the strongest authority I can invoke to support Anderson's argument on this crucial point about the particularity of nationalist desires and the generalized, modular form of the modern nation.

Chatterjee objects to Anderson's concept of nationalism as modular because this seems to label anticolonial nationalism as being forever derivative of a first-world model. Chatterjee argues, instead, that anticolonial nationalism desired to mark its *difference* with the 'modular' forms of the national society propagated by the modern West" through the demarcation of "an 'inner' domain bearing the 'essential' marks of cultural identity." At the same time, in "the domain of the 'outside,' of the economy and of statecraft . . . Western superiority had to be acknowledged and its accomplishments carefully studied and replicated."[57]

According to Chatterjee, the truly creative developments of anticolonial nationalism emerged in, or out of, the "'inner' domain" before the moment of political confrontation with colonialism. But these are now "overwhelmed and swamped by the history of the postcolonial state," which merely mimics European precedents as it lives "embedded . . . within the universal narrative of capital." Instructively, Chatterjee shifts his terms of meaningful agency to accommodate the determinations of history when he reminds us that "it is not the origins but the process of domestication of the modern state in India that is at issue; one does not, unfortunately, have the option of sending this state back to its origins." In the Philippines, antislavery ideology, like nationalism, was domesticated and naturalized through just this kind of dynamic attachment to the desires of an essential inner life.[58]

In many historic situations in the Philippines, slavery could mark the boundaries between social insiders to be protected and acquired outsiders, to whom anything could happen depending upon the circumstances. Slavery, almost everywhere, has been a condition associated with outsiders and the ritually dishonored. In Orlando Patterson's terms, it is construed as a passage through "social death."[59] That is, the practice of slavery has frequently marked a border of belonging. But the terms of bondage in Philippine societies, as in many others, could also slip in and out of a range of negotiable dependent relationships between kin, village mates, and associates.

In the early twentieth century, Filipino nationalists denied the existence of slavery throughout Philippine history in order to refute the charge that Filipinos enslaved one another as if they were not a single people who had long been civilized and Christian. Instead, they articulated an alternative model of social relations that bonded the people of the nation together—an integrated national hierarchy based on a paternalistic system of kinship and reciprocity—that remains ideologically vibrant to this day. A broad, spreading network of dependency could be made to signify a deep cultural bond between rich and poor at the heart of national life, but the history of Filipinos' ancestors enslaving one another as strangers could signal only the opposite. The idea of indigenous slavery remains incompatible with the nationalist mythos because few things are considered more abominable, or impossible, than enslaving one's own kind. Nationalism came to understand slavery, not as something that certain historical Philippine societies practiced, but as the condition of colonialism imposed on Filipinos by Spain and the United States.

At the same time that the embarrassment of slavery helped to define a distinct Filipino nation of apparently immemorial age, it also implicated the new nation more deeply in the world outside the Philippines. Nationalist discourse drew upon the rhetorical models of enslavement expressed in Christian theology, Enlightenment concepts of freedom, and imagery from the nineteenth-century Anglo-American abolitionist movements. The history of Philippine slavery and the nationalists' use of antislavery discourse therefore mark the historic heterogeneity of identity in the Philippine past. They remind us, in a most pointed way, of the underlying historicity and hybridity of modern Filipino national identity and of modern national identity in general.[60]

Slavery and emancipation thus became points of social, cultural, and political conflict in a series of intertwined American and Philippine histories. By identifying the links between modern nationalism and antislavery ideology in the Philippines, I demonstrate how Filipinos desired and thereby naturalized antislavery ideology. But it was this same naturalization of antislavery ideology that enabled it to play a hegemonic role in the consolidation of American colonial rule. The meaning of slavery emerged as an embarrassment, first for American advocates of colonialism and the colonial state in the Philippines, and then for American anti-imperialists and Filipino nationalists. By 1916, when the United States promised Philippine independence in the Jones Act and thus stabilized a symbiotic relation among these contesting groups, slavery became almost too embarrassing for any of the parties to discuss—but its specter would not go away, as William Cameron Forbes's diary entry from Dapitan attests.

In the American colonial Philippines, the powerful meaning of slavery was not merely, or only, projected as a part of colonial ideology or a manifestation of capitalism. It was also refracted in struggles over the construction of colonial hegemony and nationalist alternatives. Much as Orlando Patterson implied, the modern world's embarrassment in the face of slavery has deeply affected understandings of nationality, freedom, and the workings of various forms of dishonorable subordination, including colonialism. Like slavery in the postabolitionist world, colonialism has become an embarrassment in our postcolonial world of independent nation-states. In profoundly important ways, Americans and Filipinos find it terribly difficult to talk about slavery and the ramifications of colonialism. The controversies over slavery in the American colonial Philippines challenge us to rethink assumptions about modern identity, the peculiarity of our national histories, and the constitution of our contemporary societies.

The histories I write in this book begin in the late-nineteenth century, among very different groups of people in the United States and in the Philippines. These histories cannot be told independently, nor can they be reduced to a simple singular narrative without doing violence to the differences of the past. I have chosen to reconstruct them together as a series of overlapping accounts, divided into three parts. I hope to respect and convey some of their discontinuities through this organization while also capturing the interactions, moments of mutual recognition, and development of interdependencies that might elude more narrowly focused studies of particular Filipino or American histories.

Part I begins in the United States. It consists of an examination of the problem of slavery that pervaded the early debate over colonial rule in the Philippines and the impact of the first reports that slavery actually existed in the Moro societies. Part II is a reconstruction of the American colonial encounter with slavery in the Moro societies in the southern Philippines. I begin by reviewing the history of slavery in the Moro societies and its persistence into the twentieth century. Then I analyze the unforeseen consequences of American colonialism that ultimately led to the abolition of slavery. Part III is a dissection of the tense triangular relation among Philippine nationalism, antislavery ideology, and American colonial hegemony. After outlining the metaphorics of slavery and emancipation in early Philippine nationalist discourse, I examine the way in which allegations about the practice of slavery among the non-Christian tribes became an embarrassment for Filipino nationalists and American anti-imperialists and then for American colonialism, too. In the conclusion, I will return to consider the effects of antislavery ideology and nationalism in the modern world.

PART I

Slavery and the Colonial Question

Map 2. The Philippines and Asia, 1898 (originally published in *Harper's Weekly*, vol. 42, 11 June 1898).

CHAPTER ONE

Anticipating Slavery

In the 1890s, the Philippines was the major Pacific outpost of Spain's crumbling worldwide empire. Very few people in the United States knew much about the Philippines before 1898, although President William McKinley only feigned ignorance when he said that he could not find the islands on a map after Commodore George Dewey began the Spanish-American War with his famous victory at Manila Bay. Spain's colonies in the Americas had tempted expansionist Americans throughout the nineteenth century, from the annexation of Florida by treaty in 1819 to the Southern slaveholders' dreams of a Caribbean empire in the 1850s to the seemingly endless turmoil over slave emancipation and revolution in Cuba after 1868. While Americans focused their attention on Cuba in the early months of 1898, the McKinley administration planned a war that would extend to and, indeed, begin in the Philippines, where its naval and consular officials in Asia knew that embers still burned from the revolution of 1896.[1]

Unlike Cuba, which had its own economic, political, and moral value in the eyes of many Americans, the Philippines drew no such public attention in the early months of 1898. Apart from a few merchant houses and cordage manufacturers who purchased Manila hemp, it attracted little business. Few Americans followed the far-off and, from their point of view, obscure events of the 1896 revolution, the first modern anti-colonial revolution in the age of imperialism. But the American press, business leaders, and government officials did pay attention to China.[2]

To American observers, China seemed on the verge of being carved
up and colonized by the major European powers and Japan. The fate
of China, long heralded as a future great market for American-made
goods, worried the McKinley administration and a broader audience
concerned with the expansion of American international trade in a decade of economic troubles. Dewey's victory at Manila and the consequent collapse of Spanish authority in the Philippines under pressure
from Filipino rebels whetted an American appetite for naval bases in the
Philippines, from which the United States could project its influence into
China. Economically and strategically, McKinley's decision to take the
Philippines as an American colony grew from a larger interest in sustaining what his secretary of state, John Hay, would famously call an
"open door" into China and other markets. The decision depended,
however, on a set of broader cultural preconditions that made colonialism thinkable, practicable, and familiar. Its ramifications for Americans
and Filipinos would be far more extensive than an analysis of American
policy makers' economic and strategic calculus could reveal.[3]

Following Dewey's victory, American political society entered into a
debate over whether the United States should annex the Philippines. The
debate climaxed with the United States Senate's ratification of the Treaty
of Paris with Spain on 6 February 1899, two days after war broke out
between American troops in Manila and the surrounding army of Emilio
Aquinaldo's Republic of the Philippines. The Philippines was transferred
to the United States by Spain for $20 million, but the war in the Philip-
pines and the Americans' internal quarrel about colonialism continued.

For some Americans, the war of conquest in the Philippines seemed
barbaric for its violence and incongruity with the ideal of self-government. But only a tiny minority of critics maintained that the population
of natives and mestizos in the Philippines could be trusted to govern
themselves. The question of whether the United States should colonize the Philippines after the fashion of modern European imperialism
glossed over the more fundamental and widely shared assumption that
some modern nation-state would have to colonize Africa and much of
Asia. For most Americans, colonialism in the Philippines seemed necessary and even natural. To them, the temerity of brown-skinned Filipinos
who killed Americans in order to preserve their independence indicated
a barbarism and savagery opposed to American progress, not infre-
quently likened to that of American Indians in earlier eras of American
expansion.[4]

American colonialism in the Philippines thus appeared, simultaneously, as a departure from and a reenactment of old traditions. It was familiar and understandable in terms of well-known fables from the domestic history of the United States, but it also seemed novel as an overseas enterprise and the people of the Philippines were radically unknown. The problem of slavery in the Philippines emerged for Americans in this uncanny way.

In 1898, scarcely any Americans knew that indigenous forms of slavery had ever existed in the Philippines.[5] Then, in September of 1899, news began to filter back to the United States that General John C. Bates of the American occupation forces had negotiated a treaty with Sultan Hadji Mohammad Jamalul Kiram, recognizing the sovereignty of the United States over his sultanate based in the Sulu Islands in the southern Philippines. The McKinley administration instructed Bates to avert a war with the Moro societies by arranging a system of indirect colonial rule. This the Bates treaty accomplished in Sulu, but it also informed Americans of the existence of slavery in their new colony.

The Bates treaty provided for considerable local autonomy in governance and judicial matters. The United States pledged to respect "the rights and dignities of His Highness the Sultan and his datos [local rulers]," the religious customs of the Muslim inhabitants of the Sulu Islands, and even agreed not to interfere in judicial matters when the contest involved "crimes and offences committed by Moros against Moros." Because the political economy of the Sulu sultanate was based upon slavery, all of the provisions for local autonomy implicitly raised the thorny question of slavery. Article X, the only article of the treaty that mentioned slavery explicitly, declared that "[a]ny slave in the archipelago of Jolo shall have the right to purchase freedom by paying to the master the usual market value." Here then was an official document from the U.S. government that recognized the existence of slavery in part of the Philippine Islands.[6] In ways that no American could have predicted, the commitment of the United States to antislavery ideals became painfully entangled in the politics and ideology of imperialism less than fifty years after the question of slavery in the United States had seemingly been settled by the Civil War.

Yet, in other ways, slavery and its abolition in the Civil War were so deeply implicated in American history, culture, and ideology that their memory and legacy could not but reemerge in the debate over imperialism, much of which took shape in the vocabulary of that earlier history.

Antislavery ideology and the history of abolition shaped Americans' debate on U.S. colonial rule in the Philippines in three ways, even before news of the Bates treaty confirmed the actual existence of slavery in the Philippines.

First, slavery and its abolition were bound up in complex ways with notions of progress and barbarism, the evolution of society and the hierarchy of races, and conceptions of liberation and domination that were woven into the fabric of colonialism.[7] Second, the living memory of slavery, the Civil War, and the consequences of emancipation constituted much of the historical terrain on which the conflicts over colonial policy took place.[8] Third, the history of European colonies and the Anglo-American experience of slave emancipation were so interpreted as to produce very pessimistic assumptions about the procurement and control of labor in tropical colonies. Many white Americans doubted the practicality of free labor principles when dealing with African and Asian peoples, but few questioned the presumed necessity and legitimacy of commodity production for international markets. Though they may have disagreed on the means, most readily agreed that African and Asian peoples must be made to labor for the production of commodities. These assumptions were so deeply ingrained that the existence of slavery or some other form of involuntary servitude in tropical colonies was frequently taken for granted. Thus, for the United States, the problem of slavery in the Philippines originated in American ideology before Americans actually encountered slavery as a social practice in the Philippines.

The problem of slavery appeared in a number of different political guises. As political metaphors, slavery and emancipation structured the discourse of U.S. colonialism from its formal beginning to its end. In the founding document of American colonial authority in the Philippines, McKinley's famous Benevolent Assimilation Proclamation of 21 December 1898, the president ordered the military occupation to "proclaim in the most public manner that we come, not as invaders or conquerors, but as friends, to protect the natives in their homes, in their enjoyments, and in their personal and religious rights." He instructed them, also, "to win the confidence, respect, and affection of the inhabitants of the Philippines by assuring them in every possible way that full measure of individual rights and liberties which is the heritage of free peoples, and by proving to them that the mission of the United States is one of benevolent assimilation, substituting the mild sway of justice and right for arbitrary rule."[9]

The Benevolent Assimilation Proclamation did not mention slavery or emancipation explicitly, but the gift of individual liberty it promised from "the heritage of free peoples" resonated strongly with an American repertoire of binary oppositions between individual freedom and slavery. McKinley began to make the connection explicit just a few weeks after the start of the United States–Philippine War in February 1899. He told the Home Market Club of Boston that "[t]he future of the Philippine Islands is now in the hands of the American people . . . [the] treaty [of Paris] now commits the free and enfranchised Filipinos to the guiding hand and the liberalizing influences, the generous sympathies, the uplifting education, not of their American masters, but of their American emancipators." [10]

The prospect of the existence of slavery in the Philippines and the necessity of some form of compulsory labor to make a tropical colony economically viable became major subjects in the initial spate of literature about the new colonial policy of the United States. The war against Spain in 1898, followed by the annexation of Hawaii, Puerto Rico, and the Philippines, turned a stream of interest in the operation of colonies into a flood. The Library of Congress published extensive bibliographies of works on colonialism and the newly occupied territories. Several major studies were published that could best be called "how to" manuals for colonial rule. The first and perhaps most important of these was Allyene Ireland's *Tropical Colonization* (1899).[11]

An Englishman, Allyene Ireland led a nomadic life, travelling through British colonies in Asia and the West Indies. He worked as a journalist for newspapers and magazines in England and the United States, turning his travel observations to sustenance. It was his good fortune to arrive in the United States just at the beginning of the Spanish-American War, when the demand for literature on the colonial experience of other nations was reaching its peak. Ireland's experience and direct prose quickly earned him recognition as an expert on matters colonial. His articles in the *Atlantic Monthly* and *Popular Science Monthly* and his book were quoted as authoritative statements of the realities and problems to be encountered in tropical colonies.[12]

In the preface to *Tropical Colonization,* Ireland framed the "essential questions in regard to tropical colonization" to which he addressed his book: "(1) How to govern a tropical colony. (2) How to obtain the reliable labor absolutely necessary for the successful development of a tropical colony. (3) What does the possession of tropical colonies amount to from the standpoint of the sovereign state?" Four of the six core chapters of the book were devoted to the second question.[13]

Ireland traced the origins of what he called "the labor problem in the tropics" back to the demographic disaster of the American Indian population after the European conquest of the New World. European settlers then turned to African slave markets to find a supply of laborers who could be made to work on their plantations. Ireland did not probe deeply into the details of this history. Rather, he simply assumed the legitimacy and necessity of the demand for labor and then rationalized the system of slave labor that was created to meet the demand.[14]

Ireland's focus on the more contemporary version of the labor problem—how to get emancipated slaves and other tropical peoples to labor for colonial enterprises—lent itself to a roseate view of slavery. Under slavery, he argued, blacks in the West Indies provided a controlled, effective, and remunerative supply of labor for the plantation economy. Economically rewarding for the masters, slavery was, Ireland also maintained, beneficial to the slaves. In an instructive twist of reasoning, Ireland reconciled his rationalization of slavery with antislavery morality. "Few people to-day . . . will claim that the necessity for the abolition of slavery in the British colonies arose out of the ill-treatment to which slaves were subjected by their masters"; instead, according to Ireland, "the abolition of slavery was, in fact, merely an inevitable step in the ethical development of Great Britain, which must have been taken even though it could have been proved that each slave was as fondly cared for as the only child of loving parents."[15]

Ireland's version of antislavery ideology typified the general conservative thrust of abolitionism in the late-nineteenth-century English empire. Emancipation was still considered a progressive and disinterested act. Ireland, like many others, kept his faith in the inevitable progress of liberal economic institutions. He still believed that "apart from all other considerations the operation of economic laws would have brought slavery to an end almost as quickly as the popular clamor which did in reality lead to its abolition throughout the British dominions." But, even if abolition were inevitable in the unfolding of ethical and economic progress, this did not mean that Ireland was automatically committed to the practice of free labor and equality.[16]

Indeed, Ireland interpreted the history of the British West Indies after emancipation as a demonstration of the unqualified failure of free labor in the tropics. Consequently, he romanticized West Indian slavery as a benign and functional solution to the labor problem suitable for its time and place. Then, with a frankness born of his faith in the necessity and morality of such compulsion, he proceeded to discuss techniques of compelling people of color to provide labor that would be suitable for modern times.[17]

Ireland assumed that the production of agricultural commodities was necessary for the progress of tropical colonies and their economic success, which meant profitable trade with the metropole. The compulsion of labor was necessary, he explained, for two reasons. Using sugar for illustrative purposes, he argued first that "a perfectly reliable labor supply is the first requisite" for the production of agricultural commodities in the tropics. Especially at harvest time, when sugar cane must be cut and processed promptly, any disruption of labor would cause monumental losses to investment. Second, he repeated received wisdom when he explained that tropical peoples would not work if left to their own devices. As the history of West Indian emancipation seemed to demonstrate, tropical peoples could be made to work regularly and efficiently when compelled, but the possibility of garnering a subsistence outside of the plantation economy in bountiful tropical climates would allow them to lapse into "lazy" work routines when treated as "free labor."[18]

Significantly, the last chapter of *Tropical Colonization,* titled "The Colonial Problem of the United States," was largely devoted to the issue of labor. Because "a colony cannot buy goods until it produces goods for sale," Ireland informed his readers that "the commercial problem in the American colonies is almost entirely comprised in the one question of labor." Some form of coercion would be necessary to create and control a labor force in Hawaii, Puerto Rico, and the Philippines. As solutions, Ireland prescribed limiting access to subsistence by increasing the population and restricting access to land, and also the use of imported contract laborers forced to work by the terms of their indenture. Ireland considered one more solution: the creation of new desires. For a concise description of the concept, he quoted Dean C. Worcester, a professor of ornithology at the University of Michigan who had written one of the first works by an American on the newly acquired Philippine colony. As Worcester explained it in 1899, "[n]ature has done so much for her children in these islands that they have no need to labor hard in order to supply their few and simple wants. . . . Their laziness might be remedied by increasing their necessities."[19]

For Allyene Ireland, antislavery ideology was not an obstruction in the path of colonial rule. He believed that the labor problem could be solved in ways that did not violate ethical norms. Ironically, some of his readers in the United States used his arguments to draw implications to the contrary. David Starr Jordan, an ichthyologist and president of Stanford University, may have been the first anti-imperialist to make a specifically (rather than metaphorically) antislavery argument against U.S. colonial rule in the Philippines. Jordan's assumptions about the labor problem were derived from Ireland, whom he quoted as an authority on the problems of colonial rule.[20]

The crux of the colonial problem, Jordan told an audience at Stanford in mid-February 1899, was the labor problem. "Success in the control of the tropical races no nation has yet achieved, for no one has yet solved the problem of securing industry without force, of making money without some form of slavery." Speaking of the British West Indies, but extrapolating for all tropical regions, Jordan declared that "the natives will not work continuously unless they are forced to work as slaves." Jordan's argument ran precisely parallel to Ireland's. The only difference was that Jordan found blatantly coerced labor unacceptable.[21]

Jordan believed that slavery was "endemic in the tropics," but he did not advocate an abolitionist crusade through the newly acquired colonies. He simply wanted his countrymen to refrain from establishing tropical colonies. Neither sentimental nor ready to put much faith in colonialist schemes for regenerating ostensibly barbarous peoples, he thought about the colonial problem in stark terms.

The Philippines, Jordan warned, were "not contiguous to any land of freedom. They lie in the heart of that region which Ambrose Bierce calls 'the horrid zone, nature's asylum for degenerates.' They are," he continued, "already densely populated. . . . Their population cannot be exterminated on the one hand, nor made economically potent on the other, except through slavery." Jordan was willing to consider whether the population of the Philippines could be "exterminated" to pave the way for American settlers, much as the native population of North America had been eliminated and removed. He referred to the subjects of colonial rule as "slave races," obviously incapable of social and political development, and feared that prolonged contact with Filipinos would "corrupt and weaken us." The need for a prophylactic distance between the United States and the degenerative influences of the tropics would make colonialism as dangerous as abolitionist activity would be futile.[22]

Jordan's warnings about the degenerative influences of the tropics were more complex than might first meet the eye. Such comments are often read more or less wholly in the eugenic and medical senses of bodily contamination, to which racial segregation was a common historical response. However, in Jordan's case there was also a definite fear of the degenerative consequences of the brutal methods of social control used in "tropical colonies." That is, he believed many of the humanitarian objections to physical coercion expressed in antislavery ideology and related nineteenth-century reform movements would be unenforceable in colonial situations. The renewed use of barbaric methods, long since abolished in the metropole, would restore the threats to society and progress that had been among the targets of the original reform campaigns. Put another way, virtually all white Americans agreed (however fatuously) that American slavery had been injurious to the master class. The prospect of colonial rule in the Philippines raised the specter of a new master-slave relationship, with equivalently disastrous consequences for the new master class.

David Starr Jordan's argument about the necessity of slavery in tropical colonies carried him to another level of analysis in which he thought emancipation of a kind was possible. With echoes of Abraham Lincoln's "house divided" speech, Jordan insisted that "[w]e cannot run a republic in the West and a slave plantation in the East. We must set our bondsmen free, however unready they may be for freedom." Smoothly, Jordan moved from his fear of contact with slavery as a concrete social relationship toward a more comprehensive, metaphorical condemnation of colonialism as a kind of slavery.

Antislavery ideology wound its way into the debate over colonialism in peculiar ways. There were, in fact, extensive links between antislavery ideology, the history of abolition in the United States, and the colonial question, even when slavery as a social relationship was not at issue. The connections are particularly striking in the arguments of the anti-imperialists during the early years of the colonial question.

Genealogy linked much of the leadership of the turn-of-the-century anti-imperialist movement with the pre–Civil War antislavery movement in the United States. Not surprisingly, the concentration of leading anti-imperialists with notable antislavery backgrounds was highest in the New England–New York area. George S. Boutwell, the first president of the Boston-based Anti-Imperialist League, as well as Gamaliel Bradford Sr., Edward Atkinson, Charles Francis Adams Jr., Moorfield Storey, and Carl Schurz were active in the antislavery cause through the Civil War. Others too young to have been part of the antislavery movement, such as William Lloyd Garrison III and Oswald Garrison Villard, had names that revealed prestigious abolitionist pedigrees.[23]

The anti-imperialists with antislavery backgrounds were acutely conscious of their heritage. The Civil War, abolition, and Reconstruction were fresh memories, but their meanings could be mixed. At least a few avowed imperialists and future officials of the colonial state also had genealogical links to abolitionism. Like William Cameron Forbes, Dean C. Worcester also descended from an abolitionist family with impressive reform credentials. His grandfather was Samuel Worcester, the missionary who represented Cherokee interests in *Worcester* v. *Georgia,* a case in which the Supreme Court tried to restrain President Andrew Jackson's policy of Indian removal in 1832. Chief Justice John Marshall's decision redefined Indians as "domestic dependent wards of the nation," a concept for which the younger Worcester found new use. Worcester's and Forbes's new antislavery crusade would come later. The anti-imperialists had theirs first.[24]

At the inaugural meeting of the Anti-Imperialist League, held in Boston's Faneuil Hall on 15 June 1898, the problem of colonialism was addressed in terms of the antislavery experience. Gamaliel Bradford reminded his listeners that only "a generation has elapsed since the country by a violent effort threw off the disease of slavery," thus purifying and strengthening the Union. Now, he continued, "for the doubtful chance of raising the condition of some, no doubt, very wretched peoples," his countrymen were "willing to risk infinite disaster to the people of the United States" and also to "humanity, whose fate is bound up with our institutions." Moorfield Storey, who would be a founder of the NAACP and lead the anti-imperialists for two decades, quoted Lincoln on the national dedication "to the proposition that all men are created equal." He then asked rhetorically if Filipinos or Puerto Ricans were "less fit than were the slaves to whom we gave the ballot thirty years ago." The labor leader George E. McNeil, fearful of competition from cheap colonial labor, warned that a "slave, servile or subject class is a dangerous class" that makes republican government impossible. "The poverty of manual laborers in any community," he said, "presages the necessity of a governing class," which would lead to "monarchy."[25]

The anti-imperialist leadership thought of their struggle as the heir to the antislavery tradition. Moorfield Storey called on the Anti-Imperialist League to "revive the anti-slavery spirit" to fight the new imperial policy. The strategy of the anti-imperialist movement followed the earlier movement's reliance on suasion. As in the abolitionist movement, individualism and moralism caused repeated schisms among anti-imperialists, including a split between political independents favoring a third-party presidential candidate in 1900 and champions of the Democratic candidate William Jennings Bryan.[26]

The antislavery experience remained a reference point for the anti-imperialists, even well into the twentieth century. Carl Schurz, Moorfield Storey, Charles Francis Adams Jr., Josephine Lowell Shaw, Edward Ordway, George S. Boutwell, and others judged the progress of their cause by drawing analogies with various stages of the antislavery struggle. These analogies often conveyed a message of optimism and hope when success seemed distant. For example, in his 1909 presidential address to the annual meeting of the Anti-Imperialist League, Moorfield Storey acknowledged the apparently superior strength of the plan proposed by President William Howard Taft and governor general Forbes to bond the Philippines to the United States through a reduction of tariffs and the investment of capital in the colony. But Storey found solace in recalling that "[t]he millions of dollars invested in slaves and slave property, the millions which slaveholders owed to northern merchants, the business and social ties which bound North as well as South to the maintenance of slavery, the political hopes and interests which were founded upon it were but as dust in the balance against the irresistible demands of human freedom." Storey admitted that "we are nothing in this contest" against "the whole power of the United States." But, with a tremendous faith in progress, he was certain that "[u]pon our side are the moral and economical forces which destroyed slavery, the forces which will overthrow English domination of India . . . the love of justice, the love of freedom, the 'self-evident truths' of the Declaration, the conscience of the American people, and no barrier that capital can erect can withstand these." [27]

Analogies with the antislavery movement could also be less sanguine. In May 1899, when the volume of protest against the war of conquest in the Philippines was disappointingly low, Charles Francis Adams could not muster Storey's inveterate faith in progress. He told his younger friend that, although "the history of our country between 1852 and 1861 may be a great comfort to you . . . I grew up in that period. Unfortunately, I do not see any organization now in the field corresponding to that of the Anti-Slavery men then; and the country is [now] much larger, and morally more unwieldy." [28]

Ironically, memories of the Civil War also supplied some of the more vulgar critics of the anti-imperialists with an epithet that cut close to the hearts of old antislavery men. The Civil War, after all, caused a massive extension of federal power and it redefined the question of loyalty to the

Union. In the press and in hate mail, many anti-imperialists were re-
buked as "copperheads" for their criticism of the war in the Philippines,
the same label that Unionists once applied to Northerners reluctant to
support the Civil War. The prominence of references to slavery, abolition, and the Civil War even before Americans received news about the
existence of slavery in the southern Philippines indicates the spread of
antislavery ideology throughout American political culture.[29]

The locus and implications of discourse about slavery began to
change, however, with the signing of the Bates treaty on 30 August 1899
and its consequent publicity in the United States in September. Americans' discussion of the problem of slavery in the Philippines was now
grounded in reports of a social reality that seemed to confirm some of
the anti-imperialists' fears. Ideology had already defined slavery as a
problem of colonialism. Americans' perceptions of slavery when they
encountered it in practice were shaped by antislavery ideology, but the
ideology's effect on discourse would itself be reshaped by this encounter.

In the United States, the early reports of the Bates treaty were pro-
pelled into notoriety by Edward Atkinson. An abolitionist who, with
John Murray Forbes, had raised money to finance migration to John
Brown's bloody Kansas, Atkinson was a leading exponent of free labor
ideology throughout his long and varied career. Ironically, given his later
opposition to colonialism in the Philippines, his influential pamphlet
"Cheap Cotton by Free Labor," published in 1859, was a plea to develop cotton production in British India and Africa to compete with cotton produced in the southern United States by slaves. Active in liberal
reform causes over a long life, Atkinson was a spry seventy-one years old
at the outbreak of the Spanish-American War. Until near the end of his
days in 1905, he devoted a large share of his enormous energy to opposing U.S. colonial policy in the Philippines. The main vehicle of his efforts was an irregularly published serial, *The Anti-Imperialist*.[30]

Atkinson was the principal author, editor, publisher, and distributor
of this series of incendiary pamphlets. With his own money, support
from prominent anti-imperialists such as Andrew Carnegie and Moorfield Storey, and financial contributions of various sizes from around the
country, Atkinson mailed several printings of each of the six issues of
The Anti-Imperialist from his hometown of Brookline, Massachusetts.
His lurid indictments of colonial policy attracted a following that grew
exponentially when the postmaster general of the United States accused
Atkinson of treason and confiscated copies of *The Anti-Imperialist* in
transit to high colonial officials in Manila.[31]

The fifth issue of *The Anti-Imperialist* was distributed in late September 1899 with a striking headline on its cover: "Slavery and Polygamy Reestablished Under the Jurisdiction of the United States So Far as Can Be Done by Authority of William McKinley, in Carrying on this Effort to Deprive the People of the Philippine Islands of Their Liberty." [32] The gist of Atkinson's argument was simple and to the point. He contrasted the legal recognition of slavery embodied in the Bates treaty with the president's usual defense of colonial rule as the spread of freedom and progress: "Wherever the flag is raised it stands not for despotism and aggression, but for liberty, opportunity, and humanity," as McKinley had put it in a speech made just a few weeks before. Atkinson retorted that, if the "Island of Sulu, one of the Philippines never yet conquered by Spain, is now by cession within the jurisdiction of the United States, then all persons now held as slaves in that Island" must be freed in accordance with the Thirteenth Amendment.[33]

Atkinson contended that the McKinley administration's sponsorship of the Bates treaty was both hypocritical and unconstitutional. "Unless the undisputed terms of the treaty with the Sultan are disavowed," he warned, "the President of the United States has attempted to substitute arbitrary power for the Constitution and law of the land, and to reestablish slavery and polygamy in that part of the domain claimed by him to be under the jurisdiction of the United States." Most embarrassing of all, Atkinson informed his readers that slavery was plainly prohibited by the constitution of the Philippine Republic, the revolutionary government of the Philippines that the United States was trying to suppress and denigrate as unfit for national leadership.[34]

Coincidentally, just a day before the Bates treaty was signed on 30 August in Jolo, the capital of the Sulu sultanate, Atkinson forwarded a letter from the elderly Reverend Samuel May, a prominent antebellum abolitionist, to the editor of the *Boston Transcript*. His letter of introduction reads as if it were informed by an unaccountable premonition. "You may be willing," Atkinson suggested to the *Transcript*, "to call attention to the fact that all the old leaders of public opinion in Anti-Slavery times who are living are opposed to the policy of warfare, violence and wrong in the Philippine Islands, while some who have passed away recently,—Mssrs. John M. Forbes and Henry Lee among the number, declared themselves in urgent words against this policy." [35]

Edward Atkinson was a crafty and resourceful propagandist. He devoted much of his life to antislavery activity and the cause of civil rights for black Americans. Although Atkinson did not call on the United

States to act decisively to end slavery in the Sulu Islands, preferring, instead, that the United States abandon its venture in colonialism, his opposition to slavery was without doubt sincere. Nevertheless, Atkinson also lambasted McKinley for the Bates treaty because he believed that the tar brush of slavery would produce an excited reaction. In a request to a friend in Washington for more precise information on the content of the Bates treaty, Atkinson commented with some pleasure that the treaty "cannot be disavowed, although it is the greatest tactical blunder yet made by the Administration." His earlier pamphlets provoked charges of treason. Now Atkinson told a friend that "No. 5" of the *Anti-Imperialist* "is the highest bid that I have yet made for a residence in [the federal penitentiary at] Fort Warren." A few days before the pamphlet came back from the printer, Atkinson informed Carl Schurz that "No. 5 is the most aggressive work I have yet done and in order to make it yet more so I have today prepared a letter to the Postmaster General in which I shall enclose proof of the most aggressive part of the pamphlet." [36]

Atkinson may well have been right about pamphlet "No. 5." Responses to his attack on the Bates treaty and the McKinley administration's entire colonial policy in the Philippines ranged from applause and financial support to redoubled charges of treason. In one of the most florid pieces of hate mail to cross Atkinson's desk, the superintendent of schools in Custer County, Montana, called the elderly pamphleteer "one of the breed of cowards who, when our country was in death struggle for existence, criticized the administration of Lincoln, bemoaned the cruelty and the destruction of war, 'The Cost of a National Crime,' 'The Hell of War and Its Penalties,' 'Criminal Aggression,' etc. You and your kind were then and are now the cowardly, slimy 'copperhead' which from safe seclusion in the rear of all danger sends forth poison to destroy alike the brave soldier in the field and the homes of the people." Atkinson, of course, had actively supported the North in the Civil War. The titles the superintendent listed were those of the pamphlets Atkinson wrote denouncing conquest and colonial rule in the Philippines. Even when an anti-imperialist with impeccable antislavery credentials criticized the U.S. government's toleration of slavery in the Sulu Islands, loyalists to the McKinley administration's colonial policies were likely to express their counterattack with rhetoric from the Civil War and antislavery struggles.[37]

President McKinley did not respond to Atkinson or the other antiimperialists directly, but he did amplify the antislavery rhetoric of colonial discourse. Just a few weeks after news of the Bates treaty reached Americans through newspapers and Atkinson's pamphlets, the president told an audience in his home state of Ohio that "[o]ur flag is there [in the Philippines], not as the symbol of oppression, not as the token of tyranny, not as the emblem of enslavement, but representing there as it does here, liberty, humanity and civilization." [38] There was at once a strong sense of confident supremacy in McKinley's use of antislavery rhetoric and a note of defensiveness.

The president made his first official statement on the Bates treaty in a message sent to Congress on 5 December 1899, some two months after Edward Atkinson publicized the issue of slavery. McKinley defended the treaty, but added a "reservation" to be conveyed to the Sultan of Sulu. He affirmed the terms of Article X of the treaty, which recognized the right of slaves to purchase their freedom at market value, and then stipulated that the parties to the treaty would concur "that this agreement is not to be deemed in any way to authorize or give the consent of the United States to the existence of slavery in the Sulu Archipelago." Congress then called for the full record of communications and orders concerning the treaty negotiations. These were delivered and printed as public documents, but the Senate took no action on the Bates treaty. [39]

Anti-imperialists raised the issue of slavery in the Sulu Islands repeatedly over the next few years and recalled it periodically throughout the next decade. Slavery in the Sulu Islands and the McKinley administration's seeming complicity in its maintenance provided an opportunity to attack the constitutionality and ostensible benevolence of American colonial rule. The charges of unconstitutional action and hypocrisy were resonant precisely because the morality, legality, and social nature of slavery were decisively condemned by a remarkable consensus in the United States. Slavery occupied a central place in ideology and the memory of recent history, so the problem of slavery in the Sulu Islands touched upon many sensitive nerves.

Most of the anti-imperialists who discussed the McKinley administration's actions in the Sulu Islands directed attention to the Thirteenth Amendment. The constitutional prohibition of slavery was widely understood to be a hard-won product of the Civil War and a milestone of progress. Yet, although there was no active opposition to the Thirteenth Amendment in the United States at the turn of the century, there certainly was a movement to ignore or repeal the Fourteenth and Fifteenth amendments, which were intended to guarantee the freed American slaves' civil rights and suffrage. Racism undergirded American colonialism and the deprivation of African Americans' rights, but it also informed much of the anti-imperialist critique of colonial policy.[40]

Not surprisingly, the most comprehensive analyses of the constitutional problems posed by the Bates treaty were penned by an old, unreconstructed radical Republican. In addition to being the first president of the Anti-Imperialist League, George Boutwell had earlier served in the United States House of Representatives and Senate, in President Grant's cabinet, and a term as governor of Massachusetts. For Boutwell all of these offices paled in significance when compared with his participation in the formation of the Republican Party in 1856 and the abolition of slavery during the Civil War. Boutwell told an assembly of black Bostonians who gathered at Faneuil Hall to celebrate the fortieth anniversary of the Emancipation Proclamation that it was the most important step taken since the Declaration of Independence to advance the world to "a higher civilization." If the destruction of slavery was the greatest event of his life, then the United States's recent colonial conquests were the most ominous. He told the crowd: "You are to reach a conclusion whether the large body of voters that you represent shall co-operate with the Republican Party in the work of enslaving millions of the human race, or whether they shall accept the example of Lincoln and Grant and co-operate with those who are in favor of abandoning the policy of subjugation."[41]

Although many anti-imperialists discussed colonial rule in terms of slavery, Boutwell stands out for having used the metaphor most extensively. In January 1899, long before the existence of slavery in the Sulu Islands was brought to public attention in the United States, Boutwell was already describing colonialism as a contravention of the Thirteenth Amendment.[42] He needed to take but a small step to refocus and intensify his arguments when the practice of slavery in the Philippines was confirmed. As for his great hero, Lincoln, Boutwell's hatred of slavery coexisted with complex views of race that now drove his fears about admitting "alien" races to citizenship, labor competition, trade competition, and the fate of the principles of the Republic.

Convinced that the Supreme Court must rule in favor of unregulated trade with the Philippines in the upcoming lawsuits known as the Insular Cases, in January 1900, Boutwell declared that the imminent "decision means full freedom of trade between the islands and the states, and it means much more. The inhabitants of the islands, from Luzon to Sulu, slave and free, are made citizens of the United States, and no puny legislative scheme, such as has been proposed for Hawaii, can bar them out." Unless the Supreme Court reversed the Thirteenth Amendment and approved "vassalage," he feared there would be "ten million American citizens, all of another race, all ignorant of our language, ignorant of our traditions." And, to send a chill down the nation's spine, Boutwell asked, "If we establish our tenancy in the Philippine Islands, do not the islands become an Open Door for the ingress of the Mongolian race; peoples in no way distinguishable from the present occupants of the islands?"[43]

Boutwell's most pointed observations on the consequences of slavery in the Philippines were delivered in two speeches. The first of these, "The Enslavement of American Labor," he read at a meeting of the Boston Central Labor Union on 22 January 1902. The second, "Two Experiments," prepared sometime in 1904,[44] was an extended comparison of Reconstruction in the southern United States and U.S. colonial rule in the Philippines.

The argument of "The Enslavement of American Labor" was constructed on assumptions widely shared by both imperialists and anti-imperialists. Like Alleyne Ireland and others, Boutwell recognized that dreams of lucrative overseas markets for American goods were not apt to be brought to fruition without some reciprocal American purchase of commodities produced in the prospective market. So Boutwell admonished: "Woe to the laboring and producing populations of a country that enters into a free competition with the unnumbered millions of India and the Chinese." Competition from cheap labor working overseas was the source of danger, not the immigration of cheap labor to the United States. The evil consequences would be worse than reduced wages, or even "wage-slavery." In competition with workers "whose wages are less than sixty per cent. of the wages which are now paid to American laborers," the United States must give up the industry or its workers "must accept the wages which are now paid in Cebu and Luzon." With the opening of free trade, "the Sultan of Sulu would thus find his slave labor upon an equality with the free labor of America, while he and his harem would be in the enjoyment of a pension from the treasury of the United States." Ironically, Boutwell's faith in the power of free trade prompted an equal and opposite retreat from faith in the superior efficiency of free labor. "The Enslavement of American Labor," he predicted, would result from free and unfettered competition with slave labor in Southeast Asia.[45]

In "Two Experiments" Boutwell analyzed the challenge that American colonialism posed to "the principles of the Declaration of Independence and the doctrine laid down by President Lincoln at Gettysburg, when he said '. . . We here highly resolve that the dead shall not have died in vain . . . that the United States shall under God have a new birth of freedom, and that the government of the people, by the people and for the people shall not perish from the earth.'" Since 1898 the right of self-government had been denied in the Philippines and the denial of civil rights for blacks in the southern United States had gained momentum. The McKinley and Roosevelt administrations were reinterpreting the constitutional legacy of Reconstruction as a failure in a process that was, according to Boutwell, inextricably linked to their defense of colonial rule in the Philippines. To beat back this tide of reaction, Boutwell compared the "experiments" of Reconstruction and colonial rule. He judged Reconstruction a success and colonial rule a failure in an assessment that stressed the way in which the problem of slavery was handled in each case.[46]

Boutwell's opening wedge was the declaration by the secretary of war, Elihu Root, that the Fifteenth Amendment and accompanying legislative measures of Reconstruction were failures. By interesting logic, Boutwell extrapolated a condemnation of the Thirteenth Amendment from Root's criticism of the Fifteenth. "The liberation of four million slaves," he maintained, "could not have been justified upon the ground that they were to be transferred from one form of slavery to a condition of serfdom as disparaging to its victims and as dangerous to the country as was the system of slavery that was overthrown." Therefore the "wisdom and justice" of the Thirteenth Amendment "are necessarily impeached if the Fourteenth and Fifteenth Amendments are unworthy of confidence and support." Of course, the claim that Root, McKinley, and Roosevelt were threatening the authority of the Thirteenth Amendment could be made more directly. Boutwell asked the embarrassing question, What have they done about slavery in the Philippines?[47]

The Thirteenth Amendment had failed only once, Boutwell maintained. It was an "unqualified success within the states of the American Union, and within the territories that have been created on this continent." The failure had occurred in the Philippines, a place governed through Secretary Root's War Department. Slavery still existed there "after five years of unlimited control by the government of the United States." It was "not only tolerated by the United States government, but means have been obtained from the public treasury for the continuance of the system and the support of the men who control it and enjoy and are to enjoy the real or imaginative advantages that have been or may be

derived from it." Either Root, through negligence, was "personally responsible for the failure of which he complains," or the United States
would have to admit that it was not able to abolish slavery in the Philippines. If the latter were the case, Boutwell concluded, "then it is manifest that the policy of President McKinley has been a signal failure, not
only with reference to the Philippines, but it has carried down the Declaration of Independence and the principles on which President Lincoln
leaned for support when he announced his political axiom on the field
of Gettysburg."[48]

In the final analysis, Boutwell explained the persistence of slavery in
the Philippines without reference to negligence on the part of Secretary
Root or incapacity on the part of the government of the United States.
Boutwell located the problem in essence rather than implementation. He
repeated a common anti-imperialist refrain when he wrote: "The policy
in the Philippine Islands has been a policy of servitude. However
dignified by name, or qualified by promises, it still has been a policy of
servitude on the part of one race, and of domination through alleged superiority of attainments on the part of another race." The toleration of
the social institution of slavery in the Sulu Islands, Boutwell suggested,
was no anomaly. It was merely the logical consequence of a larger policy to keep the Filipinos in a state of colonial servitude.[49]

CHAPTER TWO

Americans Imagine
Philippine Slavery

For Americans, colonial rule in the Philippines and the encounter with slavery recalled some of the key issues of emancipation in the United States and the Caribbean. The problems of colonialism and slavery in the Philippines took shape from conflicted discourses about race, labor, and progress. In 1898, these American problems were, in fact, constructed out of ideology even before the actual practice of colonialism in the Philippines gave them material existence. As vitally important as race, labor, and the concept of progress were in American discourse, it would be a mistake for us to understand the intersection of antislavery ideology and colonialism exclusively in these terms.

The problem of controlling a "tropical" labor force was not the only association Americans made between the question of slavery in the Philippines and their own history. Indeed, for complex reasons, discussion of the labor problem receded into the background once the actual encounter with slavery in the Philippines was made. Other associations came to the fore.

When Americans learned that the Moro societies of the southern Philippines practiced slavery, through news of the Bates treaty, they immediately had a special framework at hand for interpreting that practice: Moros were Muslims. The salience of Islam pervaded American interpretations of Moro slavery. At the very beginning of American public discussion of the matter, as we have seen, Edward Atkinson linked slavery and polygamy together in the title of his incendiary anti-imperialist pamphlet. Other anti-imperialists followed suit in their efforts to embarrass the McKinley administration.

H. H. Van Meter, a member of the very active Chicago branch of the anti-imperialist movement, put the argument in pungent terms. It was not just the practice of slavery under the Bates treaty that discredited U.S. colonialism, he said, but a larger contradiction of Christian order.

> We call the world to witness . . . that the pretence that the real reason for not allowing the civilized, Christianized, intelligent Filipino native Catholics the liberty of self-government, under their own leaders, with republican institutions like our own, because of unfitness, is the most abhorrent and apparent hypocrisy. The fact that the savage, degraded barbarians and semi-Mohammedans of the Sulus and Mindanao have been allowed their own government under a most despotic rule, contrary to all our traditions, with such "religious" customs as polygamy, slavery and human sacrifice, is proof positive of this assertion.[1]

Coupled with polygamy, slavery had been one of the "twin relics of barbarism" condemned by the Republican Party's inaugural platform in 1856. The Party of Lincoln appealed to Northern voters who wanted to think of themselves as embodying a free Christian civilization, in contrast to the unChristian corruptions of the slave-owning South and the Mormon heresy, which was likened to the "false" religion of polygamous Islam. The same distinction still appealed to Americans in the early 1900s. Consequently, the seemingly obscure issue of slavery in the Sulu Islands, a small and remote part of the Philippine archipelago, did not remain the province of a group of old abolitionists deeply vested in the receding triumphs of the Civil War and Reconstruction. Slavery in the Sulu Islands became the subject of a Broadway hit.

George Ade's *The Sultan of Sulu: An Original Satire in Two Acts* followed the spirit of Karl Marx's dictum about history repeating itself as farce. A musical comedy, *The Sultan of Sulu* ran for nearly two hundred performances on Broadway after opening on 29 December 1902. The U.S. occupation of the Sulu Islands under the terms of the Bates treaty furnished Ade with a remarkable plot that drew on popular discourses about slavery, race, Islam, and colonialism.[2]

Ade, an accomplished humorist and energetic anti-imperialist, visited the Philippines in 1901 to inspect at first-hand the colonial policy he opposed. Although he did not travel to the Sulu Islands, Ade's satire combined the stories he heard around Manila with the reports that circulated in the United States and a large admixture of his own imagination. His vision of the interactions between the "Mohammedans, polygamists, and slaveholders" of the Sulu Islands and the American officials who arrived under the Bates treaty was "not an attempt to show what subsequently happened, but merely what might have happened."[3]

In the play, the Sultan of Sulu, depicted as a clown, is besieged by American soldiers and schoolteachers, and by the *datus* (local rulers) who contest his power. The Americans introduce the cocktail and the Arkansas legal code, declare the sultan's wives divorced, and free the sultan's slaves, roughly in that order. The divorces are followed by a court order to enforce the law entitling a divorced wife to collect one-half of her former husband's income as alimony. Unable to pay one-half of his income to each of his eight or nine divorced wives, the sultan finds himself in jail, literally imprisoned by the colonial imposition of a new culture.

The sultan tries various schemes to escape from his predicament. He considers reducing his income so the alimony shares shrink to nothing. He tries to return his wives to the *datus* he stole them from. He establishes a marriage agency to marry them off to American soldiers—all to no avail. Then the final blow strikes. His position as governor under the colonial regime is made elective while he is in prison and the two candidates for the office are his newly freed slaves. As the sultan gives in to despair he is suddenly rescued by a message from Washington to the American officer in command: "The Supreme Court decides that the Constitution follows the flag on Mondays, Wednesdays, and Fridays only. This being the case, you are instructed to preserve order in Sulu, but not to interfere with any of the local laws or customs." The Americans release the sultan from jail, the candidates for governor are reenslaved, and the restored slaves bring the sultan his throne. Needless to say, this was not quite the way slavery ended in the United States, but the echoes of Reconstruction and redemption must have been clear enough.[4]

Leading politicians also incorporated the problem of slavery in the Philippines into their campaign scripts. Forty years after Abraham Lincoln's election to the presidency, William Jennings Bryan made slavery an issue in his electoral contest with the incumbent McKinley in 1900. The exchange of charges and countercharges illuminates the sensitivities touched by the controversy over slavery in Sulu.

In a speech on 4 October 1900, just one month before the election, Bryan denounced the McKinley administration's actions in the Sulu Islands. "We fought then," he told the crowd, recalling the glory of the Union triumph in the Civil War, "for the adoption of a constitutional amendment that provided that no man could own a slave, and yet before the Philippine war is ended we have the Sulu treaty, which recognizes slavery." The charge was similar to the allegations made by anti-imperialists such as Atkinson and Boutwell. Colonial rule and the continuing war in the Philippines, according to these critics, were uprooting the finest traditions of the country and destroying the fruits of the Civil War.[5]

McKinley remained confidently at home and did not personally respond to Bryan's attack, while the acting secretary of war George D. Meiklejohn and the Republican congressman C. H. Grosvenor of Ohio came to the administration's defense. Meiklejohn and Grosvenor relied primarily on published Senate documents on the Bates treaty to build their replies, but an unsigned and hand-corrected memo in McKinley's papers—titled "Sulu Slavery. Was it Authorized Ratified or Affirmed by President McKinley? The Official Record in the Case"—suggests that the administration's apology was crafted with the president's attention.[6]

In his initial replies to Bryan, Meiklejohn reiterated the president's contention that the agreement with the Sultan of Sulu should not be construed as "consent . . . to the existence of slavery." He also insisted that the so-called Bates treaty was not even a real treaty, as it had never been formally approved by the president and the senate.[7] Congressman Grosvenor delivered a lengthier rebuttal than did Meiklejohn, but his arguments were similar. In a speech read at Evanston, Illinois, Grosvenor explained that "no treaty was made with the Sultan as described and asserted, but it is true that Gen. Bates, acting on behalf of the armed forces of the United States, entered into a temporary agreement with the Sultan and others, by which, if it had been approved by the President and by Congress, slavery would have been recognized and possibly fortified in that territory." Grosvenor defended the propriety of the "temporary agreement" as a means to avert hostilities in the southern Philippines while warfare continued in Luzon and the Visayas.[8]

In addition to disavowing the Bates treaty, Grosvenor used the documents McKinley submitted to Congress the previous winter to describe the social conditions in the Sulu Islands and explain how the administration planned to abolish slavery. "In the first place," he declared, "there was no such thing as slavery, within the modern and American acceptation of the term, existing in the Archipelago of Jolo." Grosvenor cited a report by the U.S. Army's inspector general in the Philippines to support his assertion that "[t]he slavery existing there was voluntary." It was a system of "domestic slavery" in which "the Moro slave, so-called, becomes a member of the owner's family, enjoying certain privileges, and that he even voluntarily sells himself to better his conditions and to secure some slight temporary individual benefit." Moreover, Grosvenor proclaimed, "[t]here lives not on this earth one man with a greater horror of slavery than William McKinley." Whatever the real nature of slavery in the Sulu Islands, the American people could rest assured that President McKinley would never tolerate it, much less give it his sanction. To substantiate this, Grosvenor read into his speech the orders given by the secretary of war Elihu Root on 27 October 1899, directing the U.S. military governor of the Philippines to plan a compensated emancipation.[9]

Root had informed the military governor of the president's desire "that you should make inquiry as to the number of persons held in slavery in the archipelago, and what arrangement it may be practicable to make for their emancipation. It is assumed that the market price referred to in the agreement of Aug. 20, 1899, is not very high at present, and it may be that a comparatively moderate sum, which Congress might be willing to appropriate for that purpose, would suffice to secure freedom for the whole number." No such compensated emancipation was ever consummated, but plans for a compensated emancipation were discussed with the sultan, causing unexpected consequences. The possibility of a handsome compensation in the near future seems to have rejuvenated the market in slaves.[10]

Only after his reelection did McKinley reply directly to his opponents' charges about the toleration of slavery in the Sulu Islands and the unconstitutionality of U.S. colonial rule in the Philippines. The reelected president from the party of Lincoln said,

> Those who profess to distrust the liberal and honorable purposes of the administration in its treatment of the Philippines are not justified. Imperialism has no place in its creed or conduct. Freedom is the rock upon which the republican party was builded and now rests. Liberty is the great Republican doctrine for which the people went to war and for which a million lives were offered and billions of dollars expended to make it the lawful legacy of all without the consent of master or slave. . . . if our opponents would only practice as well as preach the doctrines of Abraham Lincoln, there would be no fear for the safety of our institutions at home or their rightful influence in any territory over which our flag floats.[11]

McKinley's reference to Lincoln seems to have carried two meanings. The doctrines of Lincoln included, retrospectively, the abolition of slavery and the federal government's right to impose such progress on a vanquished foe over and against its objections to external rule. Anti-imperialists who called for an American withdrawal from the Philippines rejected this analogy with Reconstruction and did not propose to do anything to abolish slavery in the Sulu Islands. The Republican president proposed that his colonial policy would use the same constitutional power that Lincoln had used in the American South to abolish slavery in the southern Philippines. Unlike the Union's clear triumph over the South in the Civil War however, the United States's need to negotiate colonial power in the southern Philippines created unsettling tensions in colonial policy on slavery.

Three principal factors informed the administration's hesitant course on the problem of slavery in Sulu. In public pronouncements and confidential correspondence, the McKinley and early Roosevelt administrations indicated their desire to avoid a war in the southern Philippines, argued that slavery in the Sulu Islands was an unburdensome form of bondage, and expressed their faith that they could effect a gradual, smooth emancipation. In the administration's thinking these factors were intimately related, as Elihu Root, the secretary of war, explained in an exchange of letters with Albert Bushnell Hart, a professor of history at Harvard University.[12]

Hart was raised in an abolitionist family that instilled an antislavery commitment readily discernible in his work as an historian. In January 1902, he wrote to his friend and fellow historian Theodore Roosevelt to ask what must have been a painful question: "Why does the free United States permit slavery to continue in the Sulu Islands?"[13]

President Roosevelt referred Hart's letter to Root, who answered the query personally. Root explained that the United States was not permitting slavery to continue in the Sulu Islands; rather, it was "engaged in extirpating it." There was "no question of permitting or not permitting" slavery, but there was "a question of the best method of introducing our rule of freedom among these semi-independent and war-like tribes." The current policy was admittedly slow in its action, but, Root cautioned, "[t]here is only one alternative to the peaceful method we are now pursuing; that is a bloody war, in which we should probably find the so-called slaves themselves fighting against us, with hardly any exception."[14]

What Root understood as the "mild character of the so-called slavery among the Sulus" also justified a slow course. "We might well consider it justifiable to incur great expense and loss of life for the immediate rescue of persons who are in an intolerable condition of suffering," he reassured Hart, "while a more humane and conciliatory course of persuasion and peaceful arrangement is better adapted to the actual existing conditions of comparative comfort but little removed from ordinary voluntary domestic service." [15]

At first glance, the position outlined by Root seems a simple matter of expediency, if not calculating hypocrisy. Root, McKinley, and Roosevelt never scrupled thus about the cost in blood of the more general emancipation the United States was supposedly bringing to the Philippines in the form of colonial rule. The greater autonomy conceded the Moro societies of the southern Philippines was certainly not the product of respect or recognition, given the double force of American racism and disparagement of Islam. Indeed, once the armed resistance against the colonial regime in the north and central Philippines was reduced to relatively controllable proportions in 1902 and 1903, colonial rule in the south became more aggressive and intrusive. The first important action taken from this new, increasingly assertive stance was General Leonard Wood's antislavery decree, put into effect on 24 November 1903. Wood's decree ignited brutal warfare that continued through the decade. Given this readiness to rationalize the use of virtually unlimited force in the name of benevolence, expediency seems a plausible explanation for the United States's temporizing policy on slavery in Sulu. [16]

Expediency is not, however, an adequate historical explanation for the course of the United States's initially hesitant encounter with slavery. Several historians of emancipation in Africa have also noted that colonial depictions of "mild slavery" often originated as rationalizations that allowed officials to tolerate slavery without seeming to abandon dearly held antislavery principles. [17] But why was the rationalization persuasive, especially after the earlier humanitarian campaign against the barbarism of slavery in the Anglo-American world had successfully addressed similar claims about the mildness of slavery, especially in the U.S. South? If expedience was a factor, we need to understand the ideological as well as material preconditions that made the expedient act possible and, indeed, defined it as expedient.

The conservative tendency of Anglo-American antislavery ideology in the late nineteenth century, evident in the works of colonialists such as Alleyne Ireland and anti-imperialists such as David Starr Jordan, was founded upon the interpretation of the history of prior emancipations. As we have seen, the U.S. Civil War and Reconstruction set much of the intellectual terrain for conflicts over American colonial policy in the Philippines. The conservative shift of late-nineteenth-century antislavery ideology in the United States also had roots in a broader transformation of liberal social thought. American liberalism, in the classical sense, took a decidedly conservative turn in the late nineteenth century. The Civil War and Reconstruction were the last great radical and humanitarian acts of American classical liberalism. Evolutionary theories and the new social sciences often produced contradictory political effects. Without entering the complex debate over the nature, shape, and causes of this transformation, I would like to direct attention to the way some prominent American social theorists treated the issue of slavery in the late-nineteenth and early twentieth centuries.[18]

As liberal social thought turned more conservative and the political economy tightened after the Civil War, some began to probe the boundaries of liberalism for a more radical solution to social woes. Henry George was the most important social theorist in this group. In his phenomenally influential book *Progress and Poverty* he envisioned a utopia with true equality of opportunity. George's view of slavery did not deviate from the classical liberal model. "As for slavery," he intoned, "I cannot see how it could ever have aided in establishing freedom, and freedom, the synonym for equality, is, from the very rudest state in which man can be imagined, the stimulus and condition of progress." Slavery was always inefficient according to George, "a waste of human power" for the slave and master alike. It destroyed the roots of "inventiveness" and violated the "law of human progress." "Slavery," he concluded, "never did and never could aid improvement." Henry George would have been unlikely to perceive the toleration of slavery under the Bates treaty as expedient. His social theory apparently allowed him no means by which to legitimize a relaxed posture toward slavery.[19]

For all of his great popularity, however, George was edged out of the dominant stream of American social thought by a new generation of professional social scientists. Influenced by the evolutionary thought of Darwin, William Graham Sumner, and Herbert Spencer, trained by the historical economists of Heidelberg and Berlin, these self-conscious professionals helped to forge a new understanding of self and society in the United States. Contrary to the practice of classical liberalism, these scholars began to relativize their view of human nature in terms of race, culture, and history. The result was a new and strikingly conservative view of slavery.[20]

Richard T. Ely was one of the leading lights of the new school of political economy. A crusader against the laissez-faire tradition, Ely helped to found the study of labor economics and labor history in the United States. In addition to being a founder of the American Economics Association and a leader in the movement to professionalize the discipline of economics, Ely was a central figure in Wisconsin's renowned progressive movement. His views on slavery were representative of those prevailing among the new social scientists.[21]

Slavery, according to Ely, was "a necessary stage in the evolution of industrial society." Abandoning classical liberal dogma about a universal and constant human nature, Ely maintained that "[i]t was only in later ages, when the habits of thrift and industry had been ground into the very nature of man, that the servile bonds could advantageously be removed." With regard to the United States's new colonial possessions, Ely cautioned his readers not to expect too much of the "lower races." Liberty and freedom would be impossible and some form of slavery or compulsory labor might be necessary in places like the Philippines until a higher order of civilization could be "ground into the very nature" of the natives.[22]

By 1900, American social scientists could have declared that they were all evolutionists now. For example, one of Ely's leading opponents in the great debate over laissez-faire economic policy, Arthur Twining Hadley, shared his position on slavery. "It must not be assumed," Hadley instructed, "that emancipation is a good thing for every man or for every race. Compulsory labor is better than no labor at all." Like Ely, Hadley believed slavery to be backward and relatively inefficient in comparison with free labor, but necessary at certain stages of development. Only at higher stages could workers be left to govern themselves freely through self-control, just like advanced nations fit for independence and democratic self-government.[23]

Invidiously, evolutionary theories tended to imply that the process of abolition (like colonial "tutelage") would have to be protracted among people such as the Filipinos because they supposedly had much history to progress through before they could exercise the self-control that made freedom possible. Ely recognized the extent of his departure from classical liberal assumptions. "For a long time in this country," he reminded his readers, "under the influence of eighteenth-century philosophy, we were inclined to regard men as substantially equal, and to suppose that all could live under the same economic and political institutions. It now becomes plain that this is a theory which works disaster, and is, indeed, cruel to those who are in the lower stages, resulting in their exploitation and degradation."[24]

Evolutionary social thought taught that colonialism and obnoxious institutions of control such as slavery would have to be tolerated until the forces of progress could operate over a long duration. For Ely this was a matter of enlightened benevolence; to act upon a theory of equality would be "cruel." These beliefs were widely shared, along with their implications about the supposed unfitness of Filipinos for independence. As the progressive historian Charles Beard recalled some years later, "it was obvious to every one that such refined notions of American policy [as the constitutional rights to a free press and trial by jury], though well known to high-class Spaniards, could not be lightly applied to primitive people in tropical islands. Doubtless the Sultan of Sulu had never heard of Magna Carta."[25]

The evolutionary theories of race, slavery, and freedom embedded in the work of representative social thinkers on both the "progressive" left and laissez-faire right informed a dominant conservative bias against dramatic social transformations such as abolition. The belief that slavery was necessary in certain societies also tended to carry with it an ameliorated view of the pain of slavery. Alleyne Ireland, for example, based his defense of coerced labor in tropical colonies on a romantic portrait of slavery as a benevolent institution. The McKinley and Roosevelt administrations agreed that what was necessary could not be cruel when they insisted that slavery in the Sulu Islands was "mild," merely "domestic," or not really slavery at all. The supposed mildness of slavery, as Elihu Root explained to Albert Bushnell Hart, did not absolve the United States of the duty to abolish slavery in the name of progress, but it did remove the imperative for immediate action.[26]

Early American reports from the Sulu Islands all described the slavery there as benign. Some went so far as to say that Sulu "slavery" was really a "voluntary" arrangement that the so-called slaves would not flee even if they were granted freedom by a proclamation of abolition. Tellingly, however, most of the reports provided substantial evidence to the contrary. The reports from the early military administration in Sulu indicate clearly that one of the most important consequences of the American presence and vague portents of a coming abolition was a discernible increase in the number of runaway slaves. Much of the information sent out of the Sulu Islands by the Americans stationed there provided definite evidence, for those who might have been able and willing to see it, that slaves were by no means happily ensconced in a relationship of benign dependence.

The implications of the interpretation of slavery as benign seem clear enough given the need to avoid a war in the southern Philippines while fighting raged in the north. Yet the idea of mild slavery has been so persistent in debates and scholarship about slavery outside the Americas that we must probe deeper to understand it. I believe the ideology of race, in a rather odd way, influenced the perceptions of the colonial administration in Sulu and affected later historical accounts of non-Western slavery generally.[27]

Despite prominent discussions of the labor problem in tropical colonies and the function of New World slavery in controlling labor, turn-of-the-century Americans thought of slavery as, primarily, a racial institution. For them, as for many subsequent historians, slavery was an episode in the history of race relations and race control. In the Sulu Islands, however, almost all of the slaves were, by American definitions, the same race as their masters.[28] Except for an occasional captured European or American seaman, the slaves in nineteenth-century Sulu virtually all came from Southeast Asia. Most were probably from the Visayan Islands of the Philippines and, at the end of the nineteenth century, from the highlands of Mindanao. This practice obviously clashed with Americans' understanding of slavery as a racial institution. Colonial administrators frequently claimed that masters and slaves were indistinguishable, that slaves were assimilated into the society, and that slavery in the Sulu Islands was therefore "mild," implicitly unlike the slavery that had existed in the Southern United States. The idea of a mild slavery helped to make sense of a social institution in an unfamiliar society within the ideological framework of the observers.

To subject the perceptions of American observers in the Philippines to an analysis of their ideological content does not and should not imply that their observations had nothing to do with the reality in which they were enmeshed. However, most Americans engaged in the public discussion about slavery in the Sulu Islands had no first-hand observations to inform their views, nor do they appear often to have relied on the few published first-hand accounts of slavery in the Moro societies. Instead, their discourse on slavery in the Sulu Islands was more an expression of pure ideology than anything else. George Ade's musical provides a telling example.

Although the slaves in the Sulu Islands were almost all Southeast Asian, Ade portrayed them as Africans. Moreover, during *The Sultan of Sulu*'s long run on Broadway, the two slaves identified in the cast of characters were played by actors of Irish descent dressed in Arabian robes and made-up with blackface. The slaves were identified by their blackness.[29] How would such a racialized understanding of slavery interpret a slavery in which the slaves not only were not black, but also were of the same "race" as the masters? The idea of a mild, assimilative slavery provided a convenient way.

For Americans in the southern Philippines, the depiction of a mild slavery became less convenient through 1902 and 1903. Conditions in the Sulu Islands and the Philippines at large changed, making the abolition of slavery in the southern Philippines more practicable, if not also imperative. Then, in the months leading up to the proclamation of abolition, the colonizers' perception of slavery changed completely. Before General Wood issued his antislavery decree, American officials in the Sulu Islands and Mindanao had come to see slavery in the Moro societies as oppressive and intolerable. With the colonial state now playing the role of emancipator, the political implications of the problem of slavery in the Philippines began to favor the perpetuation of colonial rule. How and why will be the subjects of the following chapters.

PART II

Abolition by Avoidance

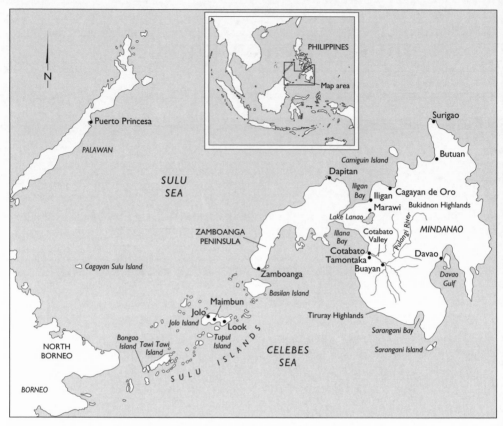

Map 3. The Sulu Islands and Mindanao, c. 1900.

CHAPTER THREE

Colonialism and Moro Slavery

To Americans, slavery in the Moro societies seemed, at once, familiar enough to embarrass the imperial administrations in Washington and exotic enough to be explained away as a "mild" form of servitude that was not intolerable to the slaves themselves. At its extremes, American antislavery discourse could constitute its subject, Moro slavery, in quite fantastical ways. But which interpretation of Moro slavery was the more fantastic, the image of benign dependency or that of harsh bondage, and how did these representations relate to the new colonial order in the Moro societies?

American representations did not and could not directly reflect the conditions of slavery in the Moro societies. The Americans who debated imperialism in the United States were spatially removed from the Moro societies and they remained minimally informed about them. Neither the anti-imperialists nor the imperial administrations in Washington commissioned special inquiries or hearings to investigate the practice of slavery in the southern Philippines. Their arguments over the nature of slavery there must therefore be understood in principally local American terms. The reports on slavery in the Sulu Islands that accompanied the Bates treaty provided a thin screen of information on which Americans projected their own ideological divisions over empire, theories of race, and presuppositions about Islam.

If the debate in the United States over the relative harshness or mildness of Moro slavery had very little to do with actual practices of bond-

age, the same was not necessarily the case for colonial knowledge produced locally in the southern Philippines. Colonial knowledge about
the Moro societies was certainly as tendentious and distanced by antislavery ideology as were the depictions of Moro slavery circulating in
the United States. Moreover, only one of the American officers in Mindanao and Sulu, Najeeb M. Saleeby, became a student of the Moro societies and sustained an abiding interest in their cultures and histories.
Nevertheless, their colonial position in the Moro societies enmeshed
them in the affairs of masters and slaves and vice versa. The political implications of Americans' antislavery ideology unfolded and changed not
only in the debate over imperialism in the Untied States, but also in relation to local politics and social relations in specific Moro societies.

When Americans first established stations in Mindanao and the Sulu
Islands after 1898, they encountered independent and semiautonomous
Moro societies that had only recently begun to buckle under the pres-
sures of colonial encroachment. Unlike other precolonial Philippine societies, the Moro societies in the south had formed indigenous state systems by adapting to local circumstances the Islamic model of sultanates
ruled by descendants of the Prophet. Two principal sultanates over-
shadowed the other Moro societies. The Taosug-dominated Sulu sultanate centered at Jolo in the Sulu Islands had long been the most powerful. Gaining in relative power in the late nineteenth century was the
Magindanao sultanate on the southern coast of Mindanao within which
two centers of power periodically vied for supremacy, one down river
at Cotabato and the other up river at Buayan. It was this state structure
and the history of the Moro societies' autonomy from Spanish colonial
rule, in combination with the exigencies of the war of conquest in the
northern and central Philippines, that prompted the American colonial authorities to negotiate the Bates treaty for indirect rule in Sulu.
The Moro societies were not, however, what the Americans expected
them to be.

To American eyes, Moros multiplied the already substantial otherness of Filipinos by being Muslim and having evaded the direct cultural
influence of Spanish colonization. Indeed, the word *Moro,* originally a
Spanish name for Muslims around the world, became a reified racial
category in the hands of the American colonial officials. By marking the
Moros as inherently different from (Catholic) Filipinos, American colonialism inscribed both groups with corporate identities founded in the
ostensibly natural distinctions of racial ancestry. This colonial delinea-
tion of identities moved in a close and sometimes tense relationship with

Philippine nationalism, which staked a similar interest in the construction of a collective Filipino identity that did not include Moros or the non-Christian tribes. For our purposes now, however, the important point is that such corporate identities were alien to the local and dyadic loyalties that obtained in specific Moro societies.

Although the sanctified office of sultan provided centers of hierarchy in the Moro societies, the Moro sultanates were segmentary in form and dyadic in structure. That is, the sultans did not govern defined territories or populations. Instead, they exercised power in shifting networks based on individual ties with local leaders who, in turn, exercised power in similar but smaller segments of the sultanate. Primary political allegiances remained fundamentally local and heterogeneous, even though the Sulu and Magindanao sultanates at times held considerable sway over distant communities of political and economic clients, as well as subordinate ethnic groups. Consequently, there was a disjuncture between the Americans' expectation that state authority would be homogeneously effective over a given territory and the fluid structure of the diverse Moro polities.

The Moro polities were also much weaker than the Americans had initially expected. As recently as the mid–nineteenth century the Sulu sultanate had been the most formidable military and economic presence in a region that stretched into the Visayas, northeastern Borneo, and beyond. Magindanao influence never spread nearly as far, yet Spain could barely establish a foothold in Magindanao in the last decades of the nineteenth century. By the 1890s the Sulu and Magindanao sultanates were neither fully vanquished nor independent. In 1898 American colonial officials encountered these polities in a state of flux, with old institutions of leadership under pressure from new economic and social circumstances. The practice of slavery and slave raiding figured prominently in these alterations.

The Sulu sultanate rose to great power in the eighteenth century through its regional control of slave raiding, slave-based commodity production for the burgeoning China trade, and a local redistributional trade that cemented the allegiance of client groups spread around the Sulu and Celebes Seas. James Warren has shown in his magisterial history of the Sulu sultanate in the eighteenth and nineteenth centuries that "[s]lavery and slave-raiding were fundamental to the state, inextricable . . . [from] the evolution of this system" of trade and power.[1]

The Sulu sultanate was perfectly situated to take advantage of new trading opportunities created by the expansion of European and American merchant capital. European colonization may have had the ancillary effect of suppressing slave raiding in some parts of Southeast Asia, but in doing so it redirected and intensified the slave trade in other areas. The spice trade created new demands for laborers in the sixteenth and seventeenth centuries, as did the rise of urban areas such as Batavia, Makassar, and Malacca. Slaves provided the principal source of labor to fill these demands, and some of the slaves sent to these invigorated markets passed through the hands of raiders and slave traders from the Sulu Islands.[2]

Through the mid–eighteenth century the Sulu sultanate struggled with military and trade competition from Brunei on the north coast of Borneo, the Spanish fortress at Zamboanga on the southwestern tip of Mindanao (continuously garrisoned after 1719), and the independent Magindanao and Iranun on Mindanao. The balance of power shifted in the later part of the eighteenth century, when the British East India Company and private "country traders" began to frequent the Sulu chain in search of cargos they could exchange in China for tea, a commodity that sold for premium prices in Europe and North America.

For at least several centuries, Chinese junks had sailed from Amoy down to the Sulu chain, and sometimes as far south as Makassar, to trade for the region's marine and jungle products. At Jolo the junks acquired cargos collected from within the Sulu Islands, Mindanao, Basilan, and the northeast coast of Borneo. These goods—camphor, pearls, mother-of-pearl, dried sea slugs, dried shark's fin, wax, tortoise shell, and edible bird's nests—found lucrative markets in China. It was this same Chinese demand that lured European and American merchant vessels into the Sulu Sea in the eighteenth century. The newcomers soon dominated the trade to China, setting in motion an expansion of commerce that had far-reaching social and political effects.[3]

The opportunities for long-distance trade and slave raiding set the stage for Sulu's rise. In exchange for regional products to be traded in China, European and American ships paying call at Jolo unloaded cloth, opium, metal products, and, most importantly, war stores. The Sultan and prominent Taosug *datus* established a virtual monopoly over external trade. This gave them control of the local redistribution of manufactured goods, including the weapons essential for warfare and slave raiding. The sultan and Taosug *datus* outfitted Iranun and Samal raiders, who took slaves from coastal regions throughout the Philippines and much of insular southeast Asia. Taosug *datus* also established settlements along the northeastern coast of Borneo, where they traded slaves to local communities from which they obtained goods for the expanding China trade.[4]

Jolo became the major regional slave market and trading port, where Taosug aristocrats redistributed the influx of slaves through their trading networks. In the process, the Taosug built ties with client groups across the region, such as the Iranun from Mindanao, seaborne and migrating Samal peoples, and Dayak and other peoples on Borneo. Sulu's control of weapons, trade, and raiding put its competitors in Brunei and Cotabato (the Magindanao) into decline and dwarfed Zamboanga's trade. By the early nineteenth century Sulu had turned its position at the center of this redistributional system into the basis of regional hegemony.[5]

The infusion of large numbers of captives enabled the sultanate to meet the production demands of long-distance trade. Warren estimates that between two hundred thousand and three hundred thousand slaves entered the Sulu sultanate during the period 1770–1870. Although highly impressionistic, the reports of foreign visitors suggest a dramatic population growth in Sulu and its dependencies. Warren estimates an increase on Jolo Island from approximately forty thousand in 1770 to two hundred thousand in 1814. By the mid–nineteenth century there may have been as many as five hundred thousand in the sultanate with slaves constituting a majority in some regions.[6] The bulk of Sulu's extraordinary population growth, according to Warren, consisted of imported slaves.

The common Taosug words for slave—*banyaga* and *bisaya*—reflected the alien nature of captives and their most common source. *Banyaga* is a common word for "foreigner" in many Philippine languages. A *bisaya* is a person from the Visayan Islands of the central Philippines. Both terms connoted outsiders in Sulu, implicitly non-Muslim foreigners in the case of *banyaga* and explicitly Christians in the case of *bisaya*.[7] The status of slaves as outsiders produced effects that other forms of servitude, such as debt-bondage, could not replicate.[8]

Debt-bondage within the sultanate could not increase the number of laborers beyond the limited size of the indigenous population. Nor could such dependents be transferred to distant lands as readily as could captives in exchange for foreign goods or currencies.[9] Captives also possessed skills otherwise unavailable within Sulu society. Some slaves, including Christians from the Philippines and a few Europeans (captured from ships and shipwrecks in the region), translated for merchants, provided medical services, and played music for their masters on European

instruments such as the violin.[10] Last, captives were the product and mediating lubricant of a system of raiding, military organization, and trading that would not have existed if internal debt-bondage could have fulfilled the need for dependents. Status in Sulu may have been shifting,
with considerable mobility for manumitted slaves and their descendents,
who often joined dominant ethnic groups, but the experiences and social functions of captives were distinctive in many ways.

Thanks to Warren, we know more about slave raiding and captives
bound for Sulu than about any other newly enslaved people in southeast
Asia. Escaped slaves picked up by European ships furnished the major
source of information. Once on board, they were routinely questioned
to secure information about raiding, leaving a written record of their experiences. Working through these materials, Warren collected biographical information and narratives of 180 *banyaga* who escaped from
Sulu between 1836 and 1864.[11]

Raiding itself was violent. Resistance and flight were common responses. Once captured, the newly enslaved were stripped, then tied
about the hands, feet, and neck. Some captives reported being bound in
stocks or tied down to the bottom of the boat. Beatings were routine, especially about the arms and legs to immobilize captives. In addition,
captives received a minimal diet of rice, sago, and brackish water that
sapped their strength. The passage to Sulu could take weeks or months,
ample time for this treatment to break many captives and kill numbers
of them. Those who survived the breaking were forced to row and haul
supplies at provisioning stops. Upon reaching Sulu they were sold and
resold, often to interior regions to prevent escape in early years. Simply
put, no matter how the occupations and social status of different kinds
of dependents might sometimes overlap, *banyaga* endured experiences
alien to the contractual terms of most debt relations.[12]

The importance of slavery and slave raiding in Sulu's rise is also underscored by their significance in Sulu's decline after the mid–nineteenth
century. Ironically, the colonial powers whose trade enabled Sulu's as-
cent now declared the sultanate a pirate state, inimical to their shipping,
colonial interests, and international law. The tide turned against Sulu in
the 1840s, when the colonial powers began to introduce new steam-
powered gunboats to combat raiding. The British attacked Iranun raiding bases in northern Borneo in 1845. A Spanish expedition in 1848 lev-
elled Balangingi Island, the major Samal raiding base in the Sulu chain.
In 1860 Manila positioned eighteen new gunboats in key sea passages
to block and guard against Samal raiders. Comparable actions by the

English and Dutch further restricted opportunities for raiding. In 1871 the Spanish successfully blockaded Jolo town. Five years later, in 1876, they razed the town and stationed a garrison there. In 1878 the sultan signed a treaty with Spain that, at least in the Spanish version, recognized Spain's titular sovereignty, promised cooperation to suppress "piracy," and stipulated annual payments from Spain to the sultan and other *datus*.[13]

By the 1870s raiding from the Sulu Islands was confined to minor clandestine operations running between Borneo, Mindanao, and the Visayas. Increasingly, the Taosug had to rely on small shipments of slaves from the powerful Datu Uto in Magindanao, who, also facing Spanish encroachment from downriver, had to turn inland to Mindanao's hill peoples for a source of slaves. This much-reduced slave trade continued to the beginning of the twentieth century.[14]

The disruption of slave raiding and commerce in Sulu displaced control of local and long-distance trade from the Taosug aristocracy to Chinese merchants. Consequently, the sultan lost much of his ability to tax commerce and direct the redistribution of goods to bind alliances. Politics fragmented in the sultanate. The hereditary office of sultan continued to carry religious significance, but in terms of power the sultan was now just one of many *datus*. The sultan could no longer unify the other *datus* behind him through patronage or expand the strength of his own following through the addition of numerous slaves and weapons.[15]

After the fall of Jolo in 1876, the town of Maimbung (Maimbun) on the southern coast of Jolo Island emerged as a new commercial port linking Sulu and Mindanao to new Chinese-dominated trading centers at Labuan and Singapore. In 1885–86 the Spanish established control over Sarangani Bay, Uto's main outlet for long-distance trade, where he had exchanged slaves, jungle products, and rice for weapons. Bakat, the main commercial point on the Pulangi River within Uto's domain, fell soon after. This restriction of trade strained Uto's alliances by displacing him from the center of redistribution, just as the fall of Jolo had displaced the sultan of Sulu. In February 1887 the Spanish destroyed Maimbung, dispersing its Chinese merchants to towns around Sulu and Muslim Mindanao. Later that year Datu Uto capitulated to Spanish forces positioned to overrun him entirely.[16]

Uto's military defeat was prepared by a Spanish policy that directly depleted his following. Unlike Sulu, where the sultan seems to have been the first significant leader to submit to terms with the Spanish, Uto was one of the last to take this step in Magindanao. Spanish influence in Sulu was practically confined to the walled town of Jolo. In Magindanao, Spain's presence at Cotabato in the Pulangi River delta made possible a campaign of "attraction" to detach slaves from their masters over a wider region.

The idea of conquering *datus* by first gradually weakening their traditional power base—the ownership of slaves—had been proposed as early as 1855. After the occupation of Cotabato in 1861, the Spanish pressed their new client, the relatively powerless official sultan of Magindanao, to free his slaves. The sultan reportedly answered "that he would rather give up his wife and children than his slaves, for lacking the latter he simply would cease to be a sultan." [17]

The new Jesuit mission at Tamontaka, near Cotabato, began to ransom young slaves in 1872, when a smallpox epidemic led to famine, causing the Magindanao to sell slaves for greatly reduced prices. Tamontaka became an agricultural colony, supported by donations and the church hierarchy in Manila. The Jesuits baptized *libertos* and enjoyed considerable success in encouraging runaway slaves to seek protection at the mission. It seems that some compensation was given masters for their runaway slaves, for in 1885 the Manila government appears to have changed this policy by declaring all runaway slaves free without any compensation to their masters. Yet, after a peace agreement signed in July 1885 by Uto and the Spanish governor of Mindanao, the Spanish forces returned runaway slaves to Uto.[18]

When war broke out in 1886 one of Uto's targets was the *liberto* dormitory at Tamontaka, soon burned to the ground by infiltrators. After Uto's surrender another spate of slave defections prompted the *datu* to plead for the return of his property. The Spanish refused to return Uto's slaves, but they made no effort to liberate slaves who did not run. In fact, Datu Ayunan, who fought with Spain against Uto, was allowed to keep captives taken in these battles, as well as maintain his existing body of slaves. Spain freed slaves as a strategic tactic in Magindanao. It never defined or attempted to execute a policy of abolition.[19]

Spain did destabilize the most powerful states and alliance systems in the Muslim southern Philippines, but it did not establish solid control over the region. The Spanish colonial occupation was most tenuous among the Maranao and Iranun and reached little beyond the garrisoned town of Jolo in Sulu and Cotabato in Magindanao. There were few converts other than the *libertos* at Tamontaka. The immigration of Spanish settlers and Philippine Christians to Cotabato and Davao had just begun. Only Zamboanga, under permanent occupation since 1719, had a significant Christian population and a sustained influence on its hinterland. *Datus* and their slaves, each in a sense defining the other, survived the late-nineteenth-century incursions of Spanish colonialism.

Spanish rule in Magindanao crumbled in 1898, as it collapsed around the Philippines under pressure of the Philippine revolution and then the United States invasion. In November the Spanish soldiers at Cotabato executed fifty Filipino troops stationed at their garrison for plotting a mutiny in support of the Philippine Republic.[20] Moro attacks on Christian settlements came in the wake of the Spanish panic. Datu Andong, the son of a *datu* who had allied himself with the Spaniards, began to threaten Tamontaka, urging the *libertos* to return to their masters' villages.[21]

The Spanish abandoned Cotabato in January 1899, leaving a coalition of Christian Filipinos, Chinese, and Moros in control of the town. Ramon Vilo, a Christian Filipino, declared himself governor in the name of the Philippine Republic, only to be overthrown by an alliance of Moros and Chinese under the Moro-Chinese mestizo Datu Piang. Once a follower of Datu Uto, Piang had pledged loyalty to Spain during the revolution. After Spain's demise and Vilo's assassination, Piang declared himself the new Sultan of Mindanao. His followers attacked churches in Cotabato, executed some Christians, and forced others to flee. During the colonial interregnum the Magindanao maintained their autonomy through alliances between Piang and other *datus,* the most important of whom was Datu Ali of Kudarangan, another former client of Uto's. When U.S. troops arrived at Cotabato in December 1899 Piang readily shifted allegiance yet again, this time to associate with the new colonial power.[22]

U.S. troops had reached Jolo earlier, in May 1899. Sultan Jamal-ul Kiram II was then on Siassi Island, just back from a pilgrimage to Mecca. The sultan remained there while several Jolo *datus* allowed the Americans into the town. Jacob Gould Schurman, president of the first Philippine Commission, visited Sulu in June. In an interview with the sultan, Schurman proposed an agreement along the lines of the 1878 treaty between the sultanate and Spain. The sultan gave preliminary oral consent to such a plan, setting the stage for the negotiation of the Bates treaty in August 1899.[23]

General Bates left Manila for Jolo in July 1899 with instructions to conclude a treaty affirming U.S. sovereignty through the offices of the sultan. According to his instructions, the sultanate had "no sustained industry," "slavery of every degree known to feudal service," and "free men . . . [who] are averse to taking wages and placing themselves on a level with slaves." In the past, the sultan and *datus* appropriated "one-fourth of the plunder taken by piracy, but when the profits of piracy ceased they lost their main source of income." This association of slavery with economic backwardness in a Muslim society evoked images antithetical to progress and, conversely, faith in the United States's progressive role. "By right and judicious conduct on the part of the United States Government," Bates was reminded, "it might be possible to build up these islands into flourishing and self-supporting communities beneficial to the United States and doubly beneficial to the inhabitants of the islands." [24]

The sultan's "notoriously deficient" income opened the possibility of forging a relationship through a monetary subsidy. In return, like Spain before it, the United States demanded a cessation of "piracy," meaning slave raiding as well as the general plundering of seaborne traffic. But, beyond the terms of the old Spanish treaty, the United States wanted to ban the import of firearms and devise a plan to abolish slavery. The instructions given Bates looked to the example of British indirect rule in the Malay states, where "slavery has been gradually abolished." Based on this and other models of gradual emancipation, the instructions supposed that "slavery might be considered and its remedy found in the free birth of all children born after a certain date." The sultan and *datus* were to be won over to this plan by explanations of the United States's "benevolent intentions" to respect local religion and customs, foster economic development, and thereby increase revenues to the sultanate. "A treaty formulated along these lines would undoubtedly maintain peace," the most important objective for imperial military authorities tied down by their war of conquest in the central and northern Philippines. [25]

General Bates and the sultan met several times at Jolo. In early August they exchanged treaty proposals. The sultan's proposal made no explicit mention of sovereignty or slavery. It authorized the display of his own flag alongside that of the United States, promised his "aid in preventing piracy," and expressly called for the sultan and *datus* to keep "arms for fighting." Article XI of the Sultan's proposal addressed a problem that would later be the source of much conflict. It required the return of fugitive "American subjects . . . to the Americans, because he [sic] may be a convict," and it mandated that "the same shall be done with our followers who run away to the Americans; they will be returned to us; but if the Americans will pay for them the price that will be agreed to, all right, but if we do not come to [an] arrangement they will be given back at once to avoid ill feeling." When the United States later refused to return runaway slaves, the refusal did indeed become a source of "ill feeling."[26]

Bates's proposal explicitly recognized U.S. sovereignty, called for the suppression of piracy, and, like the sultan's proposal, stipulated that residents of Sulu would be accountable to the law of the sultanate. But it also prohibited the importation of firearms except by special permission from the United States, promised to repatriate Moro "criminals and offenders," and included in Article X a provision for slaves to "purchase freedom by paying to the master a price not to exceed fifty (50) dollars Mexican." After several meetings during which the sultan and several *datus* raised concerns about this fixed maximum price, the parties agreed to require "the usual market value" for self-purchase. Datu Kalbi (Calbi), who had evinced some reluctance during the negotiations, told Bates on August 19 that he "never said a word against the whole treaty except that one paragraph about slaves, but . . . that has been satisfactorily settled." On 20 August 1899 the sultan and four *datus,* including Kalbi, signed a treaty based on Bates's proposal.[27]

In a report to accompany the treaty, Bates explained his expectations for Article X. He "found that the institution of slavery exists in a very mild form," such that the word "retainer" would express "this condition better than 'slave.'" Nevertheless, he did not use the word *retainer* in formulating Article X. Bates continued, "I also found that the Moros were jealous of any interference with [slavery]; but it seemed proper that steps should be at once taken looking to the abolition of the institution." Compensation for the owners of liberated slaves "seemed but fair" to Bates. "Article X," he wrote, "provides a speedy means of doing away with slavery."[28]

President McKinley approved of the treaty, with the caveat that the sultan should be advised that "this agreement is not to be deemed in any way to authorize or give the consent of the United States to the existence of slavery in the Sulu Archipelago, a thing which is made impossible by the 13th amendment to the Constitution of the United States." It remained to communicate this qualification to the sultan and to follow the president's request for an inquiry into the practicality of a compensated emancipation.[29]

The sultan received two communiqués in April 1900 that conveyed McKinley's views on the Bates treaty. In a letter to the Sultan and *datus* who signed the treaty, General Bates interpreted the president's directive to mean acceptance of the treaty except for Article X. Bates explained that "[t]he Constitution of the United States forbids slavery in any part of the United States, and it remains to find an equitable mode of abolishing the institution." The matter of "slavery or peonage," he assured the sultan, would be "reserved . . . for future consideration, determination, and agreement." [30] The commanding officer at Jolo, Major Owen J. Sweet, had Bates's letter translated into *jawi*, the Taosug-Arabic script, and appended a note of his own for the sultan.

About the matter of slavery Sweet advised the sultan, "do not let it worry you. The people of the United States are just, but are opposed to slavery, which at one time existed in America." The problem of slavery would "probably be considered in a conference between the Moros and some authorized American representative, in which your pecuniary interests in your slaves will be recognised and some method agreed on so that slavery shall cease without pecuniary loss to yourselves." This was the method of abolition used by England in several colonies, including the Malay states, of which the sultan would have had some knowledge. The process worked in those colonies, Sweet assured the sultan, "with satisfaction to all parties." [31] If the sultan and *datus* of Sulu did not at first realize that the United States intended to abolish slavery, the letters of April 1900 made that end plain.

While the sultan and *datus* awaited further negotiations over slavery, American officials began to equivocate on the nature of slavery in Sulu and the potential difficulties of emancipation. For example, through July 1900 the U.S. commander at Jolo reported that "[n]o trouble has arisen on account of slavery, but [it] is liable to occur if there is any unauthorized meddling." Despite the delicacy of the problem, he continued to believe it would not be "hard to stop slavery, as the owners get very little pecuniary benefit from them." Evading the economic significance of slaves, he stressed the problem of honor inherent in slavery. He explained that masters' interest in slavery derived from "the dignity and prestige it gives them to own some one over whom they have absolute control even of life and death." Nevertheless, the commander treated slaves as commodities while contemplating plans for a compensated emancipation. [32] This and other aspects of the American presence in Sulu produced unexpected consequences that would change American colonial estimates of Moro slavery and the feasibility of a controlled emancipation.

CHAPTER FOUR

Tolerating Slavery

The contradictory representations of slavery presented by the American colonial authorities reflected their partial understanding and observation of the institution in Sulu. Their reports and accounts capture the tenuousness of indirect rule and the false confidence of colonial authority. Contrary to their intent, the very instruments for a smooth, gradual, and controlled emancipation encouraged disruptions beyond colonial control. The crucial element here was the agency of masters and slaves. Each acted within the structure set by the colonizers' commitment to antislavery principles. Masters, on the one hand, responded to the promise of a compensated emancipation as an opportunity for profit that could be multiplied by securing new slaves. Many slaves, on the other hand, soon found that they could run to colonial authorities for protection. Indirect rule and colonial plans for an orderly emancipation foundered on the actions of masters and slaves.

Estimates of the number of slaves in Sulu in April 1900 ranged from five thousand to twenty thousand. Taosug informants told Major Sweet, the military commander in Jolo, that there were more than ten thousand slaves in a total population of about one hundred thousand, but this may have applied to the major island of Jolo and not the entire archipelago. In 1900, slaves brought prices (sometimes in currency, sometimes in trade goods) of between $50 and $150 Mexican, roughly equivalent to between $25 and $75 in United States currency.[1]

It had been more than a quarter century since the Spanish, Dutch, and British navies effectively ended the major slave trade centered in Sulu, but a small number of new slaves continued to be smuggled into the archipelago. With the supply of slaves so tightly restricted, *datus* turned to other sources of slaves and bonded followers. Slave stealing, judicial confiscation of slaves, judicial enslavement, and debt-bondage all increased in the late nineteenth century. When the *datus* of Sulu learned that the new colonizer would soon offer to buy all their slaves at a price considerate of their interests, they expected compensated emancipation to bring "from $100 to $200 [Mexican] or more money to them for every slave they possess." Masters found this a most compelling reason to acquire new slaves.[2]

The trade in new captives from Mindanao seems to have accelerated in 1900. In Cotabato, nine Moros and two Christian Filipinos were apprehended between March 1900 and February 1901 in separate incidents of kidnapping children to sell them as slaves. This activity appears to have been related to the demand for slaves in Sulu. The military commander at Cotabato then required all *datus* at the mouth of the Pulangi River to report the arrival of ships from Jolo and ordered Moros on board the vessels to carry a passport that would warn colonial authorities to search the ships "for stolen children."[3]

Sometime between July and September 1900 a Moro named Lagbow agreed to take twelve people (eleven Christian Filipinos and one Moro) by boat from Cotabato to Basilan, but instead sold them as slaves at an island just northeast of Jolo. Three of the party were reportedly sold to Datu Joakanain (a signatory of the Bates treaty) or his followers.[4] The commanding officer at Malabang, on the coast north of Cotabato, apprehended a Moro from Jolo who had taken captive a local woman for sale as a slave. He reported there were "many similar cases . . . at more remote points and the Datos come to me for assistance or request permission to punish the offenders."[5] A man named Selungan (Sulungan), reputedly a relative of the sultan of Sulu, brought as many as fifteen slaves to Jolo in September 1901.[6] In June 1901 a man named Sabdani in Jolo claimed he had been "stolen" and sold as a slave by one Sankil of Panigaian (near Isabela, on Basilan). The commander at Jolo wanted "Sankil for trial as an example" to discourage other slave traders.[7]

The revival of enslavement and slave trading immediately heightened tensions between Sulu *datus* and local colonial officials. The commander at Jolo had always seen slavery as a potential problem. In May 1900 he feared that precipitous action against it would "only bring on trouble and cause a needless war." [8] By November 1900 the enthusiastic response of masters to the promise of compensation had made "slavery with its attendent evils . . . the source of the greater part of the troubles" in Sulu. "This dealing in human flesh" to multiply profits in a compensated emancipation struck the commander as "abhorrent to the civilized world . . . [and] inherently repugnant to the people of the United States." It also complicated the projected emancipation. New slaves added to the future cost of emancipation "at a rate . . . incompatible with public policy and the future civilization of the Mohammedan people in these islands." Despite efforts to keep peaceful order by assuaging the concerns of masters, the colonial state's actions against enslavement and slave trading intruded ever more abrasively into relations between masters and slaves.[9]

Colonial opposition to slave raiding was neither new nor a surprise to the sultan and *datus*. They did not object to the provisions against "piracy" in the Bates treaty and there is no record of objections to the apprehension of slave raiders. But the colonial state went beyond this. In November, the commander in Jolo announced that only those slaves acquired before 13 April 1900, the date of his letter assuring the sultan of remuneration for freed slaves, would be considered legitimate for purposes of compensation. Retroactive to that date, all people in Sulu were to be protected against "newly enforced bondage." Disputes erupted as soon as colonial officials tried to deny the masters access to persons they claimed as slaves.[10]

Selectively freeing slaves initiated conflicts about property, social relations between masters and slaves, and the moral status of ethnoreligious communities. Datu Joakanain "was not well pleased" when Major Sweet "freed a slave who had been a free man since childhood; who had been a Christian for 27 years and until recently, did not know he was born a slave." This man had been re-enslaved or reclaimed as a slave by Joakanain, but the man's Christian wife, whom the commander also freed along with two children, "was born free and had never been enslaved until recently." Sweet told Joakanain "the United States was not pleased that Christians should be enslaved, and that slavery was applicable to Moros only." [11] It seems that Sweet did not recognize that the notion of Moros enslaving Moros was, at least in the abstract, as odious to Moros as the thought of Christians held in slavery was to Americans.[12]

During the initial years of occupation the colonial regime made a special point of securing the freedom of Christians held as slaves. In Cotabato, the United States military commander worked through February

1901 to recover all "Filipinos," by which he meant Christians, held by Magindanao *datus*. He secured the release of Christian slaves from Datu Uto and Datu Ali, among others.[13] The civil governor of the Philippines, William Howard Taft, displayed a similar special concern for the release of Christian slaves mixed with hesitation about any more general action against slavery. Referring to Magindanao and environs in 1901, he told Elihu Root, the secretary of war, that "[t]here were some Filipinos enslaved by the Morros [*sic*], but by order of the military they were released. I have no doubt that contact with civilization will reduce the practice of slavery very much, and that in the course of two or three years, we can secure the emancipation of all the slaves at a comparatively small sum, but if Congress goes at it hammer and tongs, it may produce a religious war which would be chiefly disastrous."[14]

By regulating the status of slaves the colonial state intruded into the affairs of people of all ranks. Even the Sultan of Sulu was not immune. Early in 1900 the commander at Jolo compelled the sultan to give up a Visayan Christian named Pascol. The commander later interceded against the sultan's claim over a Moro widow, her three married daughters, and one child. Still, the sultan managed to secure one of the daughters, prompting the commander to demand her "freedom, as he had no right by law, Koran, or Custom to this family." When the sultan offered to ransom his claim to the family for $650 Mexican, the commander stepped in again to forbid this practice.[15]

While the colonial government claimed special authority to demand the release of certain slaves, masters demanded the return of others. A Moro named Ysom had lived under U.S. protection in Jolo town since the beginning of the military occupation, working as an employee of the colonial government since July 1900. Ysom's old master did not recognize this arrangement as conferring a release from slavery. In September 1900 the old master sold Ysom for $50 Mexican. Ysom's new master went to the authorities in Jolo to claim his property. Major Sweet refused and warned the titular slave owner that he "had no right to work up such a scheme against any Moro in a government employ and under United States protection." The category of persons not liable to be claimed as slaves thus expanded to include colonial employees and, most significantly, anyone said to receive U.S. protection.[16]

The protection of slaves at American garrisons became a source of great anxiety for masters. Once slaves realized that they would be protected against return to bondage, more began to flee their masters, much as the masters feared they would. In growing numbers slaves ran from

masters of all ranks, further complicating plans for a compensated emancipation. Their receipt of protection aggravated the *datus'* relations with
the colonial state, for the refusal to return runaways undermined the
masters' power over slaves by giving the slaves a practicable option of
escape. Even the sultan could not recover runaway slaves, no matter how
much he pleaded with colonial officials about the terms of the Bates
treaty, the promise of a compensated emancipation, and the danger to
his precarious authority.

Flight had long been a common form of direct resistance to slavery in
Sulu, though its feasibility and forms were always determined by local
circumstances. We know that hundreds of slaves, and probably many
more, managed to escape from bondage in the Sulu sultanate during the
nineteenth century. The most common means of escape was to seek protection on a European ship paying call in the Jolo roadstead. Slaves also
sometimes made the passage to the Spanish fort at Zamboanga by small
boat. This route was convenient, but many escaped slaves soon found
themselves held at Zamboanga for long periods and put to hard labor.
There are several known cases of slaves from Sulu who refused passage
out of bondage through Zamboanga for this reason; in one instance, a
group of slaves picked up at sea by an English ship threatened to throw
themselves overboard if the captain took them to Zamboanga. Some
slaves undertook the great risk of finding their way home by small boat,
many doubtlessly perishing en route. A few may have found protection
with the Spanish in Jolo town during the last decades of the century, but
the slight evidence in this regard sharply differentiates Jolo from Magindanao, where the Spanish offered protection to large numbers of slaves
as a deliberate policy.[17]

Given the segmentary nature of Sulu society, factional competition
opened another option for slaves. They could flee from one master to
another, in hope of better treatment. Unless they left Sulu entirely, slaves
had to attach themselves to another master for protection, for they
could be recaptured and were sometimes killed for running away. Beatings and restraints were common on the middle passage to Sulu; they
were also known as punishments within the islands. Yet the slaves' ability to run to other masters gave them an element of power in negotiat-
ing the terms of their servitude. Masters sometimes sold slaves on their
request, lest the slave run away leaving the master with a total loss. Location shaped the slaves' ability to maneuver this way; the more isolated
or strange the location, such as the Borneo coast, the fewer the opportunities to run. If the risk of provoking slaves to run away sometimes

caused masters to be more lenient, the masters also used the threat of sale to inland parts of Mindanao and Borneo to keep slaves in check.[18]

U.S. colonial rule altered the circumstances of slavery in Sulu by its very presence. Slaves found the military stations offered them a new option for escape within Sulu. Some slaves fled their masters in the first year of the occupation, but the number was probably small. In September 1900, General William A. Kobbe, the military commander for all of Mindanao and Sulu, reported that "[i]n a few cases slaves have sought the protection of our troops, and have been claimed by their owners; but if the slave preferred to remain, he has always been allowed to do so."[19] By March 1901, when Governor Taft and the Philippine Commission toured the southern Philippines, the situation had changed. At Jolo, Major Sweet told the commission that "practically all the slaves favor emancipation. Applications for freedom are received almost daily, eight or ten having been received within the past few days."[20]

Colonial tolerance for indirect rule grew thinner as a result of problems associated with slavery, the weakness of the sultan, and violent factional struggles. General Kobbe began to voice growing disenchantment with indirect rule in Sulu during the Philippine Commission's visit in 1901. Like Major Sweet in Jolo, Kobbe had learned that the sultan was no more powerful than a weak *datu* in terms of practical politics, a sultan only "in name through heredity." He told Taft that the Bates treaty was an "embarrassment" that a brief and easy war in Sulu would remove. Yet, he continued to advise against "any radical legislation relating to slavery." Such action, he warned, "would probably give rise to resistance and be ineffective."[21]

Taft would come to share Kobbe's opinion of the Bates treaty over the next two years. At the time, he did not see the treaty as an impediment to U.S. sovereignty or an embarrassment, although he did find "slavery . . . a difficult problem with which to cope." To the relief of his conscience, colonial officials protected runaways and he believed they had "not recognized slavery." This much was simple and in accord with antislavery principles. "But slavery," continued Taft, "is a domestic institution in which the slaves form part of the household of the master and many of the slaves would not know what to do if they were free." The difficulty, Taft seemed to say, lay in the slaves' incapacity for emancipation. Nevertheless, he suggested that the colonial government "might safely pass a law abolishing slavery in the Philippines so far as the Jolo archipelago is concerned," with compensation for the masters. For Mindanao, Taft thought abolition "would present much greater difficulties," not because the freed slaves would not know what to do, but because *datus* in Mindanao "would make a much more formidable resistance" than those in Jolo.[22]

As it happened, Taft and the commission took no action against slavery in Sulu or Mindanao after their investigation in 1901. Taft remained ambivalent on the matter. "I had thought that the issue was easy of solution after leaving Jolo," he informed Root, "but was a good deal perplexed about it again when we reached Zamboanga and Cottabato in Mindanao, where we looked further into the institution."[23]

Taft's hopes for a peaceful emancipation were once again buoyed when a *datu* in Zamboanga issued an abolition proclamation shortly after the commission's departure from Mindanao. Datu Mandi had allied himself with the Spanish and fought with them against the Maranao and then the mutinous Filipino troops at the time of the Philippine revolution. He immediately gave his allegiance to the United States in 1899. Mandi was not born a *datu*. He grew up in Zamboanga town, spoke Spanish, married into an important Samal family, and made himself into a *datu* with Spanish support.[24] There were far fewer slaves within the ken of Mandi's influence on the Zamboanga Peninsula than in Sulu, Magindanao, or among the Maranao. Alert to his new patrons' feelings about slavery, on 19 April 1901 Mandi circulated a declaration in *jawi* script addressed to the *datus* of Zamboanga. The translation made for General Kobbe announced Mandi's opposition to slavery: "In view of the fact that slavery never has and never will bring any progress with it, you shall prevent Moros to have [*sic*] slaves of their own or other race."[25] Taft thought Mandi's proclamation was "the beginning of the end of slavery." He expected *datus* in Magindanao to "follow Mandi, and while slavery may not be entirely eradicated for years, it will be discouraged."[26]

Taft's renewed confidence in the course of a slow abolition had grown stronger by the time he wrote his annual report in October 1901. Noting that "[t]he question of how best to deal with slavery among the Moros has attracted wide attention in the United States," Taft explained his prescription in some detail. Slavery was "widespread among the Moros, but . . . in an extremely mild form." Slave raiding had "nearly ceased," almost all Christians had been freed, and American troops protected runaways. Most slaves were actually in debt-bondage, according to Taft. Most also were "treated kindly," could earn money to redeem themselves, and they could not be distinguished from their masters by a "casual observer." At bottom, "Moro slaves were, on the whole, so well satisfied with their present lot that if they were all set free the majority of them would promptly return to their old masters and voluntarily take up their old life again." Taft hastened to add that this was "not advanced as a defense of . . . slavery," but to illustrate "the difficulties to be encountered in abolishing it." A forceful abolition "would inevitably provoke a fierce conflict . . . and, so far as the slaves are concerned, would meet with little appreciation." A gradualist policy would produce abolition "in a generation," without a war or a bitter legacy.[27]

Slavery did not die the peaceful death that Taft expected. Confrontations between slaves, masters, and colonial officials continued to irritate affairs in Sulu and Mindanao. Sixteen slaves fled from masters on Tawi Tawi, Simunul, and Banaran Islands to the colonial garrison at Bongao at the end of 1901. Some left behind small children that U.S. troops retrieved by taking them from the masters.[28] In October 1901 the new commander in Jolo, Major C. B. Williams, reported that "cases are constantly presented and each brings with it serious and delicate questions." He warned that it did "not seem possible that the general subject can be treated evasively much longer." Reflecting on the abolition of slavery in the United States with a combination of arrogant superiority and humility, Williams wrote: "History has shown that a people much more advanced in civilization were not to be turned away from it by peaceful means." In short, the commander at Jolo began to see war over abolition as inevitable precisely at the time officials in Washington, Manila, and Zamboanga reaffirmed gradualism.[29]

General George W. Davis, the commander of the district of Mindanao and Sulu, now opined that the Bates treaty "should never have been made" and recommended its dissolution because it encouraged the Sulu sultan's belief in his sovereignty. Davis also believed, wrongly, that the rejection of Article X by the United States took away the slaves' former right to self-redemption. Still, mindful of the potential for conflict over slavery, Davis did not call for immediate abolition and direct rule. Quite the opposite: "The worst misfortune that could befall a Moro community and the nation responsible for good order among the Moros," he wrote, "would be to upset and destroy the patriarchal despotism of their chiefs, for it is all they have and all they are capable of understanding. . . . It seems to me to be our duty to respect this conservatism and deeply rooted prejudice, to utilize it and to use these Dattos in our efforts to lead these people away from slavery, polygamy, piracy, and despotic rule, just as the Dutch have in Java and the English in India."[30]

Davis also likened his position in Mindanao and Sulu to the United States's relations with American Indians. This familiar analogy caught the attention of officials in Manila. The commanding general of U.S. military forces in the Philippines endorsed Davis's report with the note: "It seems to me the most feasible plan in exercising control over the Moros would be to follow as closely as practicable the general rule of conduct that governed our administrations of the North American Indian; and the less we interfere with the so-called rights and privileges of the individual Moro the better we will be able to control them as a whole." [31] Dean C. Worcester also endorsed the report, recommending its submission to the Philippine Commission to inform future policy regarding Moros. Worcester made no reference to slavery or abolition, but he did specifically approve Davis's desire to reduce the sultan "to the status of a datto" without claim to "sovereign rights." [32]

In 1902 General Davis took the first step toward instigating a crisis over sovereignty and slavery in the Moro societies. In early March he issued an order to promote the exploration of Mindanao and Sulu. He wanted to purchase local products, hire local laborers, and open markets "through peaceful means . . . to overcome the desire of these people to remain isolated and to exclude Americans." This much could be accommodated within indirect rule. But in an aggressive departure from the status quo, he also ordered the military "to impress upon the natives the fact that the taking and selling of slaves is forbidden by our laws, and to inform those who from Spanish times have been holding slaves, and those who are held as slaves, that the United States does not recognize the right of any man to own another, and that those who wish to leave their masters will be protected against recapture and forcible return to bondage." [33] This verged on immediate abolition.

The new commander at Jolo, Colonel William Wallace, recognized immediately the implications of Davis's directive if it were to be applied in Sulu. Wallace had watched helplessly while factional disputes between Datu Joakanain, Datu Hegasan, Maharajah Indanan, and the sultan led to armed battles, plundering, and the burning of houses within view of Jolo town. What little colonial order Wallace maintained through alliances would be destroyed by intrusive action against slavery.[34]

The sultan and *datus* had been assured by Bates and Sweet that slavery would be the subject of negotiation, so Wallace asked if the new order was meant to apply to the Sulu Islands. In reply, Davis amended the order. Runaway slaves were to be protected, but this should not be "in-

terpreted in a manner that would be a violation of any provision of the
Bates Agreement." Masters and slaves should be informed that protection would be given to "those who leave their masters," not to the
broader circle of those who might "wish to leave their masters," as stipulated in the original. To clarify the retreat from the precipice of abolition, Davis explained: "It is not intended to disturb the relations existing between Moros and their slaves who wish to remain so, nor is it
intended to invite persons held as slaves to flee." Davis underscored the
distinction by later adding, "[t]his is not ordering an emancipation."[35]

At first, Wallace did not publicize the American commitment to protect runaway slaves, but he was soon drawn into the confrontation that
he wanted to avoid. In early May some of the sultan's slaves either ran
away or were stolen. The exact circumstances are unknown, but the
missing slaves eventually came into the custody of the sultan's rivals,
Datu Kalbi and Datu Joakanain. The *datus* refused to return the slaves,
so the sultan petitioned Colonel Wallace to help recover his property.
Wallace demurred, explaining that "slavery is not recognized by the
United States." He reviewed colonial policies on slavery for the sultan,
including the promises made by General Bates and Major Sweet that its
final disposition would be subject to negotiation, and he added two new
items: Wallace promised to provide the owners of protected runaways
with letters so that they could claim future compensation and he excluded from protection runaway "people who have agreed to work for
a certain person for a certain length of time to cancel a debt." Debtors
under a labor contract, he explained, "are not slaves." If they ran away,
"such people . . . might be compelled to return and complete their
contract."[36]

The flight of more of the sultan's slaves in June eventually brought the
matter to a head. While the sultan was away from Jolo, seven of his
slaves appealed to Wallace for protection. The sultan requested their return and objected to Wallace's protection of the slaves as an infringement
of agreements to treat the matter of slavery in negotiations. Only now,
in response to the sultan's demand to know by what authority he acted,
did Wallace make public the amended order of March 1902 to protect
runaway slaves.[37]

Openly stating the right of slaves to leave their masters was indeed
inflammatory. The sultan immediately complained to the military governor of the Philippines. Other masters protested the liberation of their
slaves, but no direct record of the content of their petitions remains. The
sultan's letter of complaint, in *jawi* and court translation, is one of the few

extant documents about slavery penned by a Moro. It is invaluable as an insider's commentary on the institution of slavery, as well as an indicator of the frictions caused by runaway slaves and the colonial presence.

The sultan reviewed the events. The seven runaways were a family, who were all "my slaves since they were born." When he called for them, they went instead to Colonel Wallace, who "gave them a letter of protection and sent me a copy of it." The sultan based his claim for the return of the slaves on precisely those traditions the Bates treaty promised to respect: "This letter of protection," he explained, "takes away my rights over these seven persons, who are my slaves according to Moro law, custom and the Mohammedan religion." Here the sultan indicated the broad cultural challenge inherent in any action against slavery, a social relation and institution mediated through law, custom, and religion.[38]

The sultan also left no doubt that slavery had an economic dimension. "Slaves are a part of our property," he declared. "To have this property taken away from us would mean a great loss to us." Therefore, he reasoned, General Davis's "order to protect escaped slaves . . . is not just to me and my people" and Colonel Wallace's protection of the seven slaves "is not right, and is showing bad faith on the part of the United States." These actions violated the Bates treaty, the understanding that slavery would be discussed in a conference, and Major Sweet's assurance that masters would be compensated for freed slaves. From the perspective of the sultan and, one can assume, of masters generally, it seemed the United States now intended to abolish slavery without compensation, for "to protect slaves who refuse to return to their rightful owner is just the same as to free them." So the sultan pleaded with the military governor to "keep mutual faith, do not encourage our slaves to run away from their rightful owners and then protect them so the owner cannot get them back, but let the matter be settled as is said in the letter of my father General Bates"—that is, by a negotiated compensation.[39]

The route of the sultan's appeal passed through Zamboanga, where General Davis added his own evaluation of the situation. Davis would not return runaway slaves because "slavery cannot be recognized by the United States." In fact, he now went back to his earlier more aggressive views on the matter, suggesting that slaves "should be encouraged to abandon their masters." This left the issue of compensation. He thought the "avaricious and shrewd" sultan's "real purpose" in the affair was to establish "a claim for indemnity." This was "a situation that must be met sooner or later," as the tensions of the present case amply demon-

strated. Davis advised against a compensated emancipation. It would be
"quite impracticable to secure the freedom of slaves by remuneration of
the owners," not because of costs, the difficulty of administration, or the
willingness of masters to accept payment, but because he believed the
slaves and their society were incapable of freedom. "If the slaves were
all made free tomorrow," he claimed,

> many thousands, probably hundreds of thousands, would continue in volun-
> tary servitude, for they could not now exist in freedom in most of the Moro
> country. They are not specially unhappy as slaves, for they have few wants or
> necessities, save those that are felt by all animals, and these their sultans, dat-
> tos and owners find it to be in their interest to provide. . . . [Slavery] will never
> be eradicated in these islands until public sentiment in the communities is op-
> posed to it, and this sentiment will be of slow growth.[40]

The case of the sultan's runaway slaves reached Washington, where
the secretary of war Elihu Root approved the decision to protect fugitive
slaves but did not discuss the issue of abolition.[41] The military governor
in Manila replied to the sultan's protest with the unconsoling reminder,
"[o]f course you know that the President of the United States and all the
people whom he governs do not believe it right for one person to own
another person as his slave." Runaway slaves, including the sultan's, had
to be protected. Not to do so "would severely wound the sensibilities of
the President of the United States and all the people of that country."
This did not mean that the colonial regime planned an imminent abolition. Rather, the military governor assured the sultan, "[m]y soldiers
will not seek to induce your slaves to leave you."[42]

Although the colonial authorities retreated from their flirtation with
a more active antislavery stance, the situation in Sulu remained volatile.
As the prospect of compensation for slave owners faded, the untenabil-
ity of indirect rule became all the more apparent. Neither the sultan nor
the American troops exercised territorial authority. Ever since the
demise of Taosug-sponsored trade and slave raiding, the sultan had little
patronage to distribute to build clientage. Now, in the face of the im-
plicit colonial challenge to slavery, the sultan appeared even weaker. The
colonial policy on slavery demonstrated that the sultan no longer functioned as an effective intermediary between *datus* and the outside world,
as he had during the sultanate's heyday.

CHAPTER FIVE

From Mild Slavery
to Harsh

If Americans associated with the colonial regime deceived themselves into thinking they could control a smooth and gradual emancipation, the sultan, *datus,* and slaves knew better. The sultan plainly recognized that "to protect slaves who refuse to return to their rightful owner is just the same as to free them." Even for slaves who did not flee, the option to "refuse" the most basic demands of a "rightful owner" would degrade a master's authority.

At least some slaves who fled understood the transformation they helped to create. A group of freed slaves in Bongao expressed this in a petition to the colonial governor at Jolo, pleading that the military garrison there not be vacated:

> [Y]our petitioners (natives who were formerly slaves, and who have had their liberties from the American and Spanish governments) feel sorely distressed, as your petitioners are quite certain that they and their families would be recaptured again by their former owners and be sold again as slaves, like sheep, and be treated like dogs, and possibly killed for having escaped before, and also they would be separated from their families as before the Americans came here. When the Spanish left they were treated in this manner, and up to the present time some of your petitioners (natives) have not seen or heard of their families, as they were sold to some distant places as slaves, and your petitioners (natives) may perhaps never see them again during their lifetime.[1]

When slaves ran from their masters they were quite literally making their own history in a context not exactly of their own choosing. While

the colonial regime hesitated to act decisively on its antislavery commitments, the slaves who ran took their fate into their own hands. The very
fact that the runaways appear in the colonial record indicates that the
slaves made history in another sense, too. Their actions and the responses of masters redefined the context in which the colonial authorities had to act, just as the United States military presence had redefined
the context in which masters and slaves lived and in which slaves effected their own emancipation.

Runaway slaves and the masters who tried to reclaim them engaged
in a struggle inexplicable within the official colonial image of "mild slavery." Like the Bates treaty, the belief in a distinctly benign species of slavery permitted American colonial officials to avoid conflict in the southern Philippines while the war of conquest continued in the northern
islands. The concept of "mild slavery" remained tenable in the face of
contradictory aspects of slavery, such as struggles between masters and
slaves, because it could either screen out these features or redefine them
as familiar tensions within acceptable norms of hierarchy, subordination, and servitude.

From Zamboanga in September 1900, General Kobbe reported instances of masters coming to reclaim runaway slaves, but hastened to
add, "In each case the master appeared indifferent to the [Americans']
decision" to give slaves protection. This passage on runaways is embedded within a larger argument that "[s]lavery as the term is usually understood does not exist among" the Moros. To Kobbe, slaves resembled
and seemed to live like their masters. "Apparently or really," he wrote
with an uncharacteristic glimmer of ambivalence, "social equality exists
between the slaves and the free retainers and often with the masters."
Except for their service in warfare, Kobbe thought the slaves "receive
greater benefits from [their master] than he from them."[2]

Despite the Sulu *datus'* obvious interest in the recovery of runaways
and compensation for freed slaves, Kobbe stressed the Moros' supposed
willingness to discuss "with indifference plans for altering or abolishing
the institution."[3] Nor did he alter his opinions when the commander in
Jolo informed him that slavery "with its attendant evils" proved quite
troublesome to colonial rule in Sulu. Except for the reported increase of
enslavement in preparation for a compensated emancipation, Kobbe
thought "undue importance" was given to the matter of slavery. "So-
called slavery among the Moros is distinctive," he explained, for three
reasons: "1st.—Because slaves are almost exclusively of the same race as
their masters, 2nd.—Because there is no wide social inequality or man-

ner of living apparent between master and slaves, 3rd.—Because servitude is, as a rule, voluntary. 'Slaves' are frequently willing retainers, do not perform hard labor, receive greater benefits than they confer and often transfer their allegiance unhindered."[4] In other words, the institution appeared to lack those characteristics that defined slavery as "usually understood" and made it a moral affront to Americans.

Western ideologies of race certainly made slavery in Sulu and Mindanao appear distinctive to Americans, who assumed from their own experience that slavery constituted a relation between racially different peoples, typically African and European. Hence the prominence Kobbe and others gave to the somatological similarity of masters and slaves. These white Americans, it is essential to remember, came from an intensely race-conscious culture that tended to portray its own historic forms of slavery in a softened, often romantic light. It was precisely the sense of great social distance between masters and slaves that made possible the historian U. B. Phillips's famous interpretation of the slave plantation as a benevolent school of civilization.[5] The category of racial difference enabled many white Americans to view their own historic institutions of slavery as something other than the unmitigated horror of abolitionist literature, but American colonial officials held the apparent *absence* of racial and social distance in southern Philippine slavery to indicate a "mild" type of bondage distinct from that which was practiced in the New World.

Between the colonizers' political interests and the limitations of their racialist understanding of slavery there remained much room for misunderstanding, ignorance, and confusion. For example, Kobbe thought that the "'slaves' are frequently willing retainers," exemplifying the problem of distinguishing slaves (*banyaga* or *bisaya*) from a *datu's* locally recruited followers or people in debt bondage. Unfamiliarity and the focus on race blinded colonial officials to the salient distinctions that identified slaves as outsiders and inferiors in a society in which somatological concepts of race had no meaning. Thus the early American colonial officials seem never to have commented on the use of the words *banyaga* (connoting foreigner) and *bisaya* (a Filipino from the Visayan Islands) to signify slave. Likewise, in their horror at the thought of Muslims holding Christian slaves, they did not recognize religion as a determinant of legitimate enslavement within Moro societies.

By concentrating on selective perceptions of treatment, colonial officials shifted their attention away from what their own society proscribed—the social practice of owning, selling, and taking people as slaves. Instead, the most often discussed variable for determining action against slavery was whether the slaves' position could be construed as being within the broad range of hierarchy, subordination, and servitude that white Americans accepted as proper for the Moro peoples. The secretary of war Elihu Root employed this shift of focus from the prohibited to the legitimate in his attempt to reassure a skeptical Albert Bushnell Hart in early 1902. "The mild character of the so-called slavery among the Sulus" did not alter the United States's commitment to abolish slavery, but it did shape "the method which we should pursue in enforcing our prohibition of [it]." Drastic action, justifiable if to relieve "an intolerable condition of suffering," would not be appropriate for "the actually existing conditions of comparative comfort but little removed from ordinary voluntary domestic service." Other than the fact of their "so-called slavery," effectively reduced to a semantic issue by its categorization as "mild," Root found little objectionable in the slaves' social situation.[6]

The construction and sustenance of the category "mild slavery" can be traced in detail through the interviews conducted during the Philippine Commission's tour of the southern islands in 1901 and its subsequent report. Although the interviewees described a variable range of conditions and treatment in slavery, all parties—Taft and the commission, local colonial officials, and *datus*—claimed that relations between masters and slaves were harmonious. No slaves or former slaves were interviewed. The participants at each level, from the *datus* up to Taft, screened out progressively more contradictory information until, in the commission's summary report, few details contradicting the representation of "an extremely mild form" of slavery remained.

The commission first visited Jolo, where it interviewed Major Sweet. He reported that virtually all the slaves desired emancipation, yet he "did not think the slaves were treated with great cruelty; at times being whipped and at times killed outright if they displeased the 'datto.'" Sweet saw that slavery entailed "social inequality." The "slaves were looked down upon," but "manumitted slaves could rise to positions of trust and honor." As an example, Sweet related "the case of the man Janarin, who was a slave and notorious liar, whose mouth had been slit from ear to ear, but was subsequently, though a slave, placed in charge of a village" to collect taxes for his master.[7]

At Zamboanga, the commissioners interviewed Major Jasper N. Morrison, who "had been all around the islands . . . to make inquiries concerning the people." He told them that "most of the Moros obtain slaves by stealing children or by making war and capturing them." In Tawi Tawi, Morrison had been invited to purchase young female slaves and he also reported a trade in slaves from the area of Iligan Bay on the north coast of Mindanao. The conclusion of Morrison's testimony was particularly noteworthy in several respects. He recognized the ethno-religious distinctions between Moro masters and the slaves taken from "the hill tribes," emphasized the difference between retainers and slaves, and claimed special authority to evaluate slavery based on his experience in the United States.

> I was raised in a slave state; I know about slave laws. I can not see any difference between these and those of the States. If for a retinue, that is different. A retinue is one thing and slaveholding another. A retinue is a kind of voluntary service; they consider it an honor. They treat slaves in families well, because they value them and they become more or less attached to them. They live together, and it is hard for a stranger and one who does not speak the language to distinguish them. Even if they were all freed at once, I do not know but that, as they had been raised in slavery, they would continue it, and in practically the same condition. The only ones who wish to escape are those who have been taken for debt or who were captured as slaves after growing up.[8]

Except for the references to retinues, the similarity in appearance of masters and slaves, and debt bondage, Morrison's relatively nuanced description of slavery in Mindanao and Sulu resembled contemporary portrayals of slavery in the southern United States as benignly paternalistic.[9] His commander in Zamboanga accentuated the paternalistic aspects of slavery, omitting Morrison's qualifications and more subtle insights. To General Kobbe, it seemed there was "no well-defined difference" between masters and slaves, who all lived "together as a family." He did add, in the course of a discussion of polygamy, that a *datu* "had every power over his female slaves." In sum, Kobbe told the commission that "[t]he system [of slavery] was patriarchal; did not believe it cruel in any respect; did not know of slaves being sold from one family to another." He recommended against "any radical legislation relating to slavery."[10]

The statements of Sweet, Morrison, and Kobbe, in ascending order, provided information already interpreted to accord with the image of "mild slavery." Not coincidentally, this order followed their proximity to slavery, Kobbe in Zamboanga town being the most removed from daily contact. Conversely, when the commission interviewed *datus,* they heard testimony based upon direct experience as masters. The *datus'* descriptions were not yet assimilated into the interpretive structure of colonial ideology, but they did come in response to the commissioners' prompts and questions. When the *datus* spoke of relations between masters and slaves, they did so in terms of their own idealized conceptions of legitimate hierarchy. The colonizers accepted the masters' ideology of slavery with little critical comment. They even embellished it to better conform to their own conception of "mild slavery."

Attos, the chief of a Bagobo (a non-Muslim ethnic group) village in the hills above Davao Gulf, told the commission that "each man has one, two, three, or four slaves in his work." The slaves were "bought . . . for arms and working tools from the tribes to the north." Speaking for the other non-Moro ethnic groups in the Davao region, Attos said "all the slaves are Atas," members of a non-Muslim ethnic group. When the commissioners asked if "any of those lowland people" (meaning Christian Filipinos) were slaves, Attos replied, "There are some. I don't know how many there are, but I have three myself." [11] The commission also interviewed some Moro *datus* at Davao, probably from the Manobo people. Their slaves were also "all from . . . the weak pagans of the interior," purchased from "the datos of the interior." The commissioners asked only one question about the treatment of slaves: "Has the master a right to kill him?" A Manobo *datu* replied, "They have no right to kill their slaves. [But] they die, of course, very fast." [12]

At Cotabato, the commission met with Datu Piang. He said the Magindanao no longer kept Christian Filipinos as slaves, although the neighboring Maranao took Christians as captives during the recent Spanish times. About one-quarter of the people in the Magindanao region were "slaves," the *datu* said, entering the relationship through debt, "purchased from other slaveholders," or born into the status. The commissioners asked "whether slaves live in the household?" Piang said this "depends upon circumstances"; slaves lived "inside the house with the family" only if masters had "perfect trust" in them; all others resided outside the master's immediate household. Asked, "Do they treat their slaves well?" Piang answered, "That depends entirely upon the master. If he is a good-hearted man he will treat his slaves well. If he is not, he will not; and that is the reason why slaves who have hard taskmasters run away." [13]

Of all the commission's interviews, the most extensive was with Datu Mandi in Zamboanga. After discussing religious and civil offices among the Moros, the *datu* and commissioners turned to the subject of slavery. Asked, "Does slavery prevail among the Moros?" Mandi answered, "Yes." He estimated that slaves comprised "about one-eighth of the Moro population." In his domain on the Zamboanga Peninsula, Mandi said the "slaves" were held for debts or were the children of debtors.[14] But as the interview progressed, it became less clear that "slaves" were always or even typically Moros held for debts.

Q: Are the slaves in this island all Moros now?

A: Yes, sir.

Q: No Filipinos?

A: No, sir.

Q: Are there any of the Pagan races who are slaves to the Moros?

A: They are generally the slaves—they are the slaves of the Moros.

Q: Do they change their religion when they become slaves?

A: No.

Q: How do they make those people slaves; by capture or by debt?

A: Only by debt.

Q: How long is it since you have given up the practice of capturing?

A: A short time ago.

Q: I suppose the Lake Moros [Maranao] go on capturing as they used [to]?

A: Yes.[15]

The commissioners' anxious inquiries about Christians ("Filipinos") held in slavery were, in effect, questions about treatment. Muslim enslavement of Christians entailed a violation of categories, a reversal of the order of progress central to colonial ideology, that could not be reconciled to a view of slavery as "mild," "benign," or paternal. Enslaving "Pagan races" might be considered wrong, but it did not transgress Christian hierarchies of civilization. The commission reiterated this hierarchy in its annual report. After proclaiming slavery in the southern Philippines "extremely mild," it explained: "The old slave-hunting expeditions have nearly ceased. The Moro datos claim they no longer occur at all, but it is known that this statement is not strictly true, as the Moros of Mindanao still occasionally capture members of wild tribes in the interior of that island. The Filipinos formerly held as slaves have practically all been liberated by our troops, although it is possible that a few may still remain in bondage in the Lake Lanao region."[16] By the next paragraph of the report all recognition of the ethnic and religious differences between Moros and slaves from "Pagan races" and "wild tribes" had vanished. The commissioners referred to "Moro slaves," reverting to the assumption of "social equality" between indistinguishable masters and slaves.[17]

The commissioners pursued the issue of treatment at length with Datu Mandi, but asked only one question about the work performed by slaves. Their questions presumed the mildness of slavery and their reactions to Mandi's answers evaded contradictory information or assimilated it to standards of acceptable subordination.

Q: How are the slaves used and how are they treated?
A: Very much all kinds of work in the fields and in the house.
Q: How are they treated?
A: Very well.

Then the commissioners asked if slaves were "members of the family," but they inadvertently diverted Mandi from this topic by also asking him about the average debt of "slaves" in his domain. They soon returned to the subject of treatment.

Q: Do [the slaves] eat at the same table with their masters?
A: No, sir.
Q: Do the Moros eat at a table?
A: Some at a table and some on the floor.
Q: Are the children permitted to go to school?
A: Yes, sir. [Mandi earlier said few Moros attended school and those who did attended Muslim schools for religious instruction.]
Q: Do they have as good food as the rest of the family?
A: Being slaves, no.[18]

Colonial officials, insensitive to the discrepancies in status that seemed natural to Mandi, maintained their preconception that slaves were "members of the family" and thus on a nearly equal social footing. The commissioners queried Mandi about masters' sexual rights over female slaves, a subject of frequent comment in colonial reports. To colonial officials, sexual relations with female slaves fell within the category of family relations, in contrast to the older American abolitionist portrayal of American slavery as a relation of sexual abuse and depravity. Somewhat cryptically, Mandi said that a female "may be a slave for domestic uses, but for no other." Later, while discussing slave prices, Mandi explained that female slaves sold for up to twice the price of males, "because they say that in the matter of work a woman is worth more than a man." Women did much of the agricultural work in Moro societies, in addition to their value in social and sexual reproduction. But the commissioners asked no questions about slave women's roles in these spheres. Rather than treat sexual exploitation as an objectionable feature of slavery, they seem to have perceived it as a natural part of Moro life and an ameliorating influence upon slavery.[19]

In the most striking part of the interview, the commissioners and Mandi discussed the treatment of slaves in connection with local legal procedures. The exchange reveals the standards of appropriate discipline and severity applied by colonial officials in evaluating the harshness of slavery.

Q: Do masters have any special power over their slaves? If a slave commits a crime, could a master kill him or would he have to present the case to the courts?

A: Exactly the same.

Q: Could a master put a slave to death if he chose?

A: The owner could increase the debt of the slave by lending him more money.

Q: Could he kill him?

A: No; he could punish him but not kill him.

Q: Could he cut open his face? [perhaps a reference to Sweet's story of the slave Janarin]

A: No; he would have to present the case to the courts.

Q: Suppose that a slave was impudent to him and refused to obey him, what could he do?

A: He thrashes him with a rod.

Q: But could not mutilate?

A: No.

Q: Are the slaves generally content?

A: Yes.[20]

Neither Mandi nor the commissioners thought beating an insubordinate slave unduly harsh. The commissioners asked if treatment of slaves varied among "the tribes of the Moros? For instance, here they treat them mildly, but the Lake Moros are more severe, are they not?" Mandi replied, "Yes, sir. The treatment accorded slaves is according to the good heart of the master." He also agreed with the commissioners that slaves on Jolo were not treated as well as those at Zamboanga, but the implication that slavery in the Sulu Islands might be relatively harsh, like the suggestion that the treatment of slaves varied with the "heart" of the master, did not make a mark on colonial thought at this time.[21]

Colonial perceptions of slavery in the southern Philippines eventually began to shift in mid-1902. Until then, descriptions of slavery and discussions of what should be done about it almost always emphasized its "mild" nature. Afterward, in a reversal of meanings, the features that once marked slavery as mild began to make it appear intolerable. There is no evidence to suggest a corresponding change in the practice of slavery. The transformation can be traced to a complex alteration in the relation between colonial officials and Moro polities.

Events in the Philippines and the United States contributed to the new view of slavery. In June 1902, the sultan's protest over the protection of runaway slaves brought together before the colonizers' eyes the issues of slavery and the inefficacy of indirect rule through the sultan. In July, President Roosevelt signed into law the Philippine Organic Act, a measure to organize civil government for the Christian areas of the colony. Although it did not apply to the Moro peoples, the act spoke to American concerns over slavery by incorporating the language of the Thirteenth Amendment to the United States Constitution: "That neither slavery, nor involuntary servitude, except as a punishment for crime whereof the party shall have been duly convicted, shall exist in said islands."[22] Then Roosevelt declared that the "insurrection" against the U.S. conquest of the Philippines had ended. The deterioration of indirect rule in the Sulu Islands coincided with the official end of warfare in the northern islands and the regularization of civil government for the colony. Moreover, when Governor Taft testified before the House and Senate committees considering the Organic bill in February and March 1902, the issue of slavery had proved somewhat embarrassing.

Over two days in March 1902 the House Committee on Insular Affairs questioned Governor Taft extensively about slavery. Taft responded with an apology for colonial inaction against slavery. "It has been described properly as a mild form of slavery, if you can have a mild form of that institution, not that it ought to be encouraged, or not suppressed because it is mild, but because I mention it in order to show that its continuance until we can eradicate it is not going to be productive of the horror and severity that it would if they were more mistreated."[23]

Taft agreed that the Thirteenth Amendment must apply to the Philippines as territory "under the jurisdiction of the United States," in the words of the amendment. Yet, he had to admit more than once that colonial authorities "have not directed that slavery must cease."[24] He emphasized that the colonial regime "never recognized" slavery. It protected runaways, "required the delivery up of all Christian Filipino slaves," and, Taft claimed, "by force prevented and suppressed all slave traffic." With slave raiding and trading cut off, the Moros' slaves were now, he claimed, "generally Moros themselves . . . taken for debt." Taft reemphasized the "mild form" of this slavery, and again felt he had to defend his apparent toleration of slavery.

> Understand me, I do not favor and do not want to be put in the attitude of favoring a continuance of slavery, even of those who are willing to have it continued and be subject to it, but the question is, is it better to end that relation, which is not physically cruel, by the loss of life, the loss of treasure, and the destruction of property, or is it better in the course of a few years to eradicate it, as I believe we may eradicate it, by the influence which the United States is rapidly acquiring; I mean the paternal and authoritative influence that it is acquiring among the Moros.[25]

In fact, Taft regarded the situation as so "hopeful" that he believed a gradual abolition could be effected "without even the recognition involved in the purchase of slaves" to compensate masters. Compensation should be unnecessary, Taft explained to the committee, because "the Moro expects control [and] the exercise of authority over him. He respects force, and I believe the United States is gaining control over them and that the evil of slavery can be eradicated."[26]

One can already see in Taft's testimony the beginnings of a transformation in the colonial regime's stance toward the Moros and slavery. Taft used familial terms to describe both colonial rule and slavery in Moro societies. Slaves were "treated as members of the family, and it is very difficult to distinguish between one and the other."[27] Colonial rule constituted a "paternal and authoritative influence" among the Moros. When colonial officials looked with relative favor upon Moro societies, they described slavery and the power of the *datus* as patriarchal.

Taft's paternalistic colonialism encompassed and excused the use of violence at the same time that it constituted expressions of putatively benevolent or "mild" relationships. About the punishment of slaves, Taft told the committee: "Whipping is not unknown among them, though the relation [slavery] is described as a mild one."[28] And, as for the "paternal" colonial influence on the Moros, Taft explained, "[t]he fact is that troops will always be needed in the Moro settlements. The Moros do not understand any other mode of authority."[29] While Taft held out hope for a peaceful, gradual abolition of slavery, he also reinforced an ideological structure that designated Moro societies as intractable except in the face of naked force.

When queried about the autonomy allowed the Moros, Taft explained the system of indirect rule. "It takes them just as you [i.e., the Congress] take the Indian tribes here, and treats them as Indian tribes and lets their tribal governments continue." [30] This common frame of reference presupposed Taft's oscillating representations of noble and ignoble savages, as well as his use of paternalistic and familial metaphors in a situation of conquest, subordination, and potential genocide.[31] Taft's testimony embraced both poles of the contradiction in relatively equal proportion: Moros as perfect colonial subjects, entirely obedient to paternal authority; and Moros as perfect subjects for colonial conquest, resistant to all influences but violence.

From 1899 to the middle of 1902, colonial officials emphasized the benign patriarchy of Moro society. Images of "mild" slavery and peaceful obedience to the colonial patriarch served to legitimize the autonomy allowed Moros through indirect rule while the United States fought a brutal war to enforce direct rule over the supposedly more "civilized" Christians of the northern islands. Then, after July 1902, little more was said about benign aspects of Moro societies.

Whereas Taft used the model of "Indian tribes" to signify the dependent autonomy of Moro societies, in August 1902 General Davis employed the analogy to justify an entirely different course of action. In an advisory report for the reorganization of colonial government in Mindanao and Sulu, Davis suggested that "the region in question may be regarded as we formerly regarded an Indian reservation whose inhabitants were hostile or unruly . . . when the President was obliged to call in the army to discipline and govern its hostile or unfriendly savage inhabitants." To Davis, the position of the Moros in relation to the colonial government was akin to the position of Apaches at his old post, Fort Sill, "i.e., they are nominally prisoners." [32]

Davis underscored the Organic Act's contrast between Christian Filipinos fit for civil government and Moros (and other "non-Christians") too "uncivilized" for that privilege. "There is no civilized inhabitant of the Philippines, American, Spanish or Filipino," he attested, "who would even suggest that the Moros are capable of civilized and enlightened self-government, for a government of law—i.e., regulated liberty—is absolutely unknown to and unthinkable by them." [33] Religion marked this morally invidious division between "civilized" and "uncivilized." On one side stood Christians: Americans, Spaniards, and Filipinos with the capacity to develop "regulated liberty" through the legitimate paternalism of colonial rule. On the other side stood their antitheses, "non-Christians" and autonomous Muslim societies that practiced slavery and polygamy, unfit for "civilized and enlightened self-government."

> With a people who have no conception of government that is not arbitrary and absolute, who hold human life as no more sacred than the life of an animal; who have become accustomed to acts of violence; who are constrained by fear from continuing the practice of piracy; who still carry on the slave trade; who habitually raid the homes of mountain natives and enslave them; who habitually make slaves of their captives in war, even when of their own race; who not uncommonly make delivery of their own kindred as slaves in satisfaction of a debt . . . who habitually observe the precept of the Koran which declares that female slaves must submit to their masters, it is useless to discuss a plan of government that is not based on force, might, and power.[34]

Davis now represented slavery not as a fading and paternalistic institution, but as the epitome of Moro corruption, deeply rooted in the traditions and laws of Islam. His justification of colonial "force, might, and power" relied on a litany of Moro transgressions against the norms of "civilized" hierarchy, yet each item of the litany had earlier been used as evidence for the peculiar mildness of Moro slavery.

Like Taft and most other colonial officials, Davis had once argued the slaves were contented, "for they have few wants or necessities, save those that are felt by all animals."[35] He now projected this as a characteristic of all Moros, with dehumanizing effects. The image of a people who ignored the "sacred" distinction between human and animal life replaced the image of readily accommodated slaves. The absence of racial difference between masters and slaves, formerly construed as a prime indicator of the mildness of that slavery in contrast to New World slavery, now became emblematic of abomination. The prevalence of debt bondage (here only partially distinguished from slavery) no longer exemplified the voluntary, temporary, and therefore tolerable nature of servitude. Rather, by making "delivery of their own kindred as slaves in satisfaction of a debt," the violation of moral boundaries of self extended from the Moros' "own race" to "their own" families. And, whereas slavery had been portrayed as "domestic" and familial, these benevolent adjectives were replaced by stereotypes of Islamic prescriptions for the sexual violation of female slaves. In other words, an image of religiously sanctioned incest displaced the earlier depiction of an undemanding paternal slavery. "With such a class of people," Davis concluded, "it is useless to quote the bill of rights or to assert the sin and wrong of slavery."[36]

The new representation of slavery as an odious institution did not by any means constitute a fuller understanding of slavery as practiced in the southern Philippines. An analysis of slavery in terms of the absence of racial distinction, whether taken to imply the mildness of the bondage or the abhorrence of enslaving one's own kind, could not bring observers closer to the salient distinctions of religion, ethnicity, and kinship that defined outsiders as suitable for enslavement. Tracing the incidence of sexual relations between masters and female slaves to precepts of the Koran bypassed the connections between slavery, reproduction, and power that combined with women's productive value to make them more valuable slaves than men.

Much of this colonial discourse about the harshness versus mildness of slavery engaged in a distancing of the American self from the other by constantly opposing New World and southern-Philippine slaveries. Suppositions of difference are not necessarily wrong and there are obvious empirical reasons for the necessity of American scholars to attend to matters of difference in a study of Philippine societies. Yet, unwavering concentration on oppositions can make invisible the complexities of slavery, such as varying combinations of harshness and mildness within even a single master-slave relationship, dialectics of control and resistance, and contradictions between the slaves' being as people (to some extent incorporated into society) and their hypostatization as things (nonpeople, outsiders, to be exchanged or used as an extension of a master's will).

The distance between self and other preoccupied the early-twentieth-century American colonial discourse on Philippine slavery, in keeping with colonialism's exclusive definitions of civilization, moral community, and identity. Even the anti-imperialists' use of the slavery issue in propaganda against colonialism shared this structural feature with pro-colonial discourse, whether it construed slavery as mild or harsh. The politics of colonialism, in the broadest cultural sense, set the context for Americans' observations of slavery and permeated their interpretive frameworks.

Within the field of colonial representations of Moro slavery, Davis's advisory report marked a turning point in the political implications of antislavery ideology. Plotting American and Moro societies at distant points along a scale of moral hierarchy, Davis declared that "Americans have come here to teach and convince these people that all men are born free and equal, and that there is no such thing as inherited caste or privilege." This required "upsetting the whole system of tribal and patriarchal government among the Moros, but they do not fully realize this." [37] As we have seen, however, Sultan Kiram indicated otherwise in his letters of June 1902.

Antislavery ideology shaped Davis's view of the U.S. mission to the Moros. It targeted slavery as the central problem to be eradicated and projected the internalization of order in civil society as its replacement, with special emphasis on a capitalist work ethic to promote commodity production. "If the Moro and Pagan lands are ever to become productive," Davis explained, "the native inhabitants must be taught that labor is honorable, and its remuneration certain. To that end every effort should be used to restrain the savage and bloody impulses of these people, to encourage industry, to desist from slave hunting and holding and to secure for them as rapidly as they show a capacity for it a participation in community affairs, in short, to begin an organization of what we call a society that is not held together by the dicta of a Sultan, Datto, or Priest." [38] For the first time, intrusive action to eliminate actual (not just metaphorical) slavery became an explicit rationalization of American colonialism in the Philippines.

By August 1902, after three years of fitful attempts to accommodate antislavery principles to the structure of Moro society within a system of indirect rule, the colonial regime had developed a more aggressive attitude toward slavery and colonial control in the southern Philippines. This shift in perspective did not by itself determine the process of emancipation. Nor did it even yield a declaration of abolition, which would not be made until the last months of 1903. Colonial officials still hoped for a gradual emancipation that would not disrupt their tenuous control. They always understood that abolishing slavery involved power and the reordering of social relationships. Simple laws and decrees would not suffice. After all, the 1902 Organic Act forbade slavery as certainly as did the Thirteenth Amendment. That was "the most important section of [the Organic Act] affecting Moros," but, as General Davis instructed the Philippine Commission:

> The Declaration of Congress will have no immediate effect upon the institution of slavery as practiced. The Dattos and Sultans will not liberate the slaves, and if they did, in many cases the freed slaves would not leave their masters. That the Sultan will demand remuneration from the United States for their slaves is very probable, but it will be without avail unless Congress further legislates on this subject. The invariable rule of the military has been

not to return escaping slaves and not to permit their recapture, and also, not to invite slaves to flee their masters. This is about as far as any government over the Moros can effectively go.[39]

Another year of struggle between slaves and masters pushed the colonial regime toward abolition. The process of emancipation was shaped by the slaves who fled their bondage, the masters who fought to retain their property and autonomy, and a new colonial military commander, General Leonard Wood, who suppressed this resistance with ruthless force.

CHAPTER 6

Abolition and Colonialism

While American colonial officials were beginning to chafe under the limitations of indirect rule, neither the sultan nor the *datus* in Sulu attempted to alter the modus vivendi of the Bates treaty during the tense days of 1902. The situation in Mindanao was similar, though without the formal codification of a treaty. Datu Piang maintained predominance in Magindanao while cooperating with the new colonizers. With the partial exception of Maranao resistance against several military expeditions into the Lake Lanao region, no Moro leaders openly organized a sustained resistance against U.S. colonial rule.

For the United States, reorganizing the terms of colonial rule over the Moros and abolishing slavery now coincided. In June 1903 the Philippine Commission enacted a plan to organize the Muslim parts of Mindanao and Sulu into a new Moro Province, under a military administration headed by General Leonard Wood.[1] The provincial government was given the specific power to "enact laws for the abolition of slavery and the suppression of all slave hunting and slave trade." On 24 September, in one of its first acts, the government passed a law defining slave holding, trading, and raiding as crimes punishable by up to twenty years imprisonment.[2]

By 1903 Governor Taft no longer spoke publicly about plans for gradual emancipation or the slaves' comfortable conditions of servitude. Reversing his view completely, Taft explained in his annual report in December 1903 that the Moro Province government constructed its antislavery law on the theory that "the announcement of the policy of the United States upon this question may as well be radical in the beginning." Nevertheless, Taft and Wood still believed that abolition could be accomplished without disruption on Mindanao. They expected some initial resistance in Sulu, but, in a phrase that slid from the punishments of slavery to the discipline of colonialism, Taft predicted that the Moros would be "easily whipped." Indeed, he reckoned a beating to enforce abolition would be a necessity and a virtue in itself: "[T]hough the whipping may have to be repeated once or twice, its effect ultimately is very salutary. Force seems to be the only method of reaching them in the first instance, and is the only preparation for the beginning of civilized restraints upon them." [3]

Taft's imputation of a rapid abolition was misleading. The Moro Province antislavery law may have seemed "radical in the beginning" as a statement in the legal and moral discourse about slavery that circulated between Manila and the United States. But then, so too were the declarations of the Organic Act in 1902, McKinley's instructions to the Philippine Commission in 1900, and the territorially comprehensive injunction of the Thirteenth Amendment. These earlier legal and official statements did not define criminal penalties, as did the new antislavery law, but they were equally contingent upon local enforcement for effectiveness.

In fact, the Philippine Commission under Taft first withheld approval of the Moro Province antislavery law in September 1903 while it considered including penalties for enslavement in a new penal code for the entire colony. This code would never be completed, a failure of the American colonial executives that set the stage for later quarrels about the adequacy of antislavery laws for the entire colony. When the commission decided a few weeks later to approve the Moro Province law in advance of the stalled penal code, Governor Wood forbade publication of it in Sulu for fear it would cause disruptions.[4] Indeed, when the Sulu *datus* first heard about the law, they immediately perceived it as a great threat, a precipitant of conflict. The antislavery law became "radical" in its effects in spite of the temperate intentions of colonial officials.

Soon after his arrival in the southern Philippines in August 1903, Wood came to the conclusion that slavery should be abolished "gradually," so that, "little by little, the people will be swung into line, almost unconsciously." When Wood visited the Sulu Islands in August, the sultan and *datus* heard him speak in vague, general terms about regulating "the question of slavery" in new laws. He told them that the United States "wanted friendship but we were going to insist upon tranquility in the island, a cessation of the slave traffic and of the vicious and brutal practices which have distinguished the conduct of affairs in Jolo since the signing of the so-called Bates Treaty." More aggressive than his predecessors in his stand against slavery as a symbol of barbarism, Wood still fell short of advocating immediate emancipation.[5]

Like his predecessors, Wood believed he could "control these people very largely through their own chief men," with the proviso that "vicious and brutal practices" must be suppressed. "The most serious" of these, he told Taft in early October, "is slavery and with this we are now dealing [in some parts of Mindanao], not with the full rigor of the new law in all cases but little by little."[6] He meant to apply the antislavery law selectively, first to Mindanao, where he felt more confident of American influence, and only later to Sulu.

When Taft announced the new "radical" policy against slavery, he expected only minor resistance in Sulu. In Mindanao he expected virtual cooperation. About the Magindanao, he wrote, "General Wood advises me orally that the proclamation of the passage of the act in the river valley above Cotabato has been received with acquiescence by the dattos."[7]

By the end of 1903 the Moros on the Zamboanga Peninsula were also, according to Taft, "pacified and make no trouble in accepting the regime under the new Moro law." As for the Maranao, Taft asserted that the military expeditions of the past two years "resulted in subduing the wild Moros of that district." An imperative to control mediated the oppositions of colonial ideology but never eradicated its fundamental racist dualism. The colonial categorization of Moros as "pacified" and subdued inevitably recalled their prior, prescriptively natural, and perhaps yet latent "wild" character. Hence, Taft cautioned, "the predatory habits of the Moro remain," surfacing "from time to time" in acts of "robbery" and assaults against colonial soldiers.[8] Nevertheless, by the end of 1903 Taft believed that the balance had shifted from wildness to a more settled, distinctly subject condition, ready to receive the colonial beneficence of abolition.

Colonial officials soon found that their confidence in the establishment of a colonial hierarchy in Mindanao and Sulu was misplaced. They misunderstood the power of some of their Moro allies as territorially comprehensive and mistook it for their own influence. Thus, with the passage of the antislavery law, Taft expressed confidence "that another year will bring improvement in conditions so great that even the Moros themselves will understand the advantage of it," [9] a prophesy that invoked the objectivity of colonial progress and thereby located Moro inferiority at its limits. Antislavery ideology helped to define a depoliticized order of progress. If this construction served to naturalize the basis of colonial authority as objectively progressive, it also constituted a screen of self-deception against an understanding of abolition (and colonial rule) as a struggle between and about different forms of power.

The Moro Province antislavery law became a "radical" measure after prominent Taosug, Maranao, and Magindanao *datus* launched rebellions against it. The first of these rebellions was led by a powerful Taosug *datu*, Panglima Hassan. Wood ordered the general dissemination of the antislavery law in the Sulu Islands only in response to Hassan's rebellion.[10] Even then, enforcement remained discretionary, falling hardest on those who openly resisted and more lightly, if at all, on masters who accommodated themselves to colonial rule.

A factional leader from the Look region of Jolo Island and a man of humble birth, Hassan had by 1902–1903 assembled the largest following and network of alliances in the Sulu Islands. In August 1903, the departing colonial commander in Jolo contrasted Hassan's strength with Sultan Kiram's inability to exert authority and told the newly arrived Wood: "Hassan claims to be friendly; if he were Sultan he would rule." [11] Wood and the newly appointed governor of Jolo, Major Hugh L. Scott, met with Hassan soon after first arriving in Jolo. Wood described him then as "[a] fine looking intelligent Moro" and "the most important chieftain in the Island of Jolo, next to the Sultan and Datu Jokanain." [12] Patronizing as this characterization might be, its relatively favorable tone is apparent when compared with Wood's vilification of Sultan Kiram for Theodore Roosevelt's edification: "He is a run down, tricky, little Oriental degenerate, with half a dozen wives and no children; a state of affairs of which I am sure you thoroughly disapprove!" [13]

Given the Americans' desire to rule through local leaders, one might have expected the colonial state to establish a cooperative relationship with Hassan, like the one with Datu Piang in Cotabato. Hassan seems to have proposed just such an alliance, but his relationship with the American authorities foundered on conflicts over runaway slaves. In June and July 1903, twelve slaves belonging to Hassan and several more owned by one of his rivals, Panglima Tahir of Parang, fled and received protection from American troops in Jolo. Hassan twice asked for their return. Colonel Wallace, the commander in Jolo at the end of July 1903, refused. "You must know the American law on this subject," he wrote to Hassan, "I have told the Chiefs many times." Yet Wallace compounded the United States's ambiguous position on slavery by advising Hassan on how to avoid such problems: "Let the people treat their slaves kindly and they will not wish to leave them." Furthermore, Wallace differentiated a slave—"a person owned by another under the Moro law"—from a debtor. "If a man says to you I owe you fifty pesos and I agree to work for you for a certain time until my debt is paid, that man is not a slave, and if he refuses to keep his promise and runs away and asks me for protection I will not protect him." Thus the colonial state offered positive enforcement of debt bondage, if not of slavery.[14]

Hassan did not then press further for the return of his slaves, but Panglima Tahir did. In June 1903 a man named Biroa led an armed party of Tahir's followers to forcibly recover the panglima's runaway slaves in Jolo. Biroa recaptured one girl and killed another runaway slave who tried to fight him. The commanders at Jolo demanded the return of the girl and Biroa's surrender. Biroa did not answer. Instead, he installed himself on a fortified hilltop in Parang with Panglima Tahir and a group of followers, slaves, and allies that dwindled from about two hundred in number to forty by mid-September. General Wood's assurance that Biroa would be tried by the sultan under Moro law, from which he could expect a light fine or even acquittal for killing his leader's runaway slave, had no effect.[15]

In mid-September the sultan enlisted the assistance of Maharajah Indanan to enforce his rule. Indanan recovered the girl and captured one of Biroa's accomplices, but his force of between three hundred and five hundred men did not try to storm Biroa's hilltop fortification. Instead, while surrounding the hill Indanan's men reportedly "looted all the houses in that section." When they were made to return the stolen goods, Indanan ended his siege. As a last resort, the sultan asked Hassan for assistance to capture Biroa. The sultan explained his reliance on Hassan in an interview with Scott: "Yes [they will get Biroa]. Panglima Hassan, Panglima Dammang, Panglima Ambutong, and Maharaja Indanan have taken it upon themselves. I am not like the governor; I do not have three or four hundred soldiers at my disposal; I have to depend on my chiefs."[16]

Wood and the governor in Jolo welcomed the sultan's open admission of who really wielded power on Jolo Island. They had been charged by

Taft to assemble a record of the sultan's failure to uphold the Bates treaty in order to justify its abrogation. This confirmation of the sultan's inability to maintain order would support just such a brief.

The sultan's call for aid in the apprehension of Biroa put Hassan at the center of a political realignment. Major Scott immediately asked Hassan to a meeting in Jolo town. When Hassan did not respond, Scott then demanded that he meet him in Jolo within three days. Hassan replied by letter four days later, saying that his "desire to see the governor is as yet small." The reason, he explained, was that his two requests for the return of runaway slaves had been ignored. Hassan was "very much surprised" by this because, he claimed, "the general in Manila, the general in Zamboanga, and the governor of Jolo" had agreed to return his runaway slaves. "Now, if it is really true that the white man is a man of his word," he challenged Scott, the twelve runaways should be delivered promptly.[17]

While this correspondence was being conducted, Hassan met with allies and, reportedly, mended relations with some of his enemies, too. Scott immediately concluded that Hassan "must be organizing a resistance against us." From Hassan's letter, Scott judged that "his grievance appears to be connected solely with the slave question."[18]

These events increased Scott's anxiety that the Moros regarded the Americans as "weak or afraid." To Scott, his dealings with Biroa and Hassan represented a profound moral conflict on which hinged the fate of colonial rule: "I begin to see that as long as the Moros had their own way and were not interfered with that they were more or less peaceable—but as soon as the slavery question and the breaking up of the organized looting & fining of everybody with property enough to pay a fine for the support of the chiefs and the gang that surrounds each one of them is interfered with seriously the fat will get into the fire and we must look out and either let them have the island or we must fight them about it."[19]

All of this coincided with the passage of the Moro Province antislavery law in Zamboanga on 24 September. Although the law was not to be officially publicized in Sulu for months, rumors about it circulated through Jolo almost immediately. Hadji Butu, the Sultan's *wazir,* visited Scott's office to discuss the rumors on 28 September, the day Scott himself received news of the law by the evening mail from Zamboanga. Scott said he thought that the *datus* were "very uneasy about that subject." Hadji Butu asked him if he "was going to liberate slaves without conferring with the Moros." Much like his predecessors, Scott told the

wazir he would not return runaway slaves because "the U.S. did not recognize that a human being should be the slave or property of another
man like a horse or a dog," but "neither would I go into the country to
liberate slaves without further talk with the Moros." The next day he
recommended to Wood that he formally abrogate the Bates treaty and
hold a conference "before publishing" the antislavery law.[20]

Panglima Hassan eventually went to Jolo to meet with Scott in the
first week of October. He arrived in town with two of his former enemies, Panglima Dammang and Maharajah Indanan, and, in Scott's estimate, about one thousand followers. With a retinue of seventy men behind him, Hassan called upon the governor. He explained that he could
not attend sooner because he had been travelling to see "all the chiefs."
Then the conversation turned to the fugitive Biroa.[21]

At first, Hassan represented Biroa's defense. Biroa claimed that authorities as high as Governor Wallace told him to "go and get" his runaway slaves. The slave killed in the raid was shot in self-defense. Un-
moved, the governor of Jolo demanded a seamless recognition of his
absolute authority, unlike the discontinuous and shifting authority of
traditional politics in Sulu. Scott insisted that Biroa present himself.
"When I send for anybody," he told Hassan, "I don't care who he is, he
has to come; that is what I am governor for."[22]

Scott boasted repeatedly that he would capture or kill Biroa himself
if Hassan would not. Hassan asked Scott if the sultan had abandoned
the effort, and then he asked if Scott still promised to try Biroa according to Moro law. When Scott confirmed the promise, Hassan offered to
take control of the situation. "I think if I send for him," Hassan proclaimed, "he could come to-night," but he expected reciprocity from the
Americans.[23]

In exchange for his offer to control the rival leaders, Hassan asked for
recognition as the intermediary between the governor and the powerful
men of Jolo. He also told Scott, "I would like to talk to you about something else. Two generals have told me that when slaves run away they
would be returned." The problem of slavery moved the discussion beyond the realm of the negotiable for Scott. "Certainly you are mistaken," he retorted. Returning runaway slaves would not only contra-
vene U.S. policy, but also would buck the world-historical triumph of
abolition. Scott lectured Hassan on this point.

> In our country we had much trouble ourselves about the slaves; we fought
> big battles in which more people were killed in one battle than there are in
> Jolo together. One time we have been savages; we know better now. Russia,

England, people that own half of the world and have more than half of all the money and power, have no slaves. They have determined that there be no slaves. I don't recognize slaves; no man can be the property of another, like a horse or cattle. I don't believe that the general promised you to return slaves. My Government would not allow [me] to return a slave.[24]

This was the strongest open declaration of antislavery policy made yet in Jolo. It implied complete abolition. Scott offered no soothing re-assurances about not interfering with slaves who stayed with masters. He tied abolition to civilization, progress, and the imperial authority of "the people who own half the world." And yet, Hassan still tried to ne-gotiate. "Suppose somebody comes to you to give up his person for a debt," he proposed to Scott. "What are you going to do, lose your money, take nothing?" The governor said he would take the debtor's an-imals and that he would use care in lending money. Unlike Wallace, Scott did not offer to return people working off a debt. "In that case," Hassan exclaimed, "I would be ashamed to come here to Jolo and to meet a man who owes me and run away." The conference ended, both parties exasperated by their conflicting perceptions of slavery and legit-imate authority.[25]

Fighting erupted between Hassan's followers and U.S. soldiers before the end of October. Hassan demanded that Scott "withdraw the Amer-icans because it interferes with the good people." On 12 November Has-san led more than two thousand followers into a battle that ended with his capture and subsequent escape. Wood followed with a large expedi-tionary force to chase Hassan, killing hundreds in the process. Backed by this extraordinary display of power, in late November Wood "took advantage of the occasion to proclaim the new antislavery law" to the sultan and *datus,* who, with little choice in the matter, told him that they would respect it.[26]

To be precise, Wood did not really "take advantage" of an opportu-nity to declare abolition. Rather, Hassan's rebellion pushed him to act more hastily against slavery than he had intended. He did not have im-minent plans to publicize the antislavery law in Sulu before his battle with Hassan. Like his predecessors, Wood wanted to move gradually against slavery to avoid exactly this kind of uprising. Impelled by the re-sistance of masters, Wood's militant abolitionist sentiment reached a peak during his pursuit of Hassan. "Slavery is flourishing on the islands in sight of Zamboanga," he recorded in his diary on 30 November 1903, "and the only way to check it is . . . with a heavy hand."[27] In practice,

Wood quickly tempered his abolitionism, but not his bellicosity or his use of antislavery principle to support colonial authority.

The antislavery law seems to have been imposed most aggressively in the home territory of Panglima Hassan and his allies, on the southeastern end of Jolo Island. In December, colonial troops swept this area in search of Hassan, under orders to put "copies of the slave law . . . in the hands of the principal men of the islands, and as far as is possible, in the hands of the slaves . . . in order that the people may know what the law is and that slavery has been abolished." But even here the law was to be enforced selectively, "with intelligence and discretion." If this could be done "with as little disturbance as possible of innocent people," then its announcement would complement the apprehension of Hassan. By announcing that the "close observation" of frequent patrols would continue until Hassan were captured, Wood suggested that cooperation in his apprehension would remove the disruptive presence of troops telling slaves about the antislavery law.[28]

It was not until mid-January 1904 that the colonial state first tried to disseminate the law throughout the Sulu Islands, beyond the major towns and the country being searched for rebels. Copies of the law printed in *jawi* script were distributed around most of the archipelago on 19 January. Just how quickly and extensively word of the new law spread is difficult to determine. To the extent that knowledge of the law did circulate through print or word of mouth, it seriously undercut any claim that could be made for the colonial state's legitimacy in the eyes of local leaders. Few people other than the sultan and his entourage, perhaps some Chinese merchants, and the runaway slaves held stock in the colonial regime. Most slave owners had no reason to respect the law.[29]

The Moro Province government made little further effort to liberate slaves in Sulu. Except when slave raiders and traders were intercepted, few slaves were forcibly separated from their masters. Emancipation remained a process largely initiated by the slaves themselves. The principal discernible change introduced by the law was the threat of criminal prosecution, but it appears that only four cases from the Sulu Islands went to trial through 1908. In the three for which convictions were returned, the severity of sentences decreased progressively. The first case, decided in April 1904, concerned slave raiding and trading from Mindanao to the Siassi group in the Sulu Islands. A Moro named Alam was sentenced to Bilibid Prison in Manila for twelve years of forced labor and two accomplices each received ten-year sentences. In the second case, decided in October 1904, a Moro named Batu received a three-year sentence of forced labor for capturing a woman and selling her as a slave on Jolo Island. In the last recorded conviction, in November 1905, the court sentenced Hadji Asmail to pay a fine of three hundred pesos or serve twelve months in prison for taking and trying to sell a slave.[30]

Many more cases could have been prosecuted under the antislavery law, had the colonial state been so motivated. Slaves continued to leave their masters through 1904 and 1905. More than thirty disputes involving slaves came to the attention of the governor at Jolo between January and May 1904, including complaints of enslavement and requests to be freed. In one case, two bondsmen of Maharajah Indanan filed a grievance because Indanan seized a pony as payment for their manumission. The governor ordered the pony returned, but brought no judicial action against the powerful Indanan, whose cooperation was highly valued by the colonial state.[31]

The implementation of the antislavery law in Sulu involved a series of misunderstandings, self-deceptions, and unintended consequences. Aside from the few prosecutions and a rejection of compensation for masters, colonial plans for abolition hardly changed at all. Mistakenly, Taft, Wood, and the other architects of the new policy regarded it as a radical departure that would bring slavery to a reasonably quick and peaceable end.

In January 1904 Wood assured President Roosevelt that "the slavery question among the Moros is being as peacefully settled as can be" expected. Then, to his English friend, the imperialist journalist John St. Loe Strachey (a nephew of Sir John Strachey, once governor of India), Wood declared that "[s]lavery has been abolished." He further explained, "I do not mean by this that we are chasing about the country taking people away from those with who [sic] they have lived and with whom they desire to live, but we have prohibited by most rigorous measures any further raiding or enslaving and are notifying the people broadcast that they are at liberty to go and build homes for themselves whenever they like." Strachey agreed with this approach. "What one wants is to abolish the status of slavery, not as you say to run up and down the country, trying to put salt on the tails of slaves who are quite willing to muddle on in their old relationship, and who really don't know that they are slaves." Some months later, in May 1904, Wood informed his likeminded friend that "the slavery question is gradually settling itself in this province. In the courts we are pushing only those cases which are especially flagrant and where the offenders have been thoroughly instructed in the law and warned . . . [so] it will take several years to get through with the whole thing." [32]

The process of abolition in Mindanao was hardly less contrary to colonial expectations. Compared with Sulu, there seem to have been few confrontations in Mindanao between masters and the colonial state over slaves before the last months of 1903. There were far fewer recorded cases of slaves who fled masters in Mindanao. Above all, the tensions created by intimations of an imminent abolition in Sulu seem to have had no counterpart in Mindanao—until the Moro Province announced its antislavery law.

In reporting on one case of nine runaway slaves, the commanding officer at Malabang, on the coast of Illana Bay, explained his policy of not interfering in master-slave relations and then detailed a long-term plan to sponsor "colonization" by a company that would provide the "natives" with work as a way to "gradually divorce them from their Datohs." But, in the meantime, he urged that "no restriction should be placed on the purchasing of slaves by colonists [i.e., Moros], other than a strict accountability for such purchase and government record thereof with assurance that after a fixed period of labor, say six months, they become free men." [33] No such suggestion could have been made in Sulu, given the climate created by the Bates treaty and anti-imperialist scrutiny.

While American attention focused on Sulu, much of Mindanao was simply beyond the scope of colonial surveillance. Within the colonial authorities' ken on Mindanao, there was no formal structure of relations like the Bates treaty to enable Moros or Americans to demand fulfillment of obligations, redress, or recompense. Hence there is no corresponding record of complaints, responses, and negotiations about slavery, such as survives from Sulu—until the promulgation of the antislavery law in 1903.

Beginning in early October 1903, regular military patrols through the Moro territories of Mindanao carried orders "to gradually preach the doctrine of no more slaves or slave catching," recover recently enslaved people ("especially Filipinos"), and capture slave raiders. [34] More direct than any antislavery actions in Sulu except for the campaign against Hassan, the context of slavery in Mindanao made these steps more aggressive still.

Mindanao's large land mass and complex ethnogeography provided opportunities for continued slave raiding that did not exist in the Sulu Islands. The Taosug had long depended on other ethnic groups to carry on slave raiding outside the Sulu Islands. Most of these sources were cut off and Taosug-sponsored raiding suppressed before the end of the nineteenth century. This left Sulu slave markets much more dependent upon imports from Mindanao. Although the Iranun and some other groups still did some raiding in the Visayas, they, and the Magindanao, increasingly targeted their raids on the Tiruray, Subanon, and other non-Muslim peoples from the Mindanao hills. The Maranao enjoyed a strategic inland location both remote from colonial authority (Spain was only beginning to establish a presence in the Lanao area in the 1890s) and proximate to vulnerable Christian communities on the north coast of Mindanao. Few Christians remained enslaved in Sulu, but the Magindanao had taken Christian slaves as recently as the colonial interregnum of 1899 and the Maranao continued to take Christian slaves after 1900, though in small numbers.[35]

The colonial state believed that the formation of the new Moro Province government and the consequent revocation of the Bates treaty would make Sulu more like Mindanao; actually, it had the opposite effect. The Moro Province's declaration of abolition broke the always precarious modus vivendi in Mindanao. It transgressed the social and cultural autonomy of Moro groups while simultaneously exposing the colonial illusions of subjugation, influence, and control. Magindanao, Maranao, and Iranun *datus* saw colonial tampering with slavery as an infringement upon their rights, property, and power, much as they had during their conflicts with Spain. As in Sulu, the declaration of abolition prompted open warfare in Mindanao.

Among the Maranao (and probably the Iranun, who maintained kinship and clientage relations with their lakeside neighbors), the antislavery law intensified armed resistance against the American invaders. The Lanao region had been relatively tranquil since U.S. troops had marched around the lake in April and May 1903, destroying *kotas* (fortified encampments), capturing large numbers of firearms, and killing at least several hundred Moros. To demonstrate the United States's "benevolent intentions," Captain John J. Pershing had notified Maranao *datus* in advance of this expedition by letter. He tried to smooth his way through the territory by reiterating the United States's "promise" not to interfere with "the customs, habits, government, or religion of any Moro." Having kept such promises so far, the Americans had, Pershing claimed, "demonstrated to the Moros and to the whole world that we are not here to make war, nor to dispossess the inhabitants of Lanao of their lives, property, or anything that is theirs, but are here for the good of the Moro, as representatives of our great Government, of which the Moros are a part."[36]

After fighting his way around Lake Lanao, Pershing told his superiors that "[a]s long as [the Maranao] is undisturbed in the possession of his women and children and his slaves, there need be little fear from him. As a rule he treats his so-called slaves, who are really but serfs or vassals, as members of his family; but any interference with what he thinks his right regarding them had best be made gradually by the natural process of development, which must logically come by contact with and under the wise supervision of a civilized people."[37] Weakened and divided among themselves about how to deal with the Americans, most Maranao *datus* seem to have chosen accommodation or retreat as the way to preserve spheres of autonomy under (or beyond) colonial authority. Less than half a year later the Moro Province antislavery law shattered the already problematic boundaries of Maranao autonomy.

Maranao raids on colonial outposts and patrols increased in the months after October 1903 as the colonial state spread the unwelcome news of abolition. These guerrilla attacks prompted a heightened surveillance by the colonial state to spot and suppress "petty warfare and slaving expeditions."[38] Large-scale warfare resumed by April 1904, most notably in the populous Taraka region on the eastern side of the lake, where colonial troops again demolished the *kotas* of the local *datus*. In addition to sponsoring raids on colonial troops, the Taraka *datus* had continued to take captives and refused to release enslaved Christians.[39]

More so than in Sulu and Magindanao, the Maranaos' armed resistance to colonial rule was fairly continuous through 1905. However, the extremely decentralized political structure of Maranao society tended to localize and limit the scale of conflict with the colonial state. No individual *datu* in Lanao seems to have rallied alliances to sustain a large armed resistance, but at least some Maranao *datus* resisted the U.S. occupation from the start. Although abolition was less of a discrete cause of warfare between Maranao *datus* and the colonial state, it remained a distinct source of tension and conflict for years.

A summary of trials for slavery heard by the Court of First Instance of the Moro Province lists sixteen cases from Lanao during the years 1905 to 1908, more than from any other part of the province. Ten of those cases resulted in convictions, four in acquittals or dismissed charges, and two were continued beyond the period for which records survive. Most sentences were for one year in prison or less. The court inflicted the maximum penalty of five years imprisonment only once, in the case of a *datu* named Atucan who traded a slave for a carabao.[40] Although the surviving records are fragmentary, the pattern of more numerous prosecutions and lighter penalties suggests two comparative insights about the course of abolition among the Maranao. First, the number of prosecutions might reflect a higher frequency of slave holding and slave trading among the Maranao than among other Moro groups. Second, the less severe penalties meted out in these cases seems to correlate with the Maranaos' lower political profile in the Moro Province and, by extension, in the debates and reportage about Moro slavery back in the United States.

In Magindanao, warfare over slavery began in March and April 1904, when Datu Ali led his Magindanao followers to battle in the northern half of the Pulangi River Valley, the *sa-raya* (upper valley) region that had supported the late Datu Uto's resistance against Spain. Until Datu Ali's rebellion, the Magindanao seemed to have had the most settled relations with the colonial state of all the Moro peoples. Datu Piang used his political skills and control of long-distance trade through the Chinese merchants of Cotabato to bring the other major *datus* of the valley into an accommodation with the United States. Ali was a cousin of the famed Datu Uto, for whom he had employed his martial skills. Upon Uto's decline, Ali emerged as the dominant leader of the *sa-raya* region and assembled the most powerful armed following in the valley. In January 1901 Ali married Datu Piang's daughter, bonding their alliance in ties of kinship.[41]

The Magindanao neither tried to fend off the United States, as did the Maranao, nor did they become involved in simmering disputes over slavery and indirect rule like those that increased tensions in Sulu. Quite the opposite. From early on the Magindanao eagerly offered troops to accompany U.S. expeditions to neighboring Maranao and Iranun areas because these actions coincided with Magindanao interests.

In 1900 Datu Piang sent Datu Inok and one hundred men (sixty with rifles) to accompany a smaller U.S. expedition to Malabang on the coast of Illana Bay, where Piang's men initiated a battle to retaliate for Iranun raids on a village that had client ties to the powerful Magindanao *datu*.[42] Datu Ali provided the services of his son-in-law, the "Afghan" Sharif Mohammed Afdal, to negotiate with Maranao *datus* for the colonial state in March and April 1902. When this mission failed, Piang and

Ali proposed to send two thousand armed men to fight alongside U.S. troops against the Maranao. In the event, several hundred Magindanao joined the campaign as porters, trail clearers, and camp builders.[43]

Under these circumstances the colonial regime circumvented its qualms about slavery among the Magindanao. When General Davis considered a more aggressive policy of encouraging slaves to flee their masters in Sulu, he regarded the situation in Magindanao with greater equanimity. "Of course, slavery is still practiced among them," the general remarked, "but they evince a disposition, not yet shown in Sulu, in all things to conform to our requirements in their intercourse with one another, with the Filipinos, and with our own people." [44]

Although colonial officials understood their dependence upon Datu Piang in Magindanao, they attributed his success to the beneficence and economic progress brought by U.S. rule. Colonial officials deceived themselves into believing that they had established their authority over Magindanao, rather than simply arranged an accommodation through a coincidence of interests. When the Moro Province announced the antislavery law in the last months of 1903, Wood and Taft thought that the Magindanao would continue to follow the lead of colonial progress. Instead, the declaration of abolition destroyed the political and economic system of indirect rule over the whole valley through Datu Piang in Cotabato.

Datu Piang seems not to have lodged any protests about the antislavery law. According to at least one account,[45] Piang himself kept slaves as late as 1926. The accuracy of this observation aside—because it contains no details, one might wonder if these were slaves, debtors, or other kinds of clients—the contrast between Piang's quiet response to the law and Datu Ali's decision to fight requires explanation.

Piang profited from trade at the mouth of the Pulangi River, where imports from outside Mindanao were exchanged for products from upriver and the hinterland. Upriver *datus* such as Ali were more closely tied to production, which they dominated through control of laborers. Piang could profit from his position at the bottleneck of trade no matter how the goods were produced, but not so Ali and his *sa-raya* compatriots. Their power also depended more heavily than did the Chinese mestizo Piang's on the traditional patterns of prestige, rank, and bravery, in which slavery and raiding figured prominently.[46] The antislavery law thus posed a disproportionate threat to Ali's power. As it happened, Piang supported the Americans in their pursuit of Ali and Ali's eventual fall eliminated Piang's only major rival. It is reasonable to assume the prescient Datu Piang grasped this calculus from the announcement of the law.

The colonial government in Cotabato learned of Ali's preparations for war in early 1904. At Serinaya, above his home in Kudarangan, Ali constructed the largest, most heavily armed *kota* in Mindanao. In mid-February the governor of the Cotabato district learned through informers of a meeting in Kudarangan, in which "Mastula [Mastura, son of the last sultan of Magindanao] and Talikoko [presumably the sultan of Talakuku or a *datu*-rank son] consulted together and Talikoko stated that if he had to give up his slaves, he wanted to fight and join Ali and Mastula said he would too." Mastura carried with him several allied *datus,* including the important Datu Ampatuan. Other reports noted Ali's efforts to recruit support from the Lake Lanao region, an abrupt change from his former readiness to fight against the Maranao less than two years before. Soon several thousand followers had congregated in Ali's great *kota.*

In early March 1904 Leonard Wood led a large military expedition up the Pulangi River against Ali. At Kudarangan Wood conferred with Datu Piang, who described Ali's war preparations and intention to resist the implementation of the antislavery law.[47] An "Arab priest" with Piang, Sherif Tuan, "also stated that the Moros [i.e., Ali and followers] intended to fight and had declared that they would not submit to any interference with their slave trading and holding."[48] The destruction of Ali's *kota* proceeded quickly on 10 March, but this marked only the beginning of more than a year of battles that ended in the massacre of Ali and several hundred followers in October 1905.

The opening of warfare in previously peaceful Magindanao moved the secretary of war William Howard Taft to reevaluate the "radical" course for abolition that he had announced at the end of 1903. In mid-March 1904 Taft told Wood by cable that he was "very anxious that correction of undesirable customs among the Moros shall be effected by peaceful means rather than by force. This refers also to enforcement [of] recent laws affecting slavery."[49] Taft reiterated this concern two months later, when he asked Luke E. Wright, governor of the Philippines, to request an accounting from Wood. He also asked for Wright's own opinion: "Do you think Wood has been as careful as he might be to avoid conflict?"[50]

Extraordinary violence to achieve conquest and order continued in the Moro Province, as it did sporadically in the rest of the Philippines.

Taft never objected to this in itself. The problem lay in resolving the contradiction between antislavery commitments and the imperative of colonial order so that one did not fully negate the other. In the past Taft and other colonial officials elided this dilemma through their twin faith in the mildness of slavery and the prospect of its gradual demise before the forces of progress. This particular evasion became untenable with the displacement of assumptions about mild slavery, the announcement of the antislavery law, and the consequent reality of war. From his engagement with Moro resistance Leonard Wood fashioned a new dualistic response to the problem of slavery.

Wood presented the war against Ali as a struggle against slavery and "lawlessness." But while he thus unified the opposition between abolition and order in colonial discourse, the application of the antislavery law became more restricted in practice, especially in Magindanao territory. In his analysis of Ali's rebellion, Wood reinterpreted the recent history of Magindanao to suit his identification of abolition with progress, civilization, and colonial authority. Disabused of his earlier confidence that Magindanao *datus* would accept the antislavery law, he now maintained that the failure to punish Ali for the sack of Cotabato in 1899 "left the Moros with an undue sense of their importance, with . . . attending impertinence and indisposition to obey either the Civil Governor of the District or any other authority. They have been actively engaged in slave-hunting among the hill tribes and, in short, have been doing about what they liked." That is, in Wood's eyes, Ali and his followers ("the Moros") were still wild people, not yet properly conquered, disciplined, and subordinated to a higher authority (colonial rule) outside their selves.[51]

Despite his general condemnation of Moros, Wood knew it was the antislavery law that proved the flashpoint. It "aroused a great deal of opposition among the Moro Dattos," especially Ali and his half brother Guimbangan (Djimbangan) "who by their trade in the hill people (slave trade) were making a good deal of money." The antislavery law ignited "their general contempt for American authority." As Wood reported it, all of the *datus* except Piang "united . . . in this conspiracy to resist American rule and above all the operation of the slave law."[52]

At the end of his tour as governor of the Moro Province in 1906 Wood reflected on the meaning of Datu Ali's demise. "Datu Ali's opposition to the Government, his refusal to do away with slavery and slave dealing, have been the only obstacles which have held back the progress of the valley during the past two years."[53] By 1906 the problems of slavery and colonial order had been localized in the figure of Ali, so that his death could serve as the elimination of the only obstacle to "progress." The colonial state's demonization of Ali drew attention away from slavery. Indeed, for the years after 1904 there is practically no discussion of slavery in colonial records from Magindanao except in connection with Ali. And these references rarely contain any information about relations between slaves and masters, specific slaves, or details about raiding and trading.

The extant records of prosecutions for slavery in the Cotabato district are suggestive of the politically sensitive enforcement of the antislavery law. Twelve cases of slave holding and slave trading went before the Court of First Instance between 1904 and 1907. It is striking that only two trials resulted in convictions, and these cases, adjudicated in August 1907, concerned the parties to a single slave sale—one trial for the sellers, the other for the purchaser. Notably, the lead defendant in the trial for selling slaves was Guimbangan, Datu Ali's half brother, who had been captured soon after the fall of Ali's *kota* in March 1904. The court sentenced Guimbangan to five years in prison, his two codefendants to three-year terms, and the purchaser of the slave to a two-year sentence.[54] The antislavery law was enforced selectively throughout the Moro Province, but nowhere more so than in Magindanao. Ironically, at least some of the *datus* who fought alongside Ali lived to enjoy the practical nullification of the law, precisely because their leader was put down.

The abolition of slavery in the southern Philippines did occur gradually over the following years, but it was far from orderly or peaceful. The antislavery law marked the beginning (but certainly not the only cause) of ten years of warfare in the Sulu Islands. Panglima Hassan successfully evaded colonial troops until March 1904, when he was killed in battle. Datu Usap and Datu Pala picked up the torch of resistance on Jolo Island, fighting first because of the antislavery law and then, after 1905, because of the introduction of the *cedula* (head tax) and as a more general objection to American sovereignty.[55]

The *cedula* tax individualized the population as common taxpayers in relation to the state. Its introduction was accompanied by colonial restrictions on the *datus'* power to levy fines, which had frequently produced debt bondage and judicial enslavement. Like abolition, these attempts to reconfigure the political economy of payments threatened to subvert local relations of power by cutting established bonds and reorienting them to the colonial state. Moreover, they smacked of a requirement to pay tribute to a Christian state. Although the Moro Province imposed the *cedula* even more hesitantly than it applied the antislavery law, it too provoked the rebellions that cautious implementation was meant to avoid.[56]

In 1906 colonial troops surrounded rebels on top of Bud Dajo (Mount Dajo) on Jolo Island and ended the siege with a massacre of between six hundred and one thousand men, women, and children. Large-scale conflict in Sulu subsided only after another massacre of at least five hundred people on Bud Bagsak in 1913, part of a campaign to forcibly disarm the Moro population. In the midst of this bloodshed, in a largely undocumented process, the practice of taking, trading, and holding people as slaves ceased to be an institution of the society.[57]

If the actual course of emancipation in the southern Philippines faltered and remained murky after the declaration of the antislavery law, the transformation of antislavery ideology's political implications for Americans was clear and fast. From 1899 to 1903 the existence of slavery in the southern Philippines embarrassed the colonial regime. Its need to accept at least temporary and sometimes uncomfortable compromises with the institution rendered vulnerable colonialism's pretensions to ideals of progress, morality, and civilization. By the end of 1903 the antislavery law in the Moro Province replaced apologies for inaction against "mild" slavery with a firm public statement that slavery in the southern Philippines was a criminal barbarity to be abolished. The force of the transformation is conveyed by the changing treatment of slavery in three documents.

On 15 September 1903, David P. Barrows, chief of the Ethnological Survey for the Philippine Islands (previously called and later again subsumed by the Bureau of Non-Christian Tribes), completed his annual report on the division's work: the collection of "definite information relative to the geographic character of the wilder and less known portions of the Archipelago and the tribes of these regions," a task "assisted by the continually widening occupation of the islands."[58] This was an enterprise of conquest and observation, power and knowledge, to map and control and reform "tribes representing the whole scale of culture from savagery to civilization." At the margins of "savagery" were the "tribes" that engaged in "head-hunting in the north and slavery and raiding in the south," practices that, Barrows reported, "can be stopped just as soon as a proper effort is made."[59]

Barrows's optimistic account of progressive conquest and the consolidation of scientific control over wild savages sustained the civilizing claims of U.S. colonial rule. But one sentence of his report conspicuously

did not. In a section on the late–nineteenth-century Spanish colonization of non-Christian peoples, Barrows reflected: "If we except the conquest of Lake Lanao, recently achieved by the American army, Spanish
dominion was more effective both in the North and South than our own,
and head-hunting, slavery and piracy were better controlled then, than
they are today." This sentence is crossed out in the manuscript copy on
file in the Bureau of Insular Affairs archive in Washington. An embarrassment to any who would claim that U.S. colonial rule was more progressive than Spain's, the sentence was omitted from the published version in the *Report of the Philippine Commission* for 1903.[60]

The 1903 *Report of the Philippine Commission* also announced the
Moro Province antislavery law to the American public and called for the
abrogation of the Bates treaty. Taft's annual report as civil governor of
the Philippines included an appendix prepared by Wood that enumer-
ated eight reasons to justify voiding the Bates treaty. Four of these explicitly addressed the persistence of slavery and slave raiding, the recognition of slavery in Moro law, and the importance of slavery to the ruling
elite who were recognized by the treaty. A fifth reason cited Hassan's rebellion, itself sparked by the antislavery law. The remaining three reasons were the sultan's inability to enforce order, the prevalence of theft,
and *juramentado* attacks on colonial troops (a kind of suicidal assault,
running *amok,* that Wood blamed on the connivance of Muslim
"priests" and *datus*). In sum, Wood linked slavery and Islam to evoke
images of intolerable barbarism shielded by the Bates treaty.[61]

In September 1904 Leonard Wood completed the reversal of colonial
interpretations of slavery in the southern Philippines. This would be the
last substantive discussion of slavery in the Moro Province included in a
published report by the Philippine Commission. "There has been much
said about the paternal form of Moro slavery," Wood took note. But, after "a year of almost continuous contact with the Moros," much of it in
warfare instigated by the antislavery law, he found it "difficult to imagine a worse form of slavery."[62]

Wood propagated images, not unlike those deployed in anti-imperialist propaganda after the signing of the Bates treaty, of a harsh slavery
that corrupted all it touched. And he cast them all in the past tense, as
if slavery had been completely eradicated: "The slave had absolutely no
rights. His wife, his daughters, and his property were entirely subject to
the will of his owner, and he himself could be sold or even killed with
impunity." Wood found the ramifications of slavery to be "most unfortunate, not only for the slaves but also for the owners, as the institution

seemed to paralyze all true development and to accentuate the various forms of vice to which the Moro is so commonly a victim." According to Wood, slavery in the southern Philippines was not mild, but as harsh as any that had ever existed.[63]

The characterization of slavery in the southern Philippines as a particularly harsh form of the institution needs to be interpreted as a cultural product, created by people with particular worldviews and interests in specific historical situations. To put it bluntly, by September 1904 Leonard Wood's hands were awash in blood spilt over the issue of slavery; he would have to make sense of this and rationalize it or recant his faith in colonialism.

Wood's understanding of slavery in Moro societies was shaped at the core by the same ideological complex of racial hierarchy, capitalism, and faith in progress that encouraged his country's conquest and colonization of the Philippines. The imperative to abolish a severe and inhuman form of bondage helped to define and justify the destruction of the *datus'* power base, just as it served to explain the institution of direct rule in place of the Bates treaty. Yet, despite its politically tainted origins, Wood's emphasis on the harshness of slavery had the virtue of recognizing the centrality of power in the practice of slavery as a social relationship, in contrast to the virtually complete elision of power in the image of mild slavery. Wood also left some space for the complex variability of slavery within a single society, or even in individual master and slave relationships. "There were," he admitted, "many instances where relations between slaves and owners were friendly, but accidents of this kind should not be taken as a ground for describing an institution where the owners hold absolute power of life and death over their slaves as a beneficient, kindly, or paternal one." [64] To the extent that this observation represented a deeper understanding of slavery, it need not be explained as the result of disinterested objectivity. With so "much said about the paternal form of Moro slavery," the transformation to an image of harsh slavery inevitably took a contrapuntal form—a style well suited, however inadvertently, to encompass the contradictory nature of slavery as an institution of alienation and incorporation, both vicious and "paternal."

Slavery and the National Question

CHAPTER SEVEN

Metaphorics
of Slavery and Nation

The debate in the United States over the colonial question and Americans' encounter with slavery in the Moro societies transpired against the backdrop of the Philippine revolution of 1898 and the war of conquest that destroyed it. This concatenation of events had a pronounced influence on the way Americans understood slavery as a problem in the Philippines. Meanwhile, the complex dynamics of Philippine revolutionary movements and the politics of the short-lived Philippine Republic followed another path, relatively unaffected, at first, by the conflicts over slavery in distant Mindanao and Sulu.

The Philippine revolutions of 1896 and 1898 developed in the Tagalog provinces around Manila and then spread at different rates into neighboring provinces on Luzon and in the central Visayan Islands. In the eyes of Filipino nationalists, Moros were not Filipinos, even if their homelands fell within the colonial political geography that defined the Philippines as a territorial unit. After 1903, however, questions slowly emerged among American colonial officials about the adequacy of colonial antislavery laws and the reported practice of slavery in Catholic Filipino towns bordering territories inhabited by non-Christians in northern Luzon. Their inquiries began to trouble Filipino nationalists. From being an embarrassment to an American colonial regime initially reluctant to act against slavery in the southern Philippines, reports about slavery became increasingly embarrassing to Filipino nationalists and their anti-imperialist allies in the United States. This could happen only because the metaphorics of slavery played crucial roles in Philippine nationalist discourse.

To understand the importance early Filipino nationalists gave to metaphors of slavery we must consider the way in which they imagined Philippine nationalism, dialectically, out of the experience of colonialism in the late–nineteenth century. Spanish colonial hegemony in the Philippines emerged and persisted over three centuries through the interplay of Catholicism, indigenous cosmology, and, of course, the everyday mediations of a complex political economy. As in all hegemonies, Spanish rule depended upon force as well as consent to contain conflicts and suppress them. But, perhaps more than in most, Spanish colonial hegemony depended upon a combination of legerdemain and confusion, supplied by both colonial Catholicism and indigenous Philippine cultures.

The continuous Spanish colonial presence in the Philippines began, tenuously, at Cebu in 1565. Several earlier expeditions had ended in failure. Magellan was famously killed in the Visayas in 1521 by the forces of the chieftain Lapulapu of Mactan Island, whom he had been duped into attacking by one of Lapulapu's rivals. More ignominiously, native groups captured and enslaved crew members from Magellan's and other expeditions, a few of whom can be traced through encounters with later Spanish voyagers and nearby Portuguese officials.[1] The earliest colonial settlement at Cebu and the one established at Manila in 1571 were only slightly more secure through their first decades.[2] We might think, therefore, that it was just short of miraculous that Spanish officials would claim that a force of only several hundred friars and not many more officials and Spanish soldiers had succeeded in converting most of the lowland population of Luzon and the Visayas into loyal Catholic subjects of the crown by 1650.[3]

The estimates of loyal converts were based on counts of baptisms and annual tributes paid. Both marked moments of responsiveness that might not indicate permanent submission or a change in belief. The ease with which such indicators of loyalty could be misread and overestimated certainly exaggerated the success of Spanish colonization, but the fact that, to the Spaniards, these indicators were the most meaningful also suggests the minimal intrusiveness of their early presence among most of the Philippine population. There were not more than a few thousand Spaniards in the Philippines until the outbreak of the 1896 revolution and most were concentrated in Manila and a few other towns. Except in the towns and the heavily churched Tagalog provinces, most natives rarely encountered Spanish friars or officials.[4] And for those who did, their differing ideas about conversion and submission created what one historian has insightfully called "a colonial order that seemed to be premised on a mutual misreading of each other's intentions rather than on the unambiguous imposition of the ruler's will over the ruled."[5]

The relational focus of politics in the sixteenth-century Philippines and the fluidity of both group and personal identities contributed to the seemingly phenomenal speed of Spanish colonization. There were no territorial or stable supralocal polities in the precolonial Philippines, although networks of dyadic ties (of kinship, allegiance, and obligation) sometimes stretched over long distances. Nor were there well-defined ethnic or linguistic group identities. Instead, identities were figured in mainly local and relational ways that changed as relationships changed.[6] In more than a few cases, communities seemed to submit to Spanish rule but then confounded the Iberians' expectations by suddenly turning against them as alliances shifted.[7] Even for the large majority of the population that lived under Spanish rule for a long time, localism and fluidity of identity enabled them to accept and buffer Spanish influence by translating it into negotiable terms. Each person, each network of extended kin, and each community negotiated and renegotiated hierarchical relations among insiders and with outsiders. Spanish rule came from the outside, as did many other things in travel and trade and relations with spirits, but there was no sense in which any of these were considered peculiarly foreign and therefore automatically deserving of rejection. Quite the contrary, things from the outside could be propitiated, bargained over, and/or incorporated into local relations. People could also be taken captive, transferred by commercial transaction, bonded out by debt, or repulsed by force. Likewise, when people in the Philippines were taken captive by outsiders (who could hail from a nearby village or a distant port) or possessed by spirits, these unwanted relationships, too, could be subject to ransom and renegotiation.[8]

In the face of Spanish colonialism, the indigenous norms of reciprocity that structured social relations furnished modes of accommodation, opportunities for evasion, and grounds for resistance. Many of the most eager converts to Catholicism drove the friars to distraction by confessing a maze of sins, including those committed by others. Instead of a sacrament to unburden the individual soul, Tagalog converts, it seems, used confession as but another opportunity to expand the networks of exchange that enhanced the relational self. Paradoxically, the remoteness of this colony from the imperial center and the Spaniards' depen-

dence on Philippine allies for survival—elements of Spanish weakness—
abetted the process through which Spanish colonial hegemony was built
by forcing them to negotiate power with native intermediaries.[9]

The imperial religion described a divine hierarchy from the Spaniards' point of view. Conversion to Catholicism constituted formalized
submission to the missionaries, the Spanish king, and, of course, the
Christian God. Baptism brought with it the obligation to pay taxes and
provide labor services to the colonial state, in return for the king's protection and his support of missionary efforts to make available God's gift
of grace. In theory, becoming a Christian, and thus a subject of the king,
protected one from the demands of slavery in this world (although, in
practice, many converts remained slaves). The New Laws of the Indies
proclaimed by Philip II in 1542 required owners to prove they had
proper title to slaves or set them free. *Indios* who could become subjects
of the king were not supposed to be enslaved. For these reasons the
Spanish missionaries and the king's secular representatives struggled to
sort out the problem of just and unjust slavery in the Philippines, a distinction that would have made little sense to anyone in the Philippines
before the Spanish conquest, including the relatively recent converts to
Islam.[10]

The historian Vicente L. Rafael has shown how culturally specific understandings of submission, typified by slavery, were used by both
Spaniards and Tagalogs in the seventeenth and eighteenth centuries to
translate and thus make sense of Spanish rule. To the Spanish, the position of the *indios* was set in a fixed hierarchy of servitude and permanent gratitude, descending from God and the Spanish king through their
representatives in the Philippines down to the *indio* converts and those
reprobate peoples suitable for just slavery in this world. The Spanish
missionaries described the relation of the Christian faithful to God as a
form of slavery. In Philippine societies, submitting to the Christian God
as the source of all gifts could be understood in terms of traditional spirituality and debt relations, opening possibilities for recontextualizing
Christianity and colonialism as a series of reciprocal relationships that
the missionaries did not intend.[11]

Tagalogs tended to view hierarchies as negotiable and fluid, including relations with spirits that shared the same temporal world as the living. Death did not divide the living and the spirits, for the spirit of the
dead was expected to return to the place of the living. In sixteenth- and
seventeenth-century Tagalog culture, submitting oneself as a slave of the
Christian God and subject of the king did not necessarily imply total

subordination. This submission could be seen as a contract, to be negotiated and redeemed.

The Catholic idea of heaven as another realm where the distinction between slave and master would be erased opened the possibility of exchanging enslavement and death as payment for the ultimate gift of God, paradise. In Christian theology, enslavement to the Christian God introduced the possibility of imagining a future afterlife beyond hierarchy. Interpreted in the Tagalog context, this potential future could be construed as imminently available, just like the spirits of the dead. The means for effecting this transformation lay in reinventing death according to the model of Christ's Passion.[12]

Rafael's interpretation provides a fresh look at the antecedents of the inseparability of Catholicism and popular Philippine nationalism in the nineteenth and twentieth centuries, a subject first explored in Reynaldo Ileto's paradigm-shattering study, *Pasyon and Revolution: Popular Movements in the Philippines, 1840–1910*. The concept of slavery appears repeatedly in Ileto's sources, yet neither he nor other scholars have given direct attention to the changing meanings of slavery in relation to nationalism.

Making sense of popular movements in the Philippines has long troubled scholars, nowhere more conspicuously than in historical interpretations of the revolutions of 1896 and 1898. Ileto cut through the problem by approaching the history of popular uprisings in the politically central Tagalog region through the matrix of Tagalog folk culture, in particular, the epic Tagalog translations of the story of Christ's Passion, available since the eighteenth century. People chanted the *Pasyon* from memory in their homes during Easter week and performed the story as a drama in the towns. Translation, variations in editions, and modifications through oral tradition gave the story a distinctly Philippine flavor, evident in its extended meditations on such subjects as Jesus' relation to his mother. In some crucial ways the *Pasyon* could be lived and shared in a kind of present-tense biblical time made available by the story's localization in Tagalog and the persistent notion in folk cosmology of the immanence and recurring return of spirits.[13]

By the early nineteenth century, Ileto argued, the Tagalog *Pasyon* had become the great folk epic of the society. Rather than seeing Philippine Catholicism as an alien encrustation upon indigenous culture or a fully swallowed colonial mentality of submission, Ileto reinterpreted it as a set of practices and stories that had been appropriated and localized within popular culture. To this end, he began his study by reconsidering the Cofradía de San Jose, a Tagalog religious confraternity that became the center of a rebellion in 1840–1841, several decades before the appearance of modern Philippine nationalism.

Apolinario de la Cruz, a Tagalog *provinciano*, started the *cofradía* in Manila in 1832 when Dominican friars refused to admit him as a monk because he was an *indio*. The friars refused to sanction the *cofradía*, too, even though they commonly sponsored such native confraternities. In return, Apolinario barred mestizos, creoles, and Spaniards from the *cofradía*, which, together with some heterodox practices, only drew more suspicion upon the organization over time. For example, new members of the *cofradía* were required to recite by memory and sign a printed copy of a special prayer, the Declaration of Enslavement to the Beloved Lord Saint Joseph (*Sulat na paquiqui-alipin sa mahal na Poong San Josef*). Initiates thereby declared, "O Most Holy Joseph, my father and lord, I [name of initiate] prostrate myself before your feet, a slave [*alipin*] of Jesus of the Sacrament and of the Most Holy Virgin Mary. I come before you, humbly enslaving [*napa aalipin*] myself, so that you three Lords of mine—Jesus, Mary and Joseph—may be in my heart."[14]

As Ileto explains, the "common submission to the Holy Family was the condition that bound [the *cofrades*] together as brothers and sisters," sustaining a "deep sense of egalitarianism and fraternal love" that ultimately threatened colonial hierarchies of race and class. This act of "enslavement" also promised the abnegation of prior debt relations and an end to human sufferings in a future heaven, to be reached by reenacting Christ's Passion in the living present. The "perfect unity" of enslavement to the trinity of Jesus, Mary, and Joseph also meant "the dissolution of kinship ties on earth," which were figured in terms of a hierarchy of debt instead of pure and boundless fraternity.[15]

Spiritual enslavement thus provided both the means and justification to break even the oldest and strongest bonds between people when they blocked the pathway of Christ's Passion. Given the belief in spiritual incarnation common to Tagalog and many other Philippine cosmologies, the way was now open for leaders such as Apolinario de la Cruz to be identified, literally, as Christ himself, leading the *cofrades* in the reliving of Christ's Passion. When the Spanish repression of the *cofradía* began, it was easy for Apolinario de la Cruz to take on another aspect of Christ's persona. To his followers he reportedly became "king of the Tagalogs."[16] Many of the *cofradía*'s forms of expression would reappear in later popular movements, including the 1896 revolution, in which brothers and sisters (*kapatid*) would seek a king other than the Spanish king.

The 1896 revolution was organized and begun by the Katipunan (*Kataastaasan Kagalanggalang Katipunan ng mga Anak ng Bayan:* The highest and most honorable society of the children of the country), a secret society formed in Manila in 1892, just after Jose Rizal's arrest and exile to Dapitan. The founder and *supremo* of the Katipunan was Andres Bonifacio, a self-educated clerk who also acted in Tagalog dramas. Most of his close circle of associates in the Katipunan before 1896 came either from roughly similar occupational groupings or the ranks of disaffected students at the University of Santo Tomas and the Jesuit *colegio,* the Ateneo de Manila. The Katipunan remained a small, clandestine organization until early 1896, when the single issue of a printed broadside titled *Kalayaan*—the Tagalog neologism for "independence"—appears to have swollen its following in the Tagalog provinces.[17] The concept and desire for Philippine independence, which originated among the *ilustrados* and was communicated among them through the lingua franca, Spanish, took on additional layers of local meaning when the term *kalayaan* was coined to translate these desires into Tagalog.

The neologism *kalayaan* carried with it a series of powerful connotations in Tagalog culture, but the significance of its opposition to slavery has not been recognized. As Ileto explains, *layaw,* the root word of *kalayaan,* signified "bodily pleasure" and the "satisfaction of necessities." It connoted the kind of "pampering treatment" mothers accord their young children and also the condition of heavenly existence prefigured in Tagalog renderings of Christian salvation. *Kalayaan* was thus the opposite of suffering, but, as the Katipunan and many succeeding popular movements understood it, the redemption of *kalayaan* could be achieved only by suffering as Christ suffered, by living and sharing Christ's Passion unto death.[18] Christian salvation, however, was itself a discourse structured around metaphors of God as a father and also as a master over his slaves (*alipin*). In this sense, obtaining *kalayaan* would exchange bonds of kinship and debt that caused suffering for an ideal set of relations as God's children and servants.

Katipunan proclamations, initiation rituals, and various participants' contemporary accounts and memorializations spoke of replacing the old ties of debt to a cold and unresponsive "mother Spain" with obligations to a new "mother country" (*inang bayan*), the Philippines, who would bestow *kalayaan.* To accomplish this transformation the *Katipuneros* understood that it would be necessary to suffer and control their *loob* (inside), which they needed to engage mutually to establish an *utang na loob* relationship of love with their new mother country. Such sacrifice, and the discipline needed to make it, were thought to focus great powers enabling one to do extraordinary things. Under these conditions of a popular culture that did not separate the material from the spiritual, the execution of Jose Rizal in December 1896 did more than just greatly accelerate the spread of resentment against Spain. Rizal's exemplary life and martyrdom furnished the ultimate model of a Filipino Christ who had journeyed, preached, and serenely sacrificed his life for the redemption of his people from the slavery of colonialism.[19]

Images of slavery suffused the Katipunan's revolutionary discourse. For example, the Katipunan's single issue of *Kalayaan* included an allegorical tale about a downcast young man visited by a female spirit with a glowing halo. The woman offered the possibility of "true and perfect happiness" to ease the young man's sadness, but he did not recognize her. She explained that she was unknown to him because "it has been more than three hundred years since I visited your land." Then she introduced herself: "For my cause men unite, each one forgetting his selfish interests, seeing nothing but the good of all; *because of me slaves are rescued and lifted up from the mire of degradation and shame, the pride and malice of their cruel masters broken . . . My name is Kalayaan.*"[20]

As the story continues, the despondent young man describes the sufferings of his people, which Kalayaan then explains historically. When she was last present in the land, some three hundred years ago, "the Tagalog . . . people lived in the shade of my protection, and in my bosom [were] happy and breathed the air that gave . . . life and strength." All was well until, "one day, which must be execrated and accursed, Slavery arrived saying that she was Virtue and Justice, and promised Glory to all who would believe her." Spanish colonialism was figured as slavery and a cause of "degradation and shame." Redemption from slavery would take the form of *kalayaan,* a release from suffering and a return to a native maternal fold to be obtained by the common discipline of suffering.[21]

The popular nationalist metaphorics of slavery also circulated through the Katipunan's elaborate initiation rites. These included a series of ritual interrogations that culminated in the question, "Where have you come from?" to which the novitiate's sponsor would reply, "We have come from the mire of slavery [*sa lusak ng pagkaalipin*] . . . and now we are here calling before your holy gate in search of *kalayaan.*"[22] Memorializations and later reincarnations of the original Katipunan continued to speak of its members' passage from slavery to *kalayaan.* For example, a Katipunan active in 1900 told its initiates that "[i]t is indisputable that the [original] Katipunan Society was the beacon which guided us to the shores of liberty after four centuries of navigation in the sea of slavery."[23]

The early nationalist writings of the *ilustrados* in the 1880s and 1890s prefigured the Katipunan's condemnation of colonialism as a kind of slavery, just as they introduced the idea of a Filipino national identity and the concept of independence. Jose Rizal, certainly the most influential of all the *ilustrados,* shared with the Katipunan an emphasis on personal discipline and suffering as prerequisites for redemption. Rizal's metaphorics of slavery, expressed, however, an ambivalence that diverged from the Katipunan's usage and indicated certain underlying differences of worldview. The *ilustrados,* especially Rizal, inspired the Katipunan, but their political and cultural outlooks were not isomorphic.

Most of the *ilustrados* hailed from mestizo and creole families who had found profitable niches in the expanding nineteenth-century economy. Their parents had chafed against the favoritism shown the religious orders over native-born clergy, as well as against the friars' reactionary control of education and public communication. The friars filtered all of this mild reformism through their heightened olfactory sense for subversion and heresy, which made it smell too much like the creole revolutionary movements that had cost Spain most of her empire in the Americas earlier in the century. Spain's liberal revolution of 1868 brought a brief moment of hope for modernization and the extension of basic liberties, but, in fact, the liberal Spanish governors were dependent upon the friars for local knowledge and authority. In 1872 the hope for change was smashed by the colonial government's repression of a mutiny by shipyard workers and native soldiers at the Cavite naval arsenal, on the bay south of Manila. It was the repression, far out of proportion to the local uprising in Cavite, that turned the course of Philippine history.[24]

The friars blamed the native-born secular clergy—priests who did not belong to the religious orders—for allegedly instigating the Cavite mutiny in order to start a revolution against Spanish rule. Along with these charges, the friars also tarred many of the leading liberal families of Manila with the taint of subversion. Three Philippine-born priests racially classified as creoles and mestizos—Fathers José Burgos, Mariano Gomez, and Jacinto Zamora—were sent to the garrote. Dozens of their civilian associates suffered arrest and exile. Their male children, who might have studied for the priesthood before 1872, now sought other careers and postsecondary education in Europe.

In the 1880s, the *ilustrados* first struggled to achieve equality with *peninsulares* as citizens of greater Spain. Their parents' and teachers' earlier campaign to defend the secular clergy laid a basis for considering all Philippine-born people as a common group. Rather than thinking of themselves only as creoles or mestizos or natives, they began to call themselves *filipinos*. Stymied by the friars and resentful of Spanish racism in the Philippines, Rizal and other *ilustrados* soon turned their thoughts forward to imagine a Philippines even more fully equal to Spain, with liberty and, perhaps, independence.[25]

With few exceptions, the *ilustrados* thought revolution would be futile. They remained aloof from the Katipunan's plotting in early 1896. Filipinos, the *ilustrados* believed, had neither the material nor moral preparation to succeed in revolution at that moment. Yet, this cultivation, they made clear, would prepare them for a future emancipation. Rizal put it thus while in prison in 1896, awaiting trial for allegedly directing the Katipunan's revolution: "Countrymen, I have given proofs, as much as any one else, of desiring liberties for our country, and I still desire them. But I made them conditional on the education of the people so that by means of learning and work they would have their own personality and make themselves worthy of [such liberties]. In my writings I have recommended study and [the development of] civic virtues, without which there can be no redemption."[26]

Rizal always discussed the slavery of colonialism in terms of Filipinos' character. In contrast, the more militant popular nationalism of the Katipunan declared that Filipinos were wrongly held as slaves by the colonizer and aimed to change that condition through armed revolution. *Kalayaan* was both imminent and immanent for the Katipunan and its successors. Preparation and discipline were central to Katipunan ideas about change, too, but the Katipunan envisioned a purification of self and community in order to receive what was already there. Rizal's deification in popular culture was accomplished by reading the seemingly magical accomplishments of his life—his distant travels, his brilliance with languages and the word, his curative power as a medical doctor to restore sight—and the sacrifice of his death in these terms, as an incarnation of Christ's everpresent spirit. In turn, Rizal's spirit would be forever available, along with the spirit of *kalayaan*.[27]

Although Rizal appears to have consciously abetted the potential for his deification by cultivating the symbolism of his own martyrdom, he and his fellow *ilustrados* were personally committed to rationalism, secularism, and the ideal of progress.[28] They saw the friars and oppressiveness of Spanish rule as the antitheses of these values, and they believed that their development despite Spanish obstruction would be the precondition for freedom. To Rizal, the determination of the Philippines' future would be made over time, during which it would be necessary for Filipinos to prepare and culture themselves, in the broadest senses of the words.

The ambivalence in Rizal's metaphorics of slavery runs throughout many of his writings, but nowhere more prominently than in the two Spanish-language novels for which he was most celebrated: the viciously satirical *Noli Me Tangere,* published in 1887, which became the great Filipino national novel, and its slightly less sacralized sequel, *El Filibusterismo,* which appeared in 1891.[29] In the *Noli,* as it is popularly known, the educated mestizo Juan Crisostomo Ibarra y Magsalin returns to the Philippines after spending seven years in Europe. Asked what he found most remarkable in Europe, Ibarra begins to reply, "[f]rankly, what is surprising with these people, setting aside the national pride of each one," and then trails off and thinks before continuing to say that "[b]efore visiting a country I would strive to study *its history, its Exodus,* if I may say so, and after that I found everything natural; I saw always that the prosperity or the misery of the nations are in direct proportion to their liberties or prejudices, and consequently to the sacrifices or egoism of their ancestors." [30]

Home in the Philippines, Ibarra finds that the Spanish friars—the priestly fathers who control the colony—have pit their reactionary prejudice and selfishness against all that is true and just. The friars had condemned his respected Spanish-mestizo father to prison, where he died, for suspicion of heresy and subversion. They oppose Ibarra's efforts to spread enlightenment through instruction in Spanish, and they persecute him because he would marry a woman who is, secretly, the daughter of one of their own. In between Rizal's wicked portraits of the friars' iniquity and the vanity of the colonial social world, a romantic story of tragedy and sacrifice unfolds between Ibarra and his two symbolically linked loves, his *patria,* the Philippines, and his fiancée, Maria Clara, the beautiful fair-skinned daughter of a friar.

By the end of the novel the once loyal and high-minded Ibarra is transformed by the friars' plots to persecute him and frame him as a subversive. Ibarra escapes from his unjust imprisonment and flees to become "a *filibustero,* but a real *filibustero.*" [31] Although it is uncertain in the *Noli* whether Ibarra survives his flight from the civil guards, he does return as the central character of the novel's sequel, *El Filibusterismo.*

The *Noli* concludes by pondering the fate of Ibarra's other love, Maria Clara, who believes that Ibarra is dead. Tormented in a convent she entered to escape an arranged marriage to a loathsome Spaniard, she appears on the roof as a ghostly figure during a violent thunderstorm, "as beautiful as the Virgin," wailing her sorrows to the heavens, and is then never seen again.[32] The Katipunan's later allegory about the spectral woman, Kalayaan, played upon a similarly gendered motif of injustice, suffering, and loss.

In the sequel novel, popularly known as the *Fili,* Rizal warned of the catastrophes to be faced if Spain's failure to institute reforms made revolution the only hope. Ibarra returns as a mysterious jeweler named Simoun who has the ear of the governor general. He uses his position to foment ever more misery until he can detonate it to cause a general uprising. The metaphorics of slavery frame the central tension of the novel, which Simoun explores with two principal interlocutors: Basilio, the *indio* medical student (whose mother, as recounted in the *Noli,* went insane from grief when her other son was killed by a friar), and the native-born parish priest Father Florentino.

Basilio looks to a future world beyond patriotism, "enlightened and redeemed" by science. It would be a time "when there will no longer be races, when all the people will be free, when there will no longer be tyrants nor slaves, colonies nor empires." But Simoun chastises Basilio for wanting instruction in Spanish as a means to achieve change through education. "Instead of making yourselves free," he tells Basilio, "you will only make yourselves truly slaves," beholden to the thoughts and culture of another people. Basilio's utopia beyond nationalism would require that there be "no tyrant nations and no slave nations," and "for this," Simoun says, "it is necessary to shed much blood." Simoun urges Basilio to action, telling him that "resignation is not always a virtue, it is a crime when it encourages tyranny: there are no despots where there are no slaves." The problem was not only one of throwing off slavery from without, but also of removing its effects from within. A life of "uninterrupted slavery," Simoun tells Basilio, "of systematic humiliation, of constant prostration, eventually creates in the soul a hunch that cannot be straightened in a day's work."[33]

At the end of the novel, we find Simoun wounded and in the care of Father Florentino at the priest's house on the remote coast east of Manila. His plot for rebellion has collapsed; all that he cared for is in ruins. When he learns that he will be taken dead or alive, Simoun poisons himself in order to keep the painful secret of his identity. It falls to

Father Florentino to explain Simoun's failure and outline "what is to be done." The priest implores that "redemption presupposes virtue, virtue, sacrifice and sacrifice, love!" Simoun had believed "that what crime and iniquity had stained and deformed, another crime and another iniquity could purify and redeem," but, says the father, "[h]ate creates only monsters; crime, criminals; only love can build marvelous work, only virtue can save!" Emancipation would require acts of positive creation. "An immoral government corresponds to a demoralized people . . . [l]ike master, like slaves; like government, like country." Thus, the priest continues, "we have to conquer by being worthy of [our freedom], elevating reason and the divinity of the individual, loving what is just, good, great, even to die for it." Without this preparation, he asks, "[w]hy independence if the slaves of today will be the tyrants of tomorrow?" [34]

Rizal expressed similar sentiments when he referred to slavery in his personal correspondence. To his colleague and sometime rival, Marcelo H. Del Pilar, publisher of the influential Filipino journal *La Solidaridad* in Madrid, he complained in 1888 of the decadence of Filipinos in Europe. "Is there nothing to remind them that the Filipino does not come to Europe to gamble and enjoy himself, but to work for his liberty and for the dignity of his race? I have great fears," he told Del Pilar, "that we may be struggling for a useless illusion, and that instead of being worthy of liberty, we may only be worthy of slavery." [35] To Baldomero Roxas in December 1889, he wrote: "Without virtue there is no liberty, only virtue can redeem the slave." [36]

Rizal returned to the mutual relation between slaves and tyrants in a poem popularly known as *Mi último adiós,* written in the days before his execution. After the *Noli,* it is probably the most important literary expression of Philippine nationalism in terms of historical effect. In the last lines of the penultimate stanza, Rizal portends,

> I leave you all, all whom I love so well,
> To go where neither slaves, tormentors, nor tyrants dwell,
> Where Faith kills not, and where God reigns supreme.[37]

A reference to heaven, this has strong similarities to popular understandings of *kalayaan.* It also recalls the golden age of a preconquest past that Rizal described in his historical works, especially his annotated edition of Antonio de Morga's early seventeenth-century chronicle, *Sucesos de las Islas Filipinas.*

Like many *ilustrados* and nationalist intellectuals everywhere, Rizal was much concerned with history as the seedbed of national identity. He

dedicated his edition of Morga's chronicle "To the Filipinos," for whom
he would "make known the past, so that it may be possible to judge better the present and measure the path that has been traversed during three
centuries." He wanted the volume to awaken "the consciousness of our
past, which has been blotted out from our memories," and to rectify
"what has been falsified by calumny" so that "we can all dedicate ourselves to studying the future." History enabled Rizal to imagine a national community as already there and moving through time, from "our
past" into the future.[38] The Filipinos' exodus lay in the future yet to be
lived. Valorizing the pre-Hispanic past allowed Rizal to defend Filipino
civilization while also charting a history of decline and corruption under Spanish rule. It was Rizal's task as historian to account for the slavery from which the Filipino nation had to extricate itself.

Morga, like other early Spanish chroniclers, spent considerable effort
trying to make sense of indigenous Philippine forms of slavery. Rizal
used his annotations on these sections to make two arguments. First, the
conditions of servitude described by Morga were "very different from
that of a slave in Greece, or Rome, from that of the negro, and even
those [enslaved] in later times by Spaniards." The indigenous form of
slavery was, according to Rizal, originally a benign institution based on
debt, which the Spaniards changed but did not eliminate. Indeed, and
this was Rizal's second point, "Catholicism not only did not liberate the
poor class from the tyranny of the oppressive, but with its advent in the
Philippines increased the number of tyrants." The "slaves" described by
Morga still existed in 1890, according to Rizal: "In many provinces, and
in many towns, there is taking place, word for word, what Morga says,
it being lamented that at present not only Indios continue this usury, but
also the mestizos, the Spaniards, and even various priests. And it has
come to this that the Government itself not only permits it, but in its
turn exacts the capital and the person in payment of the debt of others"
by demanding that headmen pay the taxes of their villages.[39]

Throughout his edition of Morga, Rizal contrasted a romanticized
precolonial Philippine past with the regressive and repressive rule of
Spain. Filipinos thus owed no debt of gratitude to Spain. Just the opposite; they had paid the Spanish king with "their independence, their liberty . . . their gold, their blood, their sons . . . in order not even to have
the right to the name of Spaniards, to lose at the end of three centuries
of fidelity and sacrifices even the rare deputies and envoys who defended
them, to have no voice in the councils of the nation; to exchange their
national religion, their history, their usages and customs, for other bor-

rowed and ill-understood usages." The image, of course, is one of enslavement to Spain.[40]

Rizal and the Katipunan shared a vision of the Philippine past as a fall from a golden age into a state of slavery, but they diverged in other areas. The anticlerical and rationalist Rizal saw the emerging history of the nation as its exodus, simultaneously a process in secular time and a biblical metaphor that evoked the Katipunan's more spiritual conception of achieving *kalayaan* by following the path of Christ's Passion. Rizal and the *ilustrados* also made a qualitative distinction between forms of worldly slavery. Bondage in the pre-Hispanic Philippines was not quite to be counted as slavery, unlike European and American forms of slavery, enslavement through colonialism, and the inner character of being a slave.

In 1898 and 1899, as Spain was expelled from the Philippines by a renewed revolution and the United States, many of the cosmopolitan *ilustrados* united ever so briefly with followers of the Katipunan. Together, they formed the Philippine Republic, under the leadership of Emilio Aguinaldo, a member of the provincial gentry from Cavite Province. During the months of independence Aguinaldo echoed both Rizal's and the Katipunan's views of slavery. In his declaration of a revolutionary government on 23 June 1898, Aguinaldo announced that the "nation calls on all Filipinos, her sons, without distinction of class, and invites them to solidly unite, with the object of forming a noble association . . . [for] a nation which has given proofs of endurance and courage in tribulation and peril, and of industry and studiousness in peace, is not to be enslaved." [41] And later, in his message proclaiming the birth of the Philippine Republic on 23 January 1899, he consigned slavery to the past: "Ah, Representatives! How much pain and bitterness do those past days of the Spanish slavery bring to our minds and how much hope and joy do the present moments of Philippine liberty awaken in us." [42]

Almost as soon as it came into existence, the republic's unity began to splinter under the pressure of social conflicts, cultural differences, and the invading forces of the United States. Many *ilustrados* defected quickly, for they were highly conscious of their social class and skeptical of the abilities and trustworthiness of the provincials, peasants, and workers who were making the revolution. A few flocked to the U.S. authorities when American troops occupied Manila in August 1898; more followed close behind once the war of conquest began in February 1899. Soon, too, Aguinaldo found his government at odds with peasants and some townsfolk for whom an independent state did not exhaust all of the meanings and hopes they attached to the idea of *kalayaan*. This split widened as the provincial elites who staffed much of the officer corps of Aguinaldo's army began in large numbers to accept appointments to office under the Americans after 1901. Meanwhile, the tradition of the Katipunan persisted in movements that continued to fight the United States long after Aguinaldo's capture and surrender. In just this way, reflections on slavery again diverged.

The great *ilustrado* Dr. Trinidad H. Pardo de Tavera, a friend of Rizal's, was one of the first to ally himself with the new colonial power. He founded the *Partido Federal* in 1900, which resurrected the nineteenth-century *ilustrado* dream of union with the mother country by calling for Philippine statehood within the United States. Before long the party turned to call for independence, but always for an independence based on proper preparation. Although Pardo de Tavera was much more conservative than Rizal had been and considerably less sympathetic to indigenous Philippine culture, his rhetoric about preparation for independence closely resembled Rizal's. As Pardo de Tavera explained at a banquet honoring him upon retirement from official life in 1909: "My wishes have nothing to do with the question of whether the sovereign power shall reside in foreign hands, as now, or in our own, as we aspire: I want to prepare the people so that they can not be oppressed by Government . . . Political independence does not make a people safe from slavery." [43]

The popular nationalist plays that began to appear in 1902 and 1903 presented a radically different usage of slavery that built upon the Katipunan tradition. American colonial authorities soon declared these Tagalog plays "seditious" and persecuted their authors and casts. Playwrights such as Juan Matapanga Cruz and Aurelio Tolentino, who were members of the Katipunan and also served in Aguinaldo's government in 1898, composed allegorical dramas about the Philippines' struggle against slavery for freedom and independence.[44] Moreover, these plays also dealt with the theme of collaboration for money, sometimes figured as a reenactment of Judas's betrayal of Christ, at other times as selling one's kin into slavery. Proclamations of colonial benevolence and protection were portrayed as tricks to enslave the population. So, in Tolentino's *Kahapon, Ngayon, at Bukas* (Yesterday, Today, and Tomorrow), produced in 1903, the following dialogue occurs on the meeting of Inangbayan (mother country) and two characters representing the United States, Bagongsibol (literally, new sprout, i.e., the United States) and Malaynatin (the one we know, i.e., the United States government):

BAGONGSIBOL: Wherever our eagle rules, slavery is banished; wherever our stars shine liberty and abundance reach. . . .

MALAYNATIN: We will conduct thee to the height of liberty so that thou canst take thy place among the nations of the universe. . . .

INANGBAYAN: . . . if thou wishest to secure my sincere love, I do not need to be recompensed with great love, but that thou, Bagongsibol, will preserve safely our greatly desired liberty. Thou already knowest that in order to secure it, thousands of thousands of the lives of our sons, fathers, and illustrious brothers have been sacrificed in battle, so I beg of thy benevolence that if thou some day tryest to enslave me, thou wilt not do so, because I would prefer that thou shouldst kill me with all my descendants.[45]

Juan Matapanga Cruz's play *Hindi Ako Patay* (I am not dead), also produced in 1903, emphasized the theme of being sold into slavery by traitors allied with a transparently dangerous United States, represented by the characters Macamcam (Ambitious) and Maimbot (Greedy). Patriots vow to fight to the death for their liberty. Karangalan (Honor) asks God to "grant that my brother may understand clearly that he is selling our liberty, also, to those of our countrymen who are in a similar condition, and who are pleased with having money, the product of slavery, grant that they may change their feeling, and that their descendants may not inherit the treason of their ancestors." The "I" of the title is Tangulan (Defender), who is believed dead but returns alive at the end of the play. As a result, his countrymen exult: "Independence has returned!" "It has been saved from slavery!" Maimbot has no choice but to acknowledge the revitalization of the populace and admit that "[o]ur authority is now ended."[46]

By the end of the nineteenth century slavery had come to have a powerful significance in the elaboration of Philippine nationalist discourse, as a metaphor for colonialism and as a measure of national character. Both usages depended on a vision of history tied to an emerging sense of national identity. But, when considered as a social institution that was reputedly present in the Philippines, as in Rizal's annotations to Antonio de Morga's chronicle, slavery compelled special explanation because of its place in defining the nation and defending its honor.

The *ilustrados* had appropriated and reformulated an antislavery ideology, according to which a relationship would be unjust if it were, in fact, a form of slavery. The effects of this antislavery ideology, however, would be unlike those recognized by most historians of abolition. Instead of prompting an abolitionist movement to end slavery among

Philippine minority groups, antislavery ideology would move Filipino nationalists to deny that slavery as a social practice ever existed or could exist among Filipinos. At just the time that the "seditious plays" were incurring the wrath of colonial prosecutors for accusing the United States of enslaving the Philippines, however, the realignment of imperial politics around the official, colonial-sponsored nationalism of Filipino officeholders began to produce unanticipated consequences. The Filipino nationalist depiction of colonialism as a form of slavery would soon face an embarrassing challenge.

CHAPTER EIGHT

The Redefinition
of the Uncivilized

In February 1904, while testifying before the Committee on Insular Affairs of the House of Representatives, the secretary of war William Howard Taft was asked if slavery still existed in the Philippines. The existence of slavery in the Moro Province was widely known in the United States. So, too, were the colonial state's recent declaration of abolition and subsequent military engagements in Sulu, Cotabato, and Lanao. Taft now had confidence in the colonial regime's reputation as a force for abolition. He admitted that "slavery continues in part of the Moro Province" without any apology for the progress of emancipation in the southern Philippines. Unembarrassed, he went further, freely introducing the matter of slavery in northern Luzon.[1]

There was "some slavery in some of the Christian Filipino provinces that lie near to the mountain tribes," Taft told the committee, and "this latter [slavery] we are trying hard to eliminate." Although the original reports Taft had seen over the past year described slave raids carried on by non-Christian tribes in the mountains, he now limited himself to saying "it was not uncommon for hill tribe parents to bring their children into a Filipino village and to sell a child to a wealthy man in the village who would use him as a servant." Hiding some concerns about the inadequacy of antislavery statutes, Taft concluded by assuring the committee that these sales were "contrary to law, and we have directed prosecution in every case brought to our attention."[2] Taft's testimony represented important changes in Americans' attitude toward slavery in the Philippines and in their depictions of the people of the Philippines. Institutional shifts fundamental to the construction of American colonial hegemony lay behind the transformations.

From Taft's perspective in 1904, slavery was no longer a vexing issue in the Philippines. The colonial state seemed to have put it to rest in the southern Philippines by declaring it abolished. Although local struggles continued there, the problem of slavery and abolition in the Moro societies ceased to arouse contention in the United States. Neither the dwindling band of anti-imperialists nor the colonial state openly questioned the process of abolition after the 1903 antislavery decree.

The colonial state, of course, had no desire to undercut its claim to have established order and abolished slavery in the southern Philippines by acknowledging the shallowness of its still-contested influence. Embarrassing memories of earlier compromises with slavery in the southern Philippines were put to rest by proclaiming the institution fundamentally extinct. The anti-imperialists could have launched probes into the operation of the antislavery law as they had pursued investigations into the brutalities of the American war of conquest, but they were not so inclined. By 1903 even some of the most committed anti-imperialists could not help but say that the Moros were "unfit to govern themselves." To such backsliding the indefatigably egalitarian Moorfield Storey replied that the Moros "have been governing themselves for a great while and they are governing themselves today . . . the Bates Treaty left the Sultan and Datoes in power, and the government went on as before." But there was a catch in this proof of practical self-government. Slavery could not be defended; its abolition could not be opposed. In late 1903 Storey told his colleague Fiske Warren that the United States "certainly . . . left slavery and other evils in full swing, and I fancy there has been no change." Despite his suspicions, Storey did not publicly reproach the colonial administration for failing to take sufficient action.[3]

Although many prominent anti-imperialists were proud of their antislavery heritage, they never wanted an abolitionist crusade in the Philippines. From 1899 to 1903, the anti-imperialists had broadcast the existence of slavery in the southern Philippines to dissuade their countrymen from consummating a colonial project that would entangle them once more with the institution of slavery. The 1903 Moro Province antislavery law put them on the defensive. They could hardly propose that the United States simply abandon an emancipation in the southern Philippines that appeared well underway.

The changing political implications of antislavery ideology were related to a larger redefinition of the uncivilized that redirected anti-imperialist strategy. Whereas American critics of colonialism formerly emphasized negative arguments about the barbarities of conquest and the dangers posed by tropical races, by the end of 1902 the anti-imperialists had to accept the United States's control of the Philippines as an accomplished fact that could be changed only by legislation and rapid administrative guidance to independence.[4] This forced the small surviving band of dedicated anti-imperialists to argue more directly for the positive goal of Philippine independence. They could still muck-rake for scandal and corruption in the colonial administration, but their primary argument came increasingly to rest on the principle of national self-determination and the Filipinos' fitness for exercising it. Anti-imperialists could no longer use the colonial discourse about the uncivilized to bolster their own cause.

The consolidation of colonial hegemony around the official sponsorship of Philippine nationalism also carried repercussions for the way the colonial state represented the people of the Philippines. President Roosevelt's declaration, made on 4 July 1902, that the United States had triumphed in its war against the Philippine "insurrection" followed by days the Congress's Philippine Organic Act, which established terms for a permanent civil government based on Filipino self-representation. The colonial state had already begun to cultivate political relations with a generation of young Filipino leaders in the lowland provinces who would supplant the older, Manila-centered *ilustrados*. It first provided them access to municipal and provincial offices in 1901, then worked to facilitate their rise to national politics through the Philippine Assembly, which opened in 1907. By then Filipinos were serving at all but the highest executive level of colonial governance. These elected and appointed officials constituted a new national elite, the first to regularize a pan-Philippine politics through institutions that brought regional representatives together in Manila.[5]

American political relations with the Filipino nationalist leadership and the ideology of colonial progress required the colonial regime to change the way it depicted the people of the Philippines. American colonialism depended upon the representation of Filipinos as obedient inferiors, but it also justified itself by underwriting a discourse of progress in civilization and capacity for self-government. Instead of presenting the people of the Philippines as a hopelessly diverse lot of backward and uncivilized tribes incapable of self-direction, the colonial state, after 1902, increasingly portrayed the majority Catholic population as Filipinos progressing toward independent nationhood under American tutelage. Indeed, American colonial hegemony depended upon a redefinition of the uncivilized that would be accepted by critics of colonialism on both sides of the Pacific.[6]

Because so much was staked on the way people were classed as "civilized" or "uncivilized," official representation of the Filipino people became an uneven terrain for conflict and the negotiation of colonial power relations.[7] As colonial politics gave more recognition to the Filipino national elite, regulating the boundaries of civility became more important than measuring its degree. In this context, colonial discourse on slavery, head-hunting, and other "barbarous practices" was delimited between the Philippine national elite's demand for dignity and the colonial need for uncivilized subjects to sustain its ideology of benevolence. Under these circumstances, the non-Christian tribes took on special meaning as the inferior "other" of Filipino nationalists and special wards of the colonial state. Their position in the colonial hierarchy enabled American authorities to recognize Filipino self-government in the assembly and other institutions while grounding the need for further colonialism in the unquestionably uncivilized condition of the non-Christian tribes.

American classifications of the non-Christian tribes were far from surprising. By 1898 the hierarchical taxonomies of colonialism—race, labor discipline, political order, religion, disposition toward progress, etc.—were already deeply entrenched in American culture. The division of peoples in the Philippines, into civilized Filipinos on the one hand and uncivilized Moros and non-Christians on the other, owed as much to American ideology as it did to the legacy of Spanish colonialism in reshaping the boundaries of Philippine societies according to religious affiliation. Nevertheless, the structure of American knowledge about the non-Christian tribes changed during the course of establishing colonial institutions. Neither the simple product of inherited ideologies nor an unmediated reflection of ethnological reality, the meaning of the non-Christian tribes in colonial discourse took shape in the practical fashioning of colonial power and knowledge—a process in which Filipino nationalists played active, if unequal and often indirect, roles.[8]

To understand that meaning, it is necessary to chart the representation of the non-Christian tribes over time. As their name implies, American colonial officials classified them by what they were not. Differences among Filipinos existed outside and prior to colonial representations, but American colonialism reordered and reinterpreted these divisions, sometimes giving them new solidity through administrative boundaries, protective institutions, and the reifications of racial science. At the same time, American colonialism promised to obliterate many such distinctions by the spread of civilization, Christianity, and the nurturing of Filipino "fitness" for national independence.

The non-Christian tribes did not, at first, carry any special meaning for Americans. In his famous post hoc elucidation of reasons for annexing the Philippines and its people, President McKinley told a group of Methodist ministers that, once he had divined through prayer that "we could not leave them to themselves [because] they were unfit for self-government, . . . there was nothing left for us to do but to take them all, and to educate the Filipinos, and uplift and civilize and Christianize them, and by God's grace do the very best we could do by them, as our fellow-men for whom Christ also died." [9] By describing them as lacking progress, civilization, Christianity, and fitness for self-government, McKinley located Filipinos in a world that white Americans and Europeans divided into independent nations and subject races. Of course, the Americans quickly learned that most Filipinos were already Christian. The Christianizing impulse of American colonialism retreated from outright evangelization to more subtle anti-Catholic prejudices, racially tinged suspicions about the authenticity of Filipino Christianity, and expressions of the Protestant ethic in a secularized civilizing mission. With regard to the non-Christian tribes, however, McKinley's original vision of the colonized would remain substantially unaltered.

In 1899, the first Philippine Commission, led by Jacob Gould Schurman, president of Cornell University, emphasized the multiplicitous divisions among Filipinos. The people of the Philippines, the commission declared in its report, "belong to three sharply distinct races—the Negrito race, the Indonesian race, and the Malayan race," corresponding to hypothesized waves of successively more advanced migrations that populated the Philippines in the prehistoric past. This biological classification of separate races slipped imperfectly into distinctions between "wild tribes" and those that had been "civilized" and "Christianized" by outside influences. The Schurman Commission's report described Negritos at some length as a "disappearing" people, "weaklings of low stature, with black skin, closely-curling hair, flat noses, thick lips, and large, clumsy feet . . . at or near the bottom of the human series . . . incapable of any considerable degree of civilization or advancement." Many of the "wild tribes," both "Indonesian" and "Malayan," were said to be "pacific and quite harmless so long as they are decently treated," but "not a few were decidedly the reverse," reportedly practicing head-hunting, cannibalism, polygamy, slavery, and human sacrifice.[10]

Lest this portrait appear too grim at a time when anti-imperialists in the United States exploited issues of race and slavery for their own anti-thetical cause, the commission hurriedly added: "It should be clearly borne in mind, however, that the whole number of individuals included in the group of wild peoples is far below that composing the compara-tively few civilized tribes." Indeed, the commission's catalogue of inci-vilities in 1899 was given less to demonstrate directly the extent of some Filipinos' backwardness, which few Americans then doubted, than to emphasize the sheer diversity of the Philippines' population. The com-mission reduced its argument for the necessity of colonial rule to its con-tention that "the Filipinos do not constitute 'a nation,' or 'a people,'" as proven by a table "which gives the names of the various tribes so far as are known, the regions which they respectively inhabit, and, where prac-ticable, an estimate of the number of individuals composing each." The early significance of the non-Christian tribes in American colonial dis-course derived from their quantitative contribution to the total num-ber of "tribes" that made up the population of the Philippines, not any qualitative suppositions about their specific characteristics, cultures, or practices.[11]

When President McKinley sent William Howard Taft to establish civil government in the Philippines in 1900, his instructions reflected a newly emerging dialectic between colonial politics and ethnological classification. McKinley distinguished between Filipinos who would be allowed to participate in civil government according to their "many dif-ferent degrees of civilization and varieties of custom and capacity" and others beyond the boundary of consideration for inclusion in represen-tative institutions, whom he called "the 'uncivilized tribes' of the Is-lands." For the latter, McKinley urged Taft's revamped Philippine Com-mission "to adopt the same course followed by Congress in permitting the tribes of our North American Indians to maintain their tribal orga-nization and government . . . surrounded by a civilization to which they are unable or unwilling to conform." These "uncivilized tribes" were to be "subjected to wise and firm regulation; and, without undue or petty interference, constant and active effort should be exercised to prevent barbarous practices and introduce civilized customs."[12] McKinley's instructions set a pattern followed through the next thirteen years, in which institutional concessions to Christian Filipinos typically entailed a reciprocal consolidation of exclusive American colonial authority to represent peoples labelled "uncivilized."

Civil government replaced military administration in the "pacified" Christian provinces in 1901. That same year the Philippine Commission further specified the distinction between "civilized" and "uncivilized" peoples by renaming the latter groups "non-Christian tribes." In the act of naming it began to treat the non-Christian tribes as discrete administrative subjects, to be represented apart from the rest of the Philippine population in the commission's annual reports. The origins of this separation, like the name "non-Christian" itself, lay in the historic pattern of Spanish colonial authority and its concomitant, Christian conversion. Like the Moros in the southern Philippines, whom the commission first included in the category of non-Christian tribes (a usage soon abandoned), most non-Christian societies had maintained substantial autonomy from Spain until the last decades of the nineteenth century. After 1898 they enjoyed a rejuvenated autonomy for several years. To the new colonial state, this autonomy presented itself as a problem, an absence of colonial power and knowledge.

"There is at present," the commission announced in its report in 1901, "a lamentable lack of accurate information as to the non-Christian tribes." This referred primarily to the non-Christian peoples of Luzon and the Visayas. The colonial state had already gathered considerably more information about the Moros, whom the Philippine Commission described as "the only ones among these non-Christian peoples which could afford any serious menace to public order." The Moros had been distinguished for separate administration as early as 1899 and thenceforth characterized decisively apart from Christian Filipinos in American colonial discourse. However badly American officials misunderstood Moro societies, by 1901 they had considerably more first-hand experience in the Islamic southern Philippines than they had among other non-Christian peoples, who still lived beyond the reach of regular colonial reconnaissance and administration. Unknown and therefore uncontrolled, the non-Christian tribes were nevertheless assumed not to pose any serious threat to colonial power.[13]

The greater part of the commission's report in 1901 on non-Christian tribes discussed slavery in Moro societies as one of the "highly objectionable customs" that presented significant problems of administration. But near the end of that discussion the ethnogeographical scope expanded. "It should be understood," the commission cautioned, "that slavery in the Philippines is by no means confined to the Moros. It is common among the wild Indonesian tribes in the interior of Mindanao and among the wild Malayan tribes of northern Luzon." Interestingly, the report made only the most fleeting mention of the practice of "head-hunting" among Igorots, the name used to signify collectively most of the mountain-dwelling non-Christians of northern Luzon's Gran Cordillera Central. Head-hunting very soon became not only the most publicized of "objectionable customs" on the cordillera, but also part of an identity, as "wild" or "savage" headhunters, that the colonial regime invented for the Igorots and deliberately perpetuated, even as the state also paraded the suppression of head-hunting as a triumph of its civilizing mission.[14]

The specific practices indicated in colonial discourse as markers of incivility—slavery, head-hunting, human sacrifice, and cannibalism—were initially interchangeable in an ideological space already created by primary assumptions about the existence of "barbarous practices" and "highly objectionable customs." The knowledge that there were "wild Malayan tribes" and "wild Indonesian tribes" was enough for Americans to assume the existence of such practices, much as some Americans had earlier imagined slavery to be a problem throughout the Philippines because the islands were populated by "tropical races."

When most Americans assumed that all Filipinos were clearly unqualified for self-government, there was little point in demonstrating that some were much more, or less, civilized than others. In fact, the non-Christian population remained a low priority of the colonial regime for several years while it concentrated on defeating revolutionary movements in the Catholic lowlands. In 1901 the Philippine Commission apologized that it had "been able to give but slight attention to the interests of" non-Christian tribes while engaged in "the more important work of organizing provinces inhabited by civilized natives."[15] Thus the Filipinos' active resistance to conquest in the lowlands of Luzon and the central Philippines shaped the context in which colonial power was extended into non-Christian regions. The non-Christians were a lesser priority because they seemed to pose no substantial danger to U.S. colonial rule and, for the same reason, they could be excluded from formal concessions of self-government accorded (in very different ways) to Christian and Muslim Filipinos. This practical order of conquest and cooptation, however, soon gave the non-Christian population a special meaning in colonial discourse. It enabled the colonial state to imagine the non-Christian regions as a frontier with "wild" people in a state of nature, untainted (in American eyes) by Islam, Spain, Catholicism, or Philippine nationalism.

The very characteristics that enabled and exemplified non-Christian resistance against Spanish colonialism now reappeared as elements in the new colonizers' reconstruction of non-Christians as ideal colonial subjects. The non-Christians' seemingly natural state and wholly uncivilized condition made them theoretically amenable to total control and reformation.[16] Being the most perfect colonial wards, the non-Christian tribes became a test for colonial benevolence; would they be civilized and protected or destroyed and abused in the manner that Native American Indians had suffered during the past "century of dishonor"?

In the early years of U.S. rule it was common for white Americans to think of all Filipinos in terms of analogies to Native American Indians.[17] Quickly, the analogy narrowed to a focus on non-Christians and Moros as "tribal" peoples. This coincided with the colonial state's shift of descriptive categories for Christian Filipinos, from a conglomeration of tribes collected under the term *Filipino* as a merely geographical umbrella to a generalized use of the term *Filipino* as a national designation. The distinction between ethnological and national subjects was reflected in the literary forms officials used to describe different segments of the population.

Narratives of exploration and scientific investigation dominated colonial discourse on the non-Christian tribes throughout the years of U.S. rule. In contrast, Americans used political narratives increasingly to explain and understand their colonial relationship with Christian Filipinos. Narratives about "insurrection," negotiation, surrender, appointments to office, electoral maneuvering, and so on quickly became the prevalent form of official colonial reportage on the lowland Philippines. Racial science, as in ethnological and anthropometric studies of the Filipino population, continued to be practiced under colonial auspices, but its public prominence was much greater when it focused on non-Christians.[18]

The disjuncture of narrative styles widened as American officials responded publicly to the claims and aspirations of Philippine nationalism. These responses typically denied Filipino fitness for independence and offered colonial rule as the means to achieve nationalist desires, yet nevertheless recognized a dialogical relationship with Christian Filipinos, particularly the national and provincial elites. This relationship was compelled not only by the colonial state's need for collaboration from an indigenous ruling class after a long and costly war of conquest, but also by the Filipino national elite's access to communication with the small but determined anti-imperialist lobby in the United States. Meanwhile, non-Christians had no access to communicative and representative institutions in Manila. Without the power to speak for themselves beyond local relations, they became publicly voiceless subjects, to be represented by the scientific mission of the Bureau of Non-Christian Tribes and its successor, the Ethnological Survey.

The Philippine Commission organized the Bureau of Non-Christian Tribes in 1901 to conduct "systematic investigations, in order to ascertain the name of each tribe, the limits of the territory which it occupies, the approximate number of individuals which compose it, their social organization and their languages, beliefs, manners, and customs, with especial view to learning the most practical way of bringing about their advancement in civilization and material prosperity." This kind of "reliable information" was necessary, the commission explained, "if we are not to fail in our duty toward the savage or half-civilized Philippine peoples." [19] The Ethnological Survey and succeeding generations of independent anthropologists continued the work of creating a fund of scientific knowledge about the non-Christian tribes. In contrast, there was little formal ethnographic study of Catholic Filipinos during the colonial era and after.

The Bureau sent its first expeditions into the Gran Cordillera of central Luzon in 1902 and 1903. Until 1903, official knowledge still construed most of the regions inhabited by non-Christians as unexplored territory. This judgment changed rather dramatically by the end of the year. As early as January 1903, a representative of the bureau presented an "ethnographical exhibit" to the International Congress of Orientalists convened at the Hanoi Exposition. "The exhibit," reported David P. Barrows, the chief of the Ethnological Survey, "which consisted for the most part of photographs of racial types and maps, attracted considerable attention, especially from those interested in scientific work." [20] By September 1903, Barrows expected soon to "be able to report that a preliminary exploration of all portions of the Archipelago has been finished; that the field parties of this bureau will have explored every region of the islands, visited every non-Christian tribe, and secured the geographical and ethnological data necessary to complete our knowledge of the Archipelago." [21] Colonial authority had been sufficiently extended into the mountains of northern Luzon to facilitate the field collection of a massive exhibit for the 1904 Saint Louis World's Fair. The highlight of the Philippine exhibit was the display of "savage" villages, including the villagers themselves.

Unable to speak for themselves in the colonial center at Manila or in the metropole, non-Christian people could only be spoken for, represented in anthropometric studies and museums, or, in the quintessence of objectification, displayed alive at world's fairs. But, as consistent as these representations were in many respects, their exact meanings and implications depended upon context. For example, the Philippine Census and the Bureau of Non-Christian Tribes both displayed non-Christians as uncivilized subjects of colonialism, but their different effects provoked disparate reactions from Filipino nationalists.

The 1903 Philippine Census attempted to survey the entire population of the Philippines, including the non-Christian tribes. Like all such enterprises, the census was an objectification of the population that helped define and empower the reach of the state. To this extent the work of the Bureau of Non-Christian Tribes fit comfortably within the census, but the method of data collection and the project's consequences made the census decisively different for the Christian population. Many nationalist leaders eventually voiced loud objections to the activities of the Bureau of Non-Christian Tribes and its successors after the exhibit at Saint Louis, but none appears to have objected to the census. In fact, Filipinos were actively involved in both projects. A large staff worked as census takers, compilers, and supervisors. Filipino provincial governors and mayors also aided the Bureau in the collection of ethnographic information and exhibits for the Saint Louis fair and an ethnological museum in Manila, but non-Christians themselves do not appear to have shared any comparable role in assembling the exhibit, at least not in a formal sense.[22]

Filipinos' active participation in census taking must be understood in relation to the purpose of the census. Most importantly in this regard, the 1903 census laid the groundwork for creating a legislative body of Filipino delegates who would represent the nation. The Philippine Organic Act of 1902 provided for the establishment of the assembly two years after the publication of the census, pending presidential certification of peaceful obedience to U. S. rule. Published in 1905, the census did more than just satisfy a precondition for the assembly that opened in 1907. Both institutions represented the invidious ethnogeographic division of the Philippines. Only the "regular" provinces with "civilized" Filipino populations could elect and send delegates to the assembly. The "special" provinces populated by Muslims and non-Christians, officially classed as "wild" and "uncivilized" in the census, were not permitted to represent themselves in the assembly. They were not considered Filipinos.[23]

From the assembly's inception, the officially pro-independence *Nacionalista* Party led the deputies in a largely cooperative relationship with the U.S. administration.[24] The assembly became the meeting ground for provincial politicos and, as Benedict Anderson has astutely observed, the forum for their intermixing, intermarrying, and congealing into a national oligarchy.[25] The assembly may not have been a radical institution, but it must be taken seriously as a nationalist one.

No matter how partial the deputies may have been to particular interests, the assembly claimed to represent the nation and not a few times did so in conflict with the expectations of its American colonial sponsors. In addition to giving its members material power and patronage, the assembly became an institutional symbol of national civility. The speaker of the assembly, Sergio Osmeña, called it an "instrument of liberty." The assembly provided a podium from which nationalist speeches, resolutions, and citizens' petitions could be broadcast throughout the Philippines and abroad. Given the consensus that "fitness" was the qualification for self-government, it was also a stage on which Filipinos could demonstrate to the world that they could govern themselves.[26] As a public theater, the assembly was the principal site where American officials exchanged public recognition of the nationalist elite for the elite's collaboration with U.S. rule. At the same time, the assembly helped to reinforce the classification of non-Christian tribes as uncivilized or wild, making them an increasingly valuable ideological resource for the colonial state.

The visit of Secretary of War William Howard Taft to the Philippines to inaugurate the assembly in October 1907 illustrates that legislative body's powerful dual action in reorganizing colonial discourse. Taft had engineered the transfer of colonial patronage from the older, Manila-based *ilustrados* to the younger generation of provincial politicians led by Osmeña and Manuel L. Quezon in the *Partido Nacionalista*. His inaugural speech acknowledged the new political alliance. He corrected the impression that he had been dismayed by the election of the new *Nacionalistas* over his old friends from the *Partido Federal,* praising the assembly's leaders as good "conservatives," despite their public calls for immediate independence. Then he laid out the larger purpose of the assembly within the scheme of extending self-government through stages of discipline and surveillance.[27]

Taft advised the legislators: "As you shall conduct your proceedings and shape your legislation on patriotic, intelligent, conservative and useful lines, you will show more emphatically than in any other way your right and capacity to take part in the government and the wisdom of granting to your assembly and to the people that elected you more power." Then he asked, rhetorically, if the assembly would show its fitness for the extension of more self-government, "or shall it by neglect, obstruction, and absence of useful service make it necessary to take away its existing powers on the ground that they have been prematurely granted? Upon you falls this heavy responsibility."[28]

Taft's recognition of the Christian Filipinos' "right and capacity" for self-representation and progress toward self-government threw into bold relief the new significance he assigned to the non-Christian tribes. Shortly after returning to the United States, he remarked on their importance in a letter to the colonial secretary of the interior, Dean C. Worcester, who had created the Bureau of Non-Christian Tribes in 1901 and governed the non-Christians autocratically after they were set aside in special provinces in 1905. "Nothing," wrote Taft, "more clearly shows the inability of the Filipinos really to govern themselves as the mistreatment or utter neglect of treatment with which they visit the non-Christians . . . How little the virulent anti-imperialist realizes the difficulties of government at all in the Philippines, and how far from any possible success would an immediate independence miss the end sought!"[29] In this way the colonial state could posit a continuing and safely compartmentalized internal colonizing mission among designated minority groups even as it sponsored the escalation of self-government among the majority population of Catholic Filipinos.

Invidious comparisons of "civilized" Filipinos and "wild tribes" were not, in and of themselves, objectionable to Filipino nationalists. Colonial concessions to Filipino participation in civil government heightened and recast the meaning of distinctions between "civilized natives," who could anticipate the grant of independence through collaboration, and the "wild," "uncivilized," "non-Christian," "tribal" others, who helped to define Filipino progress toward self-government by their very exclusion. There is no record of Filipino nationalists demanding equal concessions for the non-Christians. Yet, while the inferiority of the non-Christians highlighted the civility of Catholic Filipinos, it also posed a danger to their claims of fitness for independence.

The Philippine exhibit at the Saint Louis World's Fair seems to have been the turning point after which the national elite came to regard almost all public displays and representations of the non-Christian tribes as a threat to claims for national capability and honor. Similar concerns had arisen before, most famously when an Igorot village became the central attraction at the Exposition of the Philippine Islands held at the Zoological Gardens in Madrid in 1887. The *ilustrados* resident in Europe participated in competitions in the arts and sciences, always looking for opportunities to demonstrate their own talents and advertise the best qualities and products of the Philippines. Ethnographic objects and reports about highland peoples had been circulating around Europe since at least the early part of the decade, including some accounts by Filipinos. The Madrid exposition, however, put live Igorots on display. *Ilustrados* objected that this was an assault on human dignity and a misrepresentation of the Philippines.[30]

From Berlin, Jose Rizal advised his friend Ferdinand Blumentritt, an Austrian ethnologist, to avoid the exhibit. "From what I understand," he reported, "it is not an Exposition of the Philippines at all but only of the Igorots." When a Moro woman in the exhibit died, Rizal responded more emphatically and, in some ways, inclusively. In another letter to Blumentritt he mourned: "I have worked hard against this degradation of my fellow Filipinos so that they should not be exhibited among the animals and plants! But I was helpless. One woman has just died of pneumonia . . . I would rather that they all got sick and died so they would suffer no more. Let the Philippines forget that her sons have been treated like this—to be exhibited and ridiculed!" But it was a daughter of the Philippines who had died, not a son. Graciano López Jaena, the founder of *La Solidaridad,* the leading journal of the *ilustrados'* propaganda campaign, called the treatment of the people on display an "inhumanity" and he complained that no Filipinos were involved on the commission that planned the exhibit.[31]

The people who remained subject to ridicule for years thereafter were not so much the Igorots as the *ilustrados.* When an Augustinian friar published a pamphlet claiming that the Igorot village displayed at Madrid represented the "actuality" of the pre-Hispanic Philippine life that Rizal and other *ilustrado* historians called an ancient civilization, Rizal retaliated against the friar in print by saying that "it is a humiliation for us, Igorots and *indios* though we may be, to be governed by the people Europe has discarded as representatives of darkness." Another *ilustrado,* Antonio Luna, wrote angrily about passing young women on the streets of Madrid who would stare and say, "Jesus, how horrible . . . an Igorot!" [32]

This earlier history and, one must suppose, the recent experience of struggling against American depictions of Filipinos as a congeries of tribes rather than a nation combined to stir some concerns among *ilustrado* circles in 1903, when the plan to send live people for display in Saint Louis became known. Filipino provincial administrators and scholars had been involved in the collection and preparation of materials for the exhibition from the beginning. The esteemed Dr. Leon Ma. Guerrero and Pedro A. Paterno, a fanciful historian and notorious political turncoat, led Filipino participation on the Manila-based Exposition Committee. Much like the 1903 census, the work seemed to indicate recognition of community in modern science and technical skill, until it was disrupted by the quarrel about sending live people for display. But this dispute was apparently quieted by a decision to send an Honorary Board of Filipino Commissioners to the fair. Dr. Trinidad H. Pardo de Tavera chaired the board, which consisted of more than forty leading scholars, attorneys, businessmen, and government officeholders. Many of them, such as Mariano Trias, Benito Legarda, Juan Villamor, Tomás G. Del Rosario, and Epifanio de los Santos, had held high-ranking military and civilian positions in the Philippine Republic of 1898. Although they would not be put in an exhibit, they were certainly given the opportunity to display themselves. [33]

The actual exhibit caused a series of uproars when it opened. The village displays of Negritos and highland peoples quickly became the center of attention, dismaying Filipino commentators in Manila and troubling American colonial administrators, too. The presentation of the national elite as civilized, capable, and necessary for governing the larger population was perfectly acceptable to all parties, but the representation of "uncivilized" non-Christians as central to the problem of colonialism in the Philippines was not. The Saint Louis World's Fair marked a transition in the significance of the non-Christian tribes that brought to the fore potential contradictions of meaning in the representation of Filipinos in the United States. [34] But, far from challenging the belief that the non-Christian tribes were uncivilized, this only underscored the widespread agreement that the non-Christian tribes were properly colonial subjects.

For American anti-imperialists, the exhibit highlighted the shift from an opposition to conquest frequently based on racial ideology to a long-term lobbying effort on behalf of Philippine independence. Critics of colonial rule working in the Democratic Party during this presidential election year crafted a platform that declared Filipinos "inherently unfit to be members of the American body politic," but this position precluded only the granting of U.S. citizenship and not the retention of Filipinos as colonial subjects.[35] Meanwhile, Moorfield Storey was just beginning to realize the anti-imperialists' dependence on representative Filipino nationalists who could "come to the assistance of their friends in the United States and strengthen our hands by making it perfectly clear to the American people that independence is what they wish." His desire for this assistance grew when he attended the 1904 Democratic convention in Saint Louis. He did not comment directly on the World's Fair, but expressed concern that Taft and the colonial establishment were creating "the impression that the Filipinos themselves do not desire independence but are content with their present position."[36] Indeed, the tour of the Honorary Board of Filipino Commissioners from the West Coast to the East and their presence at the World's Fair tended to reinforce such suppositions.

The board's president, Pardo de Tavera, had accepted his appointment with the promise that "all of our efforts will be directed toward strengthening the bonds that bind us to the American nation and assisting in the great work of civilization, peace, and order."[37] Even when one member of the board voiced concerns to a Saint Louis newspaper that the display of Igorots and Negritos was part of a Machiavellian plot by the Republican colonial regime "to justify their paternal grip on the islands," he stopped far short of calling for independence. Instead, he complained of the cost and need for American civil service employees in the Philippines and the deleterious effects of a "prohibitive tariff" that limited Philippine exports to the United States. (The tariff was removed in 1909 and thereafter the export sectors of the Philippine economy were tied to the U.S. market.) Moreover, he accepted fully the ethnological division represented in the Philippine Exhibit, even as he protested its portrayal and effects. The seven million Filipinos were "civilized Christians, orderly, peace-loving and law-abiding," he said, but the "anthropoids" featured at the fair were a distinct minority who, "like all backward and non-progressive races, are rapidly dying out."[38]

Storey's commitment to the ideal of equality approached a kind of cultural relativism that separated him from most of his anti-imperialist companions as well as most Filipino nationalists. He advised the Democratic presidential candidate Alton B. Parker and repeatedly cautioned fellow anti-imperialists not to discuss the matter of whether Filipinos were "fit" for independence because that "phrase implies that we have the right to determine what their fitness is and the result is that we may hold out indefinitely because our judgment is that they are not fit." Storey believed that "we have no right to deny them independence because the persons that happen to be in power think that people whom they do not understand cannot govern themselves." Yet, his rejection of colonial racial hierarchies coexisted with his growing dependence on a Philippine elite whose ability to speak in the United States was occasioned by their rise through colonial institutions.[39]

Taft and the colonial regime were aware of the racial tensions of imperial politics even as they created them. In June 1903, while still governor general of the Philippines, Taft was told by Clarence Edwards, the chief of the Bureau of Insular Affairs in Washington, "that it was rather unfortunate that we should have inserted in the printed reports of the commission the various pictures of the aborigines or savages in the Philippines. I have often heard it remarked in Congress that from the looks of the people in those photographs we ought not to bother much with the Philippines." Edwards's attempts to explain that the portraits were not representative seldom countered the initial effect of the photographs. The photographs gave "as false an impression of the people of the Philippines as would a representation of Indians and Negroes properly represent the inhabitants of the United States." For balance he urged Taft to send more "educated Filipinos" to the upcoming Louisiana Purchase Exposition. Photographic displays of the non-Christian tribes did not again appear in the commission's published reports.[40]

The ambiguous implications of the uncivilized resurfaced at the fair when the display of "wild tribes" proved the major attraction of the Philippine exhibit. Taft became concerned not to leave "any possible impression that the Philippine Government is seeking to make prominent the savageness and barbarism of the wild tribes either for show purposes or to depreciate the popular estimate of the general civilization of the islands." Negritos and Igorots were compelled to wear short pants over their G-strings and signs were posted to indicate their relative inconsequence as a proportion of the Philippine population. President Roosevelt's interest in the issue prompted much publicity, which gave leading anthropologists the stage to protest against the sartorial changes for destroying the great "scientific value of the display." Traditional dress was soon restored, the authenticity of the exhibit reinforced by the authority of anthropological science.[41]

Clarence Edwards and Taft hesitated briefly in 1905 when the commercially operated International Anthropological Exhibit Company applied for permission to furnish non-Christians for expositions around the country, but they put aside their fear that Americans would believe that "the majority of the people of the Philippines are similiar to the Igorrots and Negritos."[42] The company received its permission from Washington and then from Worcester, the secretary of the interior in Manila, with the proviso that it post a bond to cover the Igorots' well-being and promise to return the bodies of any who might die overseas.[43] Alien diseases and the climate had claimed lives at Saint Louis, as had substandard travel and other conditions.

Worcester soon turned strongly against "the running of these Igorot shows in the States which certainly do the Igorots no good." As secretary of the interior, he had direct control over the administration of the non-Christian tribes. Using his powers freely, he issued orders compelling Igorots recruited for exhibitions to reside only in their home villages, making it illegal for them to leave.[44] Worcester reserved for himself the right to decide who could represent the non-Christian tribes to the United States. He dominated public discourse about the non-Christian tribes through the remainder of his colonial service, earning a perfectly bifurcated reputation as humanitarian hero and archvillain.

To Filipino nationalists, Worcester was among the most reviled people in the Philippines. His misdeeds and insults were legion. Along with popularizing images of "wild tribes," "savages," and "head-hunters" through the Bureau of Non-Christian Tribes, he made many disparaging public remarks about the character of the Christian Filipinos, comparing them unfavorably with Moros and non-Christians. And, in 1908, when the nationalist newspaper *El Renacimiento Filipino* called into question his integrity, labeling him a "bird of prey" who used his government post to enrich himself through investments and inside deals, he bankrupted the paper through a libel suit. His brusque readiness to accuse others of malfeasance and incompetence stirred many conflicts with Americans, too, in which racial hierarchy played no part.[45]

On the other side, high officials of the colonial regime saw Worcester as a man of science and a model carrier of the white man's burden, if sometimes too abrasive. William Cameron Forbes told the visiting secretary of war in 1910 that he believed Worcester could "properly pose as the redeemer of four hundred and some odd thousands of human beings whose condition is so vastly better than it was before as to make a very, very powerful argument in favor of the American administration of the Islands."[46] Worcester energetically propagated this view of his work. He considered himself "the voice of God" among the non-Christians and unabashedly informed Taft "that not one single measure for their betterment has ever been proposed by anyone but myself."[47]

For colonial hegemony to work, the colonial state had to sustain its influence over official nationalism while maintaining that Filipinos were not fit for independence, and official nationalists had to sustain the authenticity of their nationalism while simultaneously accepting the colonial order. The colonial state, the Philippine nationalist elite, and the anti-imperialists found themselves in a triangular relationship based on the ambivalent position of official nationalism. The American colonial state partially displaced the tension between colonial racial supremacy and Filipino nationalists' demands for honor by reformulating and managing the boundaries of the uncivilized.

Worcester's unique authority over the non-Christian tribes thus positioned him at a critical juncture in the consolidation of colonial hegemony, where science and humanitarian traditions combined with state power to construct uncivilized subjects as recipients of colonial benevolence. His autocratic rule over the non-Christian tribes helped to insulate him from the everyday demands of recognizing political relations with Filipino nationalists, but it also placed him at a potential flash point for conflict. It was more than coincidence that Worcester first exhibited administrative interest in episodes of enslavement involving non-Christians in 1905, just as the development of power and knowledge over the non-Christian tribes was giving them special significance in the complex triangular relations of imperial politics.

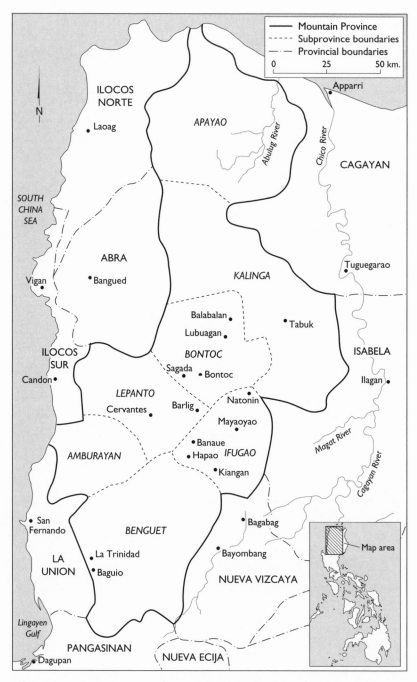

Map 4. Mountain Province, Northern Luzon, c. 1913.

CHAPTER NINE

Non-Christian Slaves and Filipino Subjects

Despite Dean C. Worcester's long involvement in the Philippines as the chief guardian and investigator of the uncivilized, he took no action against slavery until 1905. He exhibited no special concern about the issue when the first detailed reports of slave taking and trading involving non-Christians in northern Luzon reached Manila in 1903. Ten years later, when challenged by Filipino nationalists and American anti-imperialists to explain this lapse, Worcester claimed, weakly and incorrectly, that he had been out of the country at the time. He insisted that he did not learn about these conditions until, as he put it, "[m]y personal attention was forcibly drawn to this matter when I first inspected Nueva Vizcaya in 1905."[1]

Given the common American assumption that slavery was one of the "objectionable practices" endemic to the life of the "wild tribes," the changing terrain of imperial politics seems a better explanation for Worcester's delayed reaction. He developed a special interest in the problem of slavery only when it merged with his institutional mission to guard the non-Christian tribes as innocent wards of the colonial state. In 1903, however, the practice of slavery among the non-Christian tribes in northern Luzon came to the attention of American colonial officials at a transitional moment. They had not yet consolidated their new special relationship with the tribes nor had they resolved the problem of slavery in Mindanao and Sulu. Reckoning with slavery among the non-Christian tribes of northern Luzon introduced another potential source of embarrassment. In addition, the first reports of slave trading in northern Luzon presented a new problem, unlike anything faced among the Moros.

In early 1903, the American colonial state still depended upon an upward gaze from the lowlands for observations of the highland non-Christian tribes. The first reports on slavery among the non-Christians originated in the capitals of Isabela and Nueva Vizcaya Provinces in the Cagayan Valley, adjacent to the Gran Cordillera. Although these reports mentioned slave raiding and trading among the non-Christians up in the mountains, they focused on the purchase of non-Christian slaves by Catholic Filipinos in the valley towns. Furthermore, the reports implicated the Filipino governor of Isabela in slave trading at a time when plans to expand colonial self-government through the future Philippine Assembly were just beginning to unfold.

In April 1903, the American senior inspector of the Philippine Constabulary stationed in Ilagan, the capital of Isabela Province, reported that it was "a common practice to own slaves" in the province. He said that Christian Filipino landowners purchased slaves "from Igorrotes and Calingas who steal same in distant places from other tribes." Boys and girls reputedly sold for about one hundred pesos; "men 30 years old and old women [are] cheaper." After purchase, they "are generally christened and put to work on ranch or in house, and I think generally well-treated." In recent months "a number" had been sold in Ilagan, including, so he was told, three purchased by Francisco Dichoso, the provincial governor. This attracted the attention of Governor General Taft, who immediately asked to see a complete account on the matter.[2]

The senior inspector could not confirm that Governor Dichoso had actually purchased slaves, but he did describe the practice of "buying and having slaves." This was "very common during the Spanish occupation," not just in Isabela, but throughout the Cagayan Valley, from Cagayan Province in the north to Nueva Vizcaya Province in the south. The practice continued under American colonial rule.[3] The inspector collected information about twelve apparent slave sales in the provincial capital of Ilagan during the past year. He named the purchasers, the prices paid, as well as the gender and age of each person sold. The highest price went for a ten-year-old boy whom Blas Padagas, an Ilocano town councilman, purchased and resold for 180 pesos to Irineo Comaseng, a store manager, who then sent the boy to Manila, "where he now works for Irineo's sister living somewhere in Santa Cruz." The lowest price paid was 145 pesos for a twenty-five-year-old woman and a twenty-six-year-old man, purchased by another councilman, Pedro Gangan. Only the wealthy could afford to "keep slaves," and it was "apparently a good investment," thought the inspector, "as the salaries for field hands are about 4 or 5 pesetas a day, or a certain part of the crop." This kind of investment also carried risks, as a former councilman, Juan Paggao, found out when he purchased a twenty-seven-year-old man for 110 pesos, only to have him die about two weeks later.[4]

These slaves came from "the non-Christian Tribes living in this valley and surrounding Foothills and Mountains," which the inspector named as "the Calingas or Gaddanes, Igorrotes, Negritos, Ilongotes and Catalanganes." He described the "Igorrotes" and the "Calinga" (Kalinga in modern orthography) as "confirmed headhunters" who were "always at odds with their neighbors, even if they belonged to the same Tribe." In raids for heads, the inspector explained, "some prisoners are generally taken, with the idea, I think, of killing them afterwards, or selling them, as the Igorrotes do not keep slaves." These captives were then brought to lowland towns for sale, usually just one or two at a time. Once in the lowlands, the traders frequently worked through a Catholic Filipino "interpreter . . . on good terms with the Igorrotes," who could "take them around to the most likely houses in town, and no doubt gets a fee for his trouble." Sales were made for cash or goods. Traders bargained by showing "the fine points of their wares."[5]

After purchase, the inspector continued, "the slave is then put to work in the house, and shortly afterwards baptized, is treated well, learning to speak the prevailing dialect, and no doubt thoroughly appreciates the change." The inspector also reflected more critically that "the slave owner will make himself believe that he is doing a very commendable thing in rescuing an infidel, and having him brought up to become a good Christian." While he obviously concurred in this hierarchy of cultures, the inspector nonetheless recognized that a civilizing mission—though perhaps not his own—could serve as a rationalization for a master's domination. A slave was "of course assigned to the meanest and hardest work, as carrying water and the like, but nevertheless well treated, for fear that he should run away, and his only compensation is food and what little clothing he needs." If a slave did flee and looked for paying work, he would "find that nobody will employ him, as everybody in town knows that he belongs to his master, and a person doing so would incur the enmity of every slave owner." Thus the only path to liberation was "to run away to some distant place, from where his master would not be likely to get *noticias,* or where the practice of owning slaves is not prevailing."[6]

The Catholic Filipinos living in the Cagayan Valley were mainly from the Ibanag and Ilocano ethnolinguistic groups. Most grew tobacco, long a specialty of the region and virtually its only cash crop since the Spanish Tobacco Monopoly concentrated enforced production there in the early nineteenth century. The Ibanag were native inhabitants of the area who had converted to Christianity over the course of centuries of Spanish missionary work. The Ilocanos had migrated from northwestern Luzon, with encouragement from Spanish colonial administrators who wanted to relieve a labor shortage in the sparsely populated Cagayan Valley. Other immigrants, in smaller numbers, came from the hunger-plagued Batanes Islands at the northernmost tip of the Philippines and from the more heavily populated Visayas in the central Philippines. Some Moros captured by Spanish military expeditions were forcibly resettled in the Cagayan Valley, too.[7]

Slave trading continued among many of the uncolonized peoples of the Gran Cordilleras through the early nineteenth century.[8] As the demand for labor in the Cagayan Valley grew during the nineteenth century, the independent peoples of the mountains seem to have found a new, if comparatively small and clandestine, market for slaves, pawns, and other bound persons. Indeed, the disruptions of the revolutionary years and the American conquest removed some hindrances to raiding and trading in people, leading to a brief resurgence of the practice around the start of the twentieth century.[9]

In most of the Philippines, among the great majority of Filipinos who had experienced the dramatic social and cultural changes of Spanish colonization, slavery had not been practiced for almost two centuries. As we have seen, however, the institution acquired powerful new meanings as its actual social practice disappeared from daily life. Some of these meanings were evoked when, in August 1903, Governor General Taft questioned Governor Dichoso of Isabela about the reports that he had purchased slaves.

Slavery, Taft admonished the provincial governor, "is entirely contrary to the principles of the American Government and in the teeth of the Philippine [Organic] Act [of 1902], and if [the allegations are] true [it] requires action on my part." He asked Dichoso for a "frank statement of all the facts, and if slavery does prevail in your province, that we may be advised of it so that we may take radical steps to prevent its continuance." [10]

Dichoso denied ever purchasing slaves, but he did not dispute the existence of slavery in his province. "I could easily have done so [i.e., purchased slaves] in time of the late Spanish government, because I had good opportunities for doing so," he explained, and not "only one, but enough to harvest the tobacco on my plantation, and the other crops which I had planted." In Nueva Vizcaya and Isabela Provinces, "wealthy families" owned "slaves of the Ifugao tribe." In Cagayan Province to the north there were "but very few" Negrito slaves. The living conditions of these slaves had recently changed. "Under the past government there existed slaves," Dichoso acknowledged, but "since the glorious star-spangled banner has been unfolded over the province of Isabela, the slaves existing in the same, which had been purchased in that [i.e., Spanish] time and recently, are very well treated and seem to be members of the family, because the military authorities prohibited their masters from ill-treating them as they were wont to do." Many slaves ran away from cruel masters to seek "new masters who treat them well," as in the case of a forty-year-old Ifugao woman who fled from her mistress in the town of Echague in 1900, when the American military commander "enforced the prohibition of ill-treatment of slaves in said pueblo." [11]

From the details of this exchange, one aspect of Dichoso's reply should be elaborated on here, for it lay at the heart of the Philippine national elite's response to the issue of slavery over the next decade. Dichoso boldly proclaimed his "principle not to have slaves" and his desire that "personal liberty . . . reign supreme, as in every republic where the laws assure complete and real liberty, the liberty from slavery." He suggested that "an act should be passed to the end of eradicating this practice which has become general throughout the Cagayan Valley" and pledged himself "to be inexorable in the prosecution of slavery, as it is a crime and should be prosecuted as such." [12]

Taft immediately advised the secretary of commerce and police, Luke E. Wright, to include an "[a]ct denouncing slavery and kidnapping and kindred offenses as crimes" in the new penal code he was preparing to replace the Spanish colonial code of 1885.[13] Wright was a former judge from Tennessee, who had served as an officer in the Confederate Army during the Civil War. As it happened, work on the penal code bogged down in difficulties of Hispano-Philippine precedent, custom, and lack of bureaucratic will to push through a new code. The new code was never completed.

When Taft told the Committee on Insular Affairs in February 1904 that there was "some slavery in some of the Christian Filipino provinces that lie near to the mountain tribes," he told the congressmen a selectively edited story. He did not mention Governor Dichoso's alleged involvement and, where the original reports described slave raids carried on by non-Christian tribes in the mountains, Taft limited himself to saying "it was not uncommon for hill tribe parents to bring their children into a Filipino village and to sell a child to a wealthy man in the village who would use him as a servant." Hiding his concern about the inadequacy of anti-slavery statutes, Taft concluded by assuring the committee that such sales were "contrary to law, and we have directed prosecution in every case brought to our attention." [14]

Taft's selective focus on the purchase of non-Christian slaves by Christian Filipinos reflected the new significance of the non-Christian tribes. Colonial institutions had produced a new scientific knowledge about them and a refined ethnogeography of "barbarous practices." The 1904 Saint Louis World's Fair and subsequent colonial publicity made the Igorots lastingly known as headhunters, but not as practitioners of slavery. Head-hunting and slavery functioned as tropes that defined non-Christians and Moros as "uncivilized" for an American audience, though in very different ways. Slavery in the southern Philippines fit within existing European and American orientalist images of Islam that Americans unhesitatingly applied to the Moro societies. Head-hunting, in contrast, symbolized not moral corruption or tyrannical domination but an absence of law and social evolution; that is, it was a symbol of wildness.

Head-hunting could stand for an original, unrefined, and potentially benign human nature. It evoked condemnation as a practice that had to be suppressed by civilization, but, unlike slavery, it was not a social institution contrary to human nature. Head-hunting symbolized danger but not contamination, unlike finding slavery once again "under the American flag." It did not call forth comparisons with potentially troubling memories of the recent American past, as slavery inevitably did. Head-hunting allowed for a continuing American fascination without prompting anxiety about its suppression, whereas slavery had to be triumphantly and quickly abolished to avoid the kinds of embarrassments and entanglements the colonial regime had suffered in the southern Philippines. Head-hunting could be romanticized as a kind of heroic warrior individualism; any consideration of slavery would have disrupted American representations of the Igorot as noble savages by introducing elements of greed, exploitation, and illicit gain.

Although slavery and head-hunting were both thought of as barbarous practices, the distinction between them was quite important for shaping the new meaning of the non-Christian tribes under American colonial rule. The colonial regime avowed a special relationship, even friendship, with the non-Christian tribes that was based upon their reputed primitiveness as well as on their difference from Catholic Filipino nationalists. No comparable relationship was claimed with the Moros, whose antagonism against Catholic Filipinos was at least as strong. Americans were precluded by the resistance and religion of the Moros from idealizing them as they did the non-Christian tribes, but an elision of the practice of slavery was just as certainly a precondition for the sentimentalization of non-Christians in colonial discourse. Taft initiated that elision by telling congressmen that non-Christians were victims of slavery while neglecting to mention their active role in slave raiding and trading.

Despite Taft's confident assurances to Congress, such limited steps as were taken against slavery in the Cagayan Valley failed. In late 1904 the new American governor of Isabela Province informed Luke E. Wright, now the governor general, that he had been making arrests for slavery only to have the parties released by the court for lack of a law penalizing slavery as a crime. The provincial governor recommended, as Dichoso and Taft had, that "the Commission pass a law providing penalties for the sale and purchase of slaves." The request went unheeded, even though Wright had been the Philippine Commissioner charged by Taft to draft an antislavery law in 1903.[15]

When Worcester learned during his first inspection tour of the new special provinces in 1905 that young Ifugaos were being sold to Catholic Filipinos in Nueva Vizcaya Province, he called on the American provincial governor to make a detailed report. Governor Louis G. Knight sent depositions of witnesses and described the sale of several Ifugao children to Catholic Filipinos in Isabela and Nueva Vizcaya, as well as a case of two runaway slaves recaptured by municipal police and threatened with death should they flee again. Knight planned to turn the cases over to the district prosecutor, but could "find nothing whatever in the Penal Code defining or punishing as a crime the buying or selling of human beings." His report, which began by calling for the inclusion of antislavery provisions in the still-awaited new penal code, was passed on to Governor General Wright with Worcester's own admonition "that in case the Penal Code does not provide adequate punishment for such offenses, it should be so amended as to make it possible to inflict severe penalties upon those who buy and sell human beings in this Archipelago." Wright sent the papers to the attorney general, asking if the existing penal code provided "adequate punishment for such offenses." [16]

The attorney general confirmed that the cases described by Governor Knight, "in so far as they refer to the purchase and sale of human beings, are not provided for or punished under the existing Penal Code." Although there was no specific law against slavery, the attorney general advised that "such actions are punishable under that Code when they constitute either the kidnapping of a minor, illegal detention or serious threats, according to sections 481, 484, and 494 thereof." [17] With Worcester's support, three test cases were prosecuted on these grounds in the Court of First Instance at Bayombong, Nueva Vizcaya, in 1906. Convictions were returned in two cases, acquittals in the third. In one decision, the judge duly noted that, although "[t]he Congress of the United States has declared that human slavery shall not exist in these Islands, . . . no law, so far as I can discover, has yet been passed either defining slavery in these Islands, or affixing a punishment for those who engage in this inhuman practice as dealers, buyers, sellers, or derivers." [18] Still no antislavery law was decreed by the Philippine Commission.

Neither the legal questions nor the specifics of the Nueva Vizcaya cases were discussed publicly in Manila or the United States. The correspondence on slavery in northern Luzon always had bearing on the place of non-Christian tribes in colonial discourse, for discussion of slavery and abolition inevitably raised questions about progress, hierarchy, and the fulfillment of the colonial civilizing mission. The potential for political embarrassments over slavery remained minimal, however, as long as disputes about it were limited to a remote provincial court and internal correspondence. This situation changed in March 1907, when one of the convicted parties appealed to the Philippine Supreme Court.

Tomás Cabanag had been convicted for the crime of illegal detention and sentenced to eight years in prison. The provincial Court of First Instance found that he had paid one hundred pesos to Antonia Malanta, an Ifugao woman whom the court characterized as "a so-called Christian Igorrote," in exchange for a thirteen-year-old Ifugao girl named Jimaya. The young girl had for several years been living with her maternal grandmother, Oltagon, who had taken her in when her mother died and she was orphaned. Jimaya was forcibly taken from Oltagon by a male villager, Buyag, who brought her some distance to sell her to Antonia Malanta through her brother, Eusebio. Buyag claimed at the trial that he had taken Jimaya from her mother, Dudduli, who had sold Jimaya to pay her deceased husband's debts. Pawning children for debts was a custom among the Ifugao that American officials looked upon more apologetically than the kidnapping of children for sale. As it was, the court rejected Buyag's claim as inconsistent with the evidence that Jimaya was an orphan and had been living with her grandmother. Instead, it concentrated on Cabanag's disposal of the child. After holding her for a few days he told her he would take her back home, but, instead he took "the child weeping and crying and with such degree of force as was sufficient to intimidate said child and against her will carried her on horse back . . . to his residence in Cuayan in the province of Isabela . . . with the object and purpose of selling the child there into human slavery which [he did] to Mariano Lopez . . . [who] employed [her] in the manufacture of cigars, being beaten and intimidated by the wife of the said Mariano Lopez." [19]

The Supreme Court overturned the conviction of Tomás Cabanag for illegal detention because, in its opinion, the Ifugao girl he allegedly purchased and resold as a slave "was not physically confined or restrained so as to sustain a conviction for illegal detention." According to the Court, Tomás Cabanag "appears to have engaged in the business of buying in Nueva Vizcaya children to sell in the lowlands of Isabela." The transfer of children for considerations of cash or kind (typically livestock) "to pay the debts of their fathers" was, said the Court, a practice "termed a sale" in the Ifugao's "native language." Yet, the court found "no proof of slavery or even of involuntary servitude." [20]

Although Jimaya was apparently taken away against the desires of her grandmother, the Court accepted Buyag's testimony that she had actually been sold two years before by her mother, since deceased, to settle debts left by her dead father. Finding no definitive evidence of the transaction's terms "in respect of the use, treatment, and care of the child, the term of her service and her final disposition," the Court decided "the name applied to [the transaction] by the custom of the Igorots is not enough to establish that in truth and in effect it was a sale, or anything more than a contract for services." Even "if the facts in this respect be interpreted otherwise," the Court advised, "there is no law applicable here, either of the United States or of the Archipelago, punishing slavery as a crime." The Court said it found "much in this practice to condemn," but it insisted that "not even the abhorrent species of traffic apparently carried on by the accused justifies a sentence not authorized by law."[21]

Three American justices voted with the three Filipino justices to overturn Cabanag's conviction. An American justice, James B. Tracey, wrote the complex decision, which went beyond the immediate juridical question of illegal detention to discuss American and Philippine law regarding slavery as well as the historical ramifications of slavery. The Court was indeed correct about U.S. statutes. There was no law in the United States defining slavery itself as a punishable offense. When the famous Peonage Cases of the early twentieth century prompted Congress to add such a measure to the revised statutes of 1909, all that it did was revise—but not substantively alter—the Slave Kidnapping Law of 1866 and the New Mexico Anti-Peonage Law of 1867, neither of which prescribed penalties for simply holding a person in slavery. Only in 1948 would sale into slavery and holding a person in slavery become directly punishable under U.S. law.[22] As for the Philippine penal code, the Court declared that "[i]t is not unnatural that existing penal laws furnish no punishment for involuntary servitude as a specific crime." The reasons for this, it said, were to be found in Spanish and Philippine history:

> In the Kingdoms of the Spanish Peninsula, even in remote times, slavery appears to have taken but a surface root and to have been speedily cast out, the institution not having been known therein for centuries. It is only in relation to Spain's possessions in the American Indies that we find regulations in respect to slavery. In general they do not apply in their terms to the Philippine Islands where the ownership of man by his fellowman, wherever it existed, steadily disappeared as Christianity advanced. Among the savage tribes in remote parts, such customs as flourished were not the subject of legislation but were left to be dealt with by religious and civilizing influences. Such of the Spanish laws as touched the subject were ever humane and radical. In defining slavery, law 1, title 21 of the fourth *Partida,* calls it "a thing against the law of nature;" and rule 2, title 34 of the seventh *Partida* says: "It is a thing which all men naturally abhor." These were the sentiments of the thirteenth century.[23]

By extolling the supposedly humane character of medieval Spain and Spanish colonialism in the Philippines, the Court's historical survey identified the Filipinos as heirs to a Christian civilizing tradition so deep that laws against slavery had heretofore been unnecessary. The Filipinos' status as civilized Christians was thereby defined as the antithesis of slavery, a characteristic of "savage tribes."

Governor General James F. Smith had an antislavery bill drafted in response to the Cabanag decision in May 1907, but the Philippine Commission did not act on the bill.[24] It was hurriedly passing an array of other laws to preempt the jurisdiction of the Philippine Assembly, due to convene in October. This failure to act might suggest the issue of slavery was considered unimportant, yet there is substantial evidence that Worcester and other top officials considered slavery and the sufficiency of the antislavery laws consequential matters. The dynamics of colonial politics may provide at least a partial explanation for why American colonial officials evaded resolution of their own anxieties about the need for an antislavery law.

To the extent that the Philippine national elite's collaboration with U.S. colonialism did function as a historically specific variant of patron-client relations, this relationship had never been stronger than at the birth of the Philippine Assembly. Worcester, the high official most involved in the slavery prosecutions, had autonomous bailiwicks in the administration of the non-Christian tribes and colonial science. Other American officials depended far more on the Philippine national elite's cooperation in the making of colonial hegemony. Just before the Philippine Assembly convened for its inaugural meeting, William Cameron Forbes, a member of the Philippine Commission and the principal American sponsor of the leading *Partido Nacionalista* delegates, prevailed upon the assembly speaker Sergio Osmeña to have the party abandon a planned resolution calling for independence.[25] Perhaps the Philippine Commission sensed that a discussion of slavery and antislavery laws would be too volatile at a time when they wished to avoid an adverse reaction from nationalists they had just coaxed into backing off from calls for independence in the assembly. If this cannot be conclusively demonstrated for the period from 1903 to 1909, it was unmistakably the case after 1909, when the problem of slavery exposed the cultural and ideological contradictions of colonialism that were always lingering beneath the seemingly taut surface of patron-client collaboration.

Worcester eventually decided to press the Philippine Commission to act on an antislavery bill in 1909. He reintroduced the bill drafted in 1907 with a new title, An Act Prohibiting Slavery, Involuntary Servitude, Peonage or the Sale of Human Beings in the Philippine Islands. In a notice attached to the bill, Worcester explained that the Supreme Court's comments in the Cabanag decision certified the need for a new law and, he added, so did Cabanag's acquittal. Cabanag "had made a practice of buying and selling children." More importantly, Worcester argued that Cabanag was not unique. He claimed knowledge of "a considerable number of other instances of the sale of human beings," and also "a considerable number of cases in which Negrito children were held in a state of peonage closely approaching slavery."[26]

The bill proposed by Worcester prescribed a maximum five-year prison sentence for unlawful compulsion to labor, compulsion to work off debts, and the purchase, sale, or barter of human beings. It was promptly reviewed favorably by a select committee composed of two members of the Philippine Commission, Frank Branagan, an American, and Rafael Palma, a Filipino and leading member of the *Partido Nacionalista*.[27] A few minor amendments were made to the bill, which the commission accepted and passed on April 29, 1909. Two notable amendments were rejected.

The bill proposed to make it a criminal act to compel labor in return for a debt. Given the prevalence of advance payments in rural and urban labor relations, the committee feared that this prohibition would encourage "abuses on the part of farm laborers working under the share system and the employees of work shops." To preserve employers' and landlords' "legitimate" power, the committee asked that the words "compel him to labor" be replaced by "hold him to servitude."[28] Although Worcester did not accept this change, he revealed that his view on the subject of labor control was not really contrary to Branagan's and Palma's when, just a month later, the assembly passed a bill to require workers and sharecroppers to repay advances or have another employer or landlord repay the debt before they could change employment. As secretary of the interior, Worcester made a preliminary review of the bill for the commission. He was "in full and hearty sympathy with the purposes of this bill," but he believed that it provided for an unlawful imprisonment of debtors and, at the same time, did not clarify how "persons, who accept advances for labor which they are to render and then fail to render that labor, may be punished with sufficient severity to make such conduct less common than it is at present." Worcester recommended that similar but better-crafted legislation be given "very serious consideration" during the next legislative session.[29]

Branagan and Palma also wanted to include an exception to the antislavery bill's prohibition against the sale and purchase of human beings. They claimed knowledge "of one instance where a negrito child was purchased for the purpose of educating and protecting it" and proposed the exclusion of such purchases from the operation of the proposed law. They did not want to "subject a person to prosecution under this law for an act done for a good purpose." [30] The commission rejected this amendment, despite its logical similarity to the colonial civilizing mission.

In May 1909 the Philippine Assembly considered Worcester's bill for the first time. It was immediately sent to the Committee on the Revision of Laws, which agreed to approve the bill pending several amendments, the most important of which proposed that "the word 'slavery' be stricken out of the title of the Act, because it does not exist in the Philippines." The bill was returned to the full body of the assembly on May 19 and promptly tabled without further discussion. [31]

Worcester decided to address the assembly's failure to pass the law in his annual report for 1909, which would be published in the United States. He wanted to tell readers there that "[t]he stealing or the purchase of children of members of non-Christian tribes is lamentably common." It was an "infamous practice . . . carried on under the guise of *Christianizing* the children of the wild men." And, "if the conditions thus brought about are bad, those due to the peonage in which very numerous families, not only of the wild tribes but also of the more ignorant Christian peoples, are held by people of a certain class in these Islands, are worse and undoubtedly call for remedial legislation." Worcester recommended that the antislavery bill be presented to the assembly again at its next session and "a strong effort be made to secure its passage." Failing that, he recommended that the U.S. Congress take matters into its own hands to enforce the prohibition of slavery that was expressed in the Philippine Organic Act. [32]

In Washington, William Howard Taft was now president. The Bureau of Insular Affairs and the secretary of war, Jacob Dickinson, decided that the portion of Worcester's report that discussed slavery should not be published. In an internal memorandum, the assistant bureau chief Frank McIntyre raised two objections. "First," he said that "it creates the impression that slavery, involuntary servitude, peonage, and the sale of human beings are common in the Philippine Islands, have legal recognition, and cannot be prevented under existing laws"; and "[s]econd, that there is a threat, with apparent intention, of coercing the Legislative Assembly of the Philippine Islands into enacting this legislation proposed by Commissioner Worcester." McIntyre insisted that "slavery and involuntary servitude are more specifically corrected by legislation" in the Philippines than in the United States. He called Worcester's bill "an ill-digested effort" that would only make redundant the articles for illegal detention and coercion in the Philippine penal code. Rather than strengthening these statutes, the section penalizing the buying and selling of human beings would have the misguided and deleterious "effect of preventing parents from profiting from the labor of their children." [33]

With Dickinson's approval, McIntyre cabled governor general Forbes in Manila on 22 January 1910 to ask for Worcester's permission to delete the passage on slavery. "We are inclined to the opinion that reference to slavery in the Philippines is unwise," explained McIntyre. Worcester's report would "create [a] false idea here and would naturally offend the Philippine Assembly." [34] The cable arrived while Worcester was on an inspection tour, but he had given Forbes full authority to alter his report as necessary for publication. Forbes replied that he agreed it was "advisable to cut out this reference" to slavery. [35] It was excised and did not appear in the published version.

When Worcester learned of this editorial decision he raised no objection, but stood by his report and its recommendation that the matter should be dealt with by the U.S. Congress if the Philippine Assembly would not pass a law that penalized the sale of human beings at its next session. "As things stand at present," he told Forbes, "we should be placed in a somewhat embarrassing situation if any one thoroughly acquainted with the facts were to ask us what we had done to make effective the provisions of the Act of Congress [the Philippine Organic Act] prohibiting slavery." [36]

Forbes and the War Department were clearly concerned that pressuring the assembly on the matter of slavery would disrupt the politics of collaboration. Worcester, for what it is worth, was sincere in his distress about slavery in 1910, fearing that lack of action against slavery left the American colonial regime in an "embarrassing" position. The Philippine Assembly might have passed the bill minus the word *slavery,* per the recommendation of its Committee on the Revision of Laws. Instead, the bill was peremptorily dismissed from consideration. It seems that the delegates sensed a danger to their dignity in even a discussion of the question. Just two years before, Forbes had persuaded the assembly not to call for independence, even though the majority *Partido Nacionalista* had just campaigned on a platform of immediate independence. In some ways, slavery was an even more delicate matter, with an irrepressible potential for embarrassment that vacillation on the independence issue did not seem to hold for either Filipinos or Americans. Independence, on the one hand, was an issue of the present and the future. At the height of world-encompassing imperialism, the object of newly imagined nationalisms had to be projected forward, often as a utopian goal, beyond present delays and obstacles. Slavery, on the other hand, could only be an issue of the present and the past. In a progressive world dedicated to antislavery principles, slavery could not exist in the future; in the present, slavery could only be a problem to be eliminated; in the past, a problem to be explained.

For the colonial state, confronting slavery posed the potential embarrassment of exposing its own limited power and highly compromised moral position. For Filipino nationalists, allegations of slavery posed a problem for imagining the nation, not just in the present but also in the immemorial past into which nationalism projected its origins. The birth of Philippine nationalism in the late–nineteenth century was partially constituted by a new historical interest in the Philippine past, especially the state of civilization at the time of the Spanish conquest and its subsequent fate under Spanish rule. The problem of slavery thus rippled with potential embarrassments, overflowing the banks of present measures of national identity and civility to wash into the past, where the conception of a unified and civilized Philippine nation was tenuously rooted.

Governor General Forbes's political relationship with Speaker Osmeña and the assembly held together through most of 1910. By the end of the year, though, it was being stretched thin by the American regime's refusal to become more definite in its commitment to ultimate independence. This made *Nacionalista* leaders vulnerable to attacks from their left. Consequently, both the *Nacionalista* leadership and the commission came under increasing pressure to avoid the appearance of too much cooperation in public. The two legislative bodies deadlocked on many issues, including annual appropriations and the reappointment of the resident commissioners. Other issues, such as government land sales and the increase of American capital investments under the new free-trade tariff of 1909, were now debated heatedly as harbingers of the United States's intentions on the independence question. In the end, however, the Nacionalista leadership continued to betray in private its public demand for immediate independence. If the result reflected the existence of patron-client ties binding Filipino leaders to American colonial officials, then the continuing tensions between public demands for independence and private compromises indicated their limitations.[37]

By the end of 1910, the heightened tension of the independence question was loading discussion of antislavery laws with even heavier freight. In his annual address opening the legislative session in October 1910,

Forbes asked the assembly to pass the two bills Worcester had recommended during the previous session, one for the "control of labor" through enforcement of contracts and the other to penalize slavery. "While the law provides certain methods of punishing the practice of slavery, as for example, the law for illegal detention," the governor general told the delegates, it still "does not seem right that an enlightened and modern society should have no way of punishing the purchase or sale of human flesh." [38] Worcester again introduced the antislavery bill in the Philippine Commission, only to withdraw it in favor of asking the assembly to explain its actions on the bill during the previous session. No further steps were taken on either law in 1910.[39]

Worcester did not mention the antislavery law in his annual report for 1910, but he did write an extensive reply to remarks made by the secretary of war in Manila favoring the future jurisdiction of the Philippine Assembly over the non-Christian tribes. "At the outset," declared Worcester, "it should be clearly understood that the question involved is not one of the fitness of the Filipinos to govern themselves, but is one of their ability and fitness to dominate, justly control, and wisely guide along the pathway of civilization alien peoples, some of whom are warlike." The warlike aliens were, of course, the non-Christian tribes and not the Americans. Worcester reserved to the United States, and primarily himself, the fitness to colonize the non-Christian tribes properly. To stake this claim, Worcester emphasized the "progress" and "success of American rule" due to "friendly feeling," especially the "good state of public order" in which "head-hunting, slavery, and piracy are now very rare." Worcester's justification of colonial authority required the abolition of slavery, confirming his earlier perception that the problem of slavery left the regime in a potentially embarrassing position.[40]

Like the entire apparatus of colonialism, Worcester's argument for a higher level of internal colonialism within the Philippines rested on an ideology of racial and cultural supremacy. Catholic Filipinos were, he wrote, "profoundly ignorant of the wild men and their ways." They were "distinct peoples" who felt "mutual distrust and hatred." The Catholic Filipinos were thus not fit to be colonizers and so had "no just claim to ownership of the territory occupied by the wild men." Employing the wave-migration theory of Philippine settlement and colonization, Worcester argued that Negritos were the only people to have "territorial rights . . . based on title acquired by other means than conquest or purchase." Filipino nationalists who asked for control of the non-Christian tribes were "presumably actuated by high motives and a desire to promote the social development and the material prosperity of the people; but in making this claim, and at the same time denying the right of the Americans to control him [i.e., the Catholic Filipino] and his territory with a view to promoting the same desirable ends, he places himself in a somewhat anomalous logical position."[41] American rights and prerogatives thus superseded all others, by virtue of conquest, purchase, and racial superiority. The resemblance to apologies for slavery was more than just passing.

In January 1911 the commission again passed the antislavery bill, which the assembly promptly tabled by unanimous vote, without discussion. Forbes thought the assembly "showed up very badly, and acted in certain particulars very much like children." Upon reflection, he decided that he should have accepted some of the assembly's "foolish or useless but not distinctly harmful or immoral" bills, so that he could "use them as a lever to get some more important constructive work done." Perhaps, he surmised, "I came after the Assembly a little too hard."[42]

Worcester later said that he included a call for action on the antislavery bill by the assembly or the U.S. Congress in his annual report for 1911. He abided by Forbes's request to delete it, again, in order to "make a last effort to get the Assembly to act before appealing to Congress."[43] This last attempt to ease the bill through the assembly by restraining Worcester's desire to publicize the issue in the United States may have reflected concern for preserving honor and smooth interpersonal relations, as prognosticated by models of Philippine patron-client relations. But the theory behind the model is clearly insufficient to explain this history. There was something about the issue of slavery that was more important to the assembly delegates than the cultural imperative to bond with a superior power. They refused to cooperate.

In August 1911 the Philippine Commission eventually did what it had the independent power to do all along. It decreed an antislavery law for the Special Provinces—the Mountain Province and Nueva Vizcaya in northern Luzon and Agusan in eastern Mindanao—the principal homelands of most of the non-Christian population.[44]

When the legislative session began in October 1911, Governor Forbes repeated his requests for a law to penalize failure to fulfill labor contracts and an antislavery law for the provinces represented in the assembly. He prefaced the request by noting that the "non-Christian provinces" now had an antislavery law. The commission's antislavery bill for the lowland provinces was sent to the assembly in October, where it was held in committee until it was tabled, without discussion, in early February 1912.[45] The assembly did, however, pass another bill to control labor.

For the commission, the secretary of commerce and police, appropriately enough, reviewed the assembly's new bill to compel completion of labor contracts. Such legislation would be "very desirable," he advised, but probably unconstitutional. "Unfortunately," bemoaned the secretary, the U.S. Supreme Court had ruled in the recent Alonzo Bailey peonage case of 1910 "that although a statute in terms be to punish fraud, if its natural and inevitable purpose is to punish for failure to perform contracts of labor, thus compelling such performance, it violates the thirteenth amendment to the Constitution of the United States."[46] The commission then passed a modified bill prescribing criminal penalties for breach of labor contract "with intent to injure or defraud" either laborer or employer. On 20 January 1912 the assembly enacted it into law. During the next fifteen years this law was used with a predictably loose definition of "intent to injure or defraud." Thousands of workers and sharecroppers were prosecuted under what came to be known as the Peonage Act.[47]

The American colonial state's consideration of the problem of slavery was almost wholly divorced from its policies on labor control. In fact, Colonel McIntyre of the Bureau of Insular Affairs later used the so-called Peonage Act as remarkable evidence against Worcester's contention that peonage was widespread in the Philippines. "Had there been any law in the Philippine Islands under which a person could have been held in a state of peonage," McIntyre argued, "this legislation would have been unnecessary."[48] No one suggested that the Peonage Act violated the intent of the antislavery bills, nor were Filipino nationalists embarrassed by it, as they were by allegations of slavery. The assumption that Filipinos must be compelled to labor was a fundamental part of colonial ideology, as was the assumption that colonialism was legitimate because it was not slavery.

Fundamental issues of labor control could be kept separate from Worcester's allegations of slavery and peonage because nobody with an officially sanctioned voice in Philippine politics had an interest in exposing the contradiction between the colonial state's pursuit of antislavery laws and its support for repressive labor controls. The assembly delegates were virtually all men of wealth—landlords, employers, professionals, and planters. They and the American colonizers agreed on most labor issues. When the colonial state created a Bureau of Labor in 1912, its first director was Manuel Tinio, a former general in Aguinaldo's army and the owner of a hacienda in Nueva Ecija Province. A complex figure, Tinio squeezed neighboring peasants off their land through economic and legal pressure while he employed traditionally paternalistic debt relations to control labor on his own estate. Neither the Americans in the colonial regime nor the Filpino national elite wished to weaken the employers' and landlords' control of labor. The advocates of the antislavery bill never challenged these primary labor relations.[49]

The ethnogeography of colonial discourse on slavery directed attention away from labor relations in the production of major trade commodities. American investors and the wealthiest Filipino landlords were most concerned about labor in the sugar lands of Negros, Tarlac, and Pampanga, the hemp fields of the Bikol Peninsula, the coconut groves of Laguna, and the Philippine rice basket in the Central Luzon Plain. These were all lowland provinces with overwhelmingly Catholic Filipino populations. The discussion of slavery and involuntary servitude, including peonage, focused almost entirely on a commerce in people flowing from non-Christians to neighboring Christian Filipinos. When Worcester called in 1912 for the Philippine Assembly or the U.S. Congress to extend the provisions of the 1911 antislavery law to the regularly organized provinces, he said that the law's purpose was only "the adequate protection of the non-Christian tribes."[50] Politically deceptive, yes, but the struggle over antislavery laws was not a mask for an economic conflict.

If the colonial state's discourse on involuntary servitude skirted labor issues, it said little more about slavery as a relation between masters and slaves. Except for Governor Dichoso's reference to slaves harvesting tobacco and the testimony about the Ifugao girl Jimaya rolling cigars, there was scarcely any mention of commodity production in the discussion of slavery and peonage. The reports Worcester collected typically alluded vaguely to "housework" or laboring as a servant in the house of the purchaser, sometimes with the proviso that the slave was treated like a member of the family. None gave significantly detailed descriptions of the day-to-day lives of people taken as slaves, pawns, or peons. More thorough investigations of individual cases were made by constabulary officers during the height of the slavery scandal of 1912–1914, but these also concentrated on the way in which slaves and servants were acquired, with only brief questions about how they were treated and whether they were paid.

Worcester's inattention to the actual conditions of bondage stands in contrast to the colonial state's earlier fixation on the nature of relations between master and slave in the Moro societies of the southern Philippines. Colonial authorities had to attend to such relations in Mindanao and Sulu to defend their inaction against a "mild" Moro slavery. In contrast, slavery was a comparatively minor institution in northern Luzon. By 1903, the colonial state's position in the Catholic provinces of the Cagayan Valley was much more secure than it was in the southern Philippines. After the peak of the slave trade during the early 1900s, probably no more than several hundred non-Christians had been sold as slaves or pawns in the Cagayan Valley. Emancipation did cost individual masters their investment in one or two slaves, but the loss was not likely to have been devastating. Wealth was principally held in land, most labor was contracted through share tenancy, and political office depended on election or appointment from above, not on the support of retinues from below. Moreover, no frank defense of slavery was possible in the Cagayan Valley.

In contrast to the Moro leaders' open defense of slavery as a practice legitimized by authority of custom and religion, Catholic Filipino leaders such as Francisco Dichoso vocally denounced slavery. There were conflicts between masters and slaves, as evidenced by some cases of runaway slaves, but these did not present colonial officials with the kinds of political and moral dilemmas faced in the southern Philippines. The officials were not invested in defending an image of mild slavery that the runaways' actions challenged. Nor were they under pressure from critics in the United States to abolish slavery or explain their inaction, as their counterparts had been in Mindanao and Sulu.

Except for their inability to bring criminal prosecutions for engaging in slavery, Worcester and his superiors in Manila faced no other powerful constraints against their desire to end slavery in northern Luzon. There is no indication that they were concerned about emancipation causing social or political disruptions. Yet, Worcester did not order any special action when the Philippine Commission promulgated the 1911 antislavery law for the non-Christian provinces. It was not until November 1912, after the problem of slavery had been injected into public discussion of the Jones Bill in the United States, that he first began a systematic investigation of slavery and involuntary servitude.

CHAPTER TEN

Calumniating the Whole Filipino People

The lingering dispute over antislavery laws was brought to public attention in the United States by Governor General Forbes in the spring of 1912, just after the first version of the Jones bill for Philippine independence was introduced in the U.S. Congress. This changed the colonial discourse on slavery by directly tying the quarrel over antislavery laws to the question of Filipino fitness for independence. Extending the controversy to an audience in the United States, where the future of an independent Philippines might soon be decided, provoked a vocal rebuttal from Filipino nationalists.

Until the matter became public knowledge in the United States, Worcester's desire to push the Philippine Assembly to pass an antislavery law had been restrained by Forbes and the Taft administration in Washington. As long as the dispute was contained within internal channels of Philippine colonial politics, the Philippine national elite refrained from discussing the issue of slavery. The assembly simply tabled Worcester's antislavery bills without comment. But now these boundaries had been crossed and the dispute over slavery became a question of honor for Filipino nationalists. How the Philippine nation would be represented and the fate of Filipinos' quest for independence hung in the balance. This set in motion the slavery controversy of 1912–1914.

Forbes returned to the United States on leave in May 1912. He immediately organized a campaign to convince Americans to retain the Philippines as a colony indefinitely. At first he carefully protected his position within colonial politics by respecting the Filipinos' nationalist sensibilities. When Forbes sent copies of a briefing paper arguing against independence to Secretary of War Henry L. Stimson, he explained an "especial desire not to . . . express myself publicly on political matters or as to the capacity of the Filipino of whom I like to speak well and always do when I can truthfully, which is often."[1] By June his solicitous care to cultivate patron-client relations with the Philippine national elite had waned.

In an acceptance speech for an honorary degree from Harvard University, Forbes described American colonial rule as "the performance of a great work in the Philippine Islands . . . [to] bring freedom of opportunity to each and every one of the millions of these people." Forbes illustrated the United States's great success in this endeavor by pointing toward his "barometer of progress"—a collection of indices for production, trade, mileage of paved roads, the number of schoolhouses, and other categories of material improvement. Still, he cautioned against removing the force of colonial discipline too rapidly, for "the development of the individual must have progressed far enough to assure the permanence of the new order of things before the controlling hand is removed." And here Forbes drew upon antislavery principles as the ultimate measure of individual rights, progress, and readiness for self-government. The Filipinos' lack of preparation for independence was, he told the convocation, "well proven" by the assembly's repeated refusal to pass an act "prohibiting slavery and involuntary servitude." Upon "the premature withdrawal of the United States," warned Forbes, the elite would impose an oligarchic rule, "oppress the masses," and provoke popular uprisings damaging to foreign interests.[2]

Forbes's speech drew an immediate reply from Manuel Quezon, one of the two Resident Commissioners for the Philippines seated in the U.S. House of Representatives. Quezon was a leader of the dominant *Nacionalista* Party and the principal voice of Philippine nationalism heard in the United States from 1907 until he died while serving as president-in-exile during the Second World War. Like Sergio Osmeña, his sometime partner, sometime rival, Quezon rose from provincial to national politics on the basis of his own superior political skills and the sponsorship of prominent Americans, including William Cameron Forbes. And so, Quezon wrote to the Boston *Herald*, "I am sorry to have been enforced by the statement of my friend Governor Forbes, for whom I have the highest personal regard, to take issue with him. But I shall not, from personal motives, shrink from my duty of defending the interests of my people." The problem of slavery breached the boundaries of collaborative colonial politics. Quezon sent a copy of his letter to the anti-imperialist Erving Winslow, telling him "I am so provoked by the statement made by Mr. Forbes that I have lost no time in writing this answer." [3]

Of all the elements of colonial discourse Forbes employed to reinforce the necessity of Filipino subordination, Quezon singled out his remarks on slavery for rebuttal. According to Quezon, the allegations concerning the antislavery law were nothing but a contrived attack on the capacity of Filipinos for self-government. The Philippine Commission "sternly opposed . . . Philippine Independence" and also the intermediate step of expanding Filipino legislative responsibility to include the commission's duties as an upper house. For this reason, Quezon suggested, the commission passed the antislavery bill to place "the Philippine Assembly in a very awkward position." [4]

If the assembly passed the bill, it would "admit that there is such a thing as slavery and compulsory service in the Philippines, which is not a fact." But if the assembly rejected the bill, it "would be construed as indicating that the members of the Assembly were advocates of slavery." The assembly's refusal to pass an antislavery law was a decision to take the "course . . . of truth." This demonstrated the legislators' "moral courage." Pointing to Filipino participation in the same material improvements that Forbes celebrated, Quezon concluded that the assembly's record "shows conclusively that its foremost interest is to promote the welfare, uplifting, and liberty of the masses." [5]

Quezon did not rest after vindicating Filipino honor against Forbes's charges. Examining the question of slavery in more depth, Quezon turned its implications against the American colonial administration. A new antislavery law was unnecessary even if slavery existed, he said, because the Philippine Organic Act of 1902 already prohibited slavery. Thus the commission's antislavery bill "indicates either the incompetency or the negligence of the Commissioners." Nothing "akin to slavery or compulsory service" existed in the provinces under the assembly's jurisdiction, he declared, but "should there be such a thing in the territories inhabited by the few non-Christian Filipinos, which are under the exclusive control of the Philippine Commission, I am sure the slaveholders can only be the Government officials, who are appointed by the Secretary of the Interior, the Honorable Dean C. Worcester." [6]

If slavery did exist among the non-Christian tribes, then, Quezon declared, the governor general and members of the Philippine Commission were all "guilty in not enforcing and executing the constitution of the Archipelago." As for Forbes's concern that an oligarchy would "oppress the masses" in an independent Philippines, Quezon replied that the governor general's fear "would perhaps be lessened by reminding him of the fact that the present Government of the Philippines is a foreign oligarchy, and, by all laws of justice and nature, is worse than a native oligarchy." [7]

The exchange between Forbes and Quezon took place on a political terrain shaped by the hegemony of antislavery ideology. Their opposed arguments hinged on the common assumption that slavery was gravely wrong and a blot against those who practiced or permitted it. How a people responded to slavery thus became a serious test of their moral direction. This furnished Quezon with means to indict the colonial regime not just for dishonesty, but also for incompetence, negligence, and, implicitly, unfitness to govern. Neatly, Quezon reversed the very aspersions Forbes had cast on the assembly as the highest collective representative of the Philippine nation. To do this, however, Quezon allowed for the possibility that slavery existed among the "few non-Christian Filipinos." Quezon did not object to the categorization of non-Christian tribes in colonial discourse. Rather, he used their meaning as a repository of backward and uncivilized qualities by first circumscribing their representativeness with the qualifier "few" and then holding the colonizers responsible for their untoward condition.

The problem of slavery and the problem of the non-Christian tribes led, inevitably, to the problem of Worcester. A year earlier Quezon had told the American anti-imperialists that "Worcester is the man most hated by the Filipinos and yet he seems to be firmly rooted in the Philippine Government." [8] Soon afterward, Quezon began to finance the preparation of a critical history of American rule that was to be written by James H. Blount, formerly a colonial judge, who was sympathetic to Philippine nationalism. Blount's requests for repeated infusions of cash strained his relationship with Quezon, but all was smoothed over in March 1912 when he told Quezon about a "chapter subtitled 'NON-CHRISTIAN WORCESTER,' showing how that worthy digs up a new wild or 'non-Christian' tribe every now and then, photographs it, and sends it to General Edwards to publish, so as to arouse the Protestants." If the nickname "Non-Christian Worcester" could be spread through the

Philippine press, Blount thought "we could satirize him out of office." Quezon was then receiving rejection notices from potential publishers, yet he encouraged Blount. "As to the publication of your 'Non-Christian Worcester,' you can rest assured I will do everything in my power to accomplish that end." [9] If Forbes's speech gave Quezon his own opportunity to lampoon Worcester's autocratic dominion over the non-Christian tribes as a regime of "slaveholders," with Blount's help Quezon would disparage Worcester as unChristian, too.

In calling Worcester a slaveholder, Manuel Quezon drew upon and changed the nationalist tradition of depicting colonialism as a form of slavery. He did not apply the metaphor to colonialism as a whole, only to the relation between the non-Christians and Worcester. This was partly a result of his political position in colonial institutions and his role as a representative of the Philippines in the United States. He could not afford to alienate American officials by calling their rule slavery, but Worcester was a safe exception.

Other voices in the national elite were more inclined than Quezon to make militant appeals to popular nationalism. Just after the exchange between Forbes and Quezon, but still weeks before word of it reached the Philippines, *La Vanguardia,* a newspaper in Manila, published an editorial on the eve of the Fourth of July contrasting American colonials' loud celebrations of independence with the "mockery and sarcasm" they showed toward Filipinos "still struggling in the caverns of slavery . . . as if they were enjoying our being in chains." [10] *La Vanguardia* was the successor to *El Renacimiento,* the militant nationalist newspaper shut down in 1909 by Worcester's libel suit. *La Vanguardia* employed the metaphor of slavery without reservation, in keeping with the popular usage of the Katipunan tradition and seditious plays. It was possible to talk about Filipinos as slaves in this sense because popular nationalism understood the slavery of colonialism as an unwarranted state awaiting an imminent end.

Quezon's response to Forbes indicated that the developing scandal over slavery and antislavery laws would challenge the Philippine national elite's ability to articulate links between colonialism and oppression through the metaphor of slavery. Quezon played upon the slippage of meaning between actual and metaphorical slavery, but it forced him to limit the scope of his allegation that colonialism was a form of slavery to the non-Christian tribes and Worcester. The adverse meanings of slavery had to be contained at a safe distance from valued political relationships with Americans, the reputation of the Philippine Assembly, and the dignity of the Filipino people as a civilized nation progressing toward independence.

The national elite faced a dual problem. They looked upon the social institution of slavery as uncivilized and immoral, yet they also understood the status of being a slave as a reflection on the character and essence of the enslaved. Forbes argued that the assembly did not oppose slavery and that the Filipino people would be oppressed by an oligarchy if independence were granted. Because official nationalism sought to receive independence from above, it was closely attuned to the representation of the Philippines in the United States, where independence was discussed in terms of Filipino fitness for self-government. The national elite thus had to defend Filipinos against the charge that they tolerated slavery, in the double sense of holding slaves and being suited to accept the status assigned them by the slavery of colonialism. Although this impinged on their ability to make political appeals through the popular nationalist signification of colonialism as slavery, it did open another possibility. Taking colonial discourse at its word, Americans could be held responsible for Filipino freedom and, therefore, for its failure, too. If the United States would take credit for liberty in the Philippines, then, after more than a decade of colonial rule, it must also take responsibility for the persistence of slavery.

When accounts of the exchange between Quezon and Forbes reached the Philippines, the *Nacionalista* newspaper *El Ideal* published the story in August 1912 under a headline inspired by Rizal: "Where there are slaves and oppressors . . ." *El Ideal* concurred with Quezon's denial that slavery existed in the provinces under the assembly's jurisdiction. Like Quezon, it located the slaves and their American oppressors in the non-Christian territories, where, it said, "many cases could be cited to demonstrate the existence of slavery." For examples *El Ideal* referred to the employment of non-Christians in building a railroad to Baguio and the enforcement of "obligatory labor" in Davao, on Mindanao, where cruel punishments were inflicted on those who "resist this system of slavery." [11]

Two months later, *El Ideal* spoke about the antislavery bill placed before the Philippine Assembly on October 24. In an article entitled "Where There Are No Slaves," the paper again insisted that "there is no slavery in the Philippines." There was no need to pass laws for "a social ill that exists only in the imaginations of certain men, or, at the very most, in the regions that are under the exclusive control of the Commission and for which, it, with paternal solicitude, has already promulgated a law" against slavery. Perhaps, *El Ideal* wondered, the conflict over antislavery laws was "based on the interpretation given to the word *slavery*." [12]

El Ideal defined a slave as someone who had "lost consideration as a person in order to be a thing, acquirable by sale, by trade, by any of the means of acquisition that man uses in the ordinary transactions of life, and subject to the will and caprice of its owner." And so the paper asked, did "the Commission sincerely believe that men live in such deprived conditions in the Philippines?" If it did, *El Ideal* answered, "[p]arodying Rizal, we shall say: 'Where there are slaves, there are tyrants.' Where are these? What kind of government is this that, after more than twelve years of sovereignty, has not learned to guarantee the most primordial rights of the citizen?" By inverting Rizal's famous aphorism, *El Ideal* linked the character of Filipinos to that of American rule. It called on the commission to "save the sacred prestige of this people and also that of the regime, because a government that tolerates slavery for the space of more than twelve years is, in fact, a pro-slavery government." [13]

According to *La Vanguardia*, "intelligent public opinion" considered the antislavery bill "injurious, oppressive, and in the nature of an attempt to lower the democratic prestige and national pride of the race, and even the good name of the regime under which we have been governed for more than twelve years." The urgency of the matter, the paper made clear, lay in its false "reflection on the good name of our people, whose definite status is under discussion at this very hour." If the commission wrongfully convinced the American public that slavery existed in the Philippines, then the Jones bill would surely fail. "The fact is," declared *La Vanguardia*, "a people who devote themselves to certain primitive practices do not deserve the benefits of self-government." By the same token, however, the commission's imputation of slavery would be "counter to its interests," tantamount to an admission that it had done nothing about slavery for twelve years. [14]

Both *El Ideal* and *La Vanguardia* said they would support laws against forced labor or involuntary servitude, but not against slavery. It was the word *slavery* in the commission's bill that called forth special objections because of its particular associations. *La Vanguardia* also made a special point of faulting the commission for proposing a uniform law that made no "distinction between the Christian and non-Christian provinces," a distinction that *El Ideal* and Quezon were also very careful to make. To the question, "Does slavery exist at present in the Christian provinces of the Archipelago?" the editors of *La Vanguardia* answered certainly not, if by slavery one meant the existence of "the lowest social class, debased and despised," as it existed in Rome and the United States until abolished "by Christianity." Slavery could not exist anywhere in the Philippines, "much less in the Christian provinces," because "our civilization was quite advanced and humanitarian ideas regulated our social existence" long before the United States arrived. And because slavery did not exist in the present, it could not be expected to return in the future unless "Filipinos, instead of progressing, think of lapsing back into the barbarism of primitive life"—an impossibility if one believed in progress as a great natural force or a result of American colonial rule.[15]

All of the Filipino responses I have considered so far defined slavery in contradistinction to Christianity, civilization, and progress. *La Vanguardia* did this most explicitly. The rest, beginning with Quezon's rejoinder to Forbes, expressed these themes implicitly by marking the difference between Christian Filipinos and the non-Christian tribes, repudiating slavery, and assuming that the United States should be embarrassed if it had watched passively over slavery for twelve years. Slavery and the non-Christian tribes merged as representations of the "barbarism of primitive life," the threatening other against which official nationalism defined and defended itself in appealing to the United States for independence. This was why protests against the antislavery bill so often included the complaint that it made no distinction between Christian and non-Christian Filipinos.

Although official nationalism struggled to mark the Philippines apart from images of the uncivilized, it blurred the distinction between the colonial and the national. Official nationalism appealed to the United States for independence by aligning representations of Filipino desires and capabilities with American promises of future self-government. In the dispute over antislavery laws, nationalist newspapers posited a common Filipino and American interest in the reputation of the Philippines as a land without slaves or slavery. This community of interest did in fact exist with the Bureau of Insular Affairs in Washington and the anti-imperialists. The retort that allegations of slavery in the Philippines would discredit colonial claims of progress and benevolence was surely a strategic move, just as the Philippine national elite's identification with American colonial authority fit within a far more complex series of political relationships. Accepting colonial standards at face value opened the possibility of turning the charge of slavery into an embarrassment for the United States. The election of Woodrow Wilson in November 1912 emboldened Filipino nationalists to reverse the implications of slavery more explicitly because his presidency seemed to bring the promise of independence held in the Jones bill within reach. Worcester, Taft, and Forbes were prepared to campaign against the Jones bill, but Wilson's election provided the Philippine national elite with a new opportunity to access popular nationalist discourse on slavery and liberation.

Just after the American election, *La Vanguardia* announced that Wilson "will preside over our triumphal entrance into the Promised Land after redeeming us from the long captivity to which the imperial Pharaohs reduced us." *La Vanguardia* found license to refer to colonialism as slavery by identifying the new American president as the emancipator of the Philippines, a Moses figure who would guide the Philippines to independence. Similar expectations of imminent independence were expressed in marches and meetings, including a gathering in Manila of twenty thousand people who were addressed by Osmeña, Quezon, and Aguinaldo.[16]

Beyond the coincidence of rhetoric that united the Jones bill's potential promise of independence with elite and popular nationalist desires for emancipation lay profoundly different registers of meaning and purpose. Reynaldo Ileto has shown how the language of the elite nationalists' investment in the Jones bill and Wilson's election fed into popular expectations of change as a cataclysmic shift, harking back to the Katipunans' distinctive understanding of *kalayaan* and its attainment through shared sacrifice. While appeals to popular nationalism enabled *Nacionalista* leaders to rally and showcase large followings, the rhetoric of redemption and emancipation carried the dual risks of signaling the time for an upheaval and exposing the elite to charges of deceit should they accept anything less than a transformative independence.[17]

The years from 1912 to 1914 were a tense time for the Philippine elite and the American colonial regime. Mass meetings with speeches about independence and commemorations of the revolution such as Rizal Day and Balintawak Day (marking the beginning of the 1896 revolution) often threatened to get out of the elite sponsors' control. For example, on 24 August 1912, two days before Balintawak Day, the Dimas-Alang mutual aid society held a rally to support Quezon's efforts in the United States. Speakers advised the crowd of workers and peasants in the historic Katipunan meeting place of San Juan del Monte "that the people should not forget the first shout of emancipation because only with this memory can a people obtain their independence." Word quickly spread that Dimas-Alang followers would rebel on Balintawak Day, prompting its leader, Patricio Belen, to work hurriedly to restrain the rank and file.[18]

Plots, conspiracies, and rumors of popular uprisings flourished during those years, though few actually came to fruition and none got very far. The constabulary broke up several small rebellions planned for Rizal Day, 30 December 1912, and newspapers in the United States reported that "the insurrection . . . got away from the leaders," going dangerously beyond their control. Quezon sent telegrams from Washington, telling Osmeña that it was "most important to preserve tranquility" and to advise Filipinos to be "calm and patient."[19] In late January 1913, rumors spread from the Philippines to the United States that Emilio Aguinaldo would come forward to lead an uprising. Speaking in the House of Representatives, Quezon denied the reports of "disturbances" and attributed them to "enemies [of] independence" fighting against the Jones bill. On the same day, however, he sent Osmeña a coded telegram: "Advice [sic] Aguinaldo keep away from public notice."[20]

Independence politics and the power of the national elite were riven with tensions and contradictions from the beginning. The conservative leadership of the *Partido Nacionalista* needed to present an image of political unity and stability to the United States in order to obtain support for the Jones bill, but its very promotion of the bill as the path and Wilson as the guide to redemption inspired popular expectations of imminent independence. As the American director of the Philippine constabulary observed in February 1913, "The little people are firmly convinced that as soon as President Wilson assumes office, independence for the Philippines will be one of the first things that is turned out."[21] Popular nationalism interpreted these events as signs of Kalayaan's arrival, signals that the time had come to rise up like the Katipunan and offer one's life like Rizal. But there was also great potential for disillusionment in the disjunction between the national elite's public rhetoric of immediate independence and its readiness, desire even, to bargain for a compromise relationship with the United States.

From 1912 to its passage in 1916, the terms of the Jones bill deteriorated precipitously, from mandating independence in four years to eight years to merely promising independence in the future. While Nacionalista leaders had to struggle to keep control over a potentially militant popular desire for independence, they needed to find ways to preserve the credibility of their nationalist rhetoric as independence receded into the future. Quezon recognized this problem as early as May 1912. The first Jones bill had failed, an assembly election was coming up in June, and the opposition *Partido Nacional Progresista* criticized Quezon's acquiescence to the four-year transition period offered in the bill instead of demanding immediate independence. To counteract this, Quezon asked Erving Winslow of the Anti-Imperialist League to send cables to *La Vanguardia* and *El Ideal* "saying that the Progresista Party had nothing to do with the Jones Bill, and that for the final success of that bill the Filipino people should unite in electing the Nationalist Party." [22]

The gap between expectations and fulfillment grew over the following year. There was no real progress toward independence. The Jones bill was no closer to passing and the new president had not yet announced any changes in the structure or personnel of colonial administration. When Quezon sent Osmeña word in late May 1913 that Congress would not even consider the Jones bill until the next year, the speaker of the assembly replied that there "will be for some time . . . great uneasiness and embarrassment." [23] The hopes raised by Wilson's election only made the disappointment, and the feeling that Filipinos were being deceived, more acute.

Quezon expected precisely this kind of embarrassment, for he knew already in the summer of 1912 that none of the three candidates then running for the American presidency favored rapid independence for the Philippines. But Quezon could not foresee that one of his interviews with a presidential candidate would produce a much greater embarrassment by expanding the ramifications of the slavery scandal.

At the end of July, Quezon met with Theodore Roosevelt for a private interview. The meeting upset him greatly. Quezon later informed Erving Winslow that "Mr. Roosevelt told me that he does not believe the Philippine people are quite ready for self-government." [24] This was hardly news to Quezon, nor was it an intolerable view for him to work with behind the scenes. What was troublesome was the way that Roosevelt explained his position, telling Quezon that the American Episcopal bishop of the Philippines, Charles Henry Brent, said the people would be reduced to a state of peonage in an independent Philippines. The next day Quezon wrote to Brent, objecting to his views.[25] The following day Quezon visited Frank McIntyre, chief of the Bureau of Insular Affairs, to complain about Governor Forbes's speech on the antislavery laws.

Quezon's meeting with McIntyre resulted in the bureau chief's sending two letters to the acting governor in Manila. In one McIntyre ex-

plained that "Mr. Quezon is not a believer in Philippine independence."
Quezon had to speak passionately for independence in public to maintain his reputation as a nationalist in the Philippines, but in private he
was ready to conform to the views of the three presidential candidates
in the United States—Taft, Roosevelt, and Wilson—who had told him
of their opposition to independence in the near future. Instead of independence, Quezon asked for the addition of an elected upper house to
the legislature and the replacement of some of the top colonial officials
because their "personality and conduct" made the present government
"extremely unpopular." [26]

The second letter was devoted to particular Filipino "grievances"
against American officials. In fact, there were many causes of tension and conflict in Philippine colonial politics, but the only one that
McIntyre reported from his conversation with Quezon was the speech
in which "Governor Forbes very seriously criticized the Philippine Assembly for not passing a bill . . . prohibiting slavery and the sale of human beings in the Philippine Islands." McIntyre called the commission's
treatment of the assembly "a little unfair" and enclosed a copy of the
memorandum he had prepared in 1909 recommending that references
to slavery be omitted from Worcester's annual report because they
would create a "false impression." [27] Because he asked for comments on
the Bureau's position, his letter and the accompanying documents were
passed on to Worcester sometime in October.

Before Worcester replied, he introduced an antislavery bill in the
Philippine Commission for the fourth time and secured its passage by
that body on 24 October. Two days later the assembly directed the bill
to a committee, where it sat without discussion. In the lengthy rebuttal
he wrote for McIntyre, Worcester insisted on the need for a law to crim-
inalize slavery and he directly attacked McIntyre's concern that pub-
licizing the dispute over antislavery laws would create a "false impression" about conditions in the Philippines. "Involuntary servitude
and peonage *are* common in the Philippines," Worcester insisted, and
"[s]lavery and the sale of human beings are also common . . . in certain
portions of the wild man's territory . . . and are by no means very rare
in general in the territory occupied by Filipinos which borders on the
territory occupied by non-Christians." [28]

Worcester's emphasis on the existence of various forms of involuntary
servitude marked a change in his campaign for an antislavery law. Before October 1912 he always gave much more attention to the absence

of a law prescribing criminal penalties. Now his interest turned to the prevalence of bondage itself. On November 1 he began to write to provincial governors, judges, and the constabulary, requesting information about cases of slavery, peonage, and involuntary servitude. The documents Worcester collected reveal that the antislavery law passed in 1911 prompted no effective action against slavery in the Special Provinces until Worcester called for these reports. Even then, positive steps to release people from bondage seem to have been taken in only one place, the Ifugao subprovince of the Mountain Province. Ifugao's lieutenant governor Jefferson Davis Gallman (named for his uncle, the president of the Confederacy during the U.S. Civil War) was emboldened by Worcester's inquiry to go searching in Nueva Vizcaya for young Ifugaos who had been sold to the lowlands. He proceeded to "recover some forty boys and girls" who had been sold in the Cagayan Valley. In every case the master claimed they were "'hired servants,'" but when he read the antislavery law to the masters "they were easily prevailed upon to pay much long overdue salary to their 'servants,' and the latter were returned to their homes."[29]

At first, Gallman believed that his actions stopped the trade of people from Ifugao to Nueva Vizcaya, but he soon heard that young Ifugao were again being moved to the lowlands in what was now called "the business of 'hiring' boys and girls." In the recent past, the Ifugao would talk readily about the trade of captives and pawns. On several occasions American officials had even been asked to intercede when payment for slaves was not delivered. Now it had become "much more difficult to secure information than formerly, on account of the fear of the parents themselves of incurring punishment for violations of the law—this promised action on my part having been published throughout the province." Gallman concluded that extending the provisions of the antislavery law to cover Isabela Province and "a few examples of rigid enforcement of the law will result in much benefit to the Ifugao."[30]

There were no prosecutions for violation of the 1911 antislavery law in Ifugao, or any other place. Worcester never ordered or even encouraged such prosecutions. Nevertheless, slavery had ceased to exist as an open institution throughout the Philippines by the time Worcester began to write up his slavery investigations in 1913. Much like the Spanish consolidation of colonial rule in the seventeenth and eighteenth centuries, the extension of American colonial authority over the non-Christian tribes hampered traditional raiding. The suppression of slave raiding was a welcome but mostly unintended side effect. Only the vestiges of the practice remained in 1913: an occasional raid, the exchange of pawns and debtors, and some slaves still held in the possession of masters.

The practical actions taken against slavery and involuntary servitude between 1911 and 1913, including Gallman's expedition and Worcester's investigations, could have been ordered earlier because they required no special criminal law. Moreover, this all took place in the Special Provinces under Worcester's jurisdiction, where officials played loosely with colonial law, local custom, and the means of violence. If he had wanted, Worcester could have taken far more aggressive action much earlier, but he did not use any of his substantial resources to study or work against practices of enslavement until 1912. Even then, he ordered only the collection of information from officials in the provinces and government bureaus.

Worcester's investigation into slavery grew out of his long and complexly motivated concern with the problem, but it also became part of a formally planned propaganda campaign. Soon after Woodrow Wilson won the presidential election of November 1912, the defeated incumbent William Howard Taft began to work with Governor General Forbes to organize a lobby to retain the Philippines as a colony. Although Wilson had told Quezon that he opposed Philippine independence, the president-elect did not publicly contradict the Democratic Party's stand in favor of it. Most Americans and Filipinos now thought that the Jones bill would have a good chance of passing into law. Worcester was assigned a large part in the campaign to stop it because of his scientific authority, seniority in colonial service, and the political value of the non-Christian tribes.

The combative Worcester had just published his third sensationalist article on the non-Christians in the *National Geographic Magazine* in September. It was attractively titled "Head-Hunters of Northern Luzon" and profusely illustrated with photographs of decapitated bodies, scantily clothed men and women, and images depicting the success of colonial progress among the very same peoples. By December he was at work on another contribution, putting together materials for lectures and lantern-slide shows, and beginning to work on a book to answer James H. Blount's case against the colonial government. Worcester planned to use his investigation of slavery to inform a chapter in this book.

The political significance of Worcester's investigations was given focus by Bishop Brent, whose interest was further sparked by his belated reading of Manuel Quezon's indignant letter from July. Brent sent copies of Quezon's letter—which upbraided "me for saying that the Filipino people were given to peonage and were not at present ready for self-government"—to Taft, Roosevelt, Worcester, and other associates. He told them that Quezon "has given me a splendid opening which I shall not be slow to take." [31] In the ensuing months Brent met with Worcester repeatedly to examine his growing collection of documents on slavery and then to discuss the early drafts of Worcester's report. At one meeting in January they discussed the prospects for a revived Jones bill and Quezon's response to Forbes's Harvard speech of 1912. Afterwards Worcester recorded in his diary that "this might do for an opening, I think." [32] Later, after a dinner in March, Worcester read a draft of his book chapter on "slavery and peonage" to Brent and "a little stag party of men who were interested in my book." Several of the attending constabulary officers and government officials suggested that Worcester had "laid too much stress on the enslaving of the wild people [and] . . . insisted that *Filipinos* were enslaved with even greater frequency, being both bought and sold and compelled to labor without compensation." Worcester said he would investigate that, too. [33]

Another boost came from the interest of the American Humane Association—an involvement that should underscore the way in which antislavery humanitarianism could incorporate infantilizing and dehumanizing assumptions. The president of the Humane Association wrote to Worcester asking about "humane laws" in the Philippines. Worcester's reply, written in December, mentioned laws for the prevention of cruelty to animals and discussed the conflict over antislavery laws in some detail. The association's president judged the situation "too important to be passed over in silence by humanitarians." Consequently, the April 1913 issue of the *National Humane Review* printed Worcester's letter under the title, "Human Slavery Still Exists Under the United States Flag." The *Humane Review* noted Worcester's charge that slavery continued because the Philippine Assembly would not pass an antislavery law and added: "It should be borne in mind that these are the people that many well meaning persons in the United States desire to be given political independence to regulate their own affairs. It is now a question whether the United States shall permit this condition to longer exist; also whether President Wilson and Congress are willing to act, and whether public sentiment in this country will tolerate the existence of slavery under the protection of the United States flag." [34]

On 1 May 1913, Senator William E. Borah of Idaho read the article from the *Humane Review* on the floor of the Senate. His colleagues responded by passing a resolution asking the secretary of war for "any and all facts bearing directly or indirectly upon" the charge that slavery existed in the Philippines.[35] In its reply the War Department claimed that it had no records bearing on the charge "that human slavery exists *at this time* in the Philippine Islands." The only information the department said that it had was a short extract from Taft's Congressional testimony, given in 1904, about slavery among Moros and non-Christians, and a copy of the 1911 antislavery law for the non-Christian provinces printed in Worcester's annual report for that year.[36]

The Bureau of Insular Affairs and the War Department, now headed by Wilson's appointee, Lindley Garrison, did not want the discussion of slavery to go any farther. An earlier draft of the department's reply to the Senate contained much more information, including a passage about slavery and antislavery laws from Worcester's annual report for 1912, an excerpt from Governor Forbes's request that the Philippine Assembly pass an antislavery law in 1910, an account of the decision to delete mention of slavery from Worcester's annual report for 1909, and a discussion of the decision in the Cabanag case. The draft reply also noted that "a certain mild form of slavery existed among the Moros is well established, and that there may be lingering cases is quite probable, but all that could be done by stringent legislation and zealous application of the law seems to have been done to eradicate slavery in the Moro Province." And, as for the non-Christians, the draft said: "Again, among the wild, or uncivilized, tribes of the Philippine Islands, there has doubtless existed a form of slavery."[37] All of this was then excised from the document before the final copy was transmitted to the Senate.

When the Philippine Commission resolved on 19 May 1913 to ask the secretary of war to seek Congressional action on an antislavery law, the Bureau chief, McIntyre, told the secretary of war that "[t]he matter calls for no immediate action, and none is recommended."[38] The Philippine Commission's resolution was never presented to Congress. It was, however, much too late to nip the slavery scandal in the bud.

Worcester completed a draft of his book on slavery and presented it to the Philippine Commission at the end of April. He now began to revise it for publication as a special government report, including new passages on the War Department's latest efforts to suppress discussion of slavery as well as recent denials, made by Filipino and American critics, that slavery existed. These protests acted as a catalyst upon Worcester, moving him to even more inflammatory charges against the assembly, Quezon, and American adversaries.[39]

The airing of Worcester's draft report in the Philippine Commission and Senator Borah's resolution in the U.S. Senate could hardly have come at a time that was either more difficult or more opportune for the leaders of the *Nacionalista* Party. Some dissenters had always harbored suspicions of Quezon, Osmeña, and the mainline *Nacionalistas'* commitment to independence, not to mention the United States's pledge that it was preparing the Philippines for independence. More were coming to share this skepticism. The slavery scandal was a huge embarrassment, but it also created a useful crisis.

In April 1913 at a commemorative gathering to honor the Katipunan intellectual Emilio Jacinto, the old Ilocano radical Isabelo de los Reyes discounted the Democrats' promise of Philippine independence as nothing but a myth. Aurelio Tolentino, a Katipunero of 1896 and celebrated author of nationalist dramas, told the same audience that he still hoped that the United States would grant independence, but he called for recourse to arms if that hope should fail.[40] Followers of the exiled revolutionary hero General Artemio Ricarte were already organized as a secret army, waiting for the right moment to rekindle the revolution to "redeem" the Philippines. As early as February 1913, before Wilson's inauguration, Ricartistas in Manila were saying that "the promise of independence contained in the Jones bill [was] only to deceive the people."[41]

Meanwhile, in the United States, Quezon joined the Executive Committee of the Philippine Society in April, an organization founded by Edward Fallows, a businessman who was the son of an Episcopal bishop and a confidant of the Taft-Forbes circle. The Philippine Society was a private lobby for the colonial administration. Two years before, Erving Winslow had placed a picture of Quezon in his office and told the *Nacionalista* leader that "it is the picture of the liberator of his country." Now, in May 1913, Winslow and Moorfield Storey began to have their first doubts about the sincerity of Quezon's advocacy for independence.[42]

Worse still, instead of debating the Jones bill, the U.S. Senate resolved to investigate slavery in the Philippines. The juxtaposition of Worcester's image of the Philippines as a country to be freed of slavery by colonial rule with the growing crisis of Filipinos' hope for freedom from the slavery of colonialism could hardly have been more powerful. Worcester's public charges would have demanded a response under any circumstances. In the vulnerable context of 1913, when the authority of official nationalism was on the line and the prospects for even moderate reforms in favor of self-government were increasingly in doubt, the slavery scandal was especially critical for the national elite.

In Washington, Quezon used the reading of Worcester's letter to the Humane Society in the Senate as an occasion to plead publicly for a change in colonial administration. He first sent a formal letter of complaint to the secretary of war, and then passed it on to the press. Countering Worcester's claim to scientific authority, Quezon declared that he himself could "testify" that slavery did not exist "as an institution" in the Christian Provinces subject to the Assembly, and if it did exist in any part of the Philippines, "the Philippine Commission alone is responsible for the lack of proper legislation to punish this inhuman and savage crime." Thus, Quezon argued, in "blaming" the Philippine Assembly for "the existence of such [alleged] slavery" Worcester was "by innuendo calumniating the whole Filipino people." Quezon asked that all the Philippine Commissioners be removed from office, but he specially targeted Worcester, who had "certainly done enough not only in this case, but in previous ones, to merit the loss of the privilege of being one of the administrators and legislators of a people whom he finds pleasure in slandering." [43]

Moorfield Storey followed Quezon's lead some two weeks later. He asked H. Parker Willis, an anti-imperialist Democrat close to President Wilson, if he could use his influence to urge the president to replace the Philippine Commissioners, especially Worcester, whose "recent statement in regard to slavery . . . shows how entirely unfit he is to govern the Philippine Islands when he stands ready so grossly to misrepresent the Filipino people." [44]

To the Philippines, Quezon sent word that the slavery issue was being "exploited by enem[ies] [of] freedom." [45] On May 5, *El Ideal* called Worcester's allegations "the last recourse which the Insular administration has found to thwart the joint plan of Democrats and Filipinos for reforming the political status of the country." [46] In the following month, *El Ideal* warned readers "to be on the alert" for government agents investigating the employment of Negrito servants. It noted that the slavery controversy was distancing the people from the government, showing "how true it is that in a colony the interest of the governed is always contrary and opposed to the interests of the governor." [47]

CHAPTER ELEVEN

A Scandalous Report

By June 1913 the Forbes administration knew that the Jones bill would be a dead letter for at least another year and that the leading *Naciona-listas* were quite willing to accept the continuation of American colonial rule. The colonial administration also felt reassured that Wilson was a conservative who still believed, as he had written in 1902, that a long period of colonial rule would be necessary in the Philippines.[1] Nevertheless, Worcester continued his attack on the slavery issue.

The slavery controversy brought colonial politics to the breaking point, but it did not jeopardize the structure of colonial rule. Inadvertently, the scandal gave the Philippine national elite an opportunity to redirect attention from its complicity in the failure of the Jones bill. Fighting Worcester and his allegations of slavery offered a new goal for official nationalism, more easily achieved than independence and perhaps, in some ways, more important. When the Wilson administration let it be known in June that the top administrators in the colony would be changed, the Philippine national elite could claim a significant victory.

The Forbes administration remained in office and continued to collect data on involuntary servitude through September. Its status as a lame duck is significant evidence of the limits the Philippine national elite imposed on the operation of American colonial authority. But it is also a powerful testament to the solidity of American colonial hegemony because, among the national elite, the strongest opposition was limited to the question of who would administer American rule and did not extend to the immediate continuation of colonial rule itself.

For their part, Forbes and Worcester understood well the political cost they would pay for going forward with the report on slavery. While Worcester revised his draft in June, Forbes advised him to delete the names of constabulary officers who had supplied information. "The slavery matter is a question which is agitated in the public mind," said Forbes, so the use of constabulary officers' names would "probably injure their usefulness in the future." Worcester refused to comply with this request, as it would compromise his newfound abolitionist zeal. "If the time has come when it threatens the usefulness of officers or employees of the Insular Government to report over their own names the facts as to the existence of slavery in the Islands," he told Forbes, "that in itself is a significant thing which should not be passed by." [2]

Worcester did, however, agree to another modification. There were four Filipinos on the Philippine Commission: José Luzuriaga, Gregorio Araneta, Rafael Palma, and Juan Sumulong. "Their support of the anti-slavery movement," noted Forbes, "is an extremely unpopular thing and is sure to subject them to great criticism and yet they didn't flinch at all from passing" the commission's resolution in May 1913 urging congressional action. To "save the [Filipino] members of the Commission from the embarrassment of voting" to approve and publish the report on slavery, Worcester agreed to address the final version to the governor general instead of to the commission. True to form, Worcester exploited even this concession by recounting his act of grace in a footnote. [3]

Slavery and Peonage in the Philippine Islands was printed in July 1913 by the colonial government in Manila. Worcester punctuated the final version of the text with sharp invectives directed at Filipinos who denied that slavery existed. In the opening pages, after requesting congressional legislation against slavery in the Philippines, Worcester assailed Quezon for "loudly and recklessly" claiming that there was never slavery in the Christian provinces under the assembly. [4]

In a letter written in May 1913 to the *New York Evening Post,* Quezon declared: "As a Filipino familiar with the facts in the case, I do not hesitate to qualify the letter of Secretary Worcester [to the Humane Association] as being at once false and slanderous." To this Worcester replied that Quezon might be "so ignorant of conditions . . . as to be unaware" of the recent practice of slavery in Palawan, Isabela, and other regularly organized provinces, "but if so, he has no rightful claim to be a 'Filipino familiar with the facts.'" Later in the report Worcester reprinted Quezon's response to the speech that Forbes had made at Harvard in June 1912 and called his explanation of the assembly's refusal to pass an antislavery law "puerile." Worcester also reproduced police documents on two cases of runaway house servants, apparently held in debt bondage by members of the Philippine Assembly. Implying that the practice of peonage was widespread among the assembly delegates, he asked: "Is it any wonder that that body refuses to consider a law prohibiting and penalizing peonage?"[5]

Worcester sought to discredit the Philippine national elite's ability to speak for and about the people of the Philippines, reserving that authority to himself and American colonialism. In fact, *Slavery and Peonage in the Philippine Islands* contained little analysis of Philippine societies. This was not his purpose. Instead, Worcester stitched together documents on the legal and legislative history of his antislavery bills with statements by Filipino nationalists to the effect that slavery did not exist and numerous terse reports of non-Christians sold, pawned, or held in debt by Catholic Filipinos. Although the mass of documentation was substantial, it was an analytically and ethnographically shallow text.

Following the usage of much contemporary American anthropology of the Philippines, Worcester named and located Philippine societies on a unilinear evolutionary scale, but with a peculiar twist that favored certain non-Christian groups. The way that Worcester discussed Negritos and Ifugaos in his report on slavery is especially revealing of the document's grounding in the political meaning of the non-Christian tribes. Although Worcester recounted cases involving the bondage of people from various ethnic groups, mainly non-Christians but also from some Christian groups, most of the incidents he reported involved Ifugaos and Negritos.[6] This did not necessarily reflect an underlying social prevalence. In addition to the frequency of cases, Ifugaos figured prominently, in part, because they were involved in the court cases that led to the initial proposal of an antislavery law. Cases involving Negritos stood out for other reasons. Worcester reported many such cases that originated in regularly organized Catholic Filipino provinces near Manila that sent delegates to the Philippine Assembly, such as Pampanga, Tarlac, and Zambales. Small bands of Negritos lived in the hills and forests of these provinces, near much larger Catholic Filipino populations. Worcester highlighted a number of cases in which Negritos had been taken to Manila itself to work as bonded servants. And, last but not least, the Negritos' very blackness and reputedly bleak prospects for evolution and survival gave them a unique meaning.

The proximity of Negritos to the political heartland of Filipino nationalism and the finding that some were held in bondage in the capital
furthered the formulation of a comparison that Worcester used to frame
the entire report. He contrasted the Catholic Filipino relationship with
non-Christians, epitomized by the Negritos, with the American relationship with non-Christians, now typified by the Ifugao. This juxtaposition projected American colonialism's strong and progressive relationship with the Ifugaos as an effective mission of benevolence to be
preserved. It implied that the character of a prospectively independent
Philippines could be divined through an examination of Catholic Filipinos' association with Negritos and the Philippine Assembly's refusal
to pass an antislavery law.

In the conclusion to his incendiary report, Worcester proclaimed
"that the existence of slavery and peonage in the Philippines presents
the single greatest problem which there confronts the Government of the
United States, in its effort to build up a respectable and responsible electorate and to establish representative government." [7] By linking the fate
of the non-Christian tribes with the politics of slavery and antislavery
laws, Worcester attacked the Philippine elite's claim to national community and capacity for civilized self-government. While Filipino nationalists and American anti-imperialists were working for the passage of the
Jones bill to liberate the Philippines from colonial bondage, Worcester
refigured the entire colonial enterprise as an antislavery crusade.

The frontispiece of Slavery and Peonage in the Philippine Islands portrayed two young Ifugao boys, aged perhaps seven or eight, standing on
the steps of a massive stone schoolhouse. The caption underneath ran:
"Entrance to Quiangan [Kiangan] Schoolhouse." It said the stones for
the building were quarried and then set by "Ifugao boys," including the
two youngsters in the photograph, under the direction of their American teacher. Then, Worcester asked: "Should it not be made a crime to
sell or buy such children as chattels?" The only other photograph in the
report also depicted the school, but from a distance, with approximately
sixty young Ifugao boys lined up in front of the edifice to American colonial tutelage. Its caption noted that the school had been built by these
boys and then stated: "Ifugao children are sold into slavery more frequently than are the children of any other tribe except the Negritos." [8]

Worcester's assertion that there were more Negritos held in slavery
than there were Ifugaos is of doubtful validity, both in terms of sheer
numbers and also the slipperiness of distinguishing slavery from other

kinds of bondage based on debt. He presented evidence of only a few cases from Pampanga Province in which Catholic Filipinos had raided Negrito bands to take away captives and provided no evidence that Negritos themselves sold captives, although he claimed that they did.[9] Most of the cases cited by Worcester originated in pawning, debt, or the appropriation of orphaned children who then, sometimes, were transferred for cash. Some Negritos were sold or traded several times over, but these instances seem exceptional, in contrast to the well-developed pattern of multiple trades that brought children from Ifugao into the Cagayan Valley. Many of the Ifugaos sold into the lowlands had been taken as captives; most of the Negritos were not.

The theme that stands out most clearly in Worcester's discussion of Negritos held in bondage is his presumption of their total inability to care for themselves. Even more so than when discussing the Ifugao, Worcester played upon the ambiguous origins of bondage among Negritos in order to argue that they needed to be protected from themselves as well as from predatory Christian Filipino neighbors. In his eyes, the Negritos' practice of selling and pawning their children or putting them into bondage to work off a debt constituted self-endangerment. Worcester ranked the Ifugao rather highly among the non-Christian peoples of the Philippines for their magnificent mountainside rice terraces, great physiques, diligence at labor, bravery, and loyal service in their own branch of the Philippine Constabulary, but he had little respect for Negritos as people. Worcester's desire to portray the Ifugao as victims was thus mildly buffered by a need to credit their intelligence and allegiance. He felt no such limitations of conscience in writing about Negritos whom, not coincidently, he elsewhere described as occupying the lowest rungs of the evolutionary ladder.

Worcester offered several descriptions of how Negritos fell into bondage. First, he asserted that because "the Negritos are savages of very low mentality, living in families or small groups which are often hostile to each other, inhabiting the most inaccessible mountain regions and constantly wandering about, it is often easy to persuade them to undertake the kidnapping of children to be sold into slavery." Next, he explained that "[a]nother common procedure is to get Negrito parents thoroughly intoxicated with *vino*, of which they are inordinately fond, and buy their children while they are drunk." Like the Ifugao and other Philippine peoples in the past, Negrito parents were known to sell or pawn their children when food was scarce. Therefore, Worcester concluded, be-

cause the hunter-gatherer "Negritos are very improvident and consequently sometimes suffer severely from hunger . . . it is comparatively
easy to buy their children." [10]

Among twenty-seven cases of Negritos reported to be held in various
kinds of bondage in Tarlac Province, a Filipino constabulary officer said
that twenty were delivered to the master by a parent or close relative.
Worcester found it "still more remarkable . . . that in two instances
Negritos calmly walked in and presented themselves, to be held as
servants without pay!" All of "these allegations hardly need discussion," declared Worcester. "Negrito children sell readily for considerable sums, and," he added, "no one familiar with the characteristics
of Negritos can doubt that they would do this if left to follow their
inclinations." [11]

According to Worcester, if Negritos were complicitous in deliver-
ing themselves into bondage, it was only due to their own primitiveness
and ignorance. This enabled him to emphasize "the difficulty involved
in protecting these simple people," and thus the benevolence of a paternal colonial rule.[12] The character of this rule was further specified by
Worcester's attention to Filipino claims that bondspeople were adopted
and baptized. Between the practice of selling one's own children and the
use of adoption and conversion as justifications for exploitation,
Worcester defined a need for a new parental figure in the life of Filipinos
that, he insisted, only the United States could provide.

When Ifugao slaves were freed from masters in Nueva Vizcaya, several children whose parents were dead or families unknown were sent to
be wards of the American Episcopal Church's mountain missions in
Bontoc and Sagada. Jefferson Davis Gallman found that some others
had run away from their masters and become "out and out little
vagabonds" unwilling to return to their parents, "whose language in
many cases they had almost forgotten." Gallman thought "their condition was pitiable," and Worcester concurred, describing them as "pitiable in the extreme." [13] Worcester's view of Negritos who had been separated from their people by bondage was somewhat different. He
disparaged the declaration, made to the *New York Times* by retired justice James B. Tracey, that, if Negrito slaves really existed in Manila,
"their liberation could be enforced any day through a writ of habeas
corpus." In his report on slavery, Worcester replied by asking

> How, when they will without exception declare that they desire to continue
> to serve their present masters, on the one hand, and will run away at the first

good opportunity, on the other! Would setting them at liberty bring to life parents killed when children were captured? Make children desirous of returning to parents whom they have not seen since babyhood? Fit them for the wild life of their fellow-tribesmen which they have never experienced? Make up for the long years of abject servitude which have unfitted them to stand alone? [14]

Worcester believed that Negritos were fit to be emancipated, but not to be free. As for Judge Tracey, Worcester found him "unfit to discuss the customs of the wild people or the prevalence of slavery" and had "no respect whatever for his knowledge of the non-Christian tribes of the Philippines." Tracey did "not even know their names, and his ignorance of their customs is so comprehensive as to embrace practically all that there is to be known." [15] This assault on Tracey's ability to speak for and about the non-Christian tribes was much like Worcester's response to the proposal made in 1910 by the secretary of war Jacob Dickinson to give the Philippine Assembly authority over the non-Christian tribes. Worcester had then summarily declared most Christian Filipinos to be "profoundly ignorant of the wild men" and insisted that "the question involved is not one of the fitness of the Filipinos to govern themselves, but is one of their ability and fitness to dominate, justly control, and wisely guide along the pathway of civilization alien peoples." [16]

Worcester derided all claims that Christian Filipinos stood in a paternal and proselytizing relation to servants, slaves, and pawns from non-Christian ethnic groups. Yet, his only direct comments on these assertions pertained to cases involving Negritos. "The constant references to baptism in" reports on Negritos held in bondage were "worthy of note," he acknowledged, and so was "the frequency with which these little black, dwarfish, woolly-headed savages are claimed to have been 'adopted.'" [17] Worcester dismissed the veracity of these adoptions, saying that "in no single case have I been able to obtain evidence of real, legal adoption." For an illustration, he reprinted a certificate of baptism from the curate of Lubao, Pampanga, dated Christmas Day 1912. The document recorded the eighteen-year-old Negrita's new Christian name as "Juana" and reported that "the foster mother, Doña Pia Vitug, . . . received the charge as a parent to care for the spiritual welfare and other obligations." This kind of recognition by the church, commented Worcester, imposed "no legal obligation whatever on the owner of a slave, and makes no change whatever in the status of the slave, but merely serves as a basis for the claim that he or she 'is treated as a member of the family.'" Worcester's criticism of baptism addressed the question of hierarchy even more pointedly: "The belief seems common among Filipinos that the act of baptizing wild people, whether with or without their consent, affords adequate excuse for subsequently retaining them in servitude, the favor conferred by the act of baptism being so great that the fortunate ex-heathen ought to be willing to work the rest of their lives in return for it!" [18]

Worcester's analysis of baptism and adoption as legitimations of bondage is arresting, for its terms could be applied almost exactly to the justificatory ideologies of Spanish and American colonial rule. In fact, Philippine nationalists had spent much effort demystifying Spain's gift of Christianity and would do the same for the benevolent paternalism of American colonialism in the twentieth century. The early twentieth-century Tagalog nationalist dramas known as the seditious plays had already done just that, critically analyzing colonialism as a kind of bondage putatively justified by promises of salvation, progress, and assimilation into the colonizer's national (or holy) family.

The sixteenth-century Spanish clerics interested in colonization wrestled over the concepts of just and unjust enslavement to decide who had the right to enslave whom. In the end, they decided that *indios* in the Americas and the Philippines were children of nature born to a natural liberty. *Indios* were not to be enslaved by Spaniards, but colonized, converted, and subordinated to the royal patronage that supported their salvation. The *indios'* relations to Spain were regulated, in theory, by their enslavement to God, but Spaniards found legitimate sources of worldly slaves elsewhere, among Africans, Muslims, and pagans who had rejected Christianity. By the twentieth century, antislavery ideology had long since supplanted the distinction between just and unjust slavery throughout much of the world. New distinctions were made between just and unjust domination, free and unfree labor, progress and backwardness. Worcester's report on slavery played upon these moral dichotomies to reinforce his own position in an ethnological and epistemological hierarchy over all Filipinos in much the same way that Spanish clerics had rationalized the project of colonialism some three centuries earlier.

Worcester and his contemporaries assumed that slavery was always unjust, but they distinguished just and unjust forms of other modes of domination, depending on the specifics of who dominated whom, and how. To Worcester, the hierarchy of colonialism was legitimate to the extent that the superordinate power had the "ability and fitness to dominate, justly control, and wisely guide along the pathway of civilization alien peoples." *Slavery and Peonage in the Philippine Islands* counter-posed progress and just domination by American paternalism to images of false adoptions and baptisms performed by corrupt Spanish priests, Filipino slave owners, and political leaders who would imagine them-selves as the fathers of a sovereign Philippine nation.

Writing when the slavery scandal was near its peak in August 1913, Worcester said in his final annual report that "the foundation of the whole policy of the Department of the Interior in its management of the Non-Christian Tribes of the Philippines is the just and humane treat-ment of the weakest, most ignorant, and most defenceless savages." [19] To Worcester, the abolition of slavery and the United States's solicitous domination of the non-Christian tribes were of a piece. His propensity for seeing non-Christians as children, as the simple, helpless victims of Catholic Filipinos, shaped his perception of slavery in the Philippines from 1905 through the end of the controversy he stirred in 1913. If ul-terior motives transformed Worcester's investigation of slavery into a tendentious attack on Filipino nationalism, it is also clear that the basic assumptions of his argument remained fundamentally constant, rooted in antislavery ideology, the colonial ideology of benevolence, and his po-sition of power and knowledge over the non-Christian tribes. The slav-ery scandal of 1912–1914 was in many ways the culmination of Worcester's career, enabling him to "pose as the redeemer" of the non-Christian tribes before an American public about to reconsider the Jones bill for Philippine independence.

When Worcester's report reached the United States in late August 1913 the colonial bureaucracy in Washington wanted to prevent further public discussion of Philippine slavery. The Bureau of Insular Affairs briefly considered a late effort to suppress the report, but it was already in circulation, publicly in the Philippines, privately in the United States.[20] Worcester's personal authority as a scientific voice on Philip-pine affairs, the high profile of his sponsors, led by Taft, and the sensa-tionalism of his allegations insured him a hearing. Total censorship was impossible. Nor could Worcester's allegations be contained or brushed aside as easily as they had been after the Senate's request for information on slavery the previous May. The mass of detail in the report imparted to its startling charges the sense of an authoritative representation of reality. A supplementary study conducted by the Insular Auditor W. H. Phipps added weight to Worcester's contention that slavery existed in the Philippines, the more so since Phipps bitterly resented Worcester for maligning him in the pages of the report.[21] Then, in late September, Senator Borah announced that, during the next session of Congress, he would propose a bill "to abolish slavery in the islands." [22]

Once again, the American public wrestled with the meaning of slavery, this time in the context of an established colonialism legitimized by its promise of progress toward self-government. In the immediate aftermath of the Spanish-American War, anti-imperialists presented compelling images of Philippine slavery as a kind of barbarism that should not be allowed to sully the United States's realm. Now, in 1913, most American commentators interpreted reports of slavery in the Philippines through similar theories of social evolution and contamination, but held that this demonstrated the need for continued colonial rule.

Stories about slavery in the Philippines were splashed across the front pages of newspapers throughout the United States. The *Washington Star* concluded that Filipinos were "still far removed from that stage of civilization which recognizes evil in the ownership of human beings." [23] The *Philadelphia Enquirer* reasoned that the conditions reported by Worcester "must be somewhat disconcerting to those who have been insisting that the Filipinos are capable of self-government." [24] In New York, *The Sun* called for a congressional investigation, for "if the Filipino people are only slowly emerging from toleration of actual slavery and still practice peonage, certainly the facts should be established, because no people so backward in humanity and intelligence can be ready for the independence which the Democratic Party would thrust upon them." [25] The New York *Evening Sun* printed a cartoon, with the caption, "Under the Flag!" depicting a dark-skinned and curly-haired Filipino, hands shackled, standing on an auction block under a waving Stars and Stripes. [26]

The African features of the cartoon figure recall the fanciful portrayal of black slaves in *The Sultan of Sulu,* George Ade's anti-imperialist musical comedy of 1902. Many news accounts connected the present slavery scandal to the United States's own conflicts over slavery before the Civil War. According to the *Boston Post,* the American people did "not want to be saddled with degenerate dependencies, costing even more in morals than in money," so they would want to grant self-government to the Philippines as soon as possible. But, "to declare the Philippines independent today would be injudicious," because of the small number of "civilized" people there and the problem of slavery. "What are we to do with the Filipinos?" asked the *Boston Post.* "We do not want to establish another 'zone' in which human slavery shall be maintained as an essential element in our republican system," as the paper suggested had been done so far. The editors pondered whether to "give them the privilege of citizenship extended to the former slaves of the South after the Civil War," but summarily dismissed the possibility by declaring, "Enough of that!" The United States, the paper seemed to suggest, should replay Emancipation and Reconstruction in the Philippines, but this time without any thought of political equality.[27]

The *New York Tribune* warned that "Webster's famous 'Liberty and Union' would be transformed into 'Slavery and Scuttling' in the Philippines if Mr. Quezon, the protagonist of Philippine 'independence,' had his way." A precipitate end to colonial rule would "leave the Filipinos and all their 'peculiar institutions' undisturbed," an unthinkable prospect. The *Tribune*'s editors were "confident that the American nation will not so much as seriously consider the establishment of Philippine independence until those islands, by the act and assent of their own people, have been thoroughly purged of that relic of barbarism." This series of historical analogies joined Daniel Webster's evocation of a unifying American nationalism with the Republican Party's more contentious designation in 1854 of slavery as a "relic of barbarism," pitting them in opposition to Philippine independence and all the "'peculiar institutions'" that would flourish under it.[28]

The *Chicago Tribune* elaborated on the moral force that antislavery ideology now lent to colonialism. In an editorial titled "Liberty and Slavery," anti-imperialism was characterized as a "Jeffersonian determination to relinquish the Philippines," based on "a resolve to divorce this country from relations with another, which do injury to the ideals of the one and liberties of the second." Following the reports of slavery, however, it seemed "that the only method by which many of the inhabitants of the islands now in our custody can acquire and hold even so much liberty as physical freedom is offered by the United States. The Jeffersonian disposition is warm, humane, and conscientious, but Philippine liberty, in simplified spelling, would be 'slavery.'"[29]

Anti-imperialists and a few liberal newspapers sought to question Worcester's representations of Philippine slavery and the ease with which most Americans exteriorized slavery as a problem marking other people as inferior and unfit for self-government. According to the *Brooklyn Eagle,* "full faith and credit may be given to the facts alleged by Dean C. Worcester and confirmed by Auditor Phipps, as to the 'buying' of boys and girls in the Philippines, even in Luzon, without the humiliating confession that 'slavery' exists on American territory." It was, according to the title of the editorial, "A Terminology Issue." Even in

New York there were reputedly "white slaves," "child slaves," and "sweatshop slaves," but "no real 'slavery' ever existed as a system anywhere on earth, unless supported by law and sustained by the inflexible and irresistible hand of the organized community." The paper concluded, "Simply because the Eagle believes we have given on the whole a pretty good government to the Filipinos, it refuses to accept the Worcester definition of what is going on in the Philippines." [30]

Oswald Garrison Villard's anti-imperialist *New York Evening Post* replied to a letter writer who had asked, "Shall the United States launch a new republic whose society is founded on human slavery, and this under the first Southern President since the Civil War?" The paper remarked upon the existence of peonage in the southern United States, which it had played an important role in exposing. It also challenged the association of slavery with unfitness for independence by reminding readers that the United States had been recognized as "the greatest exemplification of popular government the world had ever seen" during the three-quarters of a century that slavery had existed there as a legal institution. [31]

The *Washington Times* used satire to expose the hypocrisy of "Our Own Superiority." Pointing to recent investigations of prostitution in the United States, its editors proposed that "by keeping them long enough we can get them to conduct their traffic in human beings on the plane that our white slavers have it . . . with syndicates and exchanges and stock issues and modern frills, as we do." [32] The *Detroit Free Press* also suggested that "Senor Quezon might with justice refer to the situation in the United States and point out that slavery and peonage exist in America quite as certainly as in the Philippine islands." As for Worcester's allegations, the *Detroit Free Press* thought that Filipinos should "admit the facts, and at the same time argue a constant betterment of condition. It is not perfection that the United States demands of the Filipino; a reasonable amount of progress is all that it expects." The persistence of slavery after a few years of American rule was "no serious reflection on the Filipinos." Rather, Filipinos should be given "credit that in some degree [slavery] has been obliged to seek cover, and it is no longer held to be entirely moral." [33]

Notably, most of these responses substantially conceded the "facts" presented by Worcester. American critics could recontextualize and reinterpret Worcester's data, but they could not counter Worcester's documentation and his authority to represent the reality of Philippine societies. Representative William Atkinson Jones of Virginia, the chairman of the House Committee on Insular Affairs and author of the Jones bill, was disturbed by the wide play of Worcester's report in the press and "rather surprised" by Phipps's confirmation of the charges, since he knew that Phipps had become alienated from the Forbes administration. He admitted to Moorfield Storey that "where there is slavery, ignominy unquestionably exists to some extent," but he believed there was less "slavery and peonage . . . in the civilized portions of the Philippines than . . . in the United States." If more involuntary servitude did exist in the Philippines, Congressman Jones believed that "Mr. Worcester and his associates are largely responsible" because they had sole legislative authority through 1907 and still exercised jurisdiction over the "uncivilized and unchristianized Filipinos."[34]

Jones asked Storey to "take this subject up in the papers" so that Worcester, Forbes, and their allies should not "be permitted to have everything their own way." The congressman did just that himself, telling reporters that the scandal was the product of the "animus of Commissioner Worcester," which "everybody in the Philippines understands." He repeated the comments he had made to Storey about the comparative extent of bondage in the Philippines and United States, and the responsibility of the Philippine Commission for such bondage as did exist. "It will scarcely be contended," he challenged, "that after all these years of so-called beneficent American rule slavery exists to a greater degree than it did during the years of American occupation prior to 1907." Moreover, he recollected the widely publicized reports of slavery and polygamy in the Moro societies of the southern Philippines from ten years past, and charged that "no great effort has been made to eradicate either evil. Indeed, it is well known that the government has shut its eyes to their existence."[35]

Moorfield Storey and Erving Winslow were eager to discredit Worcester's report, but their ability to do this was rather limited. Storey opined that he was "not familiar with the facts" and regretfully told Congressman Jones that his own writings could not compete with the more sensationalist tracts put out by Worcester and Forbes with the help of the Philippine Society.[36] For his part, Winslow had beseeched Manuel Quezon to reply to the slavery charges immediately upon hearing that *Slavery and Peonage in the Philippine Islands* had been published. Quezon responded testily that he had solicited information from Speaker Osmeña by telegram, but he could not yet "deny the specific facts cited by Mr. Worcester, for the simple reason that I have no counter-facts to present."[37]

Proving a negative—in this case, that slavery did not exist in the Philippines—is seldom easy. Osmeña could not provide Quezon with "facts," only broad denials and explanations. He told his compatriot in Washington that "slavery does not exist in the territory subjected to the Assembly's jurisdiction." The assembly would not pass an antislavery law because its members distrusted Worcester, whose "hostility" was well known. "Cases of purchase" were not slavery, Osmeña explained, because the subjects of sale "enjoy perfect liberty and are comparable to a domestic servant or member of the family." Others were given for adoption, to be treated "like children" according to the "moral obligation of custom and religion," or presented to "work without pay" in exchange for education. Silverio D. Cecilio, an assembly delegate whom Worcester alleged held servants in debt bondage, reportedly called the charge an "unquestionable falsehood." Likewise, Osmeña reported that the Philippine press "unanimously contradicts and denies the existence of slavery."[38] The information Osmeña cabled from Manila may have reassured Quezon, but it provided him with little new ammunition to use against Worcester.

Quezon had played a major role behind the scenes in the Wilson administration's selection of the Democratic congressman Francis Burton Harrison to replace Forbes.[39] He planned to accompany the new governor general to Manila, leaving little time to counter Worcester's propaganda campaign in the United States. The September issue of the *Filipino People*, a monthly journal Quezon published in Washington to support the cause of Philippine independence, carried articles that denied slavery existed in the Philippines and pointed out the hypocrisy of Worcester's allegations, given the history of slavery and peonage in the United States, American toleration of slavery in the southern Philippines, and the Philippine Commission's wasted years of opportunity to take legislative action against slavery. Before leaving Washington, Quezon told Erving Winslow he would do more. "When I come back," he wrote, "I shall have, I hope, enough material to show what a slanderer Worcester is."[40]

CHAPTER TWELVE

Nationalism and Antislavery

Francis Burton Harrison was a singular choice to become the Philippines' new governor and resolve a twentieth-century scandal over slavery. Although he represented a New York district in Congress, Harrison was a Virginian by birth. His father had served as Jefferson Davis's personal secretary when the latter was president of the Confederacy. Congressman Harrison's reputation with the anti-imperialists and Manuel Quezon appears to have been made in May 1913, when he wrote to Erving Winslow: "Every year I become more earnestly impressed with the necessity of our severing our bonds with the Philippines at the earliest moment practicable; . . . [we have] no justification for holding those people in bondage." [1]

By the time Harrison landed in the Philippines in early October 1913, all sides in the United States were calling for an investigation of Worcester's allegations about slavery. Worcester and the imperialist press had long wanted action from the U.S. Congress. The anti-imperialists, certain that Worcester's charges would prove baseless, requested an inquiry and statements from the Bureau of Insular Affairs, the War Department, and the newly reorganized colonial government. [2]

The Wilson administration was also anxious to discredit Worcester and quell the disturbance over slavery, especially after the release of Phipps's report added fuel to the fire. While Harrison was en route to Manila, Secretary of War Lindley Garrison and Colonel McIntyre, the chief of the Bureau of Insular Affairs, sent him instructions to act as soon as possible. "The conditions alleged to exist in these reports," they wrote, "are offensive to republican ideas and good morals." Therefore, "even though conditions are not as represented," the secretary ordered Harrison to obtain an opinion from the Philippine attorney general on the adequacy of existing antislavery laws, secure passage of a new anti-slavery law if necessary, and concurrently arrange "a fair and impartial investigation . . . to determine the facts as to slavery, peonage, and the bartering of human beings in the Philippine Islands."[3]

Upon his arrival in Manila on October 6, Harrison made a speech that caused great excitement. After reading a plainly phrased message from President Wilson promising the appointment of a Filipino major-ity to the Philippine Commission and rapid movement toward indepen-dence, Harrison added his own memorable words. He said that the United States was offering Filipinos "the opportunity for demonstrat-ing" their "capacity for self-government," which he expected Filipinos to show by "that dignity of bearing and that self-restraint which are the outward evidences of daily increasing national consciousness." Thus, the Philippines was "now on trial before an international tribunal that is as wide as the world," with the United States serving as its "ad-vocates." If the substance of this differed little from McKinley's and Taft's policy of gradually extending imperial surveillance and disci-pline through institutions of self-government, Harrison's exuberant clos-ing injected a new millennial spirit that stirred his Filipino audience: "People of the Philippine Islands! A new era is dawning! We place within your reach the instruments of your redemption. The door of op-portunity stands open and, under Divine Providence, the event is in your own hands."[4]

From one angle, the centrality of redemption in Harrison's speech needs to be understood in light of the ongoing contest over the mean-ing of slavery, dating back at least as far as William McKinley's protes-tations that the United States came to liberate and not to enslave the Fili-pinos. Harrison's usage of the word exemplifies the hegemonic power of antislavery ideology to encompass, shape, and contain both anti-colonial and procolonial potentialities, for Americans and Filipinos. Although his remarks were widely understood as a statement of anti-imperial purpose, Harrison's equation of fitness for emancipation from colonial control with the demonstration of internalized national order also confirmed the official purpose of the colonial project. The tie between independence and the demand for disciplined self-control had deep roots in the American moral reform movements of the early nineteenth century, of which abolitionism was a part. Expectations that were commonly burdened upon freed slaves in the Americas—to continue to labor for their old masters much as they did under slavery—had a strong parallel in the requirement that Filipinos, in order to be freed from colonial rule, should maintain a stable national government consonant with the territorial contours and other standards created by the colonizer. In this sense, imperialists, anti-imperialists, and elite Philippine nationalists who engaged in the debate over the fitness of Filipinos for national independence joined in naturalizing the power of the nation-state as the sine qua non of freedom.

In the context of the Philippines in 1913, however, Harrison's address had yet another set of meanings. Here was no less than the American governor general of the Philippines taking a stand against Worcester, reversing the meaning of slavery by using it as a metaphor for colonial rule. Moreover, the imagery in Harrison's speech played upon and into the symbolism of popular Philippine nationalism. "Redemption," the dawn of "a new era," participation in change, the open door to *kalayaan*—in the historian Reynaldo Ileto's words, "Bonifacio had done no better in 1896!"[5] The event marked a momentous shift in the slavery controversy. Harrison, new to the Philippines, may not have comprehended the full import of this gesture, but his travelling companion Manuel Quezon could not have missed its significance.

In contrast to Worcester's futile attempts to convince the assembly to pass an antislavery law, Harrison worked behind the scenes to secure passage of a bill in just a few weeks. He opened the new session of the assembly on October 16 and officially presented it with a copy of Worcester's report for the representatives' "consideration." On October 20 the assembly appointed a special committee of eleven members to investigate slavery and peonage. The committee was later expanded to fifteen, almost one-fifth of the total assembly. Four days later Harrison recorded his first impressions of the Philippines for the secretary of war. He identified "four big problems" demanding "immediate solution," the first being the extension of civil government in the Moro Province and the last "the question of slavery, which is perhaps politically the most important matter." By October 30, before he had even requested the attorney general's opinion on the matter, Harrison decided to "proceed as quickly as possible to pass [a] new anti-slavery and anti-peonage law strengthening existing laws." In just two weeks the assembly would, seemingly of its own free will, produce an antislavery law.[6]

On November 14 the special committee presented a preliminary report to the assembly. It reviewed most of the major laws and edicts relating to slavery in the Philippines since Spain's sixteenth-century Laws of the Indies. Although the committee interpreted the many Spanish regulations differentiating between just and unjust slavery as laws that "prohibited and punished these crimes" of slavery, peonage, and involuntary servitude, it nevertheless concluded that the array of decrees produced over three centuries "had created a certain confusion" about what laws were still in effect.[7]

"This situation," the committee advised, "has created a state of opinion, here and especially away from here, against the good name of the Filipino people and their legislators, a state of opinion that it must fight at all costs." Rather than wait for the courts to sort out the applicable statutes, the committee proposed a new law to "confirm" the Spanish "prohibition" of slavery, peonage, and involuntary servitude. It would further "augment" this prohibition by applying in the Philippines the most recent U.S. penal laws relating to slavery and peonage, which had been updated in 1909. The relevant sections of that law merely revised the U.S. Slave Kidnapping Law of 1866 and the New Mexico Peonage Law of 1867. Neither of these laws penalized the holding of someone in slavery as a crime, but reference to them did provide Filipino nationalists the means to claim perfect equality with the example of the United States in enacting criminal laws against slavery.[8]

After vigorous debate, a majority of the assembly voted for the antislavery bill on November 15, while Harrison was, intentionally, away on a tour of the southern islands. The new Philippine Commission, now staffed by a Filipino majority appointed by Harrison, approved the assembly's bill on November 22 with an amendment to include, verbatim, the text of the relevant U.S. statutes. This was enacted into law by the unanimous vote of the assembly on November 28, more than ten years after Francisco Dichoso, the Filipino governor of Isabela Province, had first suggested the need for an antislavery law.

If Harrison's discrete coordination of the antislavery law preserved the assembly's image of autonomy, his public pronouncements on the problem of slavery helped to validate the anticolonial purpose of the new law. Just days before the assembly approved the final version of the bill, Harrison appeared on a public stage in Pampanga Province with Manuel Quezon and Guillermo Rodriguez, a Negrito mestizo descended from a Negrita grandmother who had been "adopted" by a prominent family whom she "served." Thousands of Filipinos attended this event, at which Rodriguez had the honor of welcoming the new governor general to the town. Rodriguez took the opportunity to denounce Worcester's allegations of slavery by recounting how he had received an education and then inherited a substantial sum of money from the family that had taken in his grandmother. Speaking through Quezon as interpreter, Harrison told the cheering crowd, "I would be glad if each and every member of Congress were present on this occasion, in order to have arguments with which to refute the accusations made against you by Secretary Worcester." Manila's Spanish-language newspapers celebrated Harrison's denial that slavery existed. The American-run *Manila Times* asked if these reports were true. This prompted Harrison to join Quezon in a press conference to clarify his exact language, thereby reiterating his public repudiation of Worcester's report.[9]

While the antislavery bill shuttled back and forth between the assembly and the Philippine Commission under governor general Harrison's protective cover, Filipino Attorney General Ignacio Villamor delivered an opinion on the adequacy of existing laws. As had the special committee of the assembly, Villamor mistook laws that forbade Spaniards from holding *indios* native to the Philippines as slaves for laws that defined slavery itself as a crime. However, he noted that those laws had been rescinded along with all other "general laws" by the terms of the new penal code of 1887. The attorney general discussed the section of the code punishing the crime of illegal detention and how it had been used in prosecutions, including the Cabanag case. From the Supreme Court's decision in the Cabanag case he concluded, as had Worcester, "that in the provinces under the legislative control of the Philippine Legislature, there is at present no law applicable to slavery as [a] specific crime." As for peonage, Villamor judged the laws punishing it "inadequate."[10]

Governor General Harrison accepted Villamor's decision, though with some surprise. Recapping events for the secretary of war, Harrison admitted that "there seems to be good reason for doubting whether or not a slavery law really did exist in the Philippines until the passage of the bill last week." It was Harrison's judgment that the assembly's refusal "to enact the Worcester slavery law must have been due largely to their antipathy for Mr. Worcester. I can safely say that he is the most cordially hated American in the archipelago." Perhaps, Harrison now wondered privately, Worcester had some legitimate cause for requesting

a new antislavery law. More importantly, Harrison expressed appreciation "that the question is now settled for good and all."[11] Garrison
agreed. "I am pleased indeed with the way in which you handled the
question," he told the governor general. "[T]he action taken by the Legislature . . . would seem to dispose of it."[12]

Although the question of antislavery laws may have been answered
by the new act, the larger problem of slavery and its implications were
not so easily eradicated. Harrison was able to bring the political conflict
between the assembly and the American administration to a quick close,
but he could not suppress the colonial discourse on slavery. The United
States was already saturated with Worcester's slides, descriptions, and
documents. Imperial propaganda and the power of colonial knowledge
continued to propel the controversy in the United States.

The problem of slavery remained a thorn in the side of Filipino nationalists, too, but this was only partly caused by the tenacity of imperial
propaganda in the continuing debate over Philippine independence. Filipinos protested against many aspects of American colonial discourse,
but no other issue provoked as organized and passionate a response as
did Worcester's allegations about slavery. For the Philippine national
elite, the problem of slavery involved considerably more than just colonial propaganda. As the debate over the antislavery bill in the Philippine
legislature demonstrates, the ideological implications of slavery resonated deeply in the definition of national self-identity and the legitimation of elite leadership.

The assembly representatives and members of the Philippine Commission who rose to speak in the debates over the antislavery bill unanimously avowed that slavery did not exist in the Philippines. Servillano
Platón, the chairman of the assembly's investigative committee on slavery, opened the debate by explaining the committee's desire "to vindi-
cate the honor of this people that in an ill-starred hour has been out-
raged . . . [by the allegation] that it shelters and protects the institution
of slavery, peonage and involuntary servitude, institutions that our
people fortunately banished centuries ago, ever since the sublime doctrines of the Crucified one and the love of progress and civilization have
embodied our customs, practices and nature." Slavery, peonage, and involuntary servitude were, he said, "institutions that degrade and debase
the human condition." Therefore, Platón concluded, "those who really
know our character, our nature, our customs and morality, would not
dare to assert that we are for slavery." Likewise, assembly deputies who
opposed the bill insisted that "slavery never existed in the Philippine Is-

lands," nor could it in the future, "given the psychology of the people" and the ever-advancing nature of "progress." [13]

The deputies all agreed that there was no social need for an antislavery law and most believed that slavery was, certainly, already a crime under the law. One deputy did advise his colleagues that the Supreme Court's decision in the Cabanag case indicated there would be no legal basis to prosecute for the crime of slavery if, he suggested as a hypothetical example, Worcester returned to the Philippines with a slave purchased in the United States. [14] But the other representatives all maintained that ample laws against slavery had been in force since the sixteenth century. The bill had been carefully crafted as an act to "augment the efficacy" of existing laws, thereby affirming that such laws already existed while it replaced them with a copy of the revised U.S. statutes.

Assembly deputies disagreed, however, about how best to prove that Filipinos opposed slavery. Filipino nationalists had long ago recognized that the assembly's refusal to pass an antislavery law could be distorted as evidence that Filipinos tolerated slavery and were unfit for independence. They also feared that passing such a law would be portrayed as an admission that slavery did in fact exist. This double bind structured the debate over the bill in the assembly and the Philippine Commission.

The immediate issue under dispute was tactical. Deputies disagreed about how they should respond to Worcester's propaganda about slavery, but they all understood that the underlying problem was the meaning of slavery and its dangerous political implications. As one deputy put it succinctly while arguing for passage of the bill, "If it is true that slavery does not exist in the Philippines as an institution, as a social ill, it is no less true that, much to our regret, against our wishes, the mere thesis about whether or not slavery exists among us . . . actually constitutes one of our political ills, a peril to our national cause and a threat to the realization of our independence." [15]

Advocates for the bill concentrated on the dangers of a lingering controversy over antislavery laws. According to Platón, the dispute was being "used as a weapon by those who do not sympathize with our cause." In the United States, he continued, the partisans of imperialism "invoke . . . the fact the assembly does not want to vote for a law to punish slavery etc., alleging that the Filipino people, of which the assembly is the legitimate representative, is unfit to enjoy a free and independent life." If the assembly now rejected the bill, "it would give one more weapon to these enemies of our independence." Approving the bill would end the controversy and "make silent those who have given importance to the report of the ex-secretary of the interior." Platón admitted that this was a painful choice, but he reminded his colleagues that the "new politics" of the Harrison regime "demands great patriotism from the representatives of the Filipino people, and even at certain points great sacrifices of *amor propio,* like that which will be required to approve the present bill." [16]

In response, the opponents of the bill warned that its approval could be taken as evidence that the Philippine Assembly had no independent will, passed frivolous laws, or, worse still, admitted that slavery existed. José Zurbito, a deputy from Sorsogon Province, said that the "the Filipino people, which is as civilized and dignified as any other, cannot accept a bill that assaults its dignity." Like the imperialists who had once questioned the nature of slavery in the southern Philippines, Zurbito argued that "slavery can germinate only in those countries where differences of race and color exist, because the principle and belief of the natural superiority of one person over another, or of one people over another people, originates in differences of race and color." In contrast to this model of slavery based on racial hierarchy, Zurbito described Philippine social relations as a kind of benevolent mutuality in which "the rich Filipino associates with the poor, communicates his sadnesses and joys, sleeps with him in the same bed and under the same roof." Thus, he concluded that Filipinos had "naturally democratic and antislavery instincts." Filipinos would "easily reject the yoke" of any wouldbe slave master just as they had been "able to repel with valor and energy the yoke of a foreign sovereignty maintained by cannons and guns" in the revolution against Spain.[17]

At the end of the debate the assembly voted in favor of the bill for much the same reason that Harrison and the Wilson administration wanted the new law: to bring the controversy to a close. When the matter came up before the Philippine Commission, the newly appointed Commissioner Vicente Ilustre explained his vote for the bill in similar terms. Ilustre denied the existence of slavery, peonage, and involuntary servitude in the provinces subject to the assembly. He wrote a report explaining his vote because he feared that "the passage of the bill might perhaps be considered as an admission of the existence of the evil denounced." Yet, he was more concerned about the "malevolent or simply mistaken belief that the Philippine legislature refuses to pass a bill on slavery, involuntary servitude, and peonage, because it favors them." Therefore, he decided to "vote in favor of the bill solely and exclusively in order that it may not be believed that I do not condemn such transgressions of the laws, not alone penal and social, but even human, and, moreover, that it may not even be murmured that the Filipinos are a proslavery people." [18]

The debate over the bill made clear the Philippine national elite's extreme sensitivity to the problem of slavery. The assemblymen disclaimed the existence of slavery, along with peonage and involuntary servitude, in the broadest sense, virtually denying the possibility of any potentially coercive or exploitive relationship among Filipinos. Conscious of their role as a national elite, the delegates' defense of their quest for independence against imperialist charges that Filipinos tolerated slavery also served as a legitimation of their own political and social leadership within the Philippines. When Filipino nationalists employed slavery as a metaphor for colonial rule, they contrasted it with national independence and freedom. But, when slavery and peonage were alleged to exist as social relationships within the Philippines, the new national oligarchy repelled the delegitimizing connotations of slavery by justifying all Philippine social hierarchy through the rhetoric of reciprocity. Instead of contrasting slavery with ideal types of "freedom" or "free labor," as was common in the United States and England, the Philippine national elite opposed it to an idealized model of patron-client relations based on mutual affection, gifts, and benevolence. Rather than envision the Filipino nation as a comradeship of people equal in their citizenship, the elite imagined nationhood in terms of a network of paternal hierarchy.

The national elite could conceive of a passage from colonial slavery to national freedom along a linear chronology of progress, but their justification of Philippine social relations was beyond the reach of historical time, place, and circumstance. As nationalism projected Philippine identity backward into the past, it gave new meaning to history as demonstration and confirmation of nationality, national culture, and national essence. The ahistoricity of nationalist self-consciousness—finding itself everywhere throughout the history of the Philippines among historical peoples whose worldviews did not include the concept of nation or the notion of identifying themselves by the name of a sixteenth-century Spanish king—imparted a special ideological force to the slavery issue. To counteract Worcester's propaganda, the Philippine national elite could have rested its case with a simple denial that slavery had existed at any recent time in Philippine history. Instead, they responded to an even more demanding challenge of their own definition. As a point of national honor and identity, the national elite felt it necessary to deny the existence of slavery, not just in the present, but throughout all of Philippine history.

Encouraged by the new colonial administration, the Philippine Assembly took up the task of proving that slavery had never existed in the Philippines. The sympathy of the new regime was, however, still bound within the confines of colonial cultural and political relations. Worcester enjoyed the freedom supplied by imperial power to represent the Philippines to Americans more or less as he pleased, but the assembly's investigative committee had to work against the friction of accumulated documentation and the authority of imperial observation to define perceptions of Philippine social and historical reality. The power of this friction was registered by Governor General Harrison in private correspondence.

An element of doubt crept into Harrison's thoughts about the existence of slavery, perhaps following the path carved by the revelation that there had not been an adequate criminal law against slavery. Earlier in October, Harrison told Garrison, the secretary of war, that "the term 'peonage' might more exactly describe the relation between master and servant in the cases referred to by Secretary Worcester, and of course we are familiar enough with peonage in some of our own states at home." [19] By December Harrison, somewhat less certain of the exact terms of involuntary servitude in the Philippines and more cautious in qualifying its ethnogeographical location and extent, told the secretary of war that "the Assembly is continuing its investigation as to whether slavery does or does not exist, and although I have an idea that slavery as an institution does not exist in the Christian Provinces in the Islands, I imagine that there does exist still the remnant of a feudal system under which retainers of the household are not always paid wages, but merely supplied with their board and lodging in return for their services." [20] In a letter to Moorfield Storey, the governor general praised the assembly's enactment of an antislavery law and advised the anti-imperialist leader that Worcester's charge "that slavery exists as an institution in the Christian provinces is probably a gross misstatement of fact, but into that question the legislature is now making an investigation and we are awaiting their report." [21] Along with the anti-imperialists, Harrison depended on the assembly's investigative committee to counter the weight of Worcester's authority on slavery.

CHAPTER THIRTEEN

A Nation of Kith and Kin

Since 1912, the Philippine national elite's denial that slavery existed in the Philippines had been supported only by the authority of their position as leading Filipinos; as Quezon put it, he was "a Filipino familiar with the facts." The documentation of *Slavery and Peonage in the Philippine Islands* undercut the Filipinos' already tenuous ability to represent their nation before a world dominated by imperialism and colonial knowledge. Worcester's report elicited a new hunger for "facts" that would prove that slavery did not exist in the Philippines. To satisfy this need, the investigative committee on slavery presented a series of reports to the assembly, later published in a single volume of over three hundred pages under the title *Informe Sobre la Esclavitud y Peonaje en Filipinas (Report on Slavery and Peonage in the Philippines)*.

Following its initial study of laws relating to slavery, the committee embarked on three tasks. It examined the history of social relations in the Philippines as recorded since the Spanish conquest; called upon the attorney general for a legal opinion on each case of involuntary servitude indexed by Worcester; and conducted interviews and hearings in the provinces to check Worcester's allegations empirically. Whenever possible, the committee made a point of using the hegemony of imperial observation to its own advantage by calling on European and American witnesses, authors, and precedents to support its contentions. The result was a mass of argument, excerpts and summaries of interviews,

tabulated data on alleged slaves, and erudite citations of legal, historical, and sociological literature.

The *Informe Sobre la Esclavitud* contains the first devoted historical
inquiry into Philippine forms of slavery. As such, the circumstances and
motivations behind its production shed much light on the subsequent
historiography of slavery in the Philippines and its entanglement in contemporary ideological concerns. Worcester did not probe the history of
slavery in the Philippines. His interest in slavery did not extend farther
back than the last years of Spanish rule. Ironically, because the assembly
committee wanted to prove that slavery had never existed in the Philippines it opened the history of slavery all the way back to the Spanish
conquest.

The historical section of the report presented excerpts from eight
texts describing the practice of slavery in the Philippines during the sixteenth through the eighteenth centuries, followed by a few short commentaries and a conclusion. Seven of the texts were written by Spanish
missionaries and colonial officials who lived during that period. For
copies of the two oldest texts—a letter dated 1574 from Fray Martín de
Rada and a manuscript of the 1580s written by *encomendero* Miguel de
Loarca—the committee turned to *The Philippine Islands, 1493–1898*,
a fifty-five volume collection of historical documents compiled and published under the aegis of the United States colonial administration.[1] The
eighth text was an account of early postconquest Philippine societies assembled from colonial sources by the esteemed Austrian ethnologist Ferdinand Blumentritt, who befriended Jose Rizal in Europe but never visited the Philippines himself. Instead of claiming knowledge as Filipinos,
the assembly committee reproduced the "testimonies" of these colonial
observers, directly in their own words and also through the mediating
sympathies of Dr. Blumentritt's exegesis.[2]

To prove the negative—that slavery had never existed in the Philippines—required a limiting case. The committee needed to identify the
most reliable and authoritative descriptions of alleged slavery so that it
could show that even the strongest evidence actually described some
other kind of social relationship. The committee selected documents
from Spanish missionaries and colonial officials as sources of authenti-
cated facts, but they were necessarily facts about practices that these observers united in calling slavery. "According to the letter of these testimonies," the committee concluded, "slavery existed in the Philippines at
the arrival of the Spaniards, as it had existed in all the nations of antiquity, in Rome, Greece, Egypt, among the Hebrews, etc."[3] Demonstrat-

ing that slavery did not exist in the Philippines therefore required interpretation against the friction of colonial documentation.

The committee began its interpretive work by distinguishing ancient
slavery from its modern variants. In antiquity, it argued, slavery "had
arisen . . . from a necessity of the time," as opposed to the "wicked combinations" that fostered slavery as a system of "exploitation" in modern
Europe and America. Indeed, in the Philippines, where a "continuous
state of war" raged before the Spanish conquest, the committee explained that "slavery signified a step toward humanitarianism" because
it furnished an alternative to killing one's defeated enemies. Quoting
J. K. Ingram's *History of Slavery and Serfdom*, the committee maintained that such ancient slavery was "entirely consonant" with the social life of the time, unlike the "abnormal outgrowth of the system of life
. . . in the West Indies and the United States of America." Although the
committee acknowledged that all of the historical "testimonies" listed
capture in raids or warfare as one route to "that which was called slavery," it steadfastly maintained that this relationship should not properly
be called slavery.[4]

The distinction between what the Spanish chroniclers called slavery
and what the committee considered real slavery hinged on definition and
a selective reading of the historical sources. For a definition of slavery
beyond reproach the committee again resorted to imperial authority.
"The essential elements of slavery," it declared, "have been noted by the
Supreme Court of the United States" in the Civil Rights Cases of 1883.
These decisions overturned provisions of the Civil Rights Act of 1875
and thus prepared the Constitutional basis for legally mandated racial
segregation in the post-Reconstruction period. The judgments turned,
in part, on a restrictive interpretation of the Thirteenth Amendment that
denied the continuing influence of slavery upon the lives of African
Americans after emancipation. To show that discrimination in civil society did not constitute slavery or an effect of slavery, the Court delin-
eated the "inseparable incidents" of slavery, including "compulsory service of the slave for the benefit of the master, restraint of his movement
except by the master's will, disability to hold property, to make contract,
to have a standing in court, to be a witness against a white person, and
such like burdens and incapacities."[5] This stringent definition of a slave
as the virtual extension of a master's will hardly fit the complex historical reality of slavery in the United States, let alone any other place. Yet,
being a definition of slavery given by the United States's highest court, it
enabled the committee to deny the existence of slavery by selectively re-

calling evidence about the abilities, willfulness, and mobility of so-called slaves in the Philippines.

The assembly committee's historical account emphasized the significance of labor arrangements that permitted even the most dependent categories of slaves to work for themselves at times, to acquire property, and to purchase their way out of slavery. Even some of the lowest ranks of people among Tagalog *alipin* and Visayan *oripun* were reputed by the documents "to work three days for the master and one for themselves." This, the committee said, constituted "proof that they were not legally incompetent to possess property" and thus could "redeem themselves if they pleased." This was a "fact" supported by "the unanimous testimony of all the authors who have dealt with this matter." [6]

The committee presented additional sources that testified to Philippine slaves' apparently equal standing with their masters in matters of food, drink, and dress. Here the committee cited the seventeenth-century historian Bartolomé Leonardo de Argensola's opinion that "those *indios* are improperly called slaves: their masters treat and love them like children, seat them at their tables, marry them with their daughters." The committee also recounted Fray Martín de Rada's observation of 1569, that "this race is the most arrogant that has been seen, and the slaves are the most free that one can imagine, since they only do what they want." To clinch the argument, the committee reproduced a Spanish source to buttress its assertion that "even in Jolo, where the institution exists legally under Mohammedan precepts, it is only slavery in name." Throughout the Philippines, the committee concluded, slavery was nothing "more than a name" applied to "cases of adoption, care for minors, domestic service, raising children [*crianza*], etc., carried out with more or less rigor and severity." [7]

The texts reprinted in the *Informe Sobre la Esclavitud* included evidence of a far more complex practice of slavery in the early colonial Philippines than the assembly committee wanted to recognize. Bondage involved considerable violence, requisition of labor, and the pursuit of profit by slave owners and traders. All commentators agreed that slaves were made through warfare and inherited status, as well as debt incurred through fines, loans, and exchanges. The assembly committee's focus on incidents involving children helped to imply a regime of fictive-parental supervision, but the sixteenth-century sources make explicit mention of children only as the descendents of slaves—most *alipin* and *oripun* appear in the sources as adults. The sources also described a vigorous slave trade, especially in the Visayas. In the sixteenth century,

Loarca endeavored to identify the local status of Visayan slaves purchased by the Spanish, thereby revealing that Philippine slaves not in-
frequently became Spanish slaves. Dr. Antonio de Morga observed that
"slaves are the major wealth and property which the natives of these islands have, because of their being so useful and necessary for their farm-
ing and estates." He described Tagalog *alipin sa gigilid* as slaves, "like
those we have."[8] In addition, the slaves' ability to purchase their way
out of slavery could be interpreted as confirmation of the economic
value of the institution, as slaves had to pay their price in goods, gold,
or, with the coming of the Spaniards, currency.

In effect, the historical chapter of the assembly's report on slavery appropriated the concept of mild slavery invoked a decade earlier by the
colonial state when it was hestitant to act against slavery in the southern Philippines. The idea of a mild kind of bondage served as an ideological legitimation of indigenous social hierarchy against the abolitionist claims of Worcester's imperialist propaganda. Yet, its employment in
interpreting early Spanish colonial history also indicated the degree to
which the assembly committee identified with imperial observation and
the record of colonialism in the Philippines. For example, Fray Martín
de Rada's observation about the arrogance of the *indios* and the liberties taken by their slaves, heralded by the investigating committee as an
indication of slavery's leniency, could well be interpreted with reference
to de Rada's position among slave-holding Spaniards intent on the conquest of the Philippines. He had more than just an idle curiosity about
the natives' willingness to submit to authority.

The committee's identification with the gaze of Spanish colonial rule
reached its apogee in the closing paragraphs of the report's historical
section. After all of its efforts to interpret historical references as indica-
tive of a mild kind of bondage that should not be called slavery, the committee returned to Spain's laws regarding slavery for its final argument
against the existence of slavery in Philippine history. Thus, even if one
were to follow the letter of the historical documents and admit that
"slavery existed in those distant days," the committee retorted that "the
[Spanish] kings always prohibited it; and only permitted it in very special circumstances when they were dealing, for example, with very rebellious people or tribes, as happened with the Moros of Mindanao and
Joló and the Samal."[9]

Because Spain used enslavement of Muslims and recalcitrant pagans
as "a method to redeem and convert them to a Christian life," the committee excused it as a temporary status pending submission and incor-

poration into the body of colonized Christian subjects.[10] In this way, the subject of investigation changed from native forms of bondage to Spain's supposed prohibition of indigenous slavery and then to a legitimation of the exceptions in which Spain permitted enslavement. Instead of addressing the question of indigenous forms of bondage, the report's historical section concluded by discussing the relationship between colonialism and slavery from the point of view of the Spanish colonizers.

The investigative committee drew no clear distinction between indigenous forms of bondage and the slavery practiced by Spaniards with official approval. It did not distinguish between Spanish colonial hierarchy and indigenous hierarchy, and for this reason did not reflect on colonialism itself as a form of bondage. Rather, the committee denied the historical existence of Philippine slavery by adapting the old Spanish distinction between just and unjust slavery to a new, antislavery context.

The early Spanish colonial laws reproduced in the *Informe Sobre la Esclavitud* stipulated that Spaniards should not enslave the *indios* and, instead, should allow them to choose subordination to the king and to Christ. Their enslavement would have been unjust under the Spanish law. This implied that Spanish colonialism was not a kind of slavery and that Filipinos had not been slaves under Spanish rule. However, the report also explicitly defended the use of enslavement as a method of colonialism among Muslims and pagans. This would have been considered a form of just slavery by early modern Spanish monarchs and clerics, because these Muslims and pagans, like the millions of African slaves shipped to the Americas, were classified as people who had refused the offer of Christianity.

The postabolitionist conscience of elite nationalists in the Philippine Assembly could accept the Spanish enslavement of Moros and pagans only because, theoretically, it culminated in a colonial relation of submission to king and Christ that officially terminated the relation of slavery. In the assembly's report, elite nationalists refigured and accepted the history of Spanish colonialism as an antislavery narrative. Because they imagined that submission to Spain and conversion to Christianity saved Filipinos from slavery, elite nationalists' identification with the Spanish colonial heritage could be used as an argument against a similar submission to Worcester's abolitionist imperialism.

Where Spanish slavery could not be altogether denied, it was explained as a kind of mild slavery that was self-negating. This was an exact parallel to the way that the assembly committee interpreted historical sources on indigenous forms of slavery, and it also served as a model for the way the committee responded to Worcester's charges of slavery in the contemporary Philippines.

The assembly committee replied to Worcester's specific allegations in two ways. First, it printed the opinion of Ignacio Villamor, the attorney general, on whether the incidents of slavery alleged to have occurred in provinces under the assembly's jurisdiction constituted "slavery, involuntary servitude, or peonage in the legal sense of these terms." [11] Then the committee reported its own evaluation of the factuality of Worcester's charges, based on a review of documents and its own investigations, interviews, and hearings in the relevant provinces.

Villamor's contribution was an exercise in the most rigorous disciplinary reasoning. He did not directly question Worcester's narration of circumstances or events. Instead, his analysis depended on definition and the system of legal classification embedded in the penal code. The assembly committee's fieldwork did dispute some aspects of Worcester's documentation, but the committee likewise depended most heavily upon definition to carry its argument that slavery did not exist in the Philippines. When the law, restrictive definitions, and empirical investigation could not fully dispel the charge of slavery, Villamor and the assembly committee resorted to the argument that the benevolence and mutuality of Philippine social relations made real slavery an impossibility.

As a member of the executive branch of the colonial government, Villamor needed Governor General Harrison's sanction to undertake a legal analysis of Worcester's cases for the assembly committee. Harrison authorized the study on November 14, the day that the special committee proposed its antislavery bill to the full assembly. Villamor submitted his opinion on Worcester's cases to Harrison and the assembly on November 19, just three days before he would advise Harrison that the 1885 penal code had voided any effective laws penalizing slavery as a crime. Villamor did not discuss his opinion of current antislavery laws in his report for the assembly committee. Instead, he reviewed the cases cited by Worcester and demonstrated, readily, that none had been prosecuted for slavery. Although he reprinted the Philippine Supreme Court's decision in the Cabanag case, he passed over the justices' clear statement that there were no laws defining slavery as a crime.[12]

Villamor divided the cases of alleged bondage into groups involving questions of criminal law and civil law. In discussing matters relating to criminal law, he recounted details from each case, but he did not enter into a substantive evaluation of the acts and relationships described in them. He argued only that the cases "do not constitute slavery, involun-

tary servitude, or peonage as legally defined" because the alleged perpe-
trators had been prosecuted for other crimes, such as illegal detention,
kidnapping, coercion, or corruption of minors, which did "not necessarily make [the victims] slaves or place them in a state of peonage." [13]

The remaining cases fell within the purview of civil statutes regulating care of minors, adoption, contracts, and relations between masters
and servants. Villamor argued that these laws would define the nature
of the transgression if any abuses or violations had actually occurred.
For example, Villamor wrote that it was a "legal presumption that contracts have been voluntarily entered into," hence "the violation of contracts does not subject the injured party to a condition of slavery, nor
does it place him in a condition of peonage." Damages so caused could
be "redressed by the remedies provided for by the law." [14]

In the criminal cases, it was enough for Villamor to show that crimes
other than slavery had been committed, for as crimes they were simply
anomalous acts against the norms of society. The recognition that individuals might occasionally commit such crimes as kidnapping or illegal
detention did not jeopardize nationalist pride. But the civil cases Villamor grouped under the headings "adoption," "care of minors," "domestic service," and "sale of Negritos, Ifugaos and Tagbanuas" were
different. These cases reflected directly on basic social relations and institutions inevitably tied to the nationalist imagination. Consequently,
Villamor identified patterns of behavior in the civil cases that he judged
not only within the law but also commendable. The problem shifted,
then, from properly labelling offenses everyone could agree were criminal to formulating a positive explanation of social relations that would
invalidate any notion that the acquisition of people through "adoption,"
"sale," or debt carried the taint of slavery. As Villamor argued that slavery did not and could not exist, he delivered an apologia for a social hierarchy, including relations of bondage, based upon the ideology of a
characteristically benevolent, mild servitude.

After listing eleven cases cited by Worcester in which lowland Christians claimed to have baptized and adopted Negritos and Igorots, aged
from five to forty years, Villamor defended the practice on grounds of
high principle. Where Worcester questioned the rationalization of these
relations through baptism and adoption, Villamor accepted them at face
value as an expression of Filipino social mores. "The custom of the Filipinos to adopt Negritos," he explained, "even if such adoption be only
de facto—as shown in the [Worcester] report—is far from being a pre-
text to enslave them, but on the contrary it serves as a relief from or-

phanhood and poverty by providing the helpless with a family and a home where life is, at least, more bearable, if not really enjoyable; and, above all, such custom serves to foster sentiments of humanity and of charity [beneficencia]." [15]

Under the heading "care of minors," Villamor reviewed ten cases in which young Negritos and lowland Filipinos were taken in by lowland Christians, who kept some of them in their households as unpaid servants past their twentieth birthday. The penal code and civil laws stipulated obligations in the care of minors, including basic sustenance, "Christian education," and the duty to return a child upon a parent's demand. "Aside from this," Villamor continued, "the affection which naturally arises from the sacrifices of him who takes a child under his care and the gratitude of the latter create a stronger bond of affection between them than those that could otherwise be established by law." Children placed in the care of others occupied "in the Filipino family an intermediate place between an adopted child and a domestic servant." In these situations, Villamor counseled, "wages bear no importance; the principal consideration is affection and love on the part of the one, and gratitude on the part of the other." [16]

According to Villamor's reading of the law, a minor bonded to the care of a family "preserves all his freedom" to own property, leave the master's premises, return to his or her parents, and even to sue in the courts for compensation. In addition, there was surely no legal offense when a parent turned a child over to another for superior care, for the law provided for "the appointment of a guardian [tutor]" when a child's parents died or were "unfit to perform the duties devolving upon them as such." This rhetoric of affection, benevolence, and fitness to serve as a guardian, used by Villamor to justify Philippine social hierarchy, was strikingly close to the rhetoric of American colonialism. By the same token, we can imagine that colonial officials who insisted that American rule was not slavery might have asked, along with Villamor, "What kind of slaves are these who fully enjoy all the rights accorded to free persons and do not find themselves in any of the conditions which constitute slavery?" [17]

The cases Villamor grouped as "domestic service" and "sale" of non-Christians required more textured description and analysis to differentiate them from slavery. The "main distinction between a slave and a servant lies," according to Villamor, in slavery's nature as an "imposed," "inherited," and "permanent status" that denies all liberty. Servants, in contrast, enter willingly into a relation with a master through a free con-

tract. They retain the right to free contract, although the relation between master and servant presupposes "a certain bond of sympathy
greater than that which proceeds from the relation of employer and
employee."[18]

Among the twenty-eight cases of "domestic service" Villamor reviewed, he acknowledged there were some in which "it appears that the
master resorted to usury in order to oppress his servant." But these were
cases of usury, not peonage; they were, he wrote, "nothing but the vestiges of the oppression of man by man, which unfortunately prevails
among all people and in all countries." These instances of "adversity
and penury" could "only be regarded as cases of slavery, involuntary
servitude, or peonage when we use such term *in a figurative sense,*" as
when people "receive ill treatment from those of whom they should expect consideration and affection," or when workers "under the supervision of others . . . are harshly treated, etc."[19]

Villamor's willingness to admit that domestic servants were sometimes abused in a way that could be figuratively called slavery only
sharpened his awareness of the need to distinguish metaphorical from
real slavery. Referring to the labor-control law of 1912 (later known as
the Peonage Act) that prescribed criminal penalties for intentional failure to perform services paid for in advance, Villamor asked, "if a cred-
itor mistreating his debtor who has voluntarily entered his service is
guilty of the crime of peonage, what validity will the juridical relations
of men have in society?" Contracts had to be upheld above petty abuses,
for they found "sanction in the law and any abuse or annoyance committed in connection therewith is provided for by the law itself." If the
cases cited by Worcester were treated as "types of peonage or involuntary servitude, it would be equivalent to creating, as it were, a judicial
chaos in society. The contracts of loan and hiring of services would be
robbed of their legal validity, and contractual obligations would be
nothing but illusory."[20] Slavery, peonage, and involuntary servitude
were pejorative conditions of "inhumanity and subjection," according
to Villamor.[21] Therefore, he concluded, labeling the enforcement of labor to pay off debts with the word *peonage* would threaten the entire social order of contracts, debts, and obligations.

In arguing that the forty-one cases of "sale" listed by Worcester did
not constitute slavery, Villamor drew from his preceding analyses of
adoption, care of minors, and domestic service. Using the Cabanag case
as representative of all others, Villamor maintained that "the fact of the

sale alone does not show that the Ifugaos or Negritos sold were turned over to the buyers against the will of their parents or guardians, or that they were taken altogether out of the latter's control." Because slavery was prohibited by the Philippine Organic Act of 1902, human beings could not be legally bought, sold, or owned. Thus, argued the attorney general, "the term 'sale' is improperly applied" to the subjects of such transactions. "Whether it be to relieve misery, or to alleviate the burdens of a poor family, or to allow compensation for the intermediary's services in these transactions," he reasoned, "the money given for an Igorot or Negrito cannot be taken but as a payment in advance for future services to be rendered by him." [22]

Villamor made plain his distaste for the exchange of humans for cash. He called the idea of buying and selling non-Christians "inhuman," but he argued that the act of sale alone did not necessarily indicate a state of slavery or peonage. "In many of the alleged cases of sale of Negritos and Ifugaos it is said that the supposed purchasers assign them to household work—using them as servants," and therefore, he implied, not as slaves. More importantly, "cases are not wanting where they were baptized and made Christians and given their master's names," which showed that it was not their master's "intention to subject them to slavery or involuntary servitude." [23] These examples of recognition and inclusion conflicted with Villamor's sense of the legal meaning of slavery, much as conversion and baptism once marked Spanish subjects as supposedly unenslavable.

In fact, when Villamor searched for a legal definition of slavery, he found that neither the Philippine Organic Act nor the Thirteenth Amendment to the United States Constitution gave one. Consequently, he examined the use of these terms "by the courts and other authorities," such as *Webster's Dictionary, Black's Law Dictionary*, legal commentaries, and encyclopedias, all postabolitionist sources that viewed slavery externally, as an institution that had been rightfully abolished. This encouraged an idealized definition of slavery, which Villamor understood as an indelible "condition or status" of subjection to a master.[24]

Instead of seeing slavery as a relationship or process that could harbor ambiguity and flexibility, Villamor followed the postabolitionist tendency to see slaves as a particularly abject type. From this perspective, what mattered in discerning whether a person was a slave was not how one entered into or worked through a relationship, but how one ended up. Treatment, therefore, could serve as the final test of real bondage. "If the persons sold are well treated as servants or are regarded as members of the supposed purchaser's family," then, the attorney general determined, "such sales do not constitute involuntary servitude or peonage as legally defined." On the basis of his assumption that paternal benevolence made even the condition of purchased people tolerable, Villamor concluded that none of Worcester's cases constituted "slavery, involuntary servitude, or peonage in the juridical sense of these words."[25]

The assembly committee's examination of Worcester's specific allegations differed from Villamor's analysis in several respects. It emphasized empirical investigation rather than typological legal evaluation, and thus it, most directly of all the committee's work, provided Filipino nationalists with the facts they desired to refute Worcester's charges. Most importantly, this field investigation addressed the condition of specific individuals in the present, rather than the definition of social or legal status in the distant (historical) or recent (legal) past.

Slavery did not exist as a substantial institution in the Catholic Philippines at the end of 1913, when the committee sent delegations out to the provinces. Refuting Worcester's charge that slavery continued to flourish in the Philippines was thus an easier task than explaining away its existence in the past, but involuntary servitude and peonage were different matters. As a consequence of its focus on the reality of current social practices, the committee's investigators were even less willing than Villamor was to admit the existence of oppressive relationships. Despite these shades of difference, their fundamental arguments and conclusions were identical, matching those of the committee's historical review of slavery in the Philippines. That is to say, the committee's empirical investigation and description of certain social relations in the Philippines recreated many of the same contradictory identifications with colonialism, Christianity, and paternalistic hierarchy that were earlier produced through the methodologies of historical and legal analysis.

Five subcommittees fanned out into the provinces in November and December 1913 to search for the people mentioned in Worcester's report. In addition, the subcommittees inquired after the condition of domestic servants and others taken into households and solicited testimony from notable residents as to social conditions in their localities. Case by case, the subcommittees denied that any offenses or abuses had been committed. Extending the investigation beyond Worcester's specific allegations to include, in theory, any similar cases encountered in the provinces was much like the special committee's earlier move to open the subject of slavery throughout Philippine history. The openness to include all cases enabled the committee to issue an empirically founded denial that slavery, involuntary servitude, or peonage existed in any part of the Philippines within the assembly's jurisdiction, just as the historical section of the *Informe Sobre la Esclavitud* supported the claim that slavery had never existed.

Whereas Villamor evaluated groups of cases in a summary fashion, the assembly subcommittees reproduced excerpts and summaries of interviews individually. In the conclusion to the report, the committee recapitulated the findings of these interviews in tabular form. This seemed to convey a concrete record of evidence that contradicted Worcester's allegations. As a strategy, the interviews and tabulated results highlighted the presentation of facts, yet it did so in a way that represented and refracted relations of power and authority.

The reports of interviews with alleged slaves, servants, and adopted minors were seldom more than two or three sentences long and almost always presented synoptically, in the third person. The range of information provided in these interviews was rather narrow, typically limited to statements about their subjects' status as servants or members of the family, whether they were paid a salary, if they had been delivered by their parents, and so forth. Interviews with more prominent people, such as officials, businessmen, and landowners, were typically longer and occasionally presented in verbatim transcript form.

There was no discussion about whether servants felt free to speak about their condition, or if Filipino masters or employers might be rationalizing their power over social inferiors. Americans, such as constabulary officers and other officials, received special attention as witnesses who could speak with imperial authority against Worcester. The names and circumstances of adoptees, servants, and alleged slaves became data that could be presented in tables; the testimony of prominent Filipinos and Americans was recorded in substantive statements. This hierarchy had ethnic as well as class dimensions.

For example, Subcommittee No. 1, assigned to investigate northern Luzon, did not visit Nueva Vizcaya or the Mountain Province, the homes of the Ifugao, most Igorots, and some Negrito peoples. Instead, it traveled extensively in the lowland provinces of Isabela and Cagayan, where it traced and interviewed approximately two hundred formerly non-Christian people living as servants, adoptees, and so on. From this research, the committee assimilated local lowland perceptions to its own Manila-centered nationalist framework, excluding the perspective of non-Christian peoples.

According to the subcommittee, the Mountain Province "had no schools" before American rule, so parents put their children under the care of lowland Christians "who would want to take them" and provide schooling. Others were brought to the lowlands to "avoid death" during famines, and some infants were "given up" in exchange for a "gift in goods or cash." In the lowlands, these children entered society, received schooling, religious instruction, and became part of families. "As a matter of fact," the subcommittee concluded, "the Ifugaos, Igorots, Kalingas, Aetas, and others originating from the mountains and today residing in Cagayan and Isabela have bettered their condition by the fact of being in these provinces, and, in fact, enjoy a standard of culture much more elevated than that of their compatriots in the Mountain Province." [26] Not only did the non-Christians supposedly want to be Christianized and raised to a higher level of culture but also, the subcommittee argued, the Christian Filipinos of Isabela and Cagayan had done a better job of civilizing the non-Christians by taking them into their households than Spain or the United States had done by occupying their home territories. The *Informe Sobre la Esclavitud* explained the relation between Christians and non-Christians in decidedly colonial terms, using virtually the same idiom of evangelical paternalism institutionalized by Spain.[27]

Had the subcommittee charged with investigating Worcester's allegations in northern Luzon visited Nueva Vizcaya and the Mountain Province, they would have been faced with the problem of explaining the practice of trading captives and pawns among the Ifugao and others. How the special committee might have handled this can be glimpsed in the report of the fifth subcommittee, which discussed the practice of slavery in the Moro Province.

Subcommittee No. 5 visited the southern Visayas and Mindanao. Alone among the subcommittees, this body acknowledged that there were undisputed "cases of sale of human beings," which it designated as "proven cases of slavery." There were seventeen such cases in which people had been convicted for the criminal offense of slavery in the Moro Province. However, the subcommittee was quick to add, "One has to note the fact that all of the proven cases of slavery have occurred within the territory of the Moro Province, which is outside the control of the Philippine Assembly." And even then, "the relations of these supposed slaves with their masters" never presented "the true aspect of slavery," as once existed "in the United States." This assessment was supported by the American governor of the Davao district of the Moro Province, who told the subcommittee that "the slaves of the savage people in the Philippine Islands do not have just the same status as the slaves that were in the United States before the Civil War." These slaves, he said, were rarely resold because most were like "members of their master's family." [28]

Although the concept of mild slavery was employed explicitly only by Subcommittee No. 5 in its discussion of the Moro Province, it actually played a central role throughout all of the subcommittees' reports. In the tabulated results of Subcommittee No. 1's investigation, almost all of the cases of alleged bondage were explained in the language of paternalism. The greatest number were classified as effectively adopted, occupying a position "like children" in the household. The next largest group were classed according to quality of treatment and whether they received a salary. Only in the accompanying text were they identified as servants in their master's household. Some received salaries, typically less than ten pesos per month. Others received no wages. All, however, were first described as "well treated," implying again that quality of treatment was more determinative of social condition than whether one worked for wages, to pay back a debt, or out of direct physical compulsion. The third largest group of cases were labeled "*como socio*," that is, "like a partner" or "like a member." In the interview records, most of these people described a sharecropping relationship in tobacco production. Most who specified their share put it at one-quarter of the crop, a small share for a sparsely populated region, especially when compared to the half-and-half sharing typical of the more populous central Luzon Plain. In almost all of the cases listed as *como socio*, as in the cases categorized as "like children" and "well treated," the individuals in question had taken the surname of the household in which they lived.[29] Subcommittee No. 2, whose principal work was to investigate cases involving Negritos in central Luzon, used identical characterizations and reported a similar pattern of surnames.[30]

It is important to remember at this point that the principal issues at stake in the slavery controversy were political and ideological, not social or economic. The actual social relationships investigated by the subcommittees were not being challenged in any existential way. That was not the purpose of Worcester's 1913 report, nor was the Philippine Assembly concerned to preserve these relationships from dissolution.

Despite the seemingly equal standing of slavery and peonage in the title of his report, Worcester's rhetorical focus was on slavery, which no longer existed as a substantial institution anywhere in the Philippines. Moreover, Worcester's charges of slavery almost always involved non-Christians. This concentrated the ensuing debate on regions and relationships that were remote from the centers of the colonial political economy. Political symbolism, national identity, and the implications for the upcoming consideration of the Jones bill for Philippine independence were what was really at stake in the contest over slavery. Worcester's report on slavery fomented a scandal over social relations that would challenge nationalist and anti-imperialist representations of the Filipino nation without disrupting commodity production for the international market or the economic sustenance of the colonial elite.

In general, the subcommittees followed the sociogeography of Worcester's allegations, thus reinscribing his definition of the dispute as one about relations between non-Christians and Christian Filipinos. The social relationships under contention were marginal to the colonial economy, and the subcommittees investigating them further denied that they involved any exploitation from which the alleged masters acquired benefits. Subcommittee No. 1 directed its attention to cases involving Ifugaos, Igorots, and Negritos in the Cagayan Valley, a region of little economic power in the early twentieth century. Subcommittee No. 2's territorial scope did include the important sugar- and rice-producing districts of central Luzon, as well as Manila, but its almost exclusive focus on several dozen cases involving Negritos as household servants and adoptees kept larger social relations of production out of view; the subcommittee made no reference to the commercial agriculture in its district. Subcommittees Nos. 3 and 5 steered clear of major commodity-producing areas as they examined a smaller number of cases involving non-Christians and Moros, respectively, in southern Luzon and the southern Philippines. Subcommittee No. 4 was, however, an exception to this pattern. It merits closer examination to see what its difference can reveal about the *Informe Sobre la Esclavitud* as a reply to the slavery scandal.

Subcommittee No. 4 investigated the Visayas, where the center of sugar production in the Philippines was located on Negros Island. The Negros sugar boom began in the second half of the nineteenth century. By the end of 1913 the Negros planters were poised to enjoy some of their most profitable years. The first of several large centrifugal sugar mills had just been introduced, a duty-free quota of three hundred thousand tons of sugar had been set for exports to the United States, and an especially lucrative market would soon develop during the First World War. The new sugar *centrals* were among the most highly capitalized industries in the Philippines and the island's planters, mostly Philippine-born *mestizos*, were among the colony's largest private employers of labor. This workforce was created through the planters' long struggle against what they perceived as a local labor shortage on Negros.[31]

Negros had been sparsely settled by a largely non-Christian population until immigrant homesteaders and tenants began to cultivate sugar in the mid–nineteenth century. Their labor was supplemented by a stream of seasonal migrants who came from the neighboring islands of Panay to the northwest and Cebu to the east, lured from those economically difficult regions by the attraction of advance payments for work on Negros. Debt thereby became central to labor relations on Negros, the pivot on which planters' control of labor and workers' counter-struggle turned. There is some dispute among historians about the extent to which violence played a role in the early development of this labor regime. One historian reports that "whipping remained a standard practice until the 1920s," when the labor movement forced its end. But another argues that the labor regime was a more paternalistic order in which laborers benefited from the power born of their own scarcity and the crumbling weakness of the colonial state in nineteenth-century Negros. Further research is needed to ascertain the level of non-state violence exercised by planters and workers in the nineteenth century. However, it is clear that American colonialism furnished the planters with a greatly strengthened state and that the population of Negros increased markedly, from one hundred thousand in 1850 to five hundred thousand by the 1910s and then to one million by 1939. By the 1920s, then, there is no dispute that "[t]he dictates of sugar capital had become preponderant over labor."[32]

Worcester had cited only two specific charges of slavery in the region of the Visayas covered by Subcommittee No. 4. Neither case had any obvious relation to labor in the sugar industry. The first concerned a teen-age girl who was apparently exchanged for twenty pesos between members of a Chinese merchant family in Cadiz, Negros Occidental. Three years later she was brought to board a ship bound for China with her alleged owner. The American customs collector in Iloilo, the region's major seaport, informed Worcester of the incident and, in passing, recounted that he had been told that "the ownership of household slaves who are regularly bought and sold is so common . . . that it excites no special interest among foreigners who are familiar with such forms of servitude." The second case was from Romblon Island, where two men were convicted by the Court of First Instance (a decision upheld by the Philippine Supreme Court) for the crime of abducting minors in a scheme to supply servants to far-off households at ten pesos a head. The subcommittee readily disposed of both cases: the first on testimony that the young woman had voluntarily entered into a labor and then romantic relationship with the Chinese merchant, the second because the accused had been convicted for a crime other than slavery.[33] But, instead of resting with these rebuttals and some general statements about the nonexistence of slavery and peonage similar to those expounded by the other subcommittees, this one pursued the matter further.

The subcommittee visited many of the principal towns on Panay, Romblon, and in Negros Occidental. The municipal council in each town presented formal protests against Worcester's charges, insisting that slavery, involuntary servitude, and peonage did not exist. Throughout the region, prominent citizens, clerics, and resident foreigners contradicted Worcester in public meetings. Speakers at a town meeting at Dumalag in Capiz Province on Panay declared that they "have never known slavery, peonage, or involuntary servitude in their respective municipalities." A meeting of citizens in Manapla, Negros Occidental, "unanimously agreed that slavery, peonage, and involuntary servitude have never existed" in the town or in the entire province. Public assemblies in the rich sugar district of La Carlota and other towns in northern Negros produced similar statements. In the town of Silay, the American constabulary lieutenant "denied the existence of slavery, peonage, and involuntary servitude . . . in every point in the Philippines where he has been." More American officials concurred in his opinion, and in Cadiz the American owner of a lumber business was supported in this view by "many workers" from his business.[34] Similar protests were sent from places the subcommittee did not reach during its tour of the region, such as Leyte and Samar. The special committee on slavery and the assembly then began to receive similar letters of protest from dozens of municipalities and provincial boards around the Philippines.[35]

From its travels and interviews, the subcommittee crafted a short report that vehemently denied the existence of slavery and peonage in the Visayas. However, even in this brief document there were indications of a more ambiguous order of labor relations. The subcommittee reported the opinions of a few Americans, such as the publisher of the Iloilo *Enterprise Press* and the constabulary colonel stationed in Iloilo, who claimed to have heard about cases of debt bondage. Although neither could identify any specific cases by name, the constabulary officer did tell the subcommittee that his troops had "frequently" arrested debtors under the terms of Act 2098, the labor control law of 1912, later known as the Peonage Act. This, the subcommittee suggested, was "no more than an abuse by a powerful one over some of the weak," but, in a clarifying letter included in the report, the colonel still insisted that this type of labor relation "partakes of the nature of peonage." [36]

The two most revealing statements about labor, however, came from a Filipino official and planter on Negros. In San Carlos, a leading sugar district in northeastern Negros, a planter called for the abolition of Act 2098 because its effects were part of "the cause of the emigration of our workers to the interior." In its place, he wanted to prohibit the giving of advances and generalize the labor regime employed at the Central Milling Company, where they paid workers "weekly and controlled the work with total punctuality." [37] The justice of the peace in Cápiz, on the northern shore of Panay, interpreted the effects of Act 2098 differently. "Up until now," he told the subcommittee in a letter, "in the cases denounced as infractions of Law 2098 the workers are the accused and not the patrons, demonstrating that the patrons in the jurisdiction of this justice have not abused their workers." [38] Enforcing work to pay off a debt was taken for granted as a proper and normal means of labor control and, more paradoxically, as a sign of liberality among employers.

Subcommittee No. 4's report was the only contribution to the entire controversy over slavery that even touched upon labor relations in large-scale commodity production. This was a subject that Worcester had scrupulously avoided, and the special committee did the same in every other region of the Philippines. The significance of this subcommittee's report might be read in at least two ways, depending on whether one emphasizes its place within the socioeconomic context of the Negros-centered economy or its position in the Philippine Assembly's production of the *Informe Sobre la Esclavitud*.

The subcommittee's brief discussion of the labor-control law of 1912 implied a distinction between the practice of labor control through debt and police power, on the one hand, and a range of proscribed labor relations, known as slavery, peonage, and involuntary servitude, on the other. Elsewhere in the Philippines, it was the omission of any discussion about the principal relations of production in commercial activities that implicitly protected them from association with discredited forms of servitude. In this way, the discussion of slavery certainly revealed the

boundaries of permissible forms of hierarchy and labor exploitation in
the worldview of economic and political leaders tied to the Negros economy. Antislavery ideology legitimized a broad spectrum of coercive labor relations in the Visayas by defining them as other than slavery, much
as it defined the ideology of free labor in the nineteenth-century Anglo-
American world. Yet although planters, mill owners, and local officials
freely expressed their assumptions about the need for compulsory discipline of labor, the labor question was only incidental to the larger nationalist purpose of their response to Worcester's allegations of slavery.

When viewed as an element of the *Informe Sobre la Esclavitud,* the
subcommittee's report on the Visayas takes on special importance as a
boundary marker in nationalist discourse. Whereas Worcester concentrated on the non-Christian tribes in his representation of Filipinos, the
subcommittees were divided into equal bodies of three deputies each
and assigned to report on the more or less equally sized regions covering all of the Christian Philippines. Although they shouldered unequal
burdens in responding to Worcester's specific charges, within the organization of the *Informe Sobre la Esclavitud* each subcommittee enjoyed
equivalent standing as the representative for a segment of the nation. By
exceeding the ethnogeographical focus of Worcester's report and including references to labor in the sugar economy, the subcommittee reports helped to mark the *Informe Sobre la Esclavitud* as comprehensive,
filling out the boundaries of national territory.

The subcommittees had to make inquiries in all parts of the Philippines, even those Worcester did not implicate in his report, precisely because they fell within the territorial limits of the Filipino nation as represented by the assembly. To employ an idea that Benedict Anderson
borrowed from Victor Turner, I would liken the subcommittee investigations to a series of pilgrimages out to the provinces and then back that
linked those regions in a meaningful way to the center of national identity in Manila.[39] The subcommittee on the Visayas then accelerated the
communication with the national center by initiating a campaign of local protests against Worcester's report, which soon became one of the
earliest petition movements to enmesh communities all over the Philippines in a national political issue.

In addition to covering territorial space within the nation, the subcommittee investigating the Visayas also incorporated important elements of what we might call social and temporal space. Other subcommittees addressed cases in a variety of social environments. Their reports

emphasized relations between non-Christian and Christian Filipinos, but they also included discussion of non-Christian and Moro communities that the committee members called "primitive" and "savage," sharecropping in some lowland Christian areas, and domestic service in places ranging from provincial villages to Manila. These investigations demonstrated that slavery did not exist among "primitive" people in the mountains, traditional people in the countryside, or modern people in Manila households. The subcommittee report on the Visayas completed this schematic portrait of Philippine social relations by including an image, however fleeting, of one of the most commercialized and capitalized sectors in the Philippine economy. This represented another economic sector and, symbolically, the Philippines' economic future.

The conclusion to the *Informe Sobre la Esclavitud* prefaced the special committee's findings with a section that it called the "Concept and Phases of Slavery," a brief universal history of the institution. In terms of the time, place, and social structure of slavery, the survey swept from ancient Greece and Rome through serfdom and vassalage in medieval Europe to African slavery in the Americas, "white slavery" in New York and Eastern Europe, and industrial wage slavery in modern England. The committee based its survey on the authority of the historical and social sciences, assimilating the social evolutionist framework of such prominent authors as Herbert Spencer, Lester Frank Ward, J. K. Ingram, and Sir Henry Maine.[40] As a universal history, this study depended upon a single definition of slavery that could transcend the limitations of time, place, and culture. Predictably, their definition of slavery was static, essentialist, and founded on the particular manifestations of slavery emphasized by postabolitionist European and American culture—namely, a status marked by race, the concept of legal ownership, and forced labor in production.

When juxtaposed to the *Informe Sobre la Esclavitud's* investigative findings, this universal definition of slavery provided a stark contrast. Thus, the committee concluded "that if indeed slavery existed in the Philippines at the time of the conquest, it was of a very liberal and benevolent (*tan liberal y benevola*) kind that, even in its most severe form, did not nullify the personality of the slave, in notable contrast to the slavery [practiced] from primitive and yet-recent times in other countries, in which the slave has always been considered like a thing." The committee declared that in the contemporary Philippines slavery did not exist in any of its "forms and manifestations," and neither did peonage. If there were, in fact, cases in which people were sold, the committee insisted that this only happened in the special provinces that had been under Worcester's jurisdiction. Moreover, it argued, the status of "the person sold has never been that of a slave."[41]

Far more than simply arguing that slavery did not exist in the Philippines, the *Informe Sobre la Esclavitud* marked out a set of borders within which slavery could not exist in the past, present, or future. Congruent with the assembly committee's essentialist definition of slavery, it posited an essential Filipino nature that extended across time, ethnic groups, regions, and differences of social structure. It imagined an identity averse to slavery that continued throughout time, filled the boundaries of the colonial territory called the Philippines, and incorporated all ethnic groups and social relations within itself. In short, the *Informe Sobre la Esclavitud* imagined a nation in which all Christian Filipinos were members, like members of a family connected together by hierarchical relations and mutual obligation.

CHAPTER FOURTEEN

The Manumission
of the Philippines

To the Philippine national elite, it must have seemed in the early months of 1914 that the question of slavery was going to be put to rest. Governor General Harrison had taken a public stand against Worcester's report. The *Informe Sobre la Esclavitud* and the antislavery law of 1913 addressed all of Worcester's major charges. When the chairman of the special committee on slavery presented its final report to the Philippine Assembly on 28 February 1914, he told his colleagues that the document "totally belies all the accusations that have been hurled against this long-suffering people." [1] One month earlier, while the special committee was still formulating its report, an official in the colony's Executive Bureau took all of the surplus copies of Dean C. Worcester's *Slavery and Peonage in the Philippine Islands* to Manila's municipal ice plant and burned them. Manila papers reported that the volumes were "condemned to the flames." Worcester's report had been, it seemed, thoroughly destroyed. [2]

There were additional signs that the problem of slavery might be resolved in an even more far-reaching fashion than a mere repudiation of Worcester's allegations. Harrison began to fulfill his promise to advance home rule by installing a Filipino majority in the Philippine Commission and initiating a program of "Filipinization" that rapidly replaced almost all Americans in the Philippine civil service with Filipinos. Most important of all, hopes were still high that the Jones bill would soon be made law by the Democratic Congress and President Wilson, setting a date for the redemption and emancipation of the Filipino nation.

The Philippine national elite marked the shift in antislavery ideology's implications for colonial politics by giving it concrete expression in legislation. In April 1914 the Philippine Commission proposed to make the Anti-Slavery Law of 1913 apply uniformly throughout the entire Philippines, replacing the Moro Province Anti-Slavery Law of 1903 and the Anti-Slavery Law for the non-Christian tribes that was passed in 1911. The latter two laws were American decrees that identified colonial rule with antislavery principles and demarcated limits to Filipino authority. The Philippine Assembly produced the 1913 law, but it did so for fundamentally defensive purposes under the pressure of Worcester's propaganda. In the changed circumstances of 1914, however, the Philippine Commission's antislavery bill became a vehicle for nationalist objectives.

The Philippine Commission turned the bill into a nationalist achievement by reworking the connection between slavery and the non-Christian tribes. Debates over antislavery laws had always been tied to the meaning of the non-Christian tribes through antislavery ideology's association of slavery with the uncivilized, as well as the involvement of non-Christians in most alleged cases of slavery since 1904. While the slavery controversy was raging in late 1913, Worcester toured the United States with his lantern-slide show of savagery and progress under American colonial rule.[3] Then, in March, an American entrepreneur took a group of fourteen non-Christians out of the country for exhibition in the United States. When the Philippine Commission passed the new Anti-Slavery Law in 1914, it reaffirmed the close connection between slavery and concepts of the uncivilized by adding an amendment to prohibit "the exploiting or exhibiting of [non-Christians] as a spectacle." Whereas Worcester used his antislavery campaign to propagate images of non-Christians as victims in need of colonial protection, the new Anti-Slavery Law associated slavery with the display of non-Christians and prohibited both. After that, little more was said in the Philippines about slavery as a social practice, but the problem of slavery was not so easily dismissed.[4]

The Congressional debate over the Jones bill demonstrated the persistence of colonial ideology and discourse in the United States, where the *Informe Sobre la Esclavitud* had little effect. It was given virtually no circulation there, partly because it was written in Spanish, but also because it lacked the institutional powers of colonialism, science, and whiteness that authorized Worcester's voice. Indeed, while the slavery controversy seemed settled in Manila, the debate over the Jones bill in 1914 brought the question of slavery and antislavery laws in the Philippines under Congressional scrutiny, as Worcester had long desired.

The debates over the Jones bill also revealed the extent to which elite nationalists and American proponents of Philippine independence shared many of Worcester's presuppositions about the non-Christian tribes. They concurred on the need for colonialism and civilizing work among the non-Christian tribes, whom they described as subjects unfit to govern themselves. The difference between this agreement on the need for colonialism among the non-Christians and the consensus that formed around the pledge of Philippine independence in the bill was less a contradiction than a matter of degree. As proposed in 1914 (and ultimately passed in 1916), the revised bill would change only the level of colonial surveillance and discipline, not its basic design. The Filipino national elite's ready participation in formulating and backing a bill that did not set a date for independence exposed them to biting popular nationalist criticism for their bondage to colonialism.

In the early months of 1914, as the Philippine Assembly's special committee on slavery was finishing its report, Manuel Quezon took the lead behind the scenes in watering down the Jones bill. Quezon first suggested replacing provisions for a scheduled independence date with specific literacy requirements for the population and other criteria that would delay independence, he expected, for at least twenty-five years. These measurable standards were soon dropped. All that remained was an extension of home rule through Filipinization of the bureaucracy, the addition of an elected Senate to replace the Philippine Commission as the legislative upper house, an expansion of the electorate, and an unenforceable preamble that declared the United States's intent to recognize Philippine "independence as soon as stable government can be established." Quezon's public support for the new bill marked an open retreat from his previous public demands for immediate independence. This splintered the *Partido Nacionalista* and paved the way for a revival of popular nationalist rhetoric about the need for struggle and sacrifice, the danger of deceitful rulers, and the repudiation of colonialism as a kind of slavery.[5]

The revised Jones bill was introduced in the U.S. House of Representatives in the autumn of 1914. When a Republican critic proposed an amendment to include an express prohibition of peonage, the question of slavery in the Philippines was openly debated on the House floor. To prove the existence of peonage, Republicans in the House read passages from Worcester's recently published book, *The Philippines: Past and Present*, and excerpts from his *Slavery and Peonage in the Philippine Islands*. They recounted cases of enslavement and debt bondage from these texts, and they reiterated Worcester's indictment of the Philippine Assembly for refusing to pass a law against slavery. Manuel Quezon, seated in Congress as one of the resident commissioners for the Philippines, immediately replied that he had no objection to the amendment prohibiting peonage, but felt "regret . . . that the gentleman thought it necessary in the discussion of his amendment to revive the question of the supposed slavery and peonage in the Philippines." Referring to the Philippine Assembly's inquiry into slavery, Quezon told the House that Worcester's report had "been thoroughly investigated by the most unimpeachable authorities and has been fully disposed of"—though obviously not as fully as he would have liked.[6]

As he had done on many previous occasions, Quezon attacked Worcester and his claims about slavery by questioning his honesty, pretensions of disinterested benevolence, and his failure to decree an antislavery law before 1907. Anyone who read Worcester's book and report on slavery would see, Quezon told Congress, "that there is no such thing as slavery in that part of the Philippines inhabited by Christian Filipinos—certainly not in the sense that it existed in the United States prior to the Civil War." There could be no reason "for the outcries of Mr. Worcester," said Quezon, ". . . except [his] desire to unjustly depict the Filipino people—for whom he has always entertained an ill-concealed, strong dislike, if not contempt or hatred—as a people devoid of all humanitarian sentiment and moral sense and badly in need of an iron hand to keep them in good behavior."[7]

The debate that followed was in many ways an effort to avoid the embarrassment of slavery and displace it onto others. Quezon admitted that "slavery was at one time a common practice" among the Moros of the southern Philippines, but they had "always been under the exclusive control of American officials" who briefly tolerated slavery under the terms of the "shameful" Bates treaty. Slavery was soon abolished there, so that it no longer existed anywhere in the Philippines. This was fortunate for the United States, he advised the House, for if Worcester's "pathetic and shocking" allegations were really true, "what a serious charge would the American Government have to answer before the inexorable bar of history! How would the United States satisfy the enlightened opinion and humanitarian sentiment of the world horrified by the discovery that after 15 years of continuous and supreme American control of the archipelago 'human flesh is still openly bought and sold' and that this 'greatest single problem' of the islands is still unsolved?" [8]

After a selection of Worcester's report was read into the record, Congressman Clarence Miller of Minnesota tried to validate Worcester's charges by superficially depoliticizing the issue of slavery—that is, by temporarily separating slavery as an objective fact from its political implications. A Republican, Miller feared that the vague promise of a future independence would encourage militant Filipino protests for immediate action. He had visited the Philippines in 1913 and delivered a flattering farewell address to the Philippine Assembly on the day the antislavery bill was introduced there. A witness to the debates in the assembly, he now told his colleagues that he understood "the sensitiveness on the part of the Filipino people in facing the charge that slavery and peonage exist in the islands," but did "not quite appreciate the extreme sensitiveness which they do unquestionably feel." [9]

There was slavery and peonage in the Philippines, Congressman Miller said, just as there was peonage in the United States, but that constituted "no charge against the general Filipino people" or the American people. Quezon objected that the criticism of the Philippine Assembly for not passing an antislavery law was indeed meant as an indictment of the Filipino people. When Miller tried to clarify his meaning by explaining that some people in the southern United States engaged in peonage while "the people generally" opposed it, a congressman from the impugned region took offense that this was "a great injustice to the South." [10]

Congressman Jones then closed the debate on the amendment by reminding his colleagues that even the martyred President McKinley, a Republican and an imperialist, had once been "denounced here and elsewhere" for accepting the Bates treaty. "From that time to the present the question of slavery in the Philippines has been more or less agitated." Jones, like Quezon, was "very sorry that this question of slavery and peonage in the Philippine Islands has been injected into this discussion." He expressed "regret" that Worcester should be cited as an authority, as he "has for years been engaged in active controversy over this subject with the War Department, the Philippine Assembly, the Filipino people, and all the rest of mankind who did not accept his contention that slavery was practiced in the civilized and Christianized portions of the Philippines, and that there were no adequate laws to prevent it." The Thirteenth Amendment and the Philippine Organic Act of 1902 should have settled the matter long ago, Jones insisted, and any lingering doubts ought to have been put to rest by the 1913 antislavery law.[11] Jones assured his colleagues that, contrary to Worcester's claims, "the members of the Philippine Assembly have always been as much opposed to human slavery as Mr. Worcester ever professed to be."[12] With that the Democratic majority defeated the amendment to forbid peonage and soon passed the Jones bill on to the Senate.

Dean C. Worcester testified as an expert witness in the Senate committee hearings, showing the members his famous lantern slides as he lectured them on "the very widely different social strata that are represented in the Philippine Islands." There was "no such thing as a Filipino people," Worcester instructed the senators. Pointing to a projected image of "a headhunter standing before a house ornamented with human skulls," Worcester explained that this man was "not a Filipino," a term he said was "properly used to designate the civilized, Christianized inhabitants of the islands."[13]

The Ifugao "headhunter" depicted in the slide did "not represent the lowest class," according to Worcester, nor did General Aguinaldo "represent the highest class" of the population. To illustrate these extremes Worcester first showed a slide of a Negrito, "representative of the aboriginal people," whom he described as "dwarfs, . . . practically at the bottom of the human series, so far as the possibility of undergoing development is concerned." Negritos were "being eliminated by natural processes" and would "soon be a link that is missing." Then he put on a slide of Sergio Osmeña, speaker of the Philippine Assembly, whom he said "stands pretty close to the other extreme," but also did "not represent a large class of people." Although Worcester noted that "civilized, Christianized" Filipinos made up seven-eighths of the population, his lavish attention to the non-Christian peoples helped to expand the importance of their meaning beyond proportion. He asserted a kind of equivalence by discussing the non-Christians and Christian Filipinos in symmetrical pairs, as when he told the senators "there are some 25,000 men like the little black chap, the Negrito, whom I have shown you, whereas, very unfortunately, there are not 25,000 men like Speaker Osmeña in the islands."[14]

Worcester did not mention slavery in his prepared remarks, but he did spend considerable time discussing "headhunting" and other "warlike" characteristics that prevailed among the "wild people" before they were brought under the influence of American rule. His slide show included before-and-after sequences, beginning with headhunters, their tools of war and trophies, traditional settlements, women dressed in leaves or skirts without tops, and men in G-strings. These were followed by images of colonial progress and discipline: children in school, women clothed according to American norms of feminine modesty, school-houses, trails, a unit of the Mountain Province constabulary, and Igorot sanitary agents. The latter slides all implied the continuing importance of American rule, either by including in the scene symbols of American supervision or reminders of the recent past. This suggestion of imminent regression in the absence of colonial control was also conveyed in Worcester's explanation for imposing a prohibition on the sale of alcohol to non-Christian people. "If you mix a half-pint of bad whiskey with a head-hunter"—or otherwise give up firm control, he implied—"the result is apt to be pretty disastrous in his immediate vicinity." [15]

Although Worcester mocked the non-Christians—he used a picture of his personal Ifugao servant standing in traditional dress near a display of skulls to argue that the Jones bill's requirements for serving in the proposed Philippine Senate would not be stringent enough—he also emphasized the bond between them and the colonial regime. During questioning, he told the senators that the secret of his success with "primitive tribes" was "human sympathy." "We like those hill people," declared Worcester, "and they like us." In contrast to the United States's benevolent concern for the non-Christians, Worcester argued that "sympathy does not exist between the non-Christians and Filipinos." The fate of the non-Christian tribes under the Jones bill was thus the "most important thing in this bill," because it would place them under the control of the Philippine Legislature.[16]

At this point Worcester introduced the subject of slavery as the opposite of the humanitarian feelings that bonded Americans with the non-Christians. The Jones bill, he said, threatened to place the Ifugao under the control of Filipinos in Nueva Vizcaya "who formerly bought their children for slaves and with whom they used to be constantly at outs in the old days." As in his special report, Worcester focused on the practice of slavery and debt bondage in the Christian lowlands, with emphasis on the way that non-Christians, such as the Negritos, "have been especially victimized." Unlike head-hunting and other manifestations of primitivism, which could be depicted as the picaresque qualities of noble savages, slavery could elicit nothing but revulsion. In effect, Worcester suggested that Filipino rule over the non-Christians would amount to a return of slavery, both literally and figuratively.[17]

When Manuel Quezon testified before the Senate committee, he did not directly challenge Worcester's accusations of slavery and peonage as he had done before. Instead, he positioned Filipinos squarely behind all of the triumphs for which Worcester assigned credit to the United States. He acknowledged that the Moros used to take Filipinos as slaves, but he stressed that this ceased when the Spanish regime put a garrison of Filipino troops in Mindanao who stopped Moro slave raiding. As for head-hunting, he said "that also has disappeared, due to the efficient police force in the islands." Quezon credited the United States for organizing the Philippine constabulary, but was quick to add that "some Filipinos had something to do in stopping that head-hunting vice." And Quezon made it clear that a Filipino government organized under the Jones bill would continue the work of colonizing the non-Christians and Moros, who were "by no means" capable of governing themselves. "Somebody has got to govern them," he told the senators, and he later reassured the Senate that "the [Philippine] legislature will take good care of those non-Christian tribes." Instead of pursuing a debate over slavery's existence in the Philippines, Quezon shifted the meaning of slavery by placing Filipinos within an active antislavery tradition. Thus, Filipino colonial rule over the non-Christian tribes would not be slavery, but a benevolent act of "care." [18]

Quezon's argument for the Jones bill's promise of independence turned on a similar repositioning of slavery in regard to colonialism. The preamble promising independence was the principal stumbling block in the Senate debates. Without the preamble there may have been no opposition to the bill. Striking the preamble had been proposed several times, and Quezon more than once indicated in private that he would consider accepting such a measure. Once the bill was introduced, though, the preamble, hollow as it was, became too valuable as a symbol of nationalist triumph to give up. Cleverly, Quezon argued before the Senate that the preamble was the key feature that would distinguish American colonial rule from slavery because it would give the Filipino people a choice about their future. If given no choice—that is, no preamble—and told "that I cannot be independent and you establish in the Philippines any kind of liberal government," Quezon said, "I will feel that I am a slave, not a free man." If given the option of independence seemingly offered by the Jones bill, Quezon hinted at what he had privately told American leaders: "I may decide that I do not want to be independent and yet be a free man and keep my own self-respect." The ambiguity of the preamble as a commitment to end colonial rule was now matched by Quezon's intimation of ambiguity in his people's desire for independence.[19]

It was precisely this sort of politics that kept the issue of slavery alive in the discourse of popular nationalism in the Philippines. Just days before Quezon testified in Washington, followers of the exiled General Artemio Ricarte rallied their Revolutionary Army of the Philippines in an uprising that has become known as the Christmas Eve Fiasco. In Manila and surrounding towns, bands numbering from the tens up into the hundreds gathered to seize government buildings. These groups were small, disorganized, ill-armed, and quickly overwhelmed by local police and the constabulary. All the same, they marked the persistence of popular nationalism. Indeed, the mere fact that they engineered simultaneous uprisings in distant towns was quite remarkable, given that Ricarte was out of the country and the constabulary had arrested many of the Ricartista leaders in the previous few months.

Proclamations posted during the uprising called for armed rebellion as the only way to end slavery. One found in Pasay, a suburb of Manila, announced:

> For a very long time the Philippines have lain in slavery, but now it is her desire to get up again and draw once more the terrible bolo [native machete] of revolution. As the United States of America, under whose rule we have been . . . for a long time, does not know how to fulfill its promises, the Philippines have deemed it best to separate from her. So I am arousing you, my countrymen, from your sleep, and may all the golden hearts go to the aid of their country in the fight for our ideal.[20]

Defendants in the trials that followed the foiled uprising said they joined Ricarte's army "because the United States had promised independence but had failed to keep its promise." They said that they had expected more participation in the rebellion, but some members of the Revolutionary Army thought they should wait for Quezon to return and announce the United States's decision on the Philippines' future. Those who did rebel had already decided that the national elite and the colonial regime were engaged in a policy of deceit that would not lead to the light of independence, but only to the darkness of continued "slavery."[21]

Although the uprising in 1914 was not large, there is evidence that it reflected more widespread sentiments. Earlier in the year, it was disenchantment with Osmeña's and Quezon's support of the weakened Jones bill that led Teodoro Sandiko, Dominador Gomez, and other left-wing members of the *Partido Nacionalista* to break away and form the new *Partido Democrata Nacional*. From the start, they appealed to popular nationalist sympathies through their rhetoric and association with heroes from the revolution. Their party's newspaper called Governor Harrison's vaunted New Era nothing but an "Era of Deceit." Sandiko appeared at rallies with the unreconciled old Ilocano radical Isabelo de los Reyes. Together, they denounced the Jones bill, repudiated Quezon's waffling, and reminded enthusiastic crowds that rebellion might be necessary to win independence.[22]

The strength of popular nationalism lay in its powerful appeal to the culture and patriotism of common people, but it had severe weaknesses. The overwhelming odds against armed struggle were made greater by an emphasis on participation and the localism this usually implied. At the same time, the exclusion of the popular classes from the electoral process protected the dominant official nationalists from effective challenges to their institutional voice. The *Partido Democrata Nacional* sent few of its members to office and those were mostly in the Manila area. The urban labor movement and developing middle class made Manila exceptional. In the provinces, the power of Osmeña's and Quezon's *Partido Nacionalista* went unchallenged, at least on an official level. Oligarchic politics, what Benedict Anderson has called "cacique democracy," continued with few serious interruptions under the protective cover of American colonial rule.[23]

In 1915, however, a different kind of controversy erupted in the Visayas. Copra and coconut oil production was booming in response to technological improvements and the lucrative wartime market. The Visayan Refining Company, in which Dean C. Worcester owned an interest, announced that it would open a new processing mill on Mactan Island off the coast of Cebu—the place where Lapulapu's forces defeated and mortally wounded Magellan in 1521. When word circulated that Worcester would live on site as resident manager, the political leaders of Cebu organized a series of protests, including mass meetings, a threatened labor strike, and a copra boycott. Their objection was not to American capital or even to Worcester's investment, but to Worcester's presence in their midst.[24]

All of Worcester's offenses were now hurled back at him, including his destruction of *El Renacimiento,* his slide shows of non-Christian tribes, and his report on slavery. The matter became a national issue in the Philippines. The Manila daily *El Ideal* explained that "[t]he people of Cebu, together with the whole Filipino people, are against

Mr. Worcester because he has misrepresented the condition of the Filipino people, depicting them in his book *The Philippines: Past and Present* as a people afflicted with all sorts of vice, a people sanctifying crime, a people not only incapable but also utterly unworthy of leading an independent life." The threatened strikes and boycott failed; even the protest leaders, men such as Sergio Osmeña and Dionisio Jakosalem, did not follow through on the boycott. Worcester oversaw construction and opened the mill for operation in May 1916. By the end of August 1916, when the Jones bill passed and President Wilson signed it into law, Worcester's new mill had shipped out two tanker loads of oil worth $200,000 each.[25]

The Jones bill became a law amid expressions of great enthusiasm. Just before the vote in the House of Representatives, Manuel Quezon rose to explain the changes it would establish in almost millennial terms: "So I say, Mr. Speaker, this bill is a long and very decisive step toward the complete emancipation of the Filipino people." It defined "an epoch in our history," said Quezon, for "[w]e are convinced that the promise of independence contained in the bill will be faithfully fulfilled, for we know that we are dealing with a Nation in the truest sense jealous of its honor and its good name." Congressman Jones expanded on these remarks in a particularly telling way. "When the President of the United States affixes his signature to this already too long-delayed measure of justice and right," declared the triumphant author of the bill, "it will mark an epoch in the history of this Nation as well as in the Philippine Islands, for the pages of the annals of the world will be searched in vain for its counterpart. For it not only bestows upon the Philippine people a measure of self-government such as they have never enjoyed under the sovereignty of this or any other nation, but it establishes what to them is dearer than all else—the everlasting covenant of a great and generous people, speaking through their accredited representatives, that they shall in due time enjoy the incomparable blessings of liberty and freedom." [26]

To say that Quezon and Jones overstated the significance of the Jones Act is nothing new. Conservative opponents of the bill in the United States and radical critics in the Philippines said as much during the debates of 1914, long before the first critical histories were written in the 1960s. However, some of the bill's most vocal opponents from the debates in 1914 came around to support the measure in 1916 when consideration of the Clarke Amendment revived discussion of setting a proximate date for independence. In the words of one Republican Senator, the Jones Act was "simply a confirmation of our settled line of policy to install in the Philippines, step by step, the American system of self-government." The senator's remark might be more revealing than he intended.[27]

Linking the Jones Act back to the United States's first declaration of colonization, McKinley's proclamation of Benevolent Assimilation, helps to remind us of the logic of colonial benevolence. The debate over the Jones bill was framed by the discourse of benevolence, by the assumption that the United States was committed to progress and humanitarianism in the Philippines, and by the reciprocal assumption that an attachment born of gratitude would be the proper return if the United States honored its commitments. Contrary to Congressman Jones's assertion that the "annals of the world will be searched in vain for its counterpart," the popular nationalist use of slavery as a metaphor for colonialism should alert us to the existence of a precedent that shaped American colonial discourse and practice.

If Americans and Filipinos commonly talked about the Jones Act as, in Quezon's words, "a step towards the complete emancipation of the Filipino people," it is important to recognize that it was far from an abolitionist document. The distinction I want to make is not one between immediatism and gradualism, although that was present, too, in the debate over the timing of independence. What I want to emphasize is that the Jones Act did not strike against colonialism as a system, as abolitionism did against slavery. It did not look to the end of colonialism in general, but only to its local transformation in the Philippines at some time in the future. Indeed, it was premised on the assumption that colonialism would continue among the non-Christians and Moros of the Philippines, as well as other so-called subject peoples in Asia and Africa. If we interpret the Jones Act within the terms of slavery as a metaphor for colonialism, the proper analogy would be the ancient practice of promising manumission.

What Orlando Patterson has written about slavery and manumission pertains to the history of the Jones Act and the course of American colonial rule through its end in 1946. "It is not possible to understand what slavery is all about until we understand it as a process including the act of manumission and its consequence. Enslavement, slavery, and manumission are not merely related events; they are one and the same process in different phases."[28] In this way, the Jones Act confirmed and solidified the process of American colonial rule. It did not reject it.

Conclusion

Embarrassments in a World of Nations

An instructive parallel can be drawn between the American pretension that the United States's colonial rule over the Philippines was not a kind of slavery because it promised national emancipation to the Filipino people and the argument, made by Filipino nationalists in the *Informe Sobre la Esclavitud*, that Filipino "slavery" was not really slavery because the "slaves" could purchase or otherwise acquire a higher status. The prospect of improvement and manumission, they argued, was one key piece of evidence that proved that these relationships were not really species of slavery. American colonial officials had pointed in a similar way to the ostensible mildness of Moro slavery when, from 1899 to 1903, they were forced to defend themselves against anti-imperialists' allegations that they tolerated slavery in the southern Philippines.

In all of these cases, Americans and Filipino nationalists had responded to charges that they practiced or tolerated slavery by insisting, just as their accusers did, that all modern, civilized, and Christian people opposed slavery. We might think that the various exculpatory arguments about treatment and manumission merely exposed the gap between antislavery ideology and decided antislavery action, but that is not all that they did. We should recognize that the defense of slavery and the effort to abolish it are, in an important sense, parts of a single discourse. Indeed, it made no sense to defend slavery until it was attacked and, likewise, it made no sense to deny that one practiced slavery until it became embarrassing to be thought to do so. Disputes about what constituted slavery were, and continue to be, as necessary to its elimination as to its apologetics.

Abolishing slavery required an operative definition of slavery in order to sort out what would be prohibited and what would be allowed. Before the first abolitions there had long been philosophical reflections on the nature of slavery and codifications about who was or could be a slave and how they should be treated, but no definitions primarily concerned with distinguishing slavery as an institution separate from all others. Slavery was such a familiar practice that even the United States's acts of abolition in the Civil War did not include definitions of the institution. Immediately afterward, however, the problem of defining slavery haunted the legislatures and the courts.[1] The program of universal abolition prompted comparative analyses of slavery by administrators, advocates, and scholars, but the analyses have been vexed ever since by the variations of bondage and submission across cultures as well as within each one. Scholars still cannot resolve the disputes.

Distinguishing slavery as a practice to be eliminated called forth more distinctions and definitions of that which was not slavery, but these differentiations rested as much on forgetting as they did on objective difference. Nationalists in the Philippine Assembly responded to Dean C. Worcester's lurid allegations by arguing that the Filipino nation was knit together by paternalistic ties of social indebtedness that made slavery unthinkable, as if it were a giant extended family. But slavery had always been considered an institution within the household, even in the United States, until antislavery ideology defined slavery and the familial household as fully distinct institutions.[2] American political leaders and some Filipino nationalists distanced themselves from the old charge that colonialism was a form of slavery when, during the debates on the Jones bill, they said Filipinos would owe the United States gratitude for moving their nation toward independence. But gratitude was precisely the obligation slaves were expected to return to their masters for manumission. And, in the field of labor relations in the production of commodities for export, colonial officials and official nationalists agreed that their new law holding employees criminally responsible for working off advance payments from employers did not constitute peonage even as they disagreed as to whether slavery and peonage existed elsewhere in the Philippines.

The boundaries of antislavery ideology could not and cannot be taken for granted. The Filipino and American participants in the controversies over slavery discovered this precisely because antislavery functioned as a hegemonic ideology. Rather than fixing the meaning of slavery, the hegemony of antislavery ideology made the meaning of slavery into a key object of struggle. American imperialists and anti-imperialists had taken turns excoriating Philippine forms of bondage for violating the most basic of human rights, but then they also, on other occasions, bent over backwards to explain that the so-called slavery was but a domestic institution of benevolent care. Filipino nationalists insisted that the universally opprobrious characteristics of slavery could not be found in the Philippines' present, past, or future. However, Philippine nationalism itself drew upon a broad range of meanings ascribed to the Tagalog word *alipin*. To be a slave in that discourse could call forth bonds of devotion to a higher authority, the nation, and the rejection of colonialism as the worst kind of degradation and servitude. Philippine nationalism exteriorized the negative dimensions of slavery and thereby opened a new discourse about domestic submission and hierarchy, as well as freedom. The American debates over the nature of Philippine forms of slavery were also always debates about the nature of American colonialism and Americans' own unfinished reckoning with slavery. Americans and the dominant official nationalists in the Philippines then learned that the politics of antislavery ideology were potentially, and dangerously, reversible.

In this way, American colonialism and Filipino official nationalism reached a moment of commonality. The slavery scandal of 1912–1914 presaged this reciprocal recognition by exposing the parties to a period of mutual embarrassment. The controversies over slavery were briefly mentioned during the final debates on the Jones bill, but, once it was passed in 1916, dominant discourses in both the United States and the Philippines eschewed any further discussion of slavery. The Jones Act stabilized a symbiotic relationship between official nationalism in the Philippines and American colonialism, consolidating a hegemonic order that in many ways continues to the present. But that order has not gone unchallenged. Thus we should not be surprised to find that Filipinos have continued to speak about slavery—long after it ceased to exist as a social institution and, even more to the point, long after the nonexistence of slavery in Philippine societies became ingrained in historical narratives of the nation. After 1916, however, the rhetoric of slavery became the preserve of popular subaltern leaders and older Hispanophile nationalists. They stood far enough outside the dominant discourse of colonial progress toward independence so that they would not suffer the mutual Filipino and American sting of embarrassment at the mention of slavery. Yet, for the same reason, their counterhegemonic protests and actions were regularly, if tensely, channeled in directions that could be readily tolerated, contained, or suppressed with localized applications of direct force.

To illustrate these points, let us first turn back to the story from 1921 with which this book began. When the anonymous Filipino nationalist confronted the former Governor General William Cameron Forbes with the complaint that "the Filipinos didn't want to continue in slavery," he threatened to disrupt the politics of colonial progress that had been stabilized by the Jones Act. And so the stereotypically colonial Forbes "thundered at him that I resented any such description of what America had done for the Philippines," taking the nationalist to task for speaking out of his racial place and for lacking gratitude. It was in this context that Forbes recalled the long legislative battle over antislavery laws and declared that the nationalist's "characterization of the present condition of the Filipinos as slaves was an insult to the American Government and to the Filipino people." Forbes did not, however, mention the great slavery scandal of 1912–1914. The anonymous nationalist apparently acceded to Forbes's demand for a retraction and apology. Sweating and humiliated, if Forbes is to be believed, the man "proceeded lamely with what remained of his speech."

In contrast to this anonymous nationalist who delivered his speech in the modernizing language of English, others did not share his investment in American colonial progress. Philippine Senator Benigno Aquino Sr., a staunch Hispanophile, was one such nationalist. Like his father, the revolutionary General Servillano Aquino, the Senator never settled into an entirely comfortable relationship with the American colonial authorities. The elder senator's career represented one of the last hurrahs of Spanish-language nationalism in the Philippines.

In 1928, Senator Aquino's ire was raised by a bill in the Philippine legislature that proposed replacing Spanish with English as the official language for court proceedings. Foreshadowing debates that would occur fifty years later over replacing the public use of English with Filipino, a Tagalog-based national language, the senator warned his nation that "[w]e are surrendering our soul to the dictates of the sovereign master; and such a surrender, to my thinking, is the worst kind of slavery for us."[3] On the eve of the Second World War, Benigno Aquino Sr. again employed the metaphor of slavery to defend the plan for independence in 1946 established by the United States's Tydings-McDuffie Act of 1934. More conservative legislators were questioning the economic, political, and military wisdom of imminent independence. Aquino discredited the idea of remaining under colonial rule by calling it "racial slavery," while a senator from Negros questioned how he could call Filipinos an "enslaved people" when "we are free in all but form." [4] There was no significant American colonial opposition to Senator Aquino's use of the term *slavery* on either of these occasions.

During the Japanese occupation, Benigno Aquino Sr. became speaker of the assembly and director of the *Kalibapi,* a mass political organization enjoined to incorporate Philippine nationalism within the ideology of the Greater East Asia Co-Prosperity Sphere. His famously martyred son, Benigno Aquino Jr., followed a very different cultural path after Philippine independence. Benigno Jr., unlike his father, maintained close relations with American leaders and institutions throughout his career.

Protests over slavery were also heard from subaltern movements outside the formal politics of colonial progress and official nationalism. In the 1930s, one such movement was the *Sakdal,* a radical organization of workers and peasants in central Luzon that functioned as a union, a political party, and a secret revolutionary organization along the lines of the Katipunan of 1896. Its firebrand newspaper carried the masthead, "Independent with no master but the people." [5] The *Sakdal*'s leader, Benigno Ramos, invoked the image of slavery in the style of the Katipunan, declaring that he was against "darkness, autonomy and slavery (*kadimlan* [sic], *autonomia't kaalipnan* [sic])." In return, Ramos was portrayed by Sakdalistas as a figure like the Katipunan's founder, Andres Bonifacio, who would "rescue the Mother Country from excessive enslavement." At a national Meeting of the Oppressed People in 1932, the Sakdalistas closed their congress with cries of *Mabuhay ang bayang ayaw paalipin* (Long live the people who refuse to be enslaved).[6]

The *Sakdal* enjoyed early success as a political party, mainly in the Tagalog provinces. Its first three candidates for the lower house were elected in 1934, along with several municipal officials and a provincial governor for the island of Marinduque. However, Benigno Ramos's calls for immediate independence were soon countered by the ruling *Nacionalista* Party's approval of the U.S. Tydings-McDuffie Act, which promised independence would be granted ten years after the establishment of a virtually autonomous Commonwealth government. A convention in Manila drafted the requisite constitution, to be approved by President Roosevelt and a Philippine plebiscite. Ramos and the *Sakdal* opposed the constitution and called on Filipinos to boycott the plebiscite scheduled for 14 May 1935. The *Sakdal*'s calls for immediate independence had previously been tolerated, but its campaign against the plebiscite raised the stakes. In the weeks before the plebiscite, while Ramos solicited support for his party in Japan, many of the peasants and workers among his supporters began to plan for the coming confrontation according to their own lights. Following the Katipunan tradition, they expected salvation, literally and metaphorically, from the Rising Sun in the East. Benigno Ramos's travel to Japan and the legend of General Artemio Ricarte's ever-imminent return from his long exile there encouraged such hopes. On May 2 Sakdalista bands attacked state offices in provinces around Manila. Alerted by informants, the Philippine Constabulary put down the uprisings and made mass arrests, crushing the *Sakdal*. Like General Ricarte, Ramos remained in exile until they both returned to the Philippines with Japanese troops in 1942.

The records of the U.S. Bureau of Insular Affairs also speak to the continuing potential for the mention of slavery to provoke embarrassment. During the 1920s and 1930s several committees from the League of Nations asked permission to investigate bondage in the Philippines. A united front of American colonial officials and Philippine nationalists deflected them each time.

In 1925, the secretary general of the League asked the United States for information about slavery in the Philippines to be used in drafting a convention against the slave trade. The redoubtable Sir Frederick Lugard, who had equivocated so long and so deeply over the abolition of slavery in British colonial Nigeria, told the League's Committee on Slavery that the United States permitted peonage in the Philippines.[7] The American secretary of war briefed his counterpart at the State Department with this summary.

> Charges that slavery and peonage exist in the Philippine Islands have been made from time to time ever since the Islands passed under the sovereignty of the United States. It is true that slavery was the custom among the Moros, inhabiting the southern islands of the archipelago, and that conditions savoring of slavery have been met in other parts of the Islands. Instances of a system (referred to in the Islands as "caciquism") whereby a leading personage kept his community in a state of subjection and dependency reminiscent of feudalism have been encountered.
>
> However, both practices were unlawful under the Spanish regime and are unlawful now and punishable as crimes. They are remnants of social custom and will yield before the rapidly-spreading education and growing realization of individual rights.[8]

Less information was provided to the League. In 1930, the League's Committee on the Extension of the Enquiry on Traffic in Women and Children in the East held meetings in Geneva, but received no official reports from the United States on the Philippines. An American observer reported to the State Department that only "strictly confidential information was supplied" and that affairs in the Philippines appeared "at least for an oriental country in excellent condition."[9] When the committee's official report turned out to be somewhat less flattering, it was noted in an internal Bureau of Insular Affairs memorandum that "this same accusation was made at Geneva in 1925 . . . It is a subject I would *not* suggest including in a radiogram" to Manila.[10] Another meeting of the League's committee in 1936 was handled slightly differently under the new arrangements of the Commonwealth period. An invitation to participate in a conference at Bandung was forwarded to President Quezon, who responded, "As we do not have any problem on traffic of women the Philippine Government does not contemplate sending a representative."[11]

Indeed, with the inauguration of the Commonwealth government in 1935 one epoch of the traffic in Filipino bodies came to a close. Between 1907 and 1935, more than one hundred thirty thousand Filipinos, overwhelmingly male, crossed the Pacific to labor in the United States and its territories. The great majority, at least one hundred thousand, went initially to cut cane on sugar plantations in Hawaii, many on labor contracts that required them to work off the cost of their transport. Some left Hawaii for the mainland, where they were joined by a smaller number of migrants who traveled there directly. Most were employed packing fish in the canneries of the Pacific Northwest and harvesting crops in the fields of California. Most of the migrants intended to return home, but approximately one hundred thousand never did. Some were transplanted immigrants, others simply stranded. Not long after the Great Depression fuelled anti-Filipino race riots in California, the Tydings-McDuffie Act that pledged Philippine independence also set in place an immigration quota of only fifty per year. Once known by the colonial euphemism "American nationals," Filipinos were now citizens of their own Commonwealth without a special claim to migrate to the United States.[12]

Nothing so complex as a labor migration of one hundred thirty thousand people can be explained as the simple effect of a government policy. Nevertheless, the American colonial state supported the initial migration of contract labor to Hawaii for its own reasons.[13] As William

Cameron Forbes explained to Secretary of War Henry Stimson in 1911, "[t]he chief advantage which this emigration to Hawaii can have to the Philippine Islands is of advertising our labor." Forbes judged this was a success for the project of colonial tutelage because, according to the Hawaiian Sugar Planters' Association, it showed "that once the Filipino had learned to work (and it takes him several months to do so) he made as good a workman as the Japanese." The demand for Filipino labor in Hawaii would be a "great boon" to the Philippines, he told one of Hawaii's sugar barons at the start of the migration, because "it ought to encourage capital to come here." Forbes told the governor of Hawaii in 1910 that he did "not grudge the few thousand of our people that you want at all," as if they were his to give.[14]

Relative to the economy of the United States and Americans' world-wide investments, not much American capital flowed into the Philippines while it was a colony of the United States. Much more arrived after Philippine independence in 1946 under special parity rights for American investment and the Philippine Republic's relaxation of regulations on the foreign ownership of agricultural land. Then, in the 1970s, the bottom dropped out. World commodity markets for Philippine products faltered while import prices, led by oil, surged. Meanwhile, the Marcos family and their cronies honed their skills at institutional pilfering, international borrowing, and public extravagance. The country's foreign debt, already growing markedly in the 1960s, exploded twelvefold, from $2 billion in 1970 to $24 billion in 1983.[15] In response, the Philippine state turned to a new variety of mercantilism to produce foreign exchange. Rather than simply export agricultural and industrial commodities produced in the Philippines, the state began to promote the production and export of laborers on contract, making the country's newest export commodity similar in some ways to one of its oldest.[16]

Through the 1980s an average of six hundred thousand Filipinos per year left their homeland to work abroad on contract. Their destinations were concentrated most heavily in the oil-rich Middle East, but Filipino workers have established occupational niches around the world, from London and Rome to Hong Kong, Malaysia, Japan, and, of course, the United States. By the mid-1990s, almost four million Filipinos were laboring as overseas contract workers (OCWs), making the Philippines the world's largest supplier of globe-trotting migrant labor. As many as two thousand people are estimated to leave the Philippines every day.

A largely male phenomenon in the 1970s, OCWs are now equally male and female. They serve in almost every capacity, both legal and illegal, including employment as computer technicians, merchant seamen, nurses, carpenters, truck drivers, domestic workers, entertainers of the cultural kind and of the sex-industry kind. Their social composition reflects many influences, including the dynamics of international demand and the variable economic fates of different regions in the Philippines. Education has also been a major factor. Since the 1970s some aspects of tertiary education have even been tailored to help produce more exportable workers in lucrative, high-demand occupations such as nursing. Another supply-side factor of note is the English language, a colonial holdover that, in proportion to its status as a global lingua franca, increases the worldwide utility of Filipino labor.

OCWs have constituted the Philippines' single largest source of foreign exchange, surpassing the traditional agricultural export crops as well as the new industries (electronics assembly, clothing manufacture, and so on) of special Export Processing Zones. By law, OCWs have been required to remit upward of fifty percent of their foreign earnings to Philippine bank accounts through official channels. In addition, they pay income tax to the Philippines as well as special registration and exit fees.[17]

Under the crush of international debt and the strain of divided families, President Corazon Aquino called the OCWs "modern-day heroes of the Philippines" for their sacrifices and the service they provide the nation. Highly publicized cases of abuse by employers and foreign governments amplified this image, never more so than in the infamous execution in 1995 of Flor Contemplacion, a domestic worker in Singapore. Tens of thousands lined the streets of her provincial hometown for her funeral procession. Protest vigils gathered in Manila and other cities in an outpouring of national mourning not seen since the funeral of Benigno Aquino Jr., in 1983. Two cabinet ministers fell for their failure to protect Contemplacion. Much outrage followed, along with some official attempts to secure international respect for the rights of OCWs. Driven, however, by need and their own aspirations, Filipinos continue to seek contract work abroad with the active support of a national government that requires a slice of their income.

Critics of government policy do not denigrate the bravery of OCWs, but they do question official characterizations of the service OCWs provide the nation. Most commonly, they see the OCWs as servicing the

Philippines' monumental foreign debt, contracted for the nation by parasitic politicians and unequally enforced by the demands of the International Monetary Fund, World Bank, and international capital. It should not surprise us, then, that these critics see the OCWs as the literal embodiment of a new international regime of debt bondage.[18]

Of course, colonialism was not slavery in any literal sense of the word and the World Bank holds no one in debt bondage. Slavery has been abolished throughout the world, at least officially, and colonialism, it would seem, has disappeared, too. They no longer exist as formal institutions and we have tried to distance ourselves from their taint. The historical study of slavery and colonialism therefore demands an intellectual journey. We must, somehow, travel between the worldviews of the present that proscribe slavery and colonialism, and those of the past in which these institutions were accepted and acceptable facts of life, albeit conditions that one might not want imposed on oneself. In this sense there is a morphological similarity between the effects of antislavery ideology and the emergence of a dominant anticolonial ideology in the late twentieth century. What Frederick Cooper and Ann Laura Stoler say of "[t]he continuing study of colonial regimes" will sound familiar to students of slavery: it "should be more than a neoabolitionist denunciation of a form of power now safely consigned to history." [19]

How do we understand the disappearance of slavery and colonialism? Are they comparable? Are they linked? Ranajit Guha begins his recent *tour de force* critique of colonial historiography, *Dominance Without Hegemony: History and Power in Colonial India,* by discussing the world-historic abolition of slavery as a model for understanding the emergence and nature of comparable critiques of capital and colonialism.[20] Slavery is, after all, the modern world's master trope for impermissible forms of domination. Abolition and emancipation are, with revolution, the master tropes for social transformation.

According to Guha, the European bourgeoisie's triumph over "slave-owning and feudal cultures" emerged in several steps. He posits an early period of "relentless critique" that anticipated and worked toward the overthrow of the *ancien régime,* followed by the achievement of bourgeois "dominance" and then "hegemony," which he defines as a dominance in which "persuasion outweighs coercion." But, Guha argues, in colonialism the universalizing impulse of capital "hurtled itself against an insuperable barrier," a barrier of difference that made persuasion impossible. In colonialism, he concludes, there was only "dominance without hegemony." [21]

Perhaps Guha is correct that coercion outweighed persuasion in colonized India and other places. I am not sure coercion can be weighed against persuasion so easily. Coercion can persuade by example and teach new modes of thought, even in the most extreme situations. Antonio Gramsci theorized the simultaneous existence of coercion and consent, which Guha recognizes but then tears artificially asunder.[22] Unlike Guha, I am inclined to think of hegemony as a contouring of conflicts as much as a construction of direct consent. The direction of conflicts into accepted channels that preclude greater contests over dominance is as important as the quantity of direct, spontaneous consent, even when those conflicts are solved in the end by brute force.[23] Bourgeois hegemony in Europe and the United States has not been as total, homogenous, and free of violence as Guha implies. Hegemony is not the same thing as homogeneity of thought. Be that as it may, I am more struck by the logic of Guha's argument if we accept his historical premises about capital and colonialism as a set of givens.

If colonialism was dominance without hegemony and that dominance is now, presumably, gone, what then is Guha writing against in the politics of the present? If his opponents are still, after colonialism, the failed universalizing drive of capital, bourgeois ideology, and the "dominant . . . liberal-nationalist mode" of Indian historiography, what then does that mean for his argument about hegemony? Was a colonial dominance without hegemony replaced by a hegemony without colonial dominance?

Antislavery ideology became politically effective in early industrial Britain and the United States as it became part of the cultural formation of their new style of capitalism. It provided a moral rationale for much modern colonialism in the nineteenth and twentieth centuries. Yet, despite its origins and record of frequently imperialist implications, anticolonial nationalists in the Philippines, and perhaps elsewhere, appropriated antislavery ideology to create their people's rightful place in a world of nations. Antislavery ideology played a hegemonic role in consolidating hierarchies within colonial and national boundaries. Beyond those boundaries, antislavery ideology constituted part of the larger field of disciplinary power that made the modern world a place where people could overturn the old order of colonial relationships only by forming nations, for only nations had the recognized right not to be colonized.

The world's rejection of colonialism as an acceptable sociopolitical form is, perhaps, little more than a limited cultural relativism encased within the normative goal of national self-determination in politics. But the world-historical shift of decolonization has not yet been studied as much more than the serial political histories of independent movements against colonialism. There is no historiography of the end of colonialism parallel to that of the abolition of slavery. Certainly there was no central or dominant anticolonial movement in the same way that the long-running British antislavery movement has been viewed by many historians as leading a "century of progress." Anticolonial movements were widely dispersed, although they informed one another and some of their leaders and intellectuals met in metropolitan capitals such as Paris, London, and Moscow. Nor is there an analogue in the historiography of colonialism's end to David Brion Davis's classic exposition of the relatively sudden creation of movements to abolish slavery in the eighteenth century and the subsequent generalization of antislavery ideology.[24] But Benedict Anderson's analyses of the rapid generalization of nationalism do suggest the outlines of a parallel transformation in the sociopolitical forms of group belonging.[25]

Historians of antislavery ideology and abolition have often found disappointing outcomes at the end of their research. Antislavery movements challenged all manner of hierarchies in their early years and seemed to promise a utopian future of radical egalitarianism and human community. More than a few influential historical studies of emancipation conclude by pondering antislavery's conservative turn, its legitimation of capitalist labor relations, and its accommodation to white supremacy in postemancipation America and the age of high imperialism. Likewise, it has become progressively more difficult to imagine a possible history of anticolonial movements that does not end with their containment in conservative ideology, neocolonialism, and the authoritarianism of so many postcolonial states.

Historians cannot yet rewrite the end of this story. Only a history yet to happen can make that possible. But perhaps we need to rewrite the middle of the tale to recall the power of those earlier hopes and dreams. In the American colonial Philippines of the early twentieth century, the meanings of slavery and colonialism came together in ways that may help us to understand better the extent to which they still shape our world despite our conviction that they are gone forever. Let there be no misunderstanding. I believe quite strongly that the world is a better place because of the abolition of slavery and the turn against colonialism. But we need to grasp how those abolitions depended upon the reification of slavery and colonialism. To be able to abolish slavery and colonialism, it was necessary to define them very restrictively. Complex and invasive human relationships had to be reduced and refigured as things apart from a normative world of humane existence so that they could be carved like cancers out of a social body in which they were thoroughly enmeshed.

Our received notion of the abolition of slavery is, in many ways, based on a medical model of social ills as much as a juridical view of right and equality. Eighteenth- and nineteenth-century humanitarianism tended to focus on the body and the alleviation of physical pains. We should not necessarily reject this medical model, but we need to be alert to what it presupposes and implies. In the current state of medical knowledge, we know that cancers can seldom be removed without a trace and the cures can be as debilitating as the disease.

The polymath "father" of Philippine nationalism, Jose Rizal, also thought the Filipino society of his day was afflicted with a cancer of inseparably colonial and domestic origin. Trained as a medical doctor in Europe, Rizal nevertheless expressed his national(ist) diagnosis in a politically subversive novel, *Noli Me Tangere,* which he published in 1886. Poignantly, he explained his special procedure of social examination in the novel's dedication, To My Motherland:

> Recorded in the history of human sufferings there is a cancer of a character so malignant that the least contact irritates it and awakens the sharpest of pains. Well then, every time I have wanted to evoke you amidst modern civilizations, now to accompany me with your memory, now to compare you with other nations, your beloved image appeared to me afflicted with a similar social cancer.
>
> Desiring your health, which is ours, and searching for the best treatment, I will do with you as the ancients of old did with their afflicted: they exposed them on the steps of the temple so that each person who came to invoke the Divinity would propose to them a remedy.
>
> And, to this end, I will attempt to reproduce faithfully your condition without leniencies; I will lift part of the veil that conceals the evil, sacrificing all to the truth, even my own self-esteem [*amor propio*], for, as your son, I also suffer from your defects and weaknesses.

In the spirit of Rizal, then, I want us to reconsider slavery, colonialism, and the idea of abolition. Opposition to slavery without its reification opened the possibility of finding aspects of slavery in many other relationships, conditions, and states. The historical process of abolishing slavery, a unique and dramatic event from a world-historical point of view, entailed an imperfect containment of these subversive possibilities. The most dire fears of conservatives about the dissolution of society were put to rest, but, too often, so were the millennial hopes of the most radical abolitionists. Similar struggles, fears, and processes of containment accompanied the abolition of colonialism, which was made possible only by its reification as a thing that could be eliminated from a normative world order of nation-states. Unless and until we can look upon the complexity of slavery and colonialism as they have existed in history, we shall remain blind to those elements of both that live on today and deaf to the most passionate and beautiful calls for their transcendence.

Notes

References to books and articles have been shortened in the following notes; complete references may be found in the Bibliography. Because archival materials have been listed in the Bibliography only by repository and collection, references to such materials are given in full in the notes.

INTRODUCTION

1. Library of Congress, Journal of William Cameron Forbes, ser. 2, 2:138 (entry for 11 August 1921).

2. For example, all but one of Anthony Reid's several incisive analyses of slavery in Southeast Asia begin with commentary on definitional disputes and the propriety of using the word *slavery* in studies of Southeast Asian societies. See Reid, "Introduction," 1–2, *Southeast Asia in the Age of Commerce*, 131–32, and "Decline of Slavery," 64–65.

3. David Brion Davis writes that, "unlike their British predecessors, American abolitionists showed little initiative in promoting emancipation throughout the world" (*Slavery and Human Progress*, 271).

4. Ibid.; Foner, *Nothing but Freedom;* and Kolchin, *Unfree Labor.*

5. The most instructive example is the richly generative essay, "African 'Slavery' as an Institution of Marginality," by Kopytoff and Miers.

6. Some of the pitfalls of exceptionalist historiography are discussed by Fredrickson in "From Exceptionalism to Variability."

7. See the recent fascinating study by Gomez, *Exchanging Our Country Marks;* and Thornton, *Africa and Africans.* These authors stand on the shoulders of predecessors whose contributions deserve pages of recognition, but I think these most recent titles should mark a new break in the historiography of slavery and American identity.

8. For examples of attempts to explain the globalization of images of American slavery as the true definition of slavery, see Toledano, "Ottoman Concepts of Slavery," 37–63; and Prakash, *Bonded Histories, 1–12*.

9. Williams, *Tragedy of American Diplomacy;* LaFeber, *New Empire.* Some historians of the American West do raise into view the historic internationality of what is now an integral part of the domestic United States, thereby bucking the teleology of Manifest Destiny in American historiography: see, for example, Limerick, *Legacy of Conquest* and White, *Middle Ground.* On Manifest Destiny in American history, see Stephanson, *Manifest Destiny.*

10. The point is made by Hunt in "The Long Crisis in Diplomatic History: Coming to Closure," but his prognostication of closure still seems premature. Similar issues continued to be hotly debated in the same journal; see "Culture, Gender, and Foreign Policy: A Symposium."

11. See, for example, Cooper and Stoler, eds., *Tensions of Empire;* Prakash, ed., *After Colonialism;* and Dirks, ed., *Colonialism and Culture.*

12. See, for example, Kaplan and Pease, *Cultures of United States Imperialism,* which does not contain a contribution from a historian of the United States. One exception to this disciplinary rule is Rydell, *All the World's a Fair.*

13. See Fredrickson's reassertion of the United States's essential anticolonial tradition in his essay "America's Diversity in Comparative Perspective."

14. The patron-client model of Philippine society was systematized in classic works by Hollnsteiner (*Dynamics of Power*), Lande (*Leaders, Factions and Parties*), and Lynch and Guzman, eds., *Four Readings in Philippine Values.* More recent examples include May, *Battle for Batangas;* and Paredes, ed., *Philippine Colonial Democracy.*

15. In the classic social science literature see, especially, Lynch, "Social Acceptance Reconsidered."

16. For studies that question the history of the patron-client model and show that the language of reciprocity can enable protest, resistance, and even revolution, see Ileto, *Pasyon and Revolution;* Kerkvliet, *Huk Rebellion* and *Everyday Politics;* and Rafael, *Contracting Colonialism.*

17. Rosaldo (*Culture and Truth*) cautions against this kind of classic anthropological dualism, in which the anthropologized other is seen as locked into culture while the typically modern anthropologist's self is construed to exist beyond culture in a transparent rationality.

18. For example, see the essays in Paredes, ed., *Philippine Colonial Democracy,* and Stanley, *Nation in the Making.*

19. Davis, *Problem of Slavery in Western Culture,* 63–90, and *Slavery and Human Progress,* 19–22; Patterson, *Freedom,* 1:293–344; and Martin, *Slavery as Salvation.*

20. Davis, *Slavery and Human Progress,* 16–22.

21. Davis alludes to this slippage in the epilogue to *Slavery and Human Progress,* 317–20.

22. Reid explains that some "Southeast Asian scholars" refrain from using the word *slavery* because "[i]t is difficult to use the term without appearing to denigrate Southeast Asian cultural traditions which still have force and

value" ("Decline of Slavery," 64). For an analysis of this controversy in Philippine historiography, see Salman, "Ancient Philippine Slavery and Modern Ideology."

23. Scott reported that Filipino "college students and history teachers" in the 1970s believed that slavery either never existed in the non-Muslim Philippines or that it was eradicated by Spain by the early seventeenth century (*Slavery in the Spanish Philippines,* 1–2). In *The Philippines: A Past Revisited,* the most influential nationalist history of recent decades, Constantino calls slavery a "misnomer" and describes pre-Hispanic Philippine social relations as communal and without "marked differences in status" (31–34).

24. Scott, *Slavery in the Spanish Philippines, Barangay,* "Filipino Class Structure," and "*Oripun* and *Alipin.*" See also Rafael, *Contracting Colonialism,* 136–69.

25. Scott, *Slavery in the Spanish Philippines;* Rafael, *Contracting Colonialism,* 136–69.

26. Scott, *Slavery in the Spanish Philippines.*

27. Rafael, *Contracting Colonialism,* 155, 169.

28. Scott, *Slavery in the Spanish Philippines.*

29. For a sense of this economic history, see the essays in McCoy and de Jesus, eds., *Philippine Social History.*

30. Scott, "The Creation of a Cultural Minority."

31. On the rise of the *ilustrados* and their variety of nationalism, see Schumacher, *Propaganda Movement;* Guerrero, *First Filipino;* Wickberg, *Chinese in the Philippines;* and Rafael, "Nationalism, Imagery, and the Filipino Intelligentsia."

32. Ileto, *Pasyon and Revolution* and "Rizal and the Underside of Philippine History." Also see Rafael, "Nationalism, Imagery, and the Philippine Intelligentsia."

33. Finley, *Ancient Slavery,* 11.

34. There has, of course, been extensive debate about the relationship between varieties of capitalism and the success of abolitionist movements. The most intensive exchange is reproduced in Bender, *The Antislavery Debate.*

35. Kopytoff and Miers, "African 'Slavery'"; Patterson, *Slavery and Social Death,* 209–61.

36. Davis's identification of the conceptual revolution necessary to create the very idea of abolishing slavery has been one of his greatest contributions to this historiography. See Davis, *Problem of Slavery in Western Culture; Problem of Slavery in the Age of Revolution;* and his succinct statement of this crucial point in "Perils of Doing History," 306–309.

37. The global dimensions reached by the abolitionist campaign are charted in Davis, *Slavery and Human Progress,* 279–320, and in Miers, *Britain and the Ending of the Slave Trade.*

38. My ideas about the effects of a regime of compulsory nationality have been inspired by Judith Butler's concept of "compulsory heterosexuality," which she developed in *Gender Trouble* and, of course, by the idea of disciplinary power developed by Foucault in *Discipline and Punish.*

39. On nationalism's self-projection into the past, see Anderson, *Imagined Communities*, 5, 187–206. For a criticism of the self-naturalizing tendencies of the discourse of freedom, see Prakash, *Bonded Histories*.

40. Patterson, *Slavery and Social Death,* ix. Slavery is not the only embarrassing practice that nationalism confronts, evades, and effaces in its historical narratives. A catalogue of such practices, and the ethnic and cultural differences they mark, would be lengthy. For an illuminating discussion of comparable phenomena, see Duara, *Rescuing History from the Nation.*

41. For a sense of this enormous field of literature, see the exchanges between Davis and Haskell in Bender, ed., *Antislavery Debate;* Klein, "Introduction"; Prakash, *Bonded Histories,* esp. 1–12; Solow and Engerman, eds., *British Capitalism;* Roberts and Miers, "Introduction"; Drescher, *Capitalism and Antislavery* and *Econocide;* Foner, *Nothing but Freedom;* Temperly, "Capitalism, Slavery, and Ideology;" and Anstey, *Atlantic Slave Trade.* All of these writers were, in one way or another, responding to Williams's pivotal *Capitalism and Slavery.*

42. See, for example, the representative contributions to Miers and Roberts, eds., *End of Slavery in Africa;* and Klein, ed., *Breaking the Chains.*

43. The historiography on black abolitionists in the Americas is obviously different because it takes its subjects' thoughts seriously, but there is room to go much farther in analyzing how antislavery ideology affected systems of meaning and concepts of belonging among freed people in the Americas. See, for example, Quarles, *Black Abolitionists;* James, *Black Jacobins;* Genovese, *From Rebellion to Revolution;* Blackett, *Building an Antislavery Wall* and *Beating against the Barriers;* Martin, *Mind of Frederick Douglass;* and Painter, *Sojourner Truth.*

44. The literature on emancipation in the Americas is vast. For a sense of its dominant themes, see Foner, *Nothing but Freedom* and *Reconstruction;* Scott, *Slave Emancipation in Cuba;* Holt, *Problem of Freedom;* and Fields, *Slavery and Freedom.*

45. Holt, *Problem of Freedom;* McGlynn and Drescher, eds., *Meaning of Freedom;* and Scott, "Exploring the Meaning of Freedom."

46. Davis, *Slavery and Human Progress,* 19–20.

47. Sale, *Slumbering Volcano,* 23–25; and Stoler and Cooper, "Between Metropole and Colony."

48. Jameson, *Political Unconscious,* 286–91.

49. Kopytoff, "Reflections," 500–502.

50. According to one of the leading scholars of the patron-client school, interpersonal and familial relations have contributed "a strong element of continuity to the country's economic and political history over the past century." McCoy, "'An Anarchy of Families,'" 1. That is no mean interpretive claim, given the revolutions, foreign occupations, and socioeconomic changes of the past one hundred years.

51. Prakash, *Bonded Histories,* 11.

52. Ibid., 225.

53. This does not mean that slavery cannot exist or be winked at by complicitous ruling classes. But no nation-state openly defends slavery. States facing

allegations of the continued practice of slavery within their borders tend to re-act defensively if they do not themselves lead campaigns against bondage. See Prakash, *Bonded Histories,* 218–25; McDougall, "A Topsy-Turvy World," 384; Davis, *Slavery and Human Progress,* 318–20; and Klein, "Introduction," 26–27. Also see the instructively gripping and sociologically loose analysis in Bales, *Disposable People.*

54. Anderson, *Imagined Communities,* 5, 7. On the coeval origins, development, and spread of antislavery ideology, see Davis, *Problem of Slavery in the Age of Revolution.* Conceptual connections between antislavery ideology and nationalism are suggested by Anderson (48–50), and, in different ways, by Blackbourn, *Overthrow of Colonial Slavery;* James, *Black Jacobins;* Eltis, "Europeans and the Rise and Fall of African Slavery"; and Peabody, *"There Are No Slaves in France."*

Lest there by any confusion, let me underscore *the lack of any direct causal relation* between nationalism, antislavery ideology, and abolition. The history of the United States makes that point plain. And yet, the conjunction of slavery and revolutionary nationalism produced strains, tensions, embarrassments and, as not a few scholars have now established, a volatile mixture of racism and freedom. See, for examples, Davis, *Problem of Slavery in Western Culture,* 3–28; Bailyn, *Ideological Origins;* Morgan, *American Slavery, American Freedom;* Okoye, "Chattel Slavery"; Hoffman and Berlin, eds., *Slavery and Freedom;* Roediger, *Wages of Whiteness;* and Sale, *Slumbering Volcano.*

55. Smith, *Ethnic Origins of Nations.*

56. Chatterjee, *Nationalist Thought* and *Nation and Its Fragments.*

57. Chatterjee, *Nation and Its Fragments,* 5–6.

58. Chatterjee, *Nation and Its Fragments,* 11, 227, 238. Coincidentally, Chatterjee begins his last chapter by considering the multiple "ways in which the word *jāti* can be used in any modern Indian language." Taking its use in Bengali for an example, he recounts dictionary entries that define it variously as " 'origin, such as Musalman by birth' "; " 'classes of living species, such as human *jāti,* animal *jāti,* bird *jāti'* "; " '*varna* . . . such as Brahman, etc.' "; " '*vaṃśa, gotra, kula* [lineage, clan], such as Arya *jāti,* Semitic *jāti'* "; and " 'human collectivities bound by loyalty to a state or organized around the natural and cultural characteristics of a country or province,' " including " 'nation' " and " 'race' " (221). The notion of *jāti* has thus been at the center of many struggles over recognition and belonging, for the colonized, women, minorities, outcasts, and the culturally different. Its various meanings have been alternately claimed and disclaimed by the modern state, which lives "embedded . . . within the universal narrative of capital" and attempts to fix the meaning of legitimate loyalty into the disciplinary regime of the nation-state. "It is this unresolved struggle between the narratives of capital and community within the discursive space of the modern state," concludes Chatterjee, "that is reflected in our embarrassment at the many uses of *jāti*" (238–39).

59. Patterson, *Slavery and Social Death,* esp. 35–101.

60. This does not mean that contemporary national identities are false. On the contrary, it highlights the extraordinary power vested in them to remake reality.

CHAPTER 1

1. For a general introduction to the Spanish colonial Philippines, see Cushner, *Spain in the Philippines*. On Americans' earlier interest in the Caribbean, see May, *Southern Dream of a Caribbean Empire*. The McKinley administration's interest in the Philippines and its preparation to fight the Spanish-American War there is documented by LaFeber, *New Empire*, 361–62.

2. LaFeber, *New Empire*; McCormick, *China Market*.

3. The centrality of China and Hay's later concept of the Open Door has been stressed most forcefully by Williams, *Tragedy of American Diplomacy*, rev. ed. 18–57, and by LaFeber, *New Empire*.

4. By ignoring the history of American colonialism as a multifaceted relationship and concentrating on economic expansion, William Appleman Williams argued (in *Tragedy of American Diplomacy*, rev. ed. 18–57) for the ironic victory of the anti-imperialists. An alternative view of Americans' deeper intellectual engagement in the world history of colonialism is suggested, but not quite expressly argued, by Rydell in *All the World's a Fair* and by Stephanson in *Manifest Destiny*. On comparisons to American Indian resistance, see Walter L. Williams, "United States Indian Policy and the Debate over Philippine Annexation." On the anti-imperialists, see Welch, *Response to Imperialism*; Tompkins, *Anti-Imperialism in the United States*; Beisner, *Twelve against Empire*; and Miller, *"Benevolent Assimilation."*

5. Dean C. Worcester, a professor of ornithology at the University of Michigan, was one of the exceptions. He participated in two research expeditions to the Philippines, the first in 1887, the second in 1890. On both occasions he visited Mindanao and the Sulu Islands. Capitalizing on the surge of interest on the Philippines in 1898, Worcester published an article in the *National Geographic Magazine* ("Notes on Some Primitive Philippine Tribes"), another article in *Century Magazine* ("The Malay Pirates of the Philippines"), and a book titled *The Philippine Islands and Their People*. He mentioned slavery in passing in each publication.

6. U.S. Senate, *Treaty with the Sultan*. On slavery in the Sulu Islands in the eighteen and nineteenth centuries, see Warren's superb history, *Sulu Zone*.

7. Davis's *Slavery and Human Progress* explores the ambiguous and sometimes paradoxical relationship between slavery and conceptions of progress, barbarism, liberation, and domination. Although Davis's discussion of these themes with regard to the United States does not extend far beyond the early years of Reconstruction, his general approach and his treatment of British imperialism have had a great influence on my own analysis.

8. Lasch ("Anti-Imperialists") suggested that a great deal about the anti-imperialists could be learned by placing them in the context of nineteenth-century liberal reform, with special reference to the history of the antislavery movement. Schirmer, in *Republic or Empire*, pushed Lasch's suggestion a little too far by concluding that the strength of anti-imperialism in Boston "can best be understood as the last powerful thrust of abolitionism, the radical democratic ideology that spurred the North to victory over the slaveholders' power in the

middle of the nineteenth century" (257). McPherson, in *Abolitionist Legacy*, traced the careers of abolitionists and their descendants through the early twentieth century in an effort to dispel the conventional wisdom (reiterated by Lasch) that the abolitionists "abandoned the negro." Much as Lasch expected, McPherson found an important contingent of abolitionist families in the ranks of prominent anti-imperialists, but his analysis of connections at the level of ideology was truncated by his concentration on the prosopography of the abolitionists. McPherson also found that some abolitionists and their descendants supported colonial rule in the Philippines. On the Civil War and abolition as a decisive event in the development of culture in the nineteenth-century United States, see Fredrickson, *Inner Civil War.*

9. U.S. Adjutant General's Office, *Correspondence*, 858–59 (McKinley to Secretary of War, 21 December 1898).

10. National Archives, RG 350, file 141-110 ("Address of President McKinley," 16 February 1899).

11. Griffin, *List of Books.* Reinsch, *Colonial Administration* and *World Politics.* Ireland, *Tropical Colonization.*

12. See, for example, Ireland, "European Experience," "Labor Problem in the Tropics," and "Growth of the British Colonial Conception." David Starr Jordan, president of Stanford University and an ardent anti-imperialist, relied on Ireland as an authority; see the discussion of Jordan's views below.

13. Ireland, *Tropical Colonization*, vii, xi.

14. Ibid., chapter 4.

15. Ibid., 132.

16. Ibid., 128–59.

17. Ibid.

18. Ibid., 128–94, 217–28, esp. 226–28. Alatas, *Myth of the Lazy Native*, is an insightful study of racist interpretations of labor practices in colonial Southeast Asia.

19. Ireland, *Tropical Colonization*, 217–26; the passage he quoted was from Worcester's first book, *Philippine Islands and Their People.*

20. Jordan, *Question of the Philippines.* Jordan quoted from Ireland's article, "Labor Problem in the Tropics."

Although Jordan seems to have been the first to make an antislavery argument against U.S. colonial rule in the Philippines, a very similar argument was made about Spanish rule in Cuba by a group of black Americans who organized themselves as the Cuban Anti-Slavery Committee in 1872. Because they assumed slavery to be necessary to produce a profit on Cuban sugar plantations, they reasoned that the Spanish effort to suppress the Cuban revolutionaries and retain Cuba as a colony demonstrated that Spanish gestures toward abolition, such as the Moret Law of 1870, must be insincere. Keeping Cuba as a colony seemed to make no sense without slavery. The rebels, of course, promised abolition and actually freed slaves in areas under their control. The Cuban Anti-Slavery Committee called for U.S. recognition of the rebels and Cuban independence as an antislavery measure. See Cuban Anti-Slavery Committee, *Slavery in Cuba.* The histories of U.S. involvement in the end of slavery in Cuba and the actions, responses, and views of African Americans to slavery in Latin America and Africa after the Civil War are rich subjects, each large enough to require at least a book-length monograph.

21. Jordan, *Question of the Philippines,* 20, 54.

22. Ibid., 24–28, 54, 62.

23. McPherson, *Abolitionist Legacy,* 324–25. The connection between anti-imperialism and Boston's antislavery past is emphasized in Schirmer, *Republic or Empire.*

24. McPherson (*Abolitionist Legacy,* 324–25) emphasizes the anti-imperialists' pedigree, but he acknowledges several counterexamples. Also see Lasch, "The Anti-Imperialists."

25. Anti-Imperialist League, *Anti-Imperialism: Speeches . . . 1898,* 5–9, 19–21, 26–30.

26. The story of the anti-imperialist movement has been told many times. In addition to the works by Lasch, McPherson, and Schirmer cited above, see Welch, *Response to Imperialism;* Tompkins, *Anti-Imperialism in the United States;* and Beisner, *Twelve against Empire.*

27. Moorfield Storey, "Address of the President," 33. Also see New York Public Library, Edward Ordway Papers, box 1 (Josephine Shaw Lowell to Ordway, 22 September 1903); and Massachusetts Historical Society, George S. Boutwell Papers, box 1, file "ca. 1900" ("Speech as Delivered," 24 October 1902, typescript).

28. Massachusetts Historical Society, Moorfield Storey Papers, "Charles Francis Adams–Moorfield Storey Correspondence," box 3 (Adams to Storey, 27 May 1899).

29. Because of his vociferous criticism of the McKinley administration and the war in the Philippines, Atkinson drew charges of "copperhead" like a magnet. His activities and the counterattacks they provoked are discussed below. Despite his unimpeachable antislavery credentials, which included raising funds for John Brown's Immigrant Aid Society, Atkinson was probably extremely sensitive to charges that his pamphlets "smack to[o] much of Copperheadism away back in 1861–1865" (Massachusetts Historical Society, Edward Atkinson Papers, Correspondence box, 1 June 1899–4 November 1899 [Land to Atkinson, 30 October 1899]). In a letter to his friend and fellow anti-imperialist and abolitionist Thomas Wentworth Higginson, Atkinson opened his soul. "I am constantly reminded of the old times in which we worked together. My only regret regarding the past is that I was not in the fight. The burdens and duties upon me were so great that until the very last I did not even prepare to go to the war . . . Frank Lee once said to me 'You have lost much out of your life.' I feel it" (ibid., letterbook, vol. 67 [Atkinson to Higginson, 18 September 1899]).

30. The only full length biography of Atkinson is Williamson's *Edward Atkinson.* Also see Beisner, *Twelve against Empire,* 84–106, for an overview of Atkinson's activities as an anti-imperialist. Beware, however, of Beisner's misapprehension of William Appleman Williams's analysis of the anti-imperialists, his treatment of Atkinson's propaganda on the slavery issue as if Atkinson were a solitary crank, and his failure to explore Atkinson's desire to annex and ultimately absorb Cuba into the United States; see Williams, *Tragedy of American*

Diplomacy, 1–51. On Atkinson's views about Cuba, see Massachusetts Historical Society, Atkinson Papers, letterbook, vol. 65 (Atkinson to Nordhoff, 9 March 1899); and ibid., vol. 70 (Atkinson to Fowler, 21 June 1901).

31. For a description of the incident, see Welch, *Response to Imperialism,* 50–51, and Massachusetts Historical Society, Atkinson Papers, letterbook, vol. 66 (Atkinson to Nordhoff, 13 September 1899).

32. Atkinson, *The Anti-Imperialist* 1, no. 5 (15 September 1899).

33. Ibid., 4, 8–10.

34. Ibid.

35. Massachusetts Historical Society, Atkinson Papers, letterbook, vol. 66 (Atkinson to "the Editor of the 'Transcript,'" 29 August 1899).

36. See ibid., vol. 67 (Atkinson to Kennedy, 19 September 1899); and ibid., vol. 66 (Atkinson to Bookwalter, 6 September 1899, and to Schurz, 11 September 1899).

37. Ibid., Incoming Correspondence Box, 1 June 1899–4 November 1899 (Titus, Superintendent of Schools, Custer County, Montana, to Atkinson, 30 October 1899).

38. National Archives, RG 350, file 141-10 ("Speech of President McKinley at Youngstown, Ohio," 18 October 1899).

39. The excerpt from McKinley's message to Congress of 5 December 1899 is quoted from Library of Congress, William McKinley Papers, microfilm roll 14 ("Sulu Slavery. Was it Authorized Ratified or Affirmed by President McKinley?" memorandum, n.d. [c. 10 October 1899]). The papers delivered to Congress were printed as "Report and Accompanying Papers of Brigadier General John C. Bates in Relation to the Negotiation of a Treaty or Agreement Made With the Sultan of Sulu" (56th Cong., S. Doc. 136).

40. See Lasch, "Anti-Imperialists" and Fredrickson, *Black Image in the White Mind,* 305–11.

41. For insight into Boutwell's life, see his autobiography, *Reminiscences.* The quote is from Massachusetts Historical Society, Boutwell papers, pamphlets ("Address by the Hon. George S. Boutwell . . . January 1, 1903," p. 9). Boutwell expressed similar sentiments repeatedly. He developed the theme with great elegance in a speech delivered in 1904, titled "Address of the Hon. George S. Boutwell at a Meeting Held in Faneuil Hall, Monday Evening August 1$^{\underline{st}}$, To Give Adherence to the Philippine Plank of the National Democratic Platform."

> It is our happy fortune to be able to assemble in Faneuil Hall and here to express our views of freedom, justice, human equality and the universal right of self-government and on the anniversary of a day which is worthy of commemoration in the annals of liberty. The first day August, 1834 was made memorable as the day on which slavery was abolished in the British West India Islands. The act was the beginning of a series of events in the progress of human liberty of which the overthrow of slavery in America may be considered as the culmination. It was followed, however, by the emancipation of the serfs in Russia, the abolition of slavery in the Spanish and Portuguese Islands of America and in the Empire of Brazil. . . . The overthrow of imperialism in America after a contest of six years and which may continue yet many more years will be the second great event in American history since the adoption of the Federal Constitution, It will rank with the overthrow of slavery under the administration of Mr. Lincoln (Massachusetts Historical Society, Boutwell Papers, box 1, file "ca. 1900" typescript).

42. Boutwell, "Imperialists or Republicans?"

43. Boutwell, "The President's Policy," 7–9.

44. Boutwell, *Enslavement of American Labor,* Massachusetts Historical Society, Boutwell Papers, box 1, file "1904" typescript ("Two Experiments"). Many of the same arguments developed in "Two Experiments" can also be found in another speech (ibid., file "ca. 1905"; typescript), titled "Speech Delivered in Faneuil Hall, November 1, 1904."

45. Boutwell, "Enslavement of American Labor," 11–12. Boutwell used the history of the New South's displacement of New England textile mills and the shift of agricultural production to the West to illustrate the workings of comparative advantage based upon low wage rates. The example of the South after slavery could have been used to reaffirm the tenets of free labor ideology (the textile industry developed there only after slavery was eliminated), but the rest of Boutwell's analysis seems to preclude such confidence.

46. "Two Experiments," 1.

47. Ibid., 1–2.

48. Ibid., 2–3.

49. Ibid., 13. Boutwell's identification of colonialism with slavery was most fully developed in a speech aptly titled "A Slaveholder's Title and its Enforcement by the Administration and the Army" (Massachusetts Historical Society, Boutwell Papers, box 1, file "ca. 1900; typescript).

CHAPTER 2

1. Van Meter, *Truth about the Philippines,* 104.

2. Ade, *Sultan of Sulu.*

3. Ibid., introductory note. On Ade's trip to the Philippines and the production of the play, see Kelly, *George Ade,* 163–73.

4. Ade, *Sultan of Sulu,* 126.

5. Bryan's speech is quoted in a letter written by acting Secretary of War G. D. Meiklejohn to Bryan, 6 October 1900, which was printed in Meiklejohn, "Mr. Bryan and Sulu Slaves," 2.

6. Library of Congress, McKinley Papers, microfilm reel 14 ("Sulu Slavery. Was it Authorized, Ratified or Affirmed by President McKinley?" memorandum, n.d. [c. 10 October 1899]).

7. Meiklejohn to Bryan, 6 October 1900, printed in Meiklejohn, "Mr. Bryan and Sulu Slaves," 2; Bryan to Meiklejohn, 10 October 1900, excerpted in "Bryan's Reply to Meiklejohn," 2; and Meiklejohn to Bryan, 12 October 1900, printed in Meiklejohn, "Meiklejohn Writes Bryan," 3.

8. "America and Sulu Slaves," 3.

9. Ibid.

10. Ibid.

11. National Archives, RG 350, file 141-10 ("President McKinley's Letter of Acceptance to the Chairman of the Notification Committee," 8 November 1900).

12. Ibid., file 2869-1 (Hart to Roosevelt, 23 January 1902; Root to Hart, 3 February 1902).

13. Ibid. (Hart to Roosevelt, 22 January 1902); Hart, *Slavery and Abolition.*

14. National Archives, BIA papers, RG 350, file 2869-1 (Root to Hart, 3 February 1902).

15. Ibid.

16. On the fighting in Mindanao after Wood announced abolition, see Gowing, *Mandate in Moroland.*

17. For an excellent discussion of the origins of the debate over the harshness or mildness of slavery in Africa, see McSheffrey, "Slavery, Indentured Servitude." Also see the historiographical discussions by Roberts and Miers ("Introduction," 27–33, 48) and Cooper ("Problem of Slavery in African Studies" and *From Slaves to Squatters*).

18. Foner, *Free Soil, Free Labor, Free Men,* esp. 301–17; Fredrickson, *Inner Civil War;* Montgomery, *Beyond Equality.* Studies that depict a conservative shift in liberal ideology include Williams, *Contours of American History;* Kolko, *Triumph of Conservatism;* Lasch, *New Radicalism;* Weinstein, *Corporate Ideal* and Lears, *No Place of Grace.* Many others have written about this transformation of social thought in terms that differ from and sometimes oppose the analyses of the works listed above. For some interesting examples, see White, *Social Thought in America;* Wiebe, *Search for Order;* Haskell, *Emergence of Professional Social Science;* and Ross, *Origins of American Social Science.*

19. George, *Progress and Poverty,* 522–23. Thomas (*Alternative America*) provides an incisive portrait of George, his radicalism, and his limitations.

20. On the influence of evolutionary thought and professionalism, see Lears, *No Place of Grace;* White, *Social Thought in America;* Wiebe, *Search for Order;* and Haskell, *Emergence of Professional Social Science.*

21. On Ely's career and social thought, see Haskell, *Emergence of Professional Social Science;* Furner, *Advocacy and Objectivity;* and DeBrizzi, *Ideology and the Rise of Labor Theory.*

22. Ely, *Studies in the Evolution of Industrial Society,* 48, 61–62.

23. Hadley, *Economics,* 29–31, 37. Ely and many of his contemporaries put a great deal of stock in the idea of inculcating the internalization of control. Thus, about the labor movement in the United States, Ely argued that the proper goal was "industrial democracy, which means self-rule, self-control, the self-direction of the masses in their efforts to gain a livelihood" (Ely, *Outlines of Economics,* 408). Also see Ross's classic work, *Social Control.*

24. Ely, *Studies in the Evolution of Industrial Society,* 61–62.

25. Beard, *Rise of American Civilization,* 2:488.

26. For similar analyses of the ideological functions of the "mild slavery" interpretation, see McSheffrey, "Slavery, Indentured Servitude"; Roberts and Miers, "Introduction"; and Cooper, *From Slaves to Squatters.*

27. On the persistence of the "mild slavery" interpretation in late-twentieth-century historiography, see McSheffrey, "Slavery, Indentured Servitude"; Cooper, "Problem of Slavery in African Studies"; and Roberts and Miers, "Introduction."

28. On slavery in the Sulu Islands, see Warren, *Sulu Zone*.

29. Ade, *Sultan of Sulu*. This edition contains photographs from the Broadway production. The plate between pages 56 and 57 includes a view of the two "Nubian slaves" bowed before the Sultan.

CHAPTER 3

1. Warren, *Sulu Zone*, 253.

2. Ibid., 12–13; Sutherland, "Slavery and the Slave Trade," 267; Reid, "Introduction," 31–32 and *Southeast Asia in the Age of Commerce*, 133–36.

3. Warren, *Sulu Zone*, 5–16, 38–66.

4. Ibid., 38–102.

5. Ibid., 38–102, 147–81.

6. Ibid., 208–11. In addition to the influx of slaves, migrants such as the boat-dwelling Samal Bajau Laut added to the population. Estimates are further complicated by the fluidity of ethnic and territorial boundaries in the region. For example, it is not clear whether Warren includes the population of Sulu's Bornean dependencies in his estimate for the mid-nineteenth century. Estimates of the population of the Sulu Islands in the early twentieth century range from about one hundred fifty thousand to two hundred thousand. The end of raiding, several famines, and the reconfiguration of the sultanate's boundaries all reduced the total population, but in what proportions is not known.

7. Ibid., 215–16.

8. In Taosug the word for a person in debt-bondage, distinct from slavery, was *kiapangdilihan.*

9. Warren writes, "Slaves were sold over and over again. *Datus* rarely sold their own followers, but they trafficked extensively in slaves who were given to them in payment of debts or as captives by Iranun and Balingingi" (ibid., 206).

10. On the many uses, roles, and occupations of slaves see ibid., 215–36.

11. Ibid., 237–51, 299–315.

12. Ibid. Children were, naturally, the most likely to become assimilated. Warren records cases of *banyaga* who had forgotten the language of their youth as well as the exact names of their natal families. One Spanish captive reported, "I have seen them cane some boys for recollecting the memory of their parents, telling them at the same time, 'you should be content to be with us, since you will not have to pay the *tributo,* nor perform personal services'" (241).

13. Ibid., 122–25, 190–97, 200; Ileto, *Magindanao,* 34–37, 43–47. For the text of the 1878 treaty, which Taosug interpreted as paying tribute to the sultan, see Saleeby, *History of Sulu,* 124–29.

14. Warren, *Sulu Zone,* 124–25, 197, 200; Ileto, *Magindanao,* 34–37, 43–47.

15. Warren, *Sulu Zone,* 126–43, 185–86, 253–54.

16. Ileto, *Magindanao,* 30–47, 80, 83–84; Warren, *Sulu Zone,* 130–31.

17. Ileto, *Magindanao,* 50.

18. Ibid., 66–78, 91–92; Madigan and Cushner, "Tamontaka," 322–36, and "Tamontaka Reduction," 81–94; and Cushner, "Abandonment of Tamontaka Reduction," 288–96.

19. Ileto, *Magindanao*, 91–93.

20. U.S. War Department, *Annual Report*, 1902, 9:522.

21. Ileto, *Magindanao*, 96–97.

22. Ibid.; Gowing, *Mandate in Moroland*, 22–23; Beckett, "The Defiant and the Compliant," 398–401.

23. Gowing, *Mandate in Moroland*, 30–31.

24. U.S. Senate, Treaty with the Sultan of *Sulu*, 15 (Otis to Bates, 11 July 1899).

25. Ibid., 4–5, 14–15 (Otis to Bates, 3 July and 11 July 1899).

26. Ibid., 66–77; National Archives, RG 350, file 980-17 ("The Sulu Treaty," memorandum, 24 May 1901), pp. 7–8.

27. U.S. Senate, *Treaty with the Sultan of Sulu*, 26–27, 52, 59–60, 66–77; National Archives, RG 350, file 980-17, ("The Sulu Treaty," memorandum, 24 May 1901), pp. 7–8.

28. Bates to Adjutant General, Manila, 21 August 1899, in U.S. Senate, *Treaty with the Sultan of Sulu*, 25.

29. Root to Otis, 27 October 1899, ibid., 109.

30. National Archives, RG 350, file 2869-11 (Bates to Sultan of Sulu, Datu Raja Muda, Datu Attik, Datu Kalbi, and Datu Joakanain, 4 April 1900).

31. Ibid., file 2869-12 (Sweet to Sultan of Sulu, 13 April 1900). On slavery and abolition in the Malay states, see Gullick, *Indigenous Political Systems*, 97–105; Matheson and Hooker, "Slavery in the Malay Texts"; Endicott, "Effects of Slave Raiding"; and Sullivan, *Social Relations of Dependence*.

32. National Archives, RG 94, 380789 (Sweet to Adjutant General, 19 July 1900).

CHAPTER 4

1. For overall population figures, see Gowing, *Mandate in Moroland*, 43–44, a citation of the 1903 census. The more rigorous 1918 census counted 172,776 people; see Forbes, *Philippine Islands* 2:49. Information on the numbers and prices of slaves in Sulu is reported in National Archives, RG 395, file 2105-161 (Sweet to Adjutant General, 20 May 1900, record card of letter).

2. For the slaveholders' response to the expectation of compensation, see ibid., RG 94, 366585 (Sweet to Adjutant General, 9 November 1900).

3. Ibid., RG 395, file 2105-3271 (McMahon to Assistant Adjutant General, 25 February 1901).

4. Ibid., file 2105-1506 (Sweet to Adjutant General, 24 October 1900).

5. Ibid., file 2105-6133 (Hagedorn to Adjutant General, 1 August 1901).

6. Ibid., file 2105-6368 (Commanding Officer Zamboanga to Commanding Officer Jolo, 21 September [1901]). The commander at Jolo ordered the sultan to arrest Selungan and arrange for the slaves to be returned to Mindanao. "This matter," he told the sultan, "does not admit of any correspondence or argument" (ibid., RG 350, file 5075-2, p. 93 [James to sultan, 8 September 1901]). The sultan sent for Selungan, who said "if the delivery of the slaves had not been requested he would come at once . . . because he says he is innocent. It is true

slaves were brought, but they were not his, they belonged to his passengers who have all gone back to their homes on Look and Patotol." Selungan promised to bring in the slaves, but the sultan had to send a second messenger to Selungan and there is no record that he or the slaves were delivered to colonial authorities (ibid., p. 94 [Sultan to Commanding Officer, Jolo, 16 September 1901]). Also see Captain W. H. Sage, "Investigation in connection with suspicion of stealing slaves . . ." Philippine Commission, *Report,* 1903, 1: 533–35.

7. National Archives, RG 395, file 2887, p. 149 (Sweet to Pershing, 7 June 1901).

8. Ibid., file 2105-161 (Sweet to Adjutant General, 20 May 1900).

9. Ibid., RG 94, 366585 (Sweet to Adjutant General, 9 September 1900).

10. Ibid. (Sweet to Adjutant General, 9 November 1900).

11. Ibid. (9 September 1900).

12. In practice, some Muslims were held as slaves in Sulu. In much the same way, conversion to Christianity did not save Africans from slavery in the Americas. Those Muslim *banyaga* were mostly converts (or children of converts) to Islam, but most commonly slaves in Sulu were not Muslims; they were, therefore, Christians (as connoted by *bisaya*) or people unconverted to either of the region's major scriptural religions. See Warren, *Sulu Zone,* 228–29.

13. National Archives, RG 395, file 2105-3271 (McMahon to Adjutant General, 25 February 1901).

14. Ibid., RG 350, file 2869-with 1 (Taft to Secretary of War, 3 April 1901).

15. Ibid., RG 395, file 2105-1506 (Sweet to Adjutant General, 24 October 1900); ibid., RG 94, 366585 (Sweet to Adjutant General, 9 September 1900).

16. Ibid., RG 94, 366585 (Sweet to Adjutant General, 9 September 1900).

17. Warren, *Sulu Zone,* 231–36.

18. Ibid., 217–19, 231–36, 240–44.

19. U.S. War Department, *Annual Report,* 1900, vol. 1, pt. 3, pp. 269–70; National Archives, RG 350, file 980-17, p. 12 ("The Sulu Treaty," memorandum, 24 May 1901).

20. Philippine Commission, *Report,* 1901, pt. 2, p. 85 ("Synopsis of interview had by the Commission with Maj. O. J. Sweet, Commanding Officer, Jolo, P. I., March 28, 1901").

21. Library of Congress, Elihu Root Papers, container 167, pp. 7–9 (Taft to Root, 3 April 1901); Philippine Commission, *Report,* 1901, pt. 2, pp. 85, 88–89.

22. Library of Congress, Root Papers, container 167, pp. 7–9 (Taft to Root, 3 April 1901).

23. Ibid.

24. Saleeby, *History of Sulu,* 263; Philippine Commission, *Report,* 1901, pt. 2, pp. 88–89, 94, 96–102; Forbes, *Philippine Islands* 2:43–44.

25. Library of Congress, Hugh L. Scott Papers, box 55 (Datu Mandi, "To the Datos," 19 April 1901, translation). The text of Mandi's proclamation can also be found in Gowing, *Mandate in Moroland,* 55. In the document, Mandi acknowledged the existence of slaves, "some [obtained] by loan[s] made to poor families, some buying them for trading, all doubtless forgetful of the orders is-

sued by the old Government of Spain which strictly prohibited slavery." I have found no record of any such strict prohibition, although it is possible that some similar decree may have been made in Zamboanga town. Mandi prescribed fines for "illegal trading of Moro slaves and also slavery among themselves." Relations between masters and debtors would be reordered as follows: "If actually some are in such condition [of bondage] because of debt contracted for his immediate needs, he will not be considered [a] slave as such but as a hired man who receives a salary for his services and with the view of extinguishing the debt in from eight to ten months." During his interview with the touring Philippine Commission, Mandi said that pagans were "generally the slaves . . . of the Moros." They were bonded "only by debt," but he also said it was "only a short time ago" that they had been taken by capture, and he agreed that the Maranao continued to take captives. Of the nine thousand to ten thousand people he claimed to lead he estimated "less than a thousand" were what he called slaves (Philippine Commission, *Report*, 1901, pt. 2, p. 102). On this subject, Major Morrison told the commission that "[m]ost of the Moros obtain slaves by stealing children or by making war and capturing them. I do not think the Za[m]boangans deal in slaves much" (ibid., p. 95).

26. Library of Congress, Root Papers, container 167 (Taft to Root, 3 June 1901).

27. Philippine Commission, *Report*, 1901, pt. 1, pp. 36–38.

28. National Archives, RG 395, file 2105-8763 (Hardaway to Adjutant General, 3 January 1902).

29. Ibid., RG 350, file 5075-2, p. 56 (Report of Major C. B. Williams," 30 September 1901).

30. Ibid., pp. 12–13 ("Report of Brigadier-General Davis," 24 October 1901).

31. Ibid., p. 2 (Chaffe to Wright, 4 December 1901).

32. Ibid., p. 3 (Worcester to Acting Civil Governor, 7 December 1901).

33. Ibid., file 5075-5 ("General Orders, No. 12, 4 March 1902).

34. On the factional conflicts in Sulu, see Philippine Commission, *Report*, 1903, pt. 1, pp. 502–503, 511–12, 519; also see Gowing, *Mandate in Moroland*, 77–82.

35. National Archives, RG 350, file 2869-10 (Wallace to Adjutant General, 20 March 1902, telegram; and Fountain to Commanding Officer, Jolo, 20 March 1902, telegram). Davis modified his orders in a telegram of 29 May, in Philippine Commission, *Report*, 1903, pt. 1, pp. 492–93.

36. Philippine Commission, *Report*, 1903, pt. 1, pp. 493–94.

37. National Archives, RG 350, file 2869-7 (Wallace to Adjutant General, 24 June 1902); ibid., file 2869-6 (Sultan to Governor General, 13 June 1902; translated copy).

38. National Archives, RG 350, file 2869-6 (Sultan to General Chaffee, 13 June 1902; translated copy).

39. Ibid.

40. Ibid., file 2869-4 (Davis to Adjutant General, 3 July 1902). Davis tremendously exaggerated the number of slaves.

41. Ibid., file 2869-5 (Ennis to Commanding General, 27 October 1902).

42. Ibid., file 2869-15 (Chaffee to Sultan, n.d. [c. July 1902]).

CHAPTER 5

1. Philippine Commission, *Report,* 1903, 1:508–509 ("The humble petition of the residents, traders, and natives of Bongao, Tawi Tawi," 1 October 1903). The petition carried seventy-two signatures, from "Chinamen, Filipinos, and Moros."

2. U.S. War Department, *Annual Report,* 1900, vol. 1, pt. 3, pp. 269–70; National Archives, RG 350, file 980-17, p. 12 ("The Sulu Treaty," memorandum, 24 May 1907).

3. Ibid.

4. National Archives, RG 94, 366585, pp. 4–5 (Sweet to Adjutant-General, 9 November 1900; Kobbe to Adjutant-General, 20 November 1900).

5. Phillips, *Life and Labor in the Old South,* 199.

6. National Archives, RG 350, file 2869-1 (Root to Hart, 3 February 1902).

7. Philippine Commission, *Report,* 1901, pt. 2, p. 85.

8. Ibid., 95–96.

9. See, for example, the studies of slavery that Phillips began in this period and published later as *American Negro Slavery* and *Life and Labor in the Old South.*

10. Philippine Commission, *Report,* 1901, pt. 2, pp. 88–89.

11. Ibid., 114–15.

12. Ibid.

13. Ibid., 107.

14. Ibid., 96–101.

15. Ibid., 102.

16. Ibid., 37.

17. Ibid.

18. Ibid., 101.

19. Ibid., 102.

20. Ibid., 101.

21. Ibid., 102.

22. U.S., *Statutes at Large,* 1909, vol. 32, pt. 2, 692–93 (Philippine Organic Act of 1902, Section 5).

23. U.S. House, Committee on Insular Affairs, 131.

24. Ibid., 133. Later in the hearings Taft confessed that "[t]here has been no legislation passed with respect to slavery at all by the civil government and no action taken with respect to the military government. The action taken has been to secure first the release of all Christian Filipino slaves held, and that has been accomplished, and to prevent, second, raids for making slaves. There has been nothing further done with respect to the eradication of slavery except the moral influence upon the datos which has been exerted" (p. 143).

25. Ibid., 137.

26. Ibid.

27. Ibid., 131.

28. Ibid., 135.
29. Ibid., 142.
30. Ibid., 133.
31. On the position of American Indians in the world view of American colonizers in the Philippines, see Williams, "United States Indian Policy." For a brilliant analysis of the paternalistic and familial metaphors used pervasively with regard to American Indians, see Rogin, *Fathers and Children.*
32. U.S. War Department, *Annual Report,* 1902, 9:560. In his annual report made in October 1901 Davis also identified colonial rule in the southern Philippines with the conquest of and colonial rule over Native Americans, but the inflection had changed over the intervening year: "So far as I can judge from my brief opportunity for observation, our treatment of the Mindanao Moros and the pagan tribes is based on the same general rules that have always governed our actions in intercourse with the Indian tribes on our Western frontiers. We recognized their right to regulate their own interior tribal affairs according to their native rules and customs" (p. 513).
33. Ibid., 561.
34. Ibid., 562.
35. National Archives, RG 350, file 2869-4 (Davis to Adjutant General, 3 July 1902).
36. U.S. War Department, *Annual Report,* 1902, 9:561.
37. U.S. War Department, *Annual Report,* 1902, 9:561.
38. Ibid., 561, 565.
39. Ibid., 564.

CHAPTER 6

1. National Archives, RG 350, file 5075-10: "An Act Providing for the Organization and Government of the Moro Province," Philippine Commission Act 787, 1 June 1903. For a description of the creation of the Moro Province and a survey of its institutional arrangements, see Gowing, *Mandate in Moroland,* 72–76.
2. "An Act defining the crimes of slaveholding and slave hunting, and prescribing the punishment therefor." Act No. 8, Legislative Council of the Moro Province, Philippine Commission, *Report,* 1903, 1:484.
3. Taft, "Report of the Civil Governor of the Philippine Islands," Philippine Commission, *Report,* 1903, 1:81.
4. See Library of Congress, Hugh L. Scott Papers, box 55 (McCoy to Scott, 28 September 1903); ibid., Leonard Wood Papers, container 32 (Wood to Scott, 16 October and 30 October 1903); ibid., container 33 (Taft to Wood, 27 October 1903).
5. Ibid. (Wood to Taft, 5 September 1903); ibid., container 32 ("Conference between General Wood and Hadji Butu"); ibid., Wood Diary (entry for 24 August 1903).
6. Ibid., container 33 (Wood to Taft, 5 September 1903); ibid. (Wood to Taft, 7 October 1903).
7. Philippine Commission, *Report,* 1903, 1:81.

8. Ibid., 79–81.

9. Ibid., 81.

10. Library of Congress, Wood Papers, container 33 (Wood to Taft, 28 November 1903). Wood made the antislavery law public on Jolo while on a military expedition to fight Hassan.

11. Library of Congress, Scott Papers, box 55 (Wallace to Wood, 17 August 1903).

12. Library of Congress, Wood Papers, Wood Diary (entry for 28 August 1903). Wood also noted that he had been served food by an "old family slave" during the visit to Hassan's house.

13. Ibid., container 32 (Wood to Roosevelt, 20 September 1903).

14. Library of Congress, Scott Papers, box 55 (Wallace to Hassan, 31 July 1903); Philippine Commission, *Report,* 1903, 1:516–17 (Hassan to Scott, 25 September 1903).

15. For a summary of the Biroa case, see the unsigned, untitled memorandum dated 2 October 1903 and the accompanying letters and transcripts, especially "Conversation between the Civil Governor, Maj. H. L. Scott, Fourteenth Cavalry, and Hadji Butu, the Sultan's Prime Minister," 11 September 1903 (Philippine Commission, *Report,* 1903, 1:521–26).

16. Ibid.

17. Ibid., 516; ibid., 516–17.

18. Library of Congress, Wood Papers, container 33 (Scott to Wood, 27 September 1903).

19. Ibid.

20. Ibid. (Scott to Wood, 29 September 1903).

21. Ibid. (Scott to Wood, 7 October 1903); Philippine Commission, *Report,* 1903, 1:526–28.

22. Ibid.

Hadji Butu visited Scott the next day and told him of a meeting between Hassan and the sultan that seems to confirm Hassan's desire to impose a new order in Jolo, supplanting the sultan's putative temporal position.

> Hassan said we have agreed to get Birod. After Hassan, they all came to Maibun [the Sultan's residence], Panglima Dammang, Panglima Ambutong, and Maharajah Indanan, with their followers. The Sultan asked them, what have you agreed upon and why do you come with so many followers; I asked you to get Birod, that was why you had a conference; now, have you got him? The chiefs answered, the Sultan should not interfere, they would look after it themselves. They said our thoughts are not bad but good; we want to bring peace in the country, then the Sultan can live in peace also. (Philippine Commission, *Report,* 1903, 1:528–29).

23. Ibid., 526–28 ("Conference between Governor Scott and Panglima Hassan," 6 October 1903).

24. Ibid.

25. Ibid.

26. Ibid., 528–29 ("Record of a conversation between . . . Major Scott [and] . . . Hadji Butu," 7 October 1903); Library of Congress, Wood Papers, container 33 (Wood to Taft, 28 November and 16 December 1903); ibid., Diary (entry for

22 November 1903); ibid., Scott Papers, box 55 (Hassan to Scott, n.d. [received 5 November 1903]); Gowing, *Mandate in Moroland*, 157.

27. Library of Congress, Wood Papers; Wood Diary (entry for 30 November 1903).

28. Ibid., Scott Papers, box 55 (Adjutant General, Zamboanga, to Commanding Officer, Jolo, 1 December 1903).

29. Ibid. (Scott to the Secretary of the Moro Province, 30 June 1904, and McCoy to Scott, 28 September 1903).

30. The abstracts of these cases and others from Mindanao were collected from the records of the Court of First Instance in Zamboanga and sent to Dean C. Worcester for the report on slavery that he published in 1913; see National Archives, RG 350, file 2869-88 (Low to Worcester, 21 April 1913). The three convictions came in the following cases. (1) "Causa Criminal No. 31 del Distrito Zamboanga. Los Estados Unidos contra Moros Alam, Milajan y Tangigi. Por trafico de esclavos." (2) "Causa Criminal No. 28 del Distrito de Sulu. Los Estados Unidos contra Moro Batu. Por esclavitud." (3) "Causa Criminal No. 26 del Distrito de Sulu Jurisdiccion de Bongao. Los Estados Unidos contra Moro Hadjee Asmail. Por esclavitud." These cases are listed in the appendix to Worcester's *Report on Slavery*, 84–85. There is no extant record of all court cases from the Moro Province that may be checked for additional cases, but Judge Low indicated that he had searched through the files in 1913 on Worcester's request.

31. Library of Congress, Scott Papers, box 55 (Scott, "Report of cases of lawlessness"); the report covers the period 2 September 1903 through March 1904 and data for April and May 1904 are appended.

32. Library of Congress, Wood Papers, container 35 (Wood to Roosevelt, 7 January 1904); ibid., container 33 (Strachey to Wood, 10 March 1903, and Wood to Strachey, 7 January 190[4]); ibid., container 35 (Strachey to Wood, 24 February 1904, and Wood to Strachey, 9 May 1904).

33. National Archives, RG 395, file 2105-6133, pp. 1–2, 8–9 (Hagadorn to Adjutant General, 1 August 1901).

34. Library of Congress, Wood Papers, Wood Diary (entries for 10 to 16 October 1903).

35. Cushner, "Abandonment of Tamontaka Reduction"; Ileto, *Magindanao,* 96–97.

36. U.S. War Department, *Annual Report,* 1903, 3:326. On Maranao relations with the colonial state, see Gowing, *Mandate in Moroland*, 88–94, and Funtecha, *American Military Occupation,* 12–34.

37. U.S. War Department, *Annual Report,* 1903, 3:328.

38. Library of Congress, Wood Papers, Wood Diary (entries for 5 to 14 January 1904).

39. Gowing, *Mandate in Moroland,* 155; Funtecha, *American Military Occupation,* 48–55.

40. Summaries of the court records are appended to National Archives, RG 350, file 2869-88 (Low to Worcester, 21 April 1913).

41. U.S. War Department, *Annual Report,* 1902, 9:324. On the rise of Piang and Ali, also see Ileto, *Magindanao,* 95–98 and Beckett, "The Defiant and the Compliant," 399–402.

42. U.S. War Department, *Annual Report,* 1902, 9:481–82.

43. Ibid., 484, 497–98.

44. Ibid., 497.

45. Observations of J. R. Hayden, who visited Piang; see Beckett, "The Defiant and the Compliant," 401–402.

46. Ibid., 400–403, 407–408.

47. Library of Congress, Wood Papers, container 34, p. 3 (Wood, "Report of Expedition," 17 March 1904).

48. National Archives, RG 94, file 520834/C (Wood to Executive Secretary, Philippine Commission, 16 March 1904).

49. Library of Congress, Wood Papers, container 35 (Adjutant General to Wood, 15 March 1904).

50. National Archives, RG 350, file 5075-after 14 (Taft to Wright, 12 May 1904).

51. Library of Congress, Wood Papers, container 34, pp. 17–19 (Wood, "Report of Expedition," 17 March 1904).

52. Ibid.

53. Quoted in Gowing, *Mandate in Moroland,* 154.

54. Summaries of the court records are appended to National Archives, RG 350, file 2869-88 (Low to Worcester, 21 April 1913).

55. In a discussion of Taosug historical memory, the anthropologist Thomas Kiefer ("Anthropological Perspective," 60) noted that two versions of the Taosug "Ballad of Panglima Hassan" performed in the 1970s did not mention slavery at all as reason for rebellion. Instead, Hassan's "resistance is portrayed as an attempt to resist American sovereignty, his refusal to allow his cattle to be branded, his refusal to pay the head tax, and other items which failed to impress the army observers." Kiefer is no doubt right that Hassan needed to appeal to broader values to organize sustained support, but it seems clear that Hassan's rebellion began when he found the slavery question un-negotiable. Hassan and other leaders were indeed concerned about the imposition of a head tax, which would signify tribute. The Moro Province made provisions for a *cedula* in September 1903, but like the antislavery law, it was not to be implemented immediately. The first *cedula* in Jolo was collected in 1905, from the sultan himself. Likewise, systematic branding of cattle was not yet a colonial policy in 1903.

56. Gowing, *Mandate in Moroland,* 160–66.

57. Ibid., 157–66, 230–42.

58. Philippine Commission, *Report,* 1903, 2:771.

59. Ibid., 789.

60. National Archives, RG 350, BIA Library: Philippine Commission, MSS Report, 1903, 8:4 (Barrows, "Second Annual Report of the Chief of the Ethnological Survey for the Philippine Islands").

61. Philippine Commission, *Report,* 1903, 1:490.

62. Ibid., 1904, 2:575.

63. Ibid.

64. Ibid.

CHAPTER 7

1. Scott, "Filipino-Spanish Face-to-Face Contacts."

2. Scott, "Crusade or Commerce," 46–47; and "Why Did Tupas Betray Dagami?" Also see Cushner, *Spain in the Philippines.*

3. Phelan, *Hispanization of the Philippines,* 8–9, 56.

4. Ibid., 81; Cushner, *Spain in the Philippines,* 74–100; Costa, "Development of the Native Clergy."

5. Rafael, *Contracting Colonialism,* 84.

6. These insights and their implications are developed in Rafael, *Contracting Colonialism.*

7. Scott, "Creation of a Cultural Minority" and "Why Did Tupas Betray Dagami?"

8. Rafael, *Contracting Colonialism,* 188–92.

9. Ibid., 84–166.

10. See Scott, *Slavery in the Spanish Philippines,* 18–26, for a discussion of Spain's concern for distinguishing just and unjust slavery in the Philippines. The distinction Spanish law and ideology made between slavery and colonization is perspicaciously analyzed in Todorov, *Conquest of America,* 168–82.

11. Rafael, *Contracting Colonialism,* 110–69.

12. Ibid., 167–219.

13. Ileto, *Pasyon and Revolution,* 1–27.

14. See ibid., 34. Ileto here translates *paquiqui-alipin* as "submission," *alipin* as "servant," and *napa aalipin* as "submitting," but later (ibid., p. 44) and without comment, translates *paquiqui-alipin* as "enslavement" in discussing the very same prayer. The conventional specificity of the noun *alipin* signifies "slave," which is an important meaning for this study. The meanings Ileto locates in translation—submission, servant, submitting—are surely available within the modifications of *alipin.*

15. Ibid., 36.

16. Ibid., 38–39.

17. In *Inventing a Hero* (pp. 137–62), Glenn Anthony May criticizes Ileto's use of this source, which has survived only in translated and retranslated form. He argues that the stress Ileto places on particular words and phrases cannot be traced back, with absolute certainty, to the original Tagalog document. The publication of *Kalayaan* is not in doubt, nor is Bonifacio's leadership of the Katipunan. The larger point of May's study is to question the popular legitimacy of the Katipunan by exposing the historical literature about its leader, Andres Bonifacio, as crass and unsubstantiated mythology. Ileto is only one of May's targets and perhaps the most gingerly treated.

May is on firm ground to the extent that he argues that our historical knowledge about Bonifacio is inextricably laced with nationalist mythology and plagued by a dearth of reliable sources. But his critique of *Pasyon and Revolution* is weaker. That book is, in fact, much less concerned with Bonifacio, per se, than it is with analyzing the hermeneutics through which Tagalogs understood him and other leaders. May does not seem to accept the possibility that the revolution could have been experienced in a specifically Tagalog way that differs from more globally familiar narratives of battles for control of a country.

Although the authenticity of the extant translated versions of *Kalayaan* must be treated skeptically, some of May's concerns over disparate meanings in the Tagalog-to-Spanish-to-Tagalog translations do not hold up. For example, he argues that the Tagalog word *kaginhawaan* (glossed as "prosperity") does not have the same meaning as does *bienestar* ("well-being") as used in the earliest extant Spanish translation. May then, however, agrees with Ileto that *kaginhawaan* connotes " 'a general ease of life, relief from pain, sickliness, or difficulties.' " May's suggestion that this is substantially different from *bienestar*, "since *bienestar* connotes not only physical comfort but peace of mind and tranquility," is not at all convincing. The extant translations of Bonifacio's writings are similar in style to those of many other clearly original sources from other movements stretching from the 1830s to the present. This pattern constitutes important evidence for a cultural history that May misses by focusing exclusively on Bonifacio.

18. Ileto, *Pasyon and Revolution,* 86–87.

19. The emphasis on redemption from slavery is my own. On the role of the *Pasyon* in Tagalog society and the deification of Rizal, see ibid., and Ileto, "Rizal and the Underside of Philippine History."

20. Ileto, *Pasyon and Revolution,* 88–89, emphasis mine.

21. Ibid., 89–91.

22. Ibid., 94–95.

23. Ibid., 195.

24. Schumacher, *Father Jose Burgos,* 1–43.

25. Guerrero, *First Filipino;* Schumacher, *Propaganda Movement.*

26. Guerrero, *First Filipino,* 423.

27. Ileto, "Rizal and the Underside of Philippine History."

28. Ibid.

29. The quotations that follow are my own translations, taken from Rizal, *Noli* and *El Filibusterismo.*

30. Rizal, *Noli,* 70–71.

31. Ibid., 555.

32. Ibid., 554–55, 577–80.

33. Rizal, *El Filibusterismo,* 1:77–84.

34. Ibid., 2:212–15.

35. Schumacher, *Propaganda Movement,* 213.

36. Ibid., 215.

37. Veyra, *El 'Ultimo Adiós' de Rizal,* 89–90.

38. Morga, *Sucesos,* v–vi.

39. Ibid., 297–306. The quotes are taken from pp. 299–300.

40. Ibid., 362.

41. Taylor, *Philippine Insurrection,* 3:141–43.

42. Ibid., 536–38.

43. Stanley, *Nation in the Making,* 71.

44. On the seditious plays, see Lapeña Bonifacio, *"Seditious" Tagalog Playwrights,* and Riggs, *Filipino Drama.* Riggs was an American constabulary of-

ficer who investigated the performances, actors, and authors. His manuscript, which dates from 1905, provides the only extant copies of two of the plays as well as important information about their productions and responses of their audiences.

45. Riggs, *Filipino Drama*, 318.

46. Ibid., 266, 275.

CHAPTER 8

1. U.S. House, Committee on Insular Affairs, *Hearing*, 1904, 14.

2. Ibid., 14–15.

3. Massachusetts Historical Society, Moorfield Storey Papers, letterbook, vol. 5 (Storey to Warren, 9 November 1903).

4. This change in the anti-imperialists' strategy and ultimate goal was noted by Pomeroy in *American Neo-Colonialism*, 198–205.

5. Paredes, *Philippine Colonial Democracy*, 9–10; Cullinane, "Playing the Game"; Anderson, "Cacique Democracy," 10–12. The Philippine Republic of 1898 had a Congress in which *ilustrados* from Manila and surrounding provinces were appointed to represent more distant provinces.

6. Seton-Watson (*Nations and States*, 148) coined the concept of "official nationalism" to describe the Russifying nationalism of the Czarist and Soviet empires. Anderson (*Imagined Communities*, 83–111) developed it further to include similar policies by other transethnic states, empires, and dynasties, including colonial regimes. Although Anderson later (ibid., 183) recognized that "post-independence states exhibited marked continuities with their colonial predecessors," he never used the concept of official nationalism to describe the activities of anticolonial nationalists. In the Philippines, the middle-class nationalism that developed under American colonial sponsorship was also official in the sense that it took a Manila-centered Philippinizing stance toward the ethnolinguistic diversity of the country. It has emphasized, by turns and sometimes in combination, large doses of linguistic and cultural Hispanization, Americanization, and, especially, Tagalogization in the name of national identity. For an interesting comment on the Tagalog-centered historiography of 1896 and 1898, see Aguilar, "A Failure of Imagination? The Nation in Narratives of the 1896 Philippine Revolution."

7. A full study of this subject as a struggle between Filipino nationalists and colonial discourse has not yet been attempted. Some suggestive starts can be found in Rafael, "White Love"; Rydell, *All the World's a Fair*, 154–83; Kramer, "Making Concessions"; and Vergara, *Displaying Filipinos*.

8. My thinking on this issue has been influenced by Rosaldo's intriguing essay, "Utter Savages of Scientific Value." Rosaldo rightly emphasizes the deep cultural roots of American perceptions of the Negritos and other non-Christian peoples, but his analysis of American "favoritism" for pagans over Catholics ignores the crucial interplay of nationalism, colonialism, and the ideology of benevolence in redefining the identity of the uncivilized.

9. Quoted in Olcott, *Life of William McKinley*, 2:110–11.

10. Philippine Commission, *Report*, 1900, pt. 1, pp. 11–16.

11. Ibid.

12. U.S. War Department, *Annual Report*, 1900, vol. 1, pt. 1, appendix B, 72–76.

13. Philippine Commission, *Report*, 1901, pt. 1, pp. 35–36.

14. Ibid., 34–38. A full study of the colonial discourse on head-hunting remains to be made. The height of the discourse is suggested by the title of the study by the anthropologists Felix M. and Marie Keesing, *Taming Philippine Headhunters: A Study of Government and of Cultural Change in Northern Luzon*. Its romantic possibilities are also indicated by the sobriquet "Blackburn's Headhunters," given to an American-led Ifugao guerilla force in World War II (see Harkins, *Blackburn's Headhunters*). In *Ilongot Head-Hunting*, Rosaldo examines one Filipino minority group's self-conscious identification as head-hunters and, in *Culture and Truth*, 68–87, he analyzes "imperialist nostalgia" for head-hunting and other lost signs of the uncivilized.

15. Philippine Commission, *Report*, 1901, pt. 1, p. 35.

16. Rosaldo notes this inversion in "Utter Savages of Scientific Value."

17. See Williams, "United States Indian Policy."

18. For discussions of the continued study of the lowland Catholic Filipino population through racial science, see Salman, " 'Nothing Without Labor' " and Anderson, " 'Where Every Prospect Pleases.' "

19. Philippine Commission, *Report*, 1901, pt. 1, pp. 35–38.

20. Ibid., 1903, pt. 2, p. 775.

21. Ibid., 771.

22. On the census see Rafael, "White Love"; Vergara, *Displaying Filipinos*, 37–74; and U.S. Bureau of the Census, *Census of the Philippine Islands*. On the Saint Louis Exposition, see Rydell, *All the World's a Fair*, 167–78.

23. U.S. Bureau of the Census, *Census of the Philippine Islands*.

24. On relationships between U.S. colonial officials and rising Filipino politicians, see Cullinane, "Politics of Collaboration" and "Playing the Game"; and Paredes, "Origins of National Politics," 41–69.

25. Anderson, "Cacique Democracy."

26. Osmeña is quoted in Stanley, *Nation in the Making*, 216–17. Also see Stanley's coverage of independence politics during the 1907 elections and first session of the assembly in ibid., 127–38; May, *Social Engineering*, 57–62; Salamanca, *Filipino Reaction to American Rule*, 52–58; and Ileto's "Orators and the Crowd" for his examples of how assembly elections brought to the surface the "the radical 'other' " of official nationalist discourse.

27. On Taft's role in transferring colonial patronage to the Nacionalistas, see Paredes, "Origins of National Politics," 41–69. The text of Taft's inaugural speech is printed in Philippine Commission, *Report*, 1907, pt. 1, pp. 215–27.

28. Philippine Commission, *Report*, 1907, pt. 1, pp. 215–27.

29. Bentley Library, Dean C. Worcester Papers, box 1 (Taft to Worcester, 30 November 1907).

30. Scott, *Discovery of the Igorots*, 276–78.

31. Ibid.; Schumacher, *Propaganda Movement*, 66.

32. Scott, *Discovery of the Igorots*, 277; Schumacher, *Propaganda Movement*, 68.

33. Philippine Commission, *Report,* 1903, 1: 406–15; ibid., 1904, 1:356–60; Kramer, "Making Concessions," 90.

34. Kramer ("Making Concessions") astutely recognizes the tensions and instabilities that beset Americans when they confronted Filipinos at the Saint Louis World's Fair, but he does not track the effects of this history beyond the confines of the fair itself. My principal interest is in the direction the politics of the uncivilized took during the slavery controversies after 1904. A full study of Filipinos' experiences and reactions to such exhibitions remains to be written.

35. Rydell, *All the World's a Fair,* 172.

36. Massachusetts Historical Society, Storey Papers, letterbook, vol. 6 (Storey to Warren, 5 August 1904).

37. Philippine Commission, *Report,* 1904, 1:325-26 (Pardo de Tavera to Wright, 23 April 1904).

38. This protest by Vicente Nepomuceno is quoted from Kramer, "Making Concessions," 102–103. Nepomuceno's remarks and a subsequent effort to smooth over relations made by his colleague Benito Legarda did constitute, as Kramer says (p. 103), a "critique of American colonial policy," but not, I would emphasize, a rejection of colonialism or disagreement with its evolutionary order.

39. Massachusetts Historical Society, Storey Papers, letterbook, vol. 6 (Storey to Parker, 20 October 1904).

40. National Archives, RG 350, file 7395-5 (Edwards to Taft, 22 June 1903).

41. Rydell, *All the World's a Fair,* 172–74.

42. Ibid., 194.

43. Thetford Historical Society, Worcester Family Papers, file "Philippines Past and Present, 1905–1913" (Schneiderwind to Worcester, 19 June 1905 and endorsement by Worcester).

44. Ibid. (Worcester to Pack, 11 December 1909).

45. Sullivan, *Exemplar of Americanism.*

46. Houghton Library, William Cameron Forbes Papers, fMS Am 1366.1, vol. 1 (Forbes to Dickinson, 8 June 1910).

47. Worcester to Taft, 27 January 1908, quoted in Hutterer, "Dean C. Worcester," p. 151.

CHAPTER 9

1. Worcester, *Slavery and Peonage,* 22.

2. National Archives, RG 350, file 2869-84 (Sorenson, 28 April 1903, and indorsement by Taft, 9 May 1903).

3. Ibid. (Sorenson, 2 May 1903).

4. Ibid.

5. Ibid.

6. Ibid.

7. For a history of the Cagayan region, see de Jesus, *Tobacco Monopoly.*

8. Scott, *Discovery of the Igorots,* 181–90.

9. Evidence of the resurgence in slave trading will be provided below. During his journey through Lepanto and Benguet in 1882, the German ethnographer Dr. Hans Meyer was told that local residents "no longer sold children

to lowlanders as the bontocs did," but Scott (ibid., 309) astutely wondered if this meant that they had ceased such practices or "had learned to keep quiet about them."

10. National Archives, RG 350, file 2869-84 (Taft to Dichoso, 8 August 1903).

11. Ibid. (Dichoso to Taft, 9 September 1903).

12. Ibid.

13. Ibid. (Taft to Dichoso, 8 August 1903), (Sorenson to District Chief, 2 May 1903; Taft, "Fifth Indorsement"), and (Dichoso to Taft, 9 September 1903; Taft, "First Indorsement").

14. U.S. House, Committee on Insular Affairs, *Hearing,* 1904, 14–15.

15. National Archives, RG 350, file 2869-91 (Curry to Wright, 30 November 1904).

16. Worcester, *Slavery and Peonage,* 22–23. National Archives, RG 350, file 2869-86 (Knight to Executive Secretary, 28 August and 14 September 1905, and attached endorsements by Worcester, 22 September, and Wright, 29 September, 1905).

17. National Archives, RG 350, file 2869-86 (Wilfley, "Opinion of the Attorney-General," 13 October 1905).

18. Ibid. (Burritt to Ide, 7 February 1906). The quotation is taken from Burritt's decision in *United States v Tomás Cabanag,* Court of First Instance, Nueva Vizcaya Province, 16 January 1906 (attached to ibid., 5). He made a similar comment in the other conviction he handed down: *United States v Antonio Dumay and Guinalot,* Court of First Instance, Nueva Vizcaya Province, 15 January 1906 (also attached to ibid., 5–6).

19. Ibid. (*U.S. v Cabanag*).

20. *United States v Tomás Cabanag,* Supreme Court of the Philippine Islands, 16 March 1907, *Reports of Cases,* 66, 69.

21. Ibid., 64–70.

22. Daniel, *Shadow of Slavery.*

23. *U.S. v Cabanag,* Supreme Court of the Philippine Islands, 69.

24. National Archives, RG 350, file 2869-90 (Ferguson to Smith, 13 May 1907).

25. Stanley, *Nation in the Making,* 134–36.

26. National Archives, RG 350, file 2869-90 (Worcester, "Explanatory Statement, Commission Bill No. 100, Document No. 1," 21 April 1909).

27. Ibid. (Palma and Branagan, "Report of Select Committee," 27 April 1909).

28. Ibid.

29. Ibid., file 2869-68 (Worcester, "Committee Report," 19 May 1909).

30. Ibid., file 2869-90 (Palma and Branagan, "Report of Select Committee," 27 April 1909).

31. Ibid. (Velarde, "Report of the Committee on the Revision of Laws," 17 May 1909).

32. This section of his report for 1909 is reprinted in Worcester, *Slavery and Peonage,* 68.

33. The memorandum was signed by General Clarence Edwards, although it was actually written by McIntyre (National Archives, RG 350, file 2869-27 [Edwards, 29 December 1909]). McIntyre later acknowledged his authorship, ibid., file 5543-139 (McIntyre to Worcester, 13 January 1913).

34. Ibid., file 2869-91 (McIntyre to Forbes, 22 January 1910).

35. Ibid. (Forbes to Secretary of War, 26 January 1910).

36. Ibid. (Worcester, "Memorandum for the Honorable, the Governor-General," 28 February 1910).

37. Stanley, *Nation in the Making,* 139–76.

38. Houghton Library, William Cameron Forbes Papers, bMS Am 1364.4, box 1 (Forbes, "Message of the Governor-General to the Second Philippine Legislature October 17, 1909").

39. National Archives, RG 350, file 2869-90 (Worcester to Forbes, 14 October 1910); Philippine Commission, *Journal,* 4:847.

40. Worcester, *Annual Report . . . 1910,* 66, 74–80.

41. Ibid.

42. Houghton Library, Forbes Papers, fMS Am 1366.1, vol. 1 (Forbes to Dickinson, 12 February 1911).

43. Worcester, *Slavery and Peonage,* 72.

44. Philippine Commission, *Journal,* 4:865.

45. Houghton Library, Forbes Papers, bMS Am 1364.4, box 3 (Forbes, "Message of the Governor-General to the Second Philippine Legislature, October 16, 1911"); Worcester, *Report on Slavery,* 34–35.

46. National Archives, RG 350, file 2869-68 (Elliott, "Committee Report," n.d.).

47. Ibid. (Act 2098, "An Act Relating to Contracts of Personal Service and Advances Thereunder, and Providing Punishment for Certain Offenses Connected Therewith").

48. Ibid. (McIntyre, "Memorandum: Peonage in the Philippines," 23 September 1913).

49. On Manuel Tinio, see Kerkvliet, *Huk Rebellion,* 1–25 and *Everyday Politics,* 20–26.

50. Worcester, *Annual Report . . . 1912, 30.*

CHAPTER 10

1. Houghton Library, William Cameron Forbes Papers, fMS Am 1366.1, vol. 1 (Forbes to Stimson, 26 May 1912).

2. Ibid., fMS Am 1192.1, vol. 15 (Forbes, speech, Harvard University Commencement, 20 June 1892).

3. Quezon, "The Filipinos as Legislators—To the Editor," *Boston Herald,* 24 June 1912; Philippine National Library, Manuel L. Quezon Papers, series V, box 9 (Quezon to Winslow, 22 June 1912).

4. Ibid.

5. Ibid.

6. Quezon, "The Filipinos as Legislators," *Boston Herald,* 24 June 1912.

7. Ibid.

8. Philippine National Library, Quezon Papers, series V, box 2 (Quezon to Winslow, 2 March 1911).

9. Ibid., box 5 (Blount to Quezon, 13 July 1911); ibid., series VI, box 4 (contract between Quezon and Blount, 14 July 1911); ibid., series V, box 7 (Blount to Quezon, 8 March 1912); ibid., series VI, box 4 (Quezon to Blount, 10 March 1912). Blount's work was published as *The American Occupation of the Philippines, 1899–1912.*

10. Houghton Library, Forbes Papers, fMS Am 1192.1, vol. 15 ("The 'Glorious Fourth,'" *La Vanguardia* [Manila], 3 July 1912, copy of translation by the Philippine Constabulary).

11. Ibid., vol. 16 ("Donde hay esclavos y opresores," *El Ideal* [Manila], 5 August 1912, clipping).

12. Ibid., vol. 17 ("Donde no hay esclavos," *El Ideal* [Manila], 25 October 1912, clipping).

13. Ibid.

14. Ibid. ("There is no such slavery," *La Vanguardia* [Manila], 29 October 1912, translation by the Philippine Constabulary).

15. Ibid.; Houghton Library, Forbes Papers, fMS Am 1192.1, vol. 17 ("Donde no hay esclavos," *El Ideal* [Manila], 25 October 1912).

16. *La Vanguardia* [Manila], 7 November 1912, quoted in Stanley, *Nation in the Making,* 184.

17. Ileto, "Orators and the Crowd."

18. Ibid., 96–97.

19. Ibid., 98; Philippine National Library, Quezon Papers, series V, box 11 (Quezon to Osmeña, 10 January and 3 February 1913).

20. Ibid. (Quezon to *La Vanguardia* [Manila], 27 January 1913 and Quezon to Osmeña, 27 January 1913).

21. Quoted in Ileto, "Orators and the Crowd," 100.

22. Philippine National Library, Quezon Papers, series V, box 8 (Quezon to Winslow, 18 May 1912). Although Moorfield Storey was concerned about "how far we should interfere with the internal politics of the islands," the Anti-Imperialist League did finally agree to send the following cable over Storey's name: "Enthusiastically favor Jones Bill best conditions obtainable Quezon's triumph unanimous support urged." (Massachusetts Historical Society, Moorfield Storey Papers, letterbook, vol. 13 [Storey to Winslow, 20 May 1912]; Philippine National Library, Quezon Papers, series V, box 8 [Winslow to Quezon, 20 May 1912]).

23. Quoted in Stanley, *Nation in the Making,* 190.

24. Philippine National Library, Quezon Papers, series V, box 9 (Quezon to Winslow, 31 July 1912).

25. Ibid., microfilm, reel 3 (Quezon to Brent, 31 July 1912).

26. National Archives, RG 350, file 364-after 182 (McIntyre to Gilbert, 1 August 1912).

27. Ibid., file 2869-29 (McIntyre to Gilbert, 1 August 1912).

28. Ibid., file 2869-32 (Worcester to Gilbert, 28 October 1912).

29. Ibid., file 2869-91 (Gallman, "Report of the Lieutenant-Governor of Ifugao," 2 December 1912).

30. Ibid.

31. The memorandum was signed by General Clarence Edwards, although it was actually written by McIntyre. National Archives, RG 350, file 2869-27 (Edwards, 29 December 1909). McIntyre later acknowledged his authorship in ibid., file 5543-139 (McIntyre to Worcester, 13 January 1913).

32. Ibid., file 2869-91 (McIntyre to Forbes, 22 January 1910).

33. Ibid. (Forbes to secretary of war, 26 January 1910).

34. Ibid. (Worcester, "Memorandum," 15 May 1913); ibid., file 2869-33 (*The National Humane Review* [April 1913], copy).

35. S.R. 71, 63rd Congress, 2nd sess., *Congressional Record* 50, pt. 1 (1 May 1913): 877–78.

36. National Archives, RG 350, file 2869-34 (secretary of war to president of the Senate, 6 May 1913).

37. Ibid., file 2869-with 34 (War Department to president of the Senate, 5 May 1913).

38. Ibid., file 2869-46 (McIntyre, memorandum for the secretary of war, 30 June 1913).

39. Ibid., file 2869-91 (Worcester, memorandum, 15 May 1913); Worcester, *Slavery and Peonage*, 6–7, 71.

40. Ileto, "Orators and the Crowd," 108, 332 n. 73.

41. Quoted in ibid., 109.

42. Philippine National Library, Quezon Papers, series VII, box 6, file: Anti-Imperialist League (Winslow to Quezon, 16 August 1911); ibid., series V, box 12 (Winslow to Quezon, 1 May 1913), Massachusetts Historical Society, Storey Papers, manuscript box 2 (Quezon to Winslow, 4 May 1913); ibid., letterbook, vol. 14 (Storey to Winslow, 6 May 1913, and Storey to Quezon, 6 May 1913).

43. National Archives, RG 350, file 2869-40 (Quezon to Garrison, 5 May 1913); ibid., file 2869-38 (*Washington Post*, 7 May 1913, clipping).

44. Massachusetts Historical Society, Storey Papers, letterbook, vol. 14 (Storey to Willis, 14 May 1913).

45. Philippine National Library, Quezon Papers, series V, box 12 (Quezon to *La Vanguardia*, 5 May 1913).

46. Bentley Library, Dean C. Worcester Papers, box 1 ("The Last Effort," *El Ideal* [Manila], 5 May 1913; translation).

47. Houghton Library, Forbes Papers, fMS Am 1192.1, vol. 20 ("The Perpetual Conflict," *El Ideal* [Manila], 17 June 1913; clipping).

CHAPTER 11

1. Wilson, "Ideals of America."

2. National Archives, RG 350, file 2869-91 (Forbes to Worcester, 14 June 1913; Worcester to Forbes, 2 July 1913).

3. University of Michigan Library, Worcester Philippine Collection, "Slavery and Peonage," vol. 2 (Forbes to Worcester, 5 June 1913); Worcester, *Slavery and Peonage*, 4.

4. Worcester, *Slavery and Peonage*, 6.

5. Ibid., 6–7, 39, 59–63.

6. Ibid. In a text totaling 115 pages, Worcester used 15 pages to discuss cases involving Negritos (29–30, 40–47, 95–99) and 30 to recount cases involving Ifugaos (21–29, 48–51, 85–95, 100–105).

7. Ibid., 82.

8. Ibid., facing page 48.

9. Ibid., 40–42.

10. Ibid., 41–47.

11. Ibid.

12. Ibid., 30.

13. Ibid., 50; National Archives, RG 350, file 2869-83 (Gallman to Worcester, 2 December 1912).

14. Worcester, *Slavery and Peonage*, 80; National Archives, RG 350, file 2869-37 (Tracey to Editor, *New York Times*, 6 May 1913 [clipping]). For Worcester's reply, see Worcester, *Slavery and Peonage*, 80.

15. Worcester, *Slavery and Peonage*, 78–80.

16. Worcester, *Annual Report . . . 1910*, 74.

17. Ibid., p. 47.

18. Ibid.

19. Idem, *Annual Report . . . 1913*, 10.

20. National Archives, RG 350, file 2869-66 (McIntyre to secretary of war, 15 September 1913); ibid., file 2869-67 (Garrison to McIntyre, 16 September 1913).

21. Ibid., file 2869-55 (Phipps to secretary of war, 20 May 1913). Phipps also sent two supplementary reports to the secretary of war, one of which, written in August, was critical of Worcester's lack of action against slavery over the past thirteen years: see ibid., file 2869-63 (Phipps to secretary of war, 28 July 1913) and file 2869-75 (Phipps, "Slavery in the Philippine Islands: Comments upon Secretary Dean C. Worcester's Report, and Criticism of His Action in Connection with the Subject").

22. Bentley Library, Dean C. Worcester Papers, box 2 ("Law to Wipe Out Slavery Traffic in Philippines is Sought by Borah," *Buffalo Times*, 21 September 1913, clipping).

23. Ibid. (*Washington Star*, 27 August 1913, clipping).

24. National Archives, RG 350, file 2869A (*Philadelphia Enquirer*, 31 August 1913, clipping).

25. Ibid., file 2869-A3 ("Slavery in the Philippines?" *New York Sun*, 23 September 1913, clipping).

26. Ibid., file 2869A ("Under the Flag!," *New York Evening Sun*, 26 August 1913, clipping).

27. Ibid. ("The Philippine Problem," *Boston Post*, 31 August 1913, clipping).

28. Ibid., file 2869-A1 ("Shall it be 'Slavery and Scuttling' in the Philippines?" *New York Tribune,* 29 September 1913, clipping).

29. Bentley Library, Worcester Papers, box 2 (*Chicago Tribune,* 23 September 1913, clipping).

30. Ibid. ("Slavery—A Terminology Issue," *Brooklyn Eagle,* 22 September 1913, clipping).

31. Ibid., *New York Evening Post,* 25 September 1913, clipping).

32. National Archives, RG 350, file 2869-A ("Our Own Superiority," *Washington Times,* 26 August 1913, clipping).

33. Ibid. ("Philippine Slavery," *Detroit Free Press,* 28 August 1913, clipping).

34. Massachusetts Historical Society, Moorfield Storey Papers, MSS box 2 (Jones to Storey, 20 September 1913).

35. Ibid. Jones quoted in Bentley Library, Worcester Papers, box 2 ("Denies Slavery in the Philippines," *Chicago Record Herald,* 22 September 1913, clipping), and National Archives, RG 350, file 2869-A3 ("Filipino Slavery Hits Independence," *New York Sun,* 22 September 1913, clipping).

36. Massachusetts Historical Society, Storey Papers, letterbook, vol. 15 (Storey to Jones, 22 September 1913).

37. Philippine National Library, Manuel L. Quezon Papers, series V, box 13 (Winslow to Quezon, 27 August 1913); ibid., microfilm, reel 4 (Quezon to Winslow, 28 August 1913).

38. Philippine National Library, Quezon Papers, series V, box 13 (Osmeña to Quezon, 28 August 1913, and Osmeña to Quezon, 29 August 1913).

39. Stanley, *Nation in the Making,* 201.

40. *Filipino People* 2, no. 1 (1913): 15; Philippine National Library, Quezon Papers, microfilm, reel 4 (Quezon to Winslow, 28 August 1913).

CHAPTER 12

1. At least part of this letter was passed on to Quezon. Philippine National Library, Manuel L. Quezon Papers, series V, box 12 ("Extract of letter of Hon. Francis Burton Harrison to Erving Winslow," 8 May 1913).

2. Massachusetts Historical Society, Moorfield Storey Papers, MSS box 2 (Tracey to Storey, 3 October 1913); ibid., letterbook, vol. 15 (Storey to Garrison, 7 October 1913).

3. National Archives, RG 350, file 2869-70 (McIntyre to Harrison, 25 September 1913).

4. Harrison, *Inaugural Address.*

5. Ileto, "Orators and the Crowd," 100.

6. Harrison, *Inaugural Address;* Library of Congress, Francis Burton Harrison Papers, box 47 (Harrison to Garrison, 24 October 1913); National Archives, RG 350, file 2869-73 (Harrison to Garrison, 30 October 1913).

7. This first report was read into the record of the assembly and can be found in Asamblea Filipina, *Diario de Sesiones,* 14 November 1913, tomo IX, pp. 118–23. It was also included in the assembly committee's final report, Asamblea Filipina, *Informe Sobre la Esclavitud,* 10–19.

8. Ibid.; U.S., *Statutes at Large,* 1909, vol. 35, pt. 1, 1142 (An Act to Codify, Revise and Amend Penal Law, 4 March 1909).

9. Accounts of Harrison's speech in Pampanga and a subsequent press conference in Manila were published on 26 November 1913, in *El Ideal* (Manila) and *La Vanguardia* (Manila), in National Archives, RG 350, file 2869-A18 (Philippine Constabulary translation). Further information about Rodriguez was provided by the assembly committee in its report, Asamblea Filipina, *Informe Sobre la Esclavitud,* 149.

10. National Archives, RG 350, file 2869–107 (Villamor to Harrison, 22 November 1913).

11. Ibid., file 141-with 86 1/2 (Harrison to Garrison, 4 December 1913).

12. Ibid., file 2869-104 (Garrison to Harrison, 23 December 1913).

13. Asamblea Filipina, *Diario de Sesiones,* tomo IX, pp. 123, 131–32.

14. Ibid., 132–33.

15. Ibid., 144.

16. Ibid., 123, 125.

17. Ibid., 127, 128.

18. Philippine Commission, *Journal,* 7:110-11.

19. Library of Congress, Harrison Papers, box 47 (Harrison to secretary of war, 24 October 1913).

20. National Archives, RG 350, file 141-with 86 1/2 (Harrison to Garrison, 4 December 1913).

21. Library of Congress, Harrison Papers, box 34 (Harrison to Storey, 5 December 1913).

CHAPTER 13

1. Blair and Robertson, *Philippine Islands.*

2. Asamblea Filipina, *Informe Sobre la Esclavitud,* 20–54. Although the scholarly authority of Blumentritt's writings has long since passed out of date, historians continue to use the other accounts referenced by the committee as major primary sources for sixteenth- and seventeenth-century history, including the history of slavery. For instructive discussions of these sources, see Scott, "Filipino Class Structure," and Rafael, *Contracting Colonialism,* esp. pp. 136–66.

3. Asamblea Filipina, *Informe Sobre la Esclavitud,* 48.

4. Ibid., 48–49.

5. Ibid., 49.

6. Ibid., 49–51. The committee here referred to the Tagalog *alipin sa gigilid* and Visayan *ayuey.* The Tagalog word *gilid* is today used to mean edge, but was also used in the sixteenth and seventeenth centuries to mean the back of the house where the hearth was, and also where people defecated. All of these glosses fit *alipin sa gigilid* as people who were, often, recently acquired, marginal, and kept close under a master's watch (Scott, *Barangay,* 226–27). In the Visayas, the *oripun* called *ayuey* were those whom Miguel de Loarca, a Spanish *encomendero* of long residence, said were the "most enslaved" and "the ones they mostly sell to the Spaniards" (ibid., 133).

7. Ibid.

8. Ibid., 30, 32.

9. Ibid., 52.

10. Ibid.

11. Ibid., 54.

12. Ibid., 54–97.

13. Ibid., 74–75.

14. Ibid., 96–97.

15. Ibid., 77.

16. Ibid., 79–80.

17. Ibid.

18. Ibid., 89.

19. Ibid.; my emphasis.

20. Ibid., 87.

21. Ibid., 89.

22. Ibid., 93–96.

23. Ibid., 95–96.

24. Ibid., 55–56.

25. Ibid., 94–97.

26. Ibid., 98–99.

27. Ibid.

28. Ibid., 217–20, 233.

29. Ibid., 98–135, 250–55.

30. Ibid., 137–73, 258–59.

31. McCoy, "A Queen Dies Slowly"; Aguilar, *Clash of Spirits.*

32. McCoy, "A Queen Dies Slowly," 323–24; Aguilar, *Clash of Spirits,* 126–55, 220, 223.

33. Worcester, *Slavery and Peonage,* 16–21; Asamblea Filipina, *Informe Sobre la Esclavitud,* 194–96, 201–202.

34. Asamblea Filipina, *Informe Sobre la Esclavitud,* 191–214.

35. The committee listed more than one hundred such petitions and statements of protest (ibid., appendix G, 298–308).

36. Ibid., 192–93, 206–209.

37. Ibid., 200.

38. Ibid., 205.

39. Anderson, *Imagined Communities,* 53–56.

40. But they ignored Nieboer's monumental study, *Slavery as an Industrial System,* perhaps because he cited (pp. 114–15) Blumentritt and other writers attesting to the existence of slavery in the Philippines.

41. Asamblea Filipina, *Informe Sobre la Esclavitud,* 269.

CHAPTER 14

1. Asamblea Filipina, *Diario de Sesiones* (28 February 1914), tomo IX, p. 981.

2. Houghton Library, William Cameron Forbes Papers, bMS Am 1346.3., box 1 (Bowditch to Forbes, 5 January 1914); National Archives, RG 350, file 2869A-23 ("Report of Worcester Condemned to the Flames," *Consolidación Nacional* [Manila], 11 January 1914, translation by Philippine Constabulary, clipping).

3. Worcester lectured at the National Geographic Society, major universities such as Yale, Columbia, and Princeton, public auditoriums, and political clubs. For descriptions of the standing-room-only audiences, see Thetford Historical Society, Worcester Family Papers (Worcester to Catherine Worcester, 26 January and 10 March 1914). In 1914 he presented a similar lecture to the United States Senate.

4. Philippine Commission, *Journal*, 27 March 1914, 8:792–93. Library of Congress, Francis Burton Harrison Papers, box 29 (Harrison to McIntyre, 31 March 1914). Harrison asked the chief of the Bureau of Internal Affairs to seek help from immigration officers in the United States so that the "Igorots" could be returned to the Philippines. Filipinos "are greatly opposed to the taking out of the wild people here for exhibition purposes," he explained. Harrison's analysis of this reveals a great deal about the close connection between his official anticolonialism and imperialist ideology. Filipinos were opposed "particularly because the exhibition of these people gives the American public an erroneous idea of the Philippine Islands and holds the Filipinos themselves up to some ridicule at home. But the question really is the misery to which the Igorots taken to exhibitions are sometimes subjected. Occasionally they are left in positive want, and always they are more or less corrupted and spoiled by their experiences." In fact, Worcester opposed the display of Igorots in exhibitions for exactly the same reason, because "the shows in the States . . . certainly do the Igorots themselves no good." Thetford Historical Collection, Worcester Papers (file: "Philippines Past & Present, 1905–1913" [Worcester to Pack, 11 December 1909]).

5. Quezon's role in revising the Jones bill is ably covered in Stanley, *Nation in the Making*, 212–25. For a deeper understanding of the reactions in Philippine politics, see Ileto, "Orators and the Crowd."

6. *Congressional Record* (6 October 1914) 51:16216–29.

7. Ibid., 16218.

8. Ibid.

9. Ibid., 16227; Asamblea Filipina, *Diario de Sesiones* (14 November 1913), tomo IX, pp. 134–35.

10. *Congressional Record* (6 October 1914), 51:16227.

11. Ibid., 16228.

12. Ibid.

13. U.S. Senate Committee on the Philippines, *Government of the Philippines: Hearings on H.R. 18459*, 63rd Cong., 3rd sess., 1915, 269–94.

14. Ibid.

15. Ibid.

16. Ibid., 289, 347.

17. Ibid., 318, 348.

18. Ibid., 509–10.

19. Ibid., 512.

20. Ricarte, *Memoirs*, 169; Ileto, "Orators and the Crowd," 107.
21. Ricarte, *Memoirs*, 159.
22. Ileto, "Orators and the Crowd." Also see Stanley, *Nation in the Making*, 217–18.
23. Anderson, "Cacique Democracy."
24. Mojares, "Worcester in Cebu."
25. *El Ideal* is quoted in Sullivan, *Exemplar of Americanism*, 196; Mojares, "Worcester in Cebu."
26. Quoted in Kalaw, *Development of Philippine Politics*, 362–63.
27. Ibid., 361; Stanley, *Nation in the Making*, 221–25.
28. Patterson, *Slavery and Social Death*, 296.

CONCLUSION

1. Brandwein, *Reconstructing Reconstruction*.
2. On this transformation in the United States after emancipation, see the enlightening analyses in Stanley, *From Bondage to Contract*, and in Edwards, *Gendered Strife*.
3. Joaquin, *Aquinos of Tarlac*, 98.
4. Ibid., 148–49.
5. Constantino, *The Philippines: A Past Revisited*, 373.
6. The statements by Ramos and the Sakdalistas are quoted in Terami-Wada, "Benigno Ramos," 436, 440, and "Sakdal Movement," 141. On the movement, also see Fegan, "Social History of a Central Luzon Barrio," 107–11.
7. National Archives, RG 350, file 2869A-31 ("Peonage in Philippines Permitted, Is Charge," *Washington Herald*, 27 July 1925, clipping). On Lugard's role in Nigeria, see Lovejoy and Hogendorn, *Slow Death for Slavery*.
8. See National Archives, RG 350, file 2869-127 (Davis to secretary of state, 5 December 1925).
9. Ibid., file 2869-141 ("Copy of Miss Grace Abbott's report on Meeting, Geneva, August 21–25, 1930, of Committee on the Extension of the Enquiry on Traffic in Women and Children in the East").
10. Ibid., file 2826-after 143 (untitled memorandum, n.d.).
11. Ibid., file 2869-154 (Quezon to U.S. High Commissioner, 4 February 1936).
12. Takaki, *Strangers from a Different Shore* and *Pau Hana;* Chan, *Asian Americans*.
13. The investment by the American colonial state in labor migration to Hawaii was, as the following statements indicate, disciplinary in nature as well as prospectively economic. The state's programs of civilizing discipline, it insisted, would fit Filipinos for the freedoms of self-government. Colonial labor policy and the use of forced labor on state construction projects figure prominently in those programs but, like other forms of civilizing discipline under American colonial mastery, they could be justified only in so far as they were distinguished from slavery.
14. National Archives, RG 350, file 3037-32 (Forbes to Stimson, 9 August 1911); Houghton Library, William Cameron Forbes Papers, fMS AM 1366,

vol. 6 (Forbes to Judd, 8 July 1907); ibid., vol. 12 (Forbes to Frear, 2 November 1910).

15. Bello, Kinley, and Elinson, *Development Debacle;* Villegas, "The Economic Crisis"; Anderson, "Cacique Democracy"; Hawes, *Philippine State.*

16. The ensuing discussion is based on the following: Battistella and Paganoni, *Philippine Labor Migration;* Eviota, *Political Economy of Gender,* 142–44; Martin, "Migration and Trade"; Rafael, "'Your Grief is Our Gossip'"; and Choy, "Export of Womanpower."

17. Alongside the OCWs are another (approximately) 2.5 million more or less permanent emigrants residing mainly in the United States, Canada, and Australia. At the bottom of the migration flow, an unknown number of illegal workers overseas also pump additional foreign currency into the national economy.

18. See, for example, Dios and Rocamora, eds., *Of Bonds and Bondage;* Rafael, "Writing Outside," xvi.

19. Stoler and Cooper, "Between Metropole and Colony," 35.

20. Guha, *Dominance without Hegemony,* 7–23.

21. Ibid., 7–23, 72–73, 98–99.

22. Gramsci, *Selections from the Prison Notebooks,* 12–13, 55–57, 158–173; Guha, *Dominance without Hegemony,* 22–23.

23. My thoughts on hegemony owe much to Genovese's use of the concept in *Roll, Jordan, Roll,* where he employs the metaphor of a terrain that shapes conflict as well as compromise.

24. Davis, *The Problem of Slavery in Western Culture.*

25. Anderson, *Imagined Communities,* "Nationalism, Identity, and the Logic of Seriality," and "Replica, Aura, and Late Nationalist Imaginings."

Bibliography

ARCHIVAL COLLECTIONS

Archives and Historical Collections of the Episcopal Church, Episcopal Theological Seminary of the Southwest, Austin, Texas RG 76, Philippine Records
Bentley Library, Michigan Historical Collection, University of Michigan, Ann Arbor
    Papers of H. H. Bandholtz
    Papers of Dean C. Worcester
Harvard University Archives, Cambridge, Massachusetts
    Papers of Charles W. Eliot
Houghton Library, Harvard University, Cambridge, Massachusetts
    Records of the American Board Commissioners of Foreign Missions
    Papers of Gamaliel Bradford
    Papers of William Cameron Forbes
    Papers of E. L. Godkin
    Papers of Thomas Wentworth Higginson
    Papers of William James
    Papers of Charles Eliot Norton
    Papers of Oswald Garrison Villard
Library of Congress, Washington, D.C.
    Beyer-Holleman Collection of Original Sources in Philippine Customary Law
    Papers of Tasker H. Bliss
    Papers of William E. Borah
    Papers of Charles Henry Brent
    Papers of William Jennings Bryan
    Papers of Andrew Carnegie

    Papers of William A. Croffut
    Papers of Francis Burton Harrison
    Papers of William McKinley
    Papers of John J. Pershing
    Papers of Theodore Roosevelt
    Papers of Elihu Root
    Papers of Carl Schurz
    Papers of Hugh L. Scott
    Papers of Moorfield Storey
    Papers of William Howard Taft
    Papers of Woodrow Wilson
    Papers of Leonard Wood
Massachusetts Historical Society, Boston
    Papers of Charles Francis Adams Jr.
    Papers of Edward Atkinson
    Papers of George S. Boutwell
    Papers of Clarence R. Edwards
    Papers of George Frisbie Hoar
    Papers of Henry Cabot Lodge
    Papers of Moorfield Storey
    Papers of Erving Winslow
National Archives, Washington, D.C.
    RG 94 Records of the Adjutant General's Office
    RG 350 Records of the Bureau of Insular Affairs
    RG 395 Records of U.S. Army Overseas Operations and Commands
New York Public Library, New York
    Papers of Edward Ordway
Philippine National Archives, Manila
    Mindanao y Sulu
Philippine National Library, Manila Historical Data Papers Collection
    Papers of Manuel L. Quezon
Stanford University Archives, Stanford, California
    Papers of David Starr Jordan
Thetford Historical Society, Thetford, Vermont
    Worcester Family Papers
University Archives, University of the Philippines, Quezon City
    Papers of Ignacio Villamor
University of Michigan Library, Ann Arbor
    Papers of Herbert Welsh
    Erving Winslow Anti-Imperialist League Papers
    Dean C. Worcester Philippine Collection
University of Oregon Library, Eugene
    Papers of Henry Gilheuser
    Papers of John R. White
University of Virginia Library, Charlottesville
    Papers of William A. Jones

GOVERNMENT DOCUMENTS

Asamblea Filipina. *Diario de sesiónes de la assamblea filipinas.* Manila, 1907–1916.
———. *Informe Sobre la Esclavitud en la Filpinas.* Manila, 1914.
Congressional Record, 1898–1916. Washington, D.C.
Griffin, A. P. C. *Lists of Books (with References to Periodicals) Relating to the Theory of Colonialism, Government of Dependencies, Protectorates, and Related Topics.* Washington, D.C., 1900.
Harrison, Francis Burton. *Inaugural Address and Message of Governor-General Francis Burton to the Third Philippine Legislature.* Manila, 1913.
Philippine Commission. *Report of the Philippine Commission to the President of the United States.* Washington, D.C., 1900–1916.
———. *Journal of the Philippine Commission.* Manila, 1907–1914.
Supreme Court of the Philippine Islands, *Reports of Cases Determined in the Supreme Court of the Philippine Islands,* vol. 8. Manila, 1908.
U.S. Adjutant General's Office. *Correspondence Relating to the War with Spain.* Washington, D.C., 1902.
U.S. Bureau of the Census. *Census of the Philippine Islands 1903.* 4 vols. Washington, D.C., 1905.
U.S. House. Committee on Insular Affairs. *Committee Reports, Hearings, and Acts of Congress Corresponding Thereto.* 57th Cong., 2nd sess., 1902.
———. Committee on Insular Affairs. *Hearing: Statement of the Honorable W. H. Taft.* 58th Cong., 2d sess., 1904.
U.S. Senate. Committee on the Philippines. *Affairs in the Philippine Islands: Hearings before the Committee on the Philippines.* 57th Cong., 1st sess. S. Doc. 331, 1902.
———. Committee on the Philippines. *Government of the Philippines: Hearings on H.R. 18459.* 63rd Cong., 3rd sess., 1915.
———. *Treaty with the Sultan of Sulu.* 56th Cong., 1st sess. S. Doc. 136, 1900.
U.S., *Statutes at Large* vol. 32 (1902). Washington, D.C., 1903.
U.S., *Statutes at Large* vol. 35 (1909). Washington, D.C., 1909.
U.S. War Department. *Annual Reports of the War Department.* Washington, D.C., 1899–1906.
Wilfley, L. R. *Official Opinions of the Attorney General of the Philippine Islands.* Manila, 1903.
Worcester, Dean C. *Annual Report of the Secretary of the Interior of the Philippine Islands, 1910; 1911; 1912; 1913.* Washington, D.C., 1911–1913.
———. *Slavery and Peonage in the Philippine Islands.* Manila, 1913.

PUBLISHED WORKS CITED

Ade, George. *The Sultan of Sulu: An Original Satire in Two Acts.* New York: R. H. Russell, 1903.
Agoncillo, Teodoro. *Revolt of the Masses: The Story of Bonifacio and the Katipunan.* Quezon City, Philippines: University of the Philippines Press, 1956.

———, ed. *Graciano Lopez Jaena: Speeches, Articles and Letters.* Translated and annotated by Encarnacion Alzona. Manila: National Historical Commission, 1974.

Aguilar, Filomeno V. Jr. *Clash of Spirits: The History of Power and Sugar Planter Hegemony on a Visayan Island.* Honolulu: University of Hawaii Press, 1998.

———. "A Failure of Imagination? The Nation in Narratives of the 1896 Philippine Revolution." *Pilipinas,* no. 31 (Fall 1998): 31–46.

Alatas, Syed Hussein. *The Myth of the Lazy Native: A Study of the Image of the Malays, Filipinos and Javanese from the 16th to the 20th Century and its Function in the Ideology of Colonial Capitalism.* London: F. Cass, 1977.

"America and Sulu Slaves: Congressman Grosvenor Answers the Attacks on President McKinley." *New York Times,* 7 October 1900.

Anderson, Benedict. *Imagined Communities: Reflections on the Origin and Spread of Nationalism.* Rev. ed. New York: Verso, 1991.

———. "The Idea of Power in Javanese Culture." In *Culture and Politics in Indonesia,* edited by Claire Holt, 1–69. Ithaca, N.Y.: Cornell University Press, 1972.

———. "Cacique Democracy in the Philippines: Origins and Dreams." *New Left Review* 169, 3–31 (1988).

———. "Nationalism, Identity, and the Logic of Seriality." In *The Spectre of Comparisons: Nationalism, Southeast Asia and the World,* edited by Benedict Anderson, 29–45. London: Verso, 1998.

———. "Replica, Aura, and Late National Imaginings." In *The Spectre of Comparisons: Nationalism, Southeast Asia and the World,* edited by Benedict Anderson, 46–57. London: Verso, 1998.

Anderson, Warwick. "'Where Every Prospect Pleases and Only Man is Vile': Laboratory Medicine as Colonial Discourse." *Critical Inquiry* 18 (Spring 1992): 506–29.

Anstey, Roger. *The Atlantic Slave Trade and British Abolition, 1760–1810.* London: Macmillan, 1975.

Anti-Imperialist League. *Anti-Imperialism: Speeches at the Meeting in Faneuil Hall, Boston, June 15, 1898.* Boston: Anti-Imperialist League, 1898.

Bailyn, Bernard. *The Ideological Origins of the American Revolution.* Cambridge, Mass.: Belknap Press, Harvard University Press, 1967.

Bales, Kevin. *Disposable People: New Slavery in the Global Economy.* Berkeley, Calif.: University of California Press, 1999.

Battistella, Graziano, and Anthony Paganoni, eds. *Philippine Labor Migration: Impact and Policy.* Quezon City, Philippines: Scalabrini Migration Center, 1992.

Beard, Charles. *The Rise of American Civilization.* 2 vols. New York: Macmillan, 1930.

Beckett, Jeremy. "The Defiant and the Compliant: The *Datus* of Magindanao under Colonial Rule." In *Philippine Social History: Global Trade and Local Transformations,* edited by Alfred W. McCoy and Ed. C. de Jesus, 391–414. Quezon City, Philippines: Ateneo de Manila University Press, 1982.

Beisner, Robert. *Twelve against Empire: The Anti-Imperialists, 1898–1900.* New York: McGraw-Hill, 1968.

Bello, Walden, David Kinley, and Elaine Elinson. *Development Debacle: The World Bank and the Philippines.* San Francisco, Calif.: Institute of Food and Development Policy, 1982.

Bender, Thomas, ed. *The Antislavery Debate: Capitalism and Abolitionism as a Problem in Historical Interpretation.* Berkeley, Calif.: University of California Press, 1992.

Blackburn, Robin. *The Overthrow of Colonial Slavery: 1775–1848.* London: Verso, 1988.

Blackett, R. J. M. *Beating against the Barriers: Biographical Essays in Nineteenth-Century Afro-American History.* Baton Rouge, La.: Louisiana State University Press, 1986.

———. *Building an Antislavery Wall: Black Americans in the Atlantic Abolitionist Movement, 1830–1860.* Baton Rouge, La.: Louisiana State University Press, 1983.

Blair, Emma H., and James Alexander Robertson, comp. *The Philippine Islands, 1493–1898,* 55 vols. Cleveland, Ohio: A. H. Clark, 1903–1909.

Blount, James H. *The American Occupation of the Philippines, 1899–1912.* New York: G.P. Putnam's Sons, 1913.

Boutwell, George S. *Reminiscences of Sixty Years in Public Affairs.* New York: McClure, Phillips, 1902.

———. "The Enslavement of American Labor." Address Delivered in Faneuil Hall, January 22, 1902 by the Hon. George S. Boutwell Under the Auspices of the Boston Central Labor Union. Boston, Mass.: 1902.

———. "Imperialists or Republicans?" Address Before the Essex Institute, Salem, Massachusetts, January 9, 1899 by Hon. George S. Boutwell. Washington, D.C., 1899.

———. "The President's Policy, War and Conquest Abroad, Degradation of Labor at Home." Address by Hon. George S. Boutwell at the Masonic Hall, Washington, D.C., January 11, 1900. Chicago, Ill.: American Anti-Imperialist League, 1900.

Brandwein, Pamela. *Reconstructing Reconstruction: The Supreme Court and the Production of Historical Truth.* Durham, N.C.: Duke University Press, 1999.

"Bryan's Reply to Meiklejohn." *New York Times* 11 October 1900, 2.

Bulosan, Carlos. *America Is in the Heart: A Personal History.* Seattle: University of Washington Press, 1973.

Butler, Judith P. *Gender Trouble: Feminism and the Subversion of Identity.* New York: Routledge, 1990.

Chan, Sucheng. *Asian Americans: An Interpretive History.* Boston, Mass.: Twayne, 1991.

Chatterjee, Partha. *The Nation and Its Fragments: Colonial and Postcolonial Histories.* Princeton, N.J.: Princeton University Press, 1993.

———. *Nationalist Thought and the Colonial World: A Derivative Discourse.* London: Zed Books for the United Nations University, 1986.

Choy, Catherine Ceniza. "The Export of Womanpower: A Transnational History of Filipino Nurse Migration to the United States." Ph.D. diss., University of California Los Angeles, 1998.

Clymer, Kenton B. *Protestant Missionaries in the Philippines, 1898–1916: An Inquiry into the American Colonial Mentality.* Urbana, Ill.: University of Illinois Press, 1986.

Constantino, Renato. *The Philippines: A Past Revisited.* Quezon City, Philippines: Tala, 1975.

Cooper, Frederick. *From Slaves to Squatters: Plantation Labor and Agriculture in Zanzibar and Coastal Kenya, 1890–1925.* New Haven, Conn.: Yale University Press, 1980.

———. "The Problem of Slavery in African Studies." *Journal of African History* 20, no. 1 (1979): 103–25.

Cooper, Frederick, and Anna Laura Stoler, eds. *Tensions of Empire: Colonial Cultures in a Bourgeois World.* Berkeley, Calif.: University of California Press, 1997.

Costa, Horacio de la. "The Development of the Native Clergy in the Philippines." In *Studies in Philippine Church History,* edited by Gerald H. Anderson, 65–104. Ithaca, N.Y.: Cornell University Press, 1969.

Cuban Anti-Slavery Committee. *Slavery in Cuba: A Report of the Proceedings of the Meeting held at Cooper Institute, New York City, December 13, 1872.* New York: Cuban Anti-Slavery Committee, n.d.

Cullinane, Michael. "Playing the Game: The Rise of Sergio Osmeña, 1898–1907." In *Philippine Colonial Democracy,* edited by Ruby R. Paredes, 70–113. Yale Southeast Asia Studies Monograph, no. 32. New Haven, Conn. and Quezon City, Philippines, 1988.

———. "The Politics of Collaboration in Tayabas Province: The Early Career of Manuel Luis Quezon, 1903–1906." In *Reappraising an Empire: New Perspectives on Philippine-American History,* edited by Peter W. Stanley, 59–84. Cambridge, Mass.: Harvard University Press, 1984.

"Culture, Gender, and Foreign Policy: A Symposium." *Diplomatic History* 18, no. 3 (1994): 1–78.

Cushner, Nicholas. *Spain in the Philippines: From Conquest to Revolution.* Rutland, Vt.: C.E. Tuttle, 1972.

———. "The Abandonment of Tamontaka Reduction (1898–1899)." *Philippine Studies* 12, no. 2, 288–96 (1964).

Daniel, Pete. *The Shadow of Slavery: Peonage in the South 1901–1969.* New York: Oxford University Press, 1972.

Davis, David Brion. *Slavery and Human Progress.* New York: Oxford University Press, 1984.

———. *The Problem of Slavery in the Age of Revolution, 1770–1823.* Ithaca, N.Y.: Cornell University Press, 1975.

———. *The Problem of Slavery in Western Culture.* Ithaca, N.Y.: Cornell University Press, 1966.

———. "The Perils of Doing History by Ahistoric Abstractions." In *The Antislavery Debate: Capitalism and Abolitionism as a Problem in Historical In-*

terpretation, edited by Thomas Bender, 290–310. Berkeley, Calif.: University of California Press, 1992.

DeBrizzi, John A. *Ideology and the Rise of Labor Theory in America.* Westport, Conn.: Greenwood Press, 1983.

de Jesus, Ed. C. *The Tobacco Monopoly in the Philippines: Bureaucratic Enterprise and Social Change, 1766–1880.* Quezon City, Philippines: Ateneo de Manila University Press, 1980.

Dios, Emmanuel de, and Joel Rocamora, eds. *Of Bonds and Bondage: A Reader on Philippine Debt.* Manila: Transnational Institute, Philippine Center for Policy Studies, 1992.

Dirks, Nicholas, ed. *Colonialism and Culture.* Ann Arbor, Mich.: University of Michigan Press, 1992.

Drescher, Seymour. *Capitalism and Antislavery: British Mobilization in Comparative Perspective.* New York: Oxford University Press, 1987.

———. *Econocide: British Slavery in the Era of Abolition.* Pittsburgh, Pa.: University of Pittsburgh Press, 1977.

Duara, Prasenjit. *Rescuing History from the Nation: Questioning Narratives of Modern China.* Chicago: University of Chicago Press, 1995.

Edwards, Laura F. *Gendered Strife & Confusion: The Political Culture of Reconstruction.* Urbana: University of Illinois Press, 1997.

Eltis, David. "Europeans and the Rise and Fall of African Slavery in the Americas: An Interpretation." *American Historical Review* 98, no. 5 (1993): 1399–1423.

Ely, Richard T. *Outlines of Economics.* New York: Macmillan, 1908.

———. *Studies in the Evolution of Industrial Society.* New York: Macmillan, 1903.

Endicott, K. "The Effects of Slave Raiding on the Aborigines of the Malay Peninsula." In *Slavery, Bondage and Dependency in Southeast Asia,* edited by Anthony Reid, 216–45. New York: St. Martin's Press, 1983.

Eviota, Elizabeth Uy. *The Political Economy of Gender: Women and the Sexual Division of Labor in the Philippines.* London: Zed Books, 1992.

Fegan, Brian. "The Social History of a Central Luzon Barrio." In *Philippine Social History: Global Trade and Local Transformations,* edited by Alfred W. McCoy and Ed C. de Jesus, 91–130. Quezon City, Philippines: Ateneo de Manila University Press, 1982.

Fields, Barbara Jeanne. *Slavery and Freedom on the Middle Ground: Maryland during the Nineteenth Century.* New Haven, Conn.: Yale University Press, 1985.

Finley, M. I. *Ancient Slavery and Modern Ideology.* New York: Penguin Books, 1983.

Foner, Eric. *Reconstruction: America's Unfinished Revolution, 1863–1877.* New York: Harper & Row, 1988.

———. *Nothing but Freedom: Emancipation and its Legacy.* Baton Rouge, La.: Louisiana State University Press, 1983.

———. *Free Soil, Free Labor, Free Men: The Ideology of the Republican Party Before the Civil War.* New York: Oxford University Press, 1971.

Forbes, W. Cameron. *The Philippine Islands.* 2 vols. Boston: Houghton Mifflin, 1928.

Foucault, Michel. *Discipline and Punish: The Birth of the Prison,* Translated by Alan Sheridan. New York: Pantheon Books, 1977.

Fredrickson, George. *The Black Image in the White Mind: The Debate on Afro-American Character and Destiny, 1817–1914.* New York: Harper & Row, 1971.

———. *The Inner Civil War: Northern Intellectuals and the Crisis of the Union.* New York: Harper & Row, 1965.

———. "From Exceptionalism to Variability: Recent Developments in Cross-National Comparative History." *Journal of American History* 82, no. 2 (1995): 587–604.

———. "America's Diversity in Comparative Perspective." *Journal of American History* 85, no. 3 (1998): 859–75.

Fry, Howard T. *A History of the Mountain Province.* Quezon City, Philippines: New Day, 1983.

Funtecha, Henry Florida. *American Military Occupation of the Lake Lanao Region, 1901–1913.* Marawi City, Philippines: University Research Center, Mindanao State University, 1979.

Furner, Mary. *Advocacy and Objectivity: A Crisis in the Professionalization of American Social Science.* Lexington, Ky.: The University Press of Kentucky, 1975.

Genovese, Eugene. *From Rebellion to Revolution: Afro-American Slave Revolts in the Making of the New World.* Baton Rouge, La.: Louisiana State University Press, 1979.

———. *Roll, Jordan Roll: The World the Slaves Made.* New York: Vintage Books, 1976.

George, Henry. *Progress and Poverty: An Inquiry into the Cause of Industrial Depression and of Increase of Want with Increase of Wealth.* New York: 1879.

Gomez, Michael A. *Exchanging Our Country Marks: The Transformation of African Identities in the Colonial and Antebellum South.* Chapel Hill, N.C.: University of North Carolina Press, 1998.

Gowing, Peter Gordon. *Muslim Filipinos: Heritage and Horizon.* Quezon City, Philippines: New Day, 1979.

———. *Mandate in Moroland: The American Government of Muslim Filipinos, 1899–1920.* Quezon City, Philippines: Philippine Center for Advanced Studies, University of the Philippines, 1983.

Gramsci, Antonio. *Selections from the Prison Notebooks,* edited and translated by Quentin Hoare and Geoffrey Nowell Smith. New York: International Publishers, 1971.

Grossholtz, Jean. *Politics in the Philippines.* Boston: Little, Brown, 1964.

Guerrero, Leon Ma. *The First Filipino: A Biography of José Rizal.* Manila: 1963.

Guha, Ranajit. *Dominance without Hegemony: History and Power in Colonial India.* Cambridge, Mass.: Harvard University Press, 1997.

Gullick, J. M. *Indigenous Political Systems of Western Malaya,* rev. ed. London: University of London, Athlone Press, 1988.

Harkins, P. *Blackburn's Headhunters.* New York: Norton, 1955.

Harrison, Francis Burton. *The Corner-Stone of Philippine Independence: A Narrative of Seven Years.* New York: Century, 1922.

Hart, Albert Bushnell. *Slavery and Abolition, 1831–1841.* New York: Harper & Brothers, 1906.

Haskell, Thomas. *The Emergence of Professional Social Science: The American Social Science Association and the Nineteenth-Century Crisis of Authority.* Urbana, Il.: University of Illinois Press, 1977.

Hawes, Gary. *The Philippine State and the Marcos Regime: The Politics of Export.* Bloomington, Ind.: University of Indiana, 1989.

Hoffman, Ronald, and Ira Berlin, eds. *Slavery and Freedom in the Age of the American Revolution.* Charlottesville, Va.: University Press of Virginia, 1983.

Hollnsteiner, Mary R. *The Dynamics of Power in a Philippine Municipality.* Quezon City, Philippines: Community Development Research Council, University of the Philippines, 1963.

Holt, Thomas. *The Problem of Freedom: Race, Labor, and Politics in Jamaica and Britain, 1832–1938.* Baltimore, Md.: Johns Hopkins University Press, 1992.

Horsman, Reginald. *Race and Manifest Destiny: The Origins of American Racial Anglo-Saxonism.* Cambridge, Mass.: Harvard University Press, 1981.

Hunt, Michael. "The Long Crisis in Diplomatic History: Coming to Closure." *Diplomatic History* 16 (1992): 115–40.

Hutterer, Karl L. "Dean C. Worcester and Philippine Anthropology." *Philippine Quarterly of Society and Culture* 6, no. 3 (September 1978): 125–56.

Ileto, Reynaldo C. *Pasyon and Revolution: Popular Movements in the Philippines 1840–1910.* Quezon City, Philippines: Ateneo de Manila University Press, 1979.

———. *Magindanao: 1860–1888, the Career of Datu Uto of Buayan.* Marawi City, Philippines: University Research Center, Mindanao State University, n.d.

———. "Orators and the Crowd: Philippine Independence Politics, 1910–1914." In *Reappraising an Empire: New Perspectives on Philippine-American History,* edited by Peter W. Stanley, 85–114. Cambridge, Mass.: Harvard University Press, 1984.

———. "Rizal and the Underside of Philippine History." In *Moral Order and the Question of Change: Essays on Southeast Asia,* edited by David K. Wyatt and Alexander Woodside, 274–337. New Haven, Conn.: Yale University, Southeast Asia Studies, 1982.

———. "Tagalog Poetry and Perception of the Past in the War against Spain." In *Perceptions of the Past in Southeast Asia,* edited by Anthony Reid and David Marr, 379–400. Singapore: Heinemann Educational Books, 1979.

Ireland, Alleyne. *Tropical Colonization: An Introduction to the Study of the Subject.* New York: Macmillan, 1899.

———. "The Labor Problem in the Tropics." *Popular Science Monthly* 54 (February 1899): 481–90.

———. "The Growth of the British Colonial Conception." *Atlantic Monthly* 83 (April 1899): 488–97.

———. "European Experience with Tropical Colonies." *Atlantic Monthly* 80 (December 1898): 729–34.

James, C. L. R. *The Black Jacobins: Toussaint L'Overture and the San Domingo Revolution,* 2d ed., rev. New York: Vintage Books, 1963.

Jameson, Frederic. *The Political Unconscious: Narrative as a Socially Symbolic Act.* Ithaca, N.Y.: Cornell University Press, 1981.

Jenista, Frank. *The White Apos: American Governors on the Cordillera Central.* Quezon City, Philippines: New Day, 1987.

Joaquin, Nick. *The Aquinos of Tarlac: An Essay on History as Three Generations.* Manila: Cacho Hermanos, 1983.

Jordan, David Starr. *The Question of the Philippines: An Address Delivered Before the Graduate Club of Leland Stanford Junior University, February 14, 1899.* Palo Alto, Calif.: J.J. Valentine, 1899.

Kalaw, Maximo M. *The Development of Philippine Politics.* Manila: Solar, 1926.

Kaplan, Amy, and Donald E. Pease, eds. *Cultures of United States Imperialism.* Durham, N.C.: Duke University Press, 1993.

Keesing, Felix M., and Marie Keesing. *Taming Philippine Headhunters: A Study of Government and of Cultural Change in Northern Luzon.* Stanford, Calif.: Stanford University Press, 1934.

Kelley, Fred C. *George Ade: Warm-Hearted Satirist.* Indianapolis, Ind.: Dobbs-Merrill, 1947.

Kerkvliet, Benedict J. *Everyday Politics in the Philippines: Class and Status Relations in a Central Luzon Village.* Berkeley, Calif.: University of California Press, 1990.

———. *The Huk Rebellion: A Study of Peasant Revolt in the Philippines.* Berkeley and Los Angeles, Calif.: University of California Press, 1977.

Kiefer, Thomas. *The Tausug: Violence and Law in a Philippine Moslem Society.* New York: Holt, Rinehart and Winston, 1972.

———. "An Anthropological Perspective on the Nineteenth-Century Sulu Sultanate." In *Perspectives on Philippine Historiography: A Symposium,* edited by John A. Larkin, 55–64. Yale Southeast Asia Series Monograph, no. 21. New Haven, Conn.: Yale University, Southeast Asia Studies, 1979.

Klein, Martin A. "Introduction: Modern European Expansion and Traditional Servitude in Africa and Asia." In *Breaking the Chains: Slavery, Bondage, and Emancipation in Modern Africa and Asia,* edited by Martin A. Klein, 3–36. Madison, Wisc.: University of Wisconsin Press, 1993.

Kolchin, Peter. *Unfree Labor: American Slavery and Russian Serfdom.* Cambridge, Mass.: Belknap Press of Harvard University, 1987.

Kolko, Gabriel. *The Triumph of Conservatism: A Reinterpretation of American History 1900–1916.* Chicago: Quadrangle Books, 1963.

Kopytoff, Igor. "Reflections: The Cultural Context of African Abolition." In *The End of Slavery in Africa,* edited by Suzanne Miers and Richard Roberts, 485–503. Madison, Wisc.: University of Wisconsin Press, 1988.

Kopytoff, Igor, and Suzanne Miers. "Introduction: African 'Slavery' as an Institution of Marginality." In *Slavery in Africa: Historical and Anthropological Perspectives,* edited by Suzanne Miers and Igor Kopytoff, 3–81. Madison, Wisc.: University of Wisconsin Press, 1977.

Kramer, Paul. "Making Concessions: Race and Empire Revisited at the Philippine Exposition, St. Louis, 1901–1905." *Radical History Review* no. 73 (Winter 1999): 74–114.

Kroeber, A. L. *Peoples of the Philippines.* American Museum of Natural History Handbook Series, no. 8. 2d rev. ed. New York: American Museum of Natural History, 1928.

LaFeber, Walter. *The New Empire: An Interpretation of American Expansion, 1860–1898.* Ithaca, N.Y.: Cornell University Press, 1963.

Lande, Carl H. *Leaders, Factions and Parties: The Structure of Philippine Politics.* Yale Southeast Asia Studies Monograph, no. 6. New Haven, Conn.: Yale University, Southeast Asia Studies, 1965.

Lapeña-Bonifacio, Amelia. *The "Seditious" Tagalog Playwrights: Early American Occupation.* Manila: Zarzuela Foundation of the Philippines, 1972.

Lasch, Christopher. *The New Radicalism in America, 1889–1963: The Intellectual as a Social Type.* New York: Knopf, 1965.

———. "The Anti-Imperialists, the Philippines, and the Inequality of Man." *Journal of Southern History* 24 (1958): 319–31.

Lears, T. Jackson. *No Place of Grace: Antimodernism and the Transformation of American Culture, 1880–1920.* New York: Pantheon Books, 1981.

LeRoy, James A. *The Americans in the Philippines.* New York: Houghton Mifflin, 1914.

Limerick, Patricia Nelson. *Legacy of Conquest: The Unbroken Past of the American West.* New York: Norton, 1987.

Lovejoy, Paul. *Transformations in Slavery: A History of Slavery in Africa.* New York: Cambridge University Press, 1983.

Lovejoy, Paul E., and Jan S. Hogendorn. *Slow Death for Slavery: The Course of Abolition in Northern Nigeria, 1897–1936.* Cambridge: Cambridge University Press, 1993.

Lynch, Frank. "Social Acceptance Reconsidered." In *Four Readings on Philippine Values,* edited by Frank Lynch and Alfonso de Guzman II, 4th ed., rev. and enl., 1–68. Quezon City, Philippines: Ateneo de Manila University Press, 1973.

Lynch, Frank, and Alfonso de Guzman II, eds., *Four Readings on Philippine Values,* 4th ed., rev. and enl. Quezon City, Philippines: Ateneo de Manila University Press, 1973.

McCormick, Thomas J. *China Market: America's Quest for Informal Empire, 1893–1901.* Chicago: Quadrangle Books, 1967.

McCoy, Alfred W. "'An Anarchy of Families': The Historiography of State and Family in the Philippines." In *An Anarchy of Families: State and Family in the Philippines,* edited by Alfred W. McCoy, 1–32. Madison, Wisc.: University of Wisconsin, Center for Southeast Asian Studies, 1993.

————. "A Queen Dies Slowly: The Rise and Decline of Iloilo City." In *Philippine Social History: Global Trade and Local Transformations,* edited by Alfred W. McCoy and Ed. C. de Jesus, 297–358. Quezon City, Philippines: Ateneo de Manila University Press, 1982.

McCoy, Alfred W., and Ed. C. de Jesus, eds. *Philippine Social History: Global Trade and Local Transformations.* Quezon City, Philippines: Ateneo de Manila University Press, 1982.

McDougall, E. Ann. "A Topsy-Turvy World: Slaves and Freed Slaves in the Mauritanian Adar." In *The End of Slavery in Africa,* edited by Suzanne Miers and Richard Roberts, 362–88. Madison, Wisc.: University of Wisconsin Press, 1988.

McGlynn, Frank, and Seymour Drescher, eds. *The Meaning of Freedom: Economics, Politics, and the Culture of Slavery.* Pittsburgh, Pa.: University of Pittsburgh Press, 1992.

McPherson, James. *The Abolitionist Legacy.* Princeton, N.J.: Princeton University Press, 1975.

McSheffrey, Gerald. "Slavery, Indentured Servitude, Legitimate Trade and the Impact of Abolition in the Gold Coast, 1874–1901: A Reappraisal." *Journal of African History* vol. 24 no. 3 (1983): 349–68.

Madigan, Francis C., and Nicholas P. Cushner. "Tamontaka Reduction: A Community Approach to Mission Work." *Neue Zeitschrift für Missionswissenschaft* 17, no. 2 (1961): 81–94.

————. "Tamontaka: A Sociological Experiment." *The American Catholic Sociological Review* 19, no. 4 (1958): 322–36.

Manning, Patrick. *Slavery and African Life: Occidental, Oriental, and African Slave Trades.* New York: Cambridge University Press, 1990.

Martin, Dale. *Slavery as Salvation: The Metaphor of Slavery in Pauline Christianity.* New Haven, Conn.: Yale University Press, 1990.

Martin, Philip L. "Migration and Trade: The Case of the Philippines." *International Migration Review* 27, no. 3 (1993): 639–45.

Martin, Waldo. *The Mind of Frederick Douglass.* Chapel Hill, N.C.: University of North Carolina Press, 1984.

Matheson, V., and M. B. Hooker. "Slavery in the Malay Texts: Categories of Dependency and Compensation." In *Slavery, Bondage and Dependency in Southeast Asia,* edited by Anthony Reid, 182–208. New York: St. Martin's Press, 1983.

May, Glenn A. *Inventing a Hero: The Posthumous Re-Creation of Andres Bonifacio.* Madison, Wisc.: University of Wisconsin, Center for Southeast Asian Studies, 1996.

————. *Battle for Batangas: A Philippine Province at War.* New Haven, Conn.: Yale University Press, 1991.

————. *Social Engineering in the Philippines: The Aims, Execution, and Impact of American Colonial Policy, 1900–1913.* Quezon City, Philippines: New Day, 1984.

May, Robert E. *The Southern Dream of a Caribbean Empire, 1854–1861*. Baton Rouge, La.: Louisiana State University Press, 1973.

Meiklejohn, G. D. "Mr. Bryan and Sulu Slaves." *New York Times,* 10 October 1900, 2.

———. "Meiklejohn Writes Bryan." *New York Times,* 13 October 1990, 3.

Miers, Suzanne. *Britain and the Ending of the Slave Trade*. London: 1974.

Miers, Suzanne, and Richard Roberts, eds. *The End of Slavery in Africa*. Madison, Wisc.: University of Wisconsin Press, 1988.

Miller, Stuart Creighton. *"Benevolent Assimilation": The American Conquest of the Philippines, 1899–1903*. New Haven, Conn.: Yale University Press, 1982.

Mojares, Resil B. "Worcester in Cebu: Filipino Response to American Business." *Philippine Quarterly of Culture and Society* 13, no. 1 (1985): 1–13.

Montgomery, David. *Beyond Equality: Labor and the Radical Republicans, 1862–1872*. New York: Knopf, 1967.

Morga, Antonio de. *Sucesos de las Islas Filipinas,* edited by José Rizal. Paris: Garnier Hermanos, 1890.

Morgan, Edmund. *American Slavery, American Freedom: The Ordeal of Colonial Virginia*. New York: Norton, 1975.

Nieboer, H. J. *Slavery as an Industrial System: Ethnological Researches*. The Hague: M. Nijhoff, 1900.

Okoye, F. Nwabueze. "Chattel Slavery as the Nightmare of the American Revolution." *William and Mary Quarterly* 37, no. 1 (1980): 5–28.

Olcott, C. S. *The Life of William McKinley*. 2 vols. Boston: Houghton Mifflin, 1916.

Painter, Nell Irwin. *Sojourner Truth: A Life, A Symbol*. New York: W.W. Norton, 1996.

Paredes, Ruby R. "Introduction." In *Philippine Colonial Democracy,* edited by Ruby Paredes, 1–12. Yale Southeast Asian Studies Monograph, no. 32. New Haven, Conn. and Quezon City, Philippines: Ateneo de Manila University Press, 1988.

———. "The Origins of National Politics: Taft and the Partido Federal." *Philippine Colonial Democracy,* edited by Ruby Paredes, 41–69. Yale Southeast Asian Studies Monograph, no. 32. New Haven, Conn. and Quezon City, Philippines: Ateneo de Manila University Press, 1988.

———. *Philippine Colonial Democracy*. Yale Southeast Asia Studies Monograph, no. 32. New Haven, Conn. and Quezon City, Philippines: Ateneo de Manila University Press, 1988.

Patterson, Orlando. *Freedom in the Making of Western Culture*. Vol. 1. New York: Basic Books, 1991.

———. *Slavery and Social Death: A Comparative Study*. Cambridge, Mass.: Harvard University Press, 1982.

Peabody, Sue. *"There Are No Slaves in France": The Political Culture of Race and Slavery in the Ancien Régime*. New York: Oxford University Press, 1996.

Phelan, John Leddy. *The Hispanization of the Philippines: Spanish Aims and Filipino Responses, 1565–1700*. Madison, Wisc.: University of Wisconsin Press, 1959.

Phillips, Ulrich Bonnell. *Life and Labor in the Old South.* 1929. Reprint, Boston: Little, Brown, 1963.

————. *American Negro Slavery: A Survey of the Supply, Employment, and Control of Negro Labor as Determined by the Plantation Regime.* New York: Smith, 1918.

Pomeroy, William. *American Neo-Colonialism: Its Emergence in the Philippines and Asia.* New York: International Publishers, 1970.

Prakash, Gyan. *Bonded Histories: Genealogies of Labor Servitude in Colonial India.* New York: Cambridge University Press, 1990.

————, ed. *After Colonialism: Imperial Histories and Postcolonial Displacements.* Princeton, N.J.: Princeton University Press, 1995.

Quarles, Benjamin. *Black Abolitionists.* New York: Oxford University Press, 1969.

Rafael, Vicente L. *Contracting Colonialism: Translation and Christian Conversion in Tagalog Society under Early Spanish Rule.* Quezon City, Philippines: Ateneo de Manila University Press, 1988.

————. "Writing Outside: On the Question of Location." In *Discrepant Histories: Translocal Essays on Filipino Culture,* edited by Vicente L. Raphael, xiii–xxviii. Philadelphia, Pa.: Temple University Press, 1995.

————. "'Your Grief is Our Gossip': Overseas Filipinos and Other Spectral Presences." *Public Culture* 9, no. 2 (1997): 267–91.

————. "White Love: Discipline and Surveillance in the United States Colonization of the Philippines." In *Cultures of United States Imperialism,* edited by Amy Kaplan and Donald E. Pease, 185–218. Durham, N.C.: Duke University Press, 1993.

————. "Nationalism, Imagery, and the Filipino Intelligentsia in the 19th Century." *Critical Inquiry* 16, no. 3 (1990): 591–611.

Reid, Anthony. *Southeast Asia in the Age of Commerce, 1450–1680.* Vol. 1 of *The Lands Below the Winds.* New Haven, Conn.: Yale University Press, 1988.

————. "The Decline of Slavery in Nineteenth-Century Indonesia." In *Breaking the Chains: Slavery, Bondage, and Emancipation in Modern Africa and Asia,* edited by Martin A. Klein, 64–82. Madison, Wisc.: University of Wisconsin Press, 1993.

————. Introduction to *Slavery, Bondage and Dependency in Southeast Asia,* edited by Anthony Reid, 1–43. New York: St. Martin's Press, 1983.

Reinsch, Paul. *Colonial Administration.* New York: Macmillan, 1905.

Ricarte, Artemio. *Memoirs of General Artemio Ricarte.* Manila: National Heroes Commission, 1963.

Riggs, Arthur S., *The Filipino Drama,* edited and introduced by Doreen G. Fernandez. Manila, Philippines: Ministry of Human Settlements, Intramuros Administration, 1981.

Rizal, Jose. *Noli Me Tangere.* Berlin: Berliner buchdruckerei-actien-gesellschaft, 1886. Reprint, Madrid: Ediciones de Cultural Hispanicana, 1992.

————. *El Filibusterismo,* Ghent: Boekdrukkerij F. Meyer-Van Loo, 1891. Reprint, Barcelona: Casa Editorial Maucci, 1911.

Roberts, Richard, and Suzanne Miers. "Introduction: The End of Slavery in Africa." *The End of Slavery in Africa,* edited by Suzanne Miers and Richard Roberts, 3–68. Madison, Wisc.: University of Wisconsin Press, 1988.

Roediger, David. *The Wages of Whiteness: Race and the Making of the American Working Class.* New York: Verso, 1991.

Rogin, Michael Paul. *Fathers and Children: Andrew Jackson and the Subjugation of the American Indian.* New York: Knopf, 1975.

Rosaldo, Renato. *Culture and Truth: The Remaking of Social Analysis.* Boston: Beacon Press, 1989.

———. *Ilongot Head-Hunting, 1883–1974: A Study in Society and History.* Palo Alto, Calif.: Stanford University Press, 1980.

———. "Utter Savages of Scientific Value." In *Politics and History in Band Societies,* edited by Eleanor Leacock and Richard Lee, 309–26. New York: Cambridge University Press, 1982.

Ross, Dorothy. *The Origin of American Social Science.* New York: Cambridge University Press, 1991.

Ross, Edward A. *Social Control: A Survey of the Foundations of Order.* New York: Macmillan, 1901.

Rydell, Robert W. *All the World's a Fair: Visions of Empire at American International Expositions, 1876–1916.* Chicago: University of Chicago Press, 1984.

Salamanca, Bonifacio S. *The Filipino Reaction to American Rule, 1901–1913.* Quezon City, Philippines: New Day, 1984.

Sale, Maggie Montesinos. *The Slumbering Volcano: American Slave Ship Revolts and the Production of Rebellious Masculinity.* Durham, N.C.: Duke University Press, 1997.

Saleeby, Najeeb M. *The History of Sulu.* Manila: Filipiniana Book Guild, 1963.

Salman, Michael. "'Nothing Without Labor': Penology, Discipline and Independence in the Philippines under United States Rule." In *Discrepant Histories: Translocal Essays on Filipino Cultures,* edited by Vicente L. Rafael, 113–29. Philadelphia: Temple University Press, 1995.

———. "Ancient Philippine Slavery and Modern Ideology: Historical and Historiographical Issues in the Grounding of Philippine Studies." *Pilipinas,* no. 33 (Fall 1999): 1–12.

Schirmer, Daniel Boone. *Republic or Empire: American Resistance to the Philippine War.* Cambridge, Mass.: Schenkman, 1972.

Schumacher, John N., S.J. *The Propaganda Movement: 1880–1895: The Creators of a Filipino Consciousness, the Makers of Revolution.* Manila: Solidaridad Pub. House, 1973.

———. *Father Jose Burgos: Priest and Nationalist.* Manila: Ateneo de Manila University Press, 1972.

———. "The Propagandists' Reconstruction of the Philippine Past." In *Perceptions of the Past in Southeast Asia,* edited by Anthony Reid and David Marr, 264–80. Singapore: Heinemann Educational Books, 1979.

Schurz, William. *The Manila Galleon.* New York: Dutton, 1939.

Scott, Rebecca. *Slave Emancipation in Cuba: The Transition to Free Labor.* Princeton, N.J.: Princeton University Press, 1985.

———. "Exploring the Meaning of Freedom: Postemancipation Societies in Comparative Perspective." *Hispanic American Historical Review* 168, no. 3 (1988): 407–28.

Scott, William Henry. *Barangay: Sixth-Century Philippine Culture and Society.* Quezon City, Philippines: Ateneo de Manila University Press, 1994.

———. *Slavery in the Spanish Philippines.* Manila: De la Salle University Press, 1991.

———. *The Discovery of the Igorots: Spanish Contacts with the Pagans of Northern Luzon.* Quezon City, Philippines: New Day, 1974.

———. "Why Did Tupas Betray Dagami?" In *Looking for the Prehispanic Filipino and Other Essays in Philippine History,* edited by William Henry Scott, 40–63. Quezon City, Philippines: New Day, 1992.

———. "*Oripun* and *Alipin* in the Sixteenth-Century Philippines." In *Slavery, Bondage and Dependency in Southeast Asia,* edited by Anthony Reid, 138–55. New York: St. Martin's Press, 1983.

———. "Class Structure in the Unhispanized Philippines." In *Cracks in the Parchment Curtain and Other Essays in Philippine History,* edited by William Henry Scott, 127–47. Quezon City, Philippines: New Day, 1982.

———. "The Creation of a Cultural Minority." In *Cracks in the Parchment Curtain and Other Essays in Philippine Culture,* edited by William Henry Scott, 28–41. Quezon City, Philippines: New Day, 1982.

———. "Filipino Class Structure in the 16th Century." In *Cracks in the Parchment Curtain and Other Essays in Philippine History,* edited by William Henry Scott, 96–126. Quezon City, Philippines: New Day, 1982.

———. "Filipino-Spanish Face-to-Face Contacts, 1543–1545." In *Cracks in the Parchment Curtain and Other Essays in Philippine Culture,* edited by William Henry Scott, 49–59. Quezon City, Philippines: New Day, 1982.

Seton-Watson, Hugh. *Nations and States: An Enquiry into the Origins of Nations and the Politics of Nationalism.* Boulder, Colo.: Westview, 1977.

Smith, Anthony. *The Ethnic Origins of Nations.* New York: B. Blackwell, 1986.

Solow, Barbara, and Stanley I. Engerman, eds. *British Capitalism and Caribbean Slavery.* New York: Cambridge University Press, 1987.

Stanley, Amy Dru. *From Bondage to Contract: Wage Labor, Marriage, and the Market in the Age of Slave Emancipation.* New York: Cambridge University Press, 1998.

Stanley, Peter W. *A Nation in the Making: The Philippines and the United States, 1899–1921.* Cambridge, Mass.: Harvard University Press, 1974.

Stephanson, Anders. *Manifest Destiny: American Expansionism and the Empire of Right.* New York: Hill and Wang, 1995.

Stoler, Ann, and Frederick Cooper. "Between Metropole and Colony." In *Tensions of Empire: Colonial Cultures in a Bourgeois World,* 1–56. Berkeley, Calif.: University of California Press, 1997.

Storey, Moorfield. "Address of the President." *Report of the 11th Annual Meeting of the Anti-Imperialist League, Boston, November 27–30, 1909.* Boston: The Anti-Imperialist League, 1909.

Sullivan, Patrick. *Social Relations of Dependence in a Malay State: Nineteenth-Century Perak.* The Malaysian Branch of the Royal Asiatic Society. Monograph no. 10. Kuala Lumpur: Art Printing Works, 1982.

Sullivan, Rodney. *Exemplar of Americanism: The Philippine Career of Dean C. Worcester.* Ann Arbor, Mich.: University of Michigan, Center for South and Southwest Asian Studies, 1991.

Sutherland, H. "Slavery and the Slave Trade in South Sulawesi, 1660s–1800s." In *Slavery, Bondage and Dependency in Southeast Asia,* edited by Anthony Reid, 263–85. New York: St. Martin's Press, 1983.

Takaki, Ronald. *Strangers from a Different Shore: A History of Asian Americans.* Boston, Mass.: Little, Brown, 1989.

———. *Pau Hana: Plantation Life and Labor in Hawaii, 1835–1920.* Honolulu, Hawaii: University of Hawaii Press, 1983.

Tan, Samuel K. *The Filipino Muslim Armed Struggle, 1900–1972.* Manila: Filipinas Foundation, 1977.

Taylor, J. R. M. *The Philippine Insurrection Against the United States: A Compilation of Documents with Notes and Introduction.* 5 vols. Pasay City, Philippines: Eugenio Lopez Foundation, 1971–73.

Temperly, Howard. "Capitalism, Slavery, and Ideology." *Past and Present* 75, no. 1 (1977): 94–118.

Terami-Wada, Motoe. "The Sakdal Movement, 1930–34." *Philippine Studies* 36, no. 2 (1988): 131–50.

———. "Benigno Ramos and the Sakdal Movement." *Philippine Studies* 36, no. 4 (1988): 427–42.

Thomas, John L. *Alternative America: Henry George, Edward Bellamy, Henry Demarest Lloyd and the Adversary Tradition.* Cambridge, Mass.: Belknap Press, 1983.

Thornton, John. *Africa and Africans in the Making of the Atlantic World, 1400–1800.* Cambridge: Cambridge University Press, 1992.

Todorov, Tzvestan. *The Conquest of America: The Question of the Other,* translated by Richard Howard. New York: Harper Perennial, 1992.

Toledano, Ehud. "Ottoman Concepts of Slavery in the Period of Reform." In *Breaking the Chains: Slavery, Bondage, and Emancipation in Modern Africa and Asia,* edited by Martin A. Klein, 37–63. Madison, Wisc.: University of Wisconsin Press, 1993.

Tompkins, E. Berkeley. *Anti-Imperialism in the United States: The Great Debate, 1890–1920.* Philadelphia, Pa.: University of Pennsylvania Press, 1970.

Van Meter, H. H. *The Truth About the Philippines: From Official Records and Authentic Sources.* Chicago: The Liberty League, 1900.

Vergara, Benito M., Jr. *Displaying Filipinos: Photography and Colonialism in Early 20th Century Philippines.* Quezon City, Philippines: University of the Philippines Press, 1995.

Veyra, Jaime C. de. *El 'Ultimo Adiós' de Rizal: Estudio critico-expositivo.* Manila: Bureau of Printing, 1946.

Villegas, Bernardo. "The Economic Crisis." In *Crisis in the Philippines,* edited by John Bresnan, 145–75. Princeton, N.J.: Princeton University Press, 1986.

Warren, James. *The Sulu Zone, 1768–1898: The Dynamics of External Trade, Slavery and Ethnicity in the Transformation of a Southeast Asian Maritime State.* Quezon City, Philippines: 1985.

Weinstein, James. *The Corporate Ideal in the Liberal State, 1900–1920.* Boston, Mass.: Beacon Press, 1968.

Welch, Richard, Jr. *Response to Imperialism: The United States and the Philippine-American War.* Chapel Hill, N.C.: University of North Carolina Press, 1979.

White, Morton. *Social Thought in America: The Revolt against Formalism.* Boston, Mass.: Beacon Press, 1957.

White, Richard. *The Middle Ground: Indians, Empires, and Republics in the Great Lakes Region, 1650–1815.* Cambridge: Cambridge University Press, 1991.

Wickberg, Edgar. *The Chinese in Philippine Life, 1850–1898.* New Haven, Conn.: Yale University Press, 1965.

———. "The Chinese Mestizo in Philippine History." *Journal of Southeast Asian History* 5 (1964): 62–100.

———. *The Chinese in the Philippines.* New York: 1964.

Wiebe, Robert. *The Search for Order, 1877–1920.* New York: Hill and Wang, 1967.

Williams, Eric Eustace. *Capitalism and Slavery.* Chapel Hill, N.C.: 1944.

Williams, Walter L. "United States Indian Policy and the Debate over Philippine Annexation: Implications for the Origins of American Imperialism." *Journal of American History* 66, no. 4 (1980): 810–31.

Williams, William Appleman. *The Tragedy of American Diplomacy.* 2d rev. and enl. ed. New York: Dell, 1972.

———. *The Contours of American History.* Cleveland, Ohio: World Publishing, 1961.

Williamson, Harold F. *Edward Atkinson: The Biography of an American Liberal, 1827–1905.* Boston: Old Corner Book Store, 1934.

Wilson, Woodrow. "The Ideals of America." *Atlantic Monthly* 90 (December 1902): 721–34.

Worcester, Dean C. *The Philippines Past and Present.* New York: Macmillan, 1930.

———. *The Philippine Islands and Their People.* New York: Macmillan, 1899.

———. "The Malay Pirates of the Philippines." *Century Magazine* 56, no. 5 (1898): 690–702.

———. "Notes on Some Primitive Philippine Tribes." *National Geographic Magazine* 9, no. 6 (1898): 284–300.

Index

Text and display: Sabon
Compositor: G&S Typesetters, Inc.
Printer: Thomson-Shore, Inc.